The Politics of Transparency in Modern American Fiction

European Studies in North American Literature and Culture

The Politics of Transparency in Modern American Fiction

Fear, Secrecy, and Exposure

Edited by
Paula Martín-Salván and Sascha Pöhlmann

Rochester, New York

Copyright © 2024 by the Editors and Contributors

All Rights Reserved. Except as permitted under current legislation, no part of this work may be photocopied, stored in a retrieval system, published, performed in public, adapted, broadcast, transmitted, recorded, or reproduced in any form or by any means, without the prior permission of the copyright owner.

First published 2024
by Camden House

Camden House is an imprint of Boydell & Brewer Inc.
668 Mt. Hope Avenue, Rochester, NY 14620, USA
and of Boydell & Brewer Limited
PO Box 9, Woodbridge, Suffolk IP12 3DF, UK
www.boydellandbrewer.com

ISBN-13: 978-1-64014-166-7

Library of Congress Cataloging-in-Publication Data

CIP data is available from the Library of Congress.

The publisher has no responsibility for the continued existence or accuracy of URLs for external or third-party internet websites referred to in this book, and does not guarantee that any content on such websites is, or will remain, accurate or appropriate.

Contents

Acknowledgments		vii
Introduction: The Politics of Transparency Paula Martín-Salván		1
1:	Walt Whitman's Poetry of Intimacy Sascha Pöhlmann	30
2:	The Lives and Times of Henry James and F. O. Matthiessen: The Neoliberal Transparent Society and Its Liberal Enemies Julián Jiménez Heffernan	55
3:	The Intelligibility of Coming Out as Gay Tomasz Basiuk	83
4:	Invisibility and Exposure in Ralph Ellison's *Invisible Man* (1952) and George Schuyler's *Black No More* (1931) Michel Feith	104
5:	The Transparency of the Scanner, The Opacity of the Simulacra: The Politics of Vision in Philip K. Dick's Oeuvre Umberto Rossi	129
6:	"Angrier than thou": Secrecy vs. Exposure in Philip Roth's *I Married a Communist* Cristina Chevereşan	147
7:	Political Secrets in William Gibson's Sprawl Trilogy Juan L. Pérez-de-Luque	173
8:	Secrecy and Exposure in Toni Morrison's *Paradise* Alice Sundman	194
9:	Something Big and Invisible: Thomas Pynchon's *Bleeding Edge* and the Limits of Transparency Tiina Käkelä	214

10: Narrating the Community in Karen Tei Yamashita's
   I Hotel: Story, History, System 233
   Toon Staes

11: Literary Imagination at the Digital Frontier: Dave Eggers's
   Recent Technological Dystopian Novels 255
   Jelena Šesnić

12: "The Joy of Confession": Narratives of Disclosure in
   Jonathan Franzen's *Crossroads* 276
   Jesús Blanco Hidalga

13: Celebrity 2.0: Female Influencer Figures in Contemporary
   American Fiction 296
   Julia Straub

Notes on the Contributors 315

Index 319

Acknowledgments

THIS WORK WAS SUPPORTED BY research group HUM-682 from the University of Córdoba (Spain) and research project PID2019-104526GB-I00, funded by the Spanish Ministry of Science and Innovation.

Introduction: The Politics of Transparency

Paula Martín-Salván

1. Literature and the Politics of Transparency

IN THE TWENTY-FIRST CENTURY, transparency has become an ambiguous buzzword applied to both the public realm (think Wikileaks and the Snowden affair) and the private (social media). Scholarly work on the notion of transparency has placed it at the center of debates on contemporary societies, as Byung-Chul Han (2015, vii) claimed in his influential work *The Transparency Society*: "Today the word 'transparency' is haunting all spheres of life." "Transparency" appears as a defining sign of the times that witnessed the launch of the US government's portal Data.gov in 2009, as well as the massive Wikileaks case in 2010 and the PRISM scandal involving Edward Snowden in 2013. We may feel tempted to concur with Jeremy Gilbert (2007, 22) in claiming that "we live in an age of endless disclosure."

This volume explores modern and contemporary American literature's critique of such discourses of transparency, taking its cue from recent scholarly work in sociology, political theory, and cultural studies that identifies a proliferating rhetoric of transparency in public and political life. While many scholars in this emerging field routinely gesture toward literature as the realm where secrecy may work productively, they rarely actually engage with literature directly, and literary studies itself remains notably absent from these interdisciplinary debates. This collection of essays seeks to redress that lacuna by focusing on literary texts written in an American cultural tradition in which the interplay between transparency, exposure, fear, secrecy, security, surveillance, information, and disinformation has long played a determinant role in shaping cultural identities. These essays engage in the contemporary debates on the politics of transparency and yet interrogate the premise that the prevalence of such debates is unique to the contemporary world. Starting with the analysis of cultural constructions of intimacy and privacy in Walt Whitman and Henry James as early cases of a critique to transparency, the essays in this volume study how authors and texts from the twentieth and early twenty-first centuries have challenged the tendency to relate dominant views on transparency to present-day technopolitical practices.

Scholars working in the field of critical transparency studies and secrecy studies typically point to literature as a realm in which resistance to transparency is deployed creatively (Birchall 2011, 69–71; Alloa 2022, 15). More specifically, Eva Horn goes as far as claiming that "fiction is actually the only (or at least the most lucid) way to speak, as it were, 'openly' about the precise nature of political secrecy without falling into the trap of the secrecy effect" (Horn 2011, 118). In these cases, authors perceive the specific qualities of literary forms as favoring a critical reflection on the meanings of transparency. The relevance of literature for the study of transparency in general may be considered in two different senses, one thematic, the other formal. On the one hand, as several essays included in this volume show, fiction in general holds an evident potential for speculation about the tensions between secrecy and transparency when considered in terms of its ability to represent reality in a variety of ways. For example, the works by Philip K. Dick, William Gibson, Toni Morrison, or Dave Eggers explored in this volume are speculative imaginations of realities in which the current fears expressed by critical transparency studies materialize. On the other hand, literature works through the constant interplay between the transparency and opacity of the medium of language itself. A literary text plays with its own transparency and secrecy by sometimes posing as a translucent form of mimesis, while at other times highlighting its own operations of representation through the mediation of language. Thus, as explored in the essays on Walt Whitman and Philip Roth, literature offers rich ground for the exploration of what Sascha Pöhlmann, in his essay on Whitman, calls the fantasy of media transparency.

Taking a cue from Horn's (2011, 118) claim that literature may be a significant realm in searching for models where secrecy may be put to productive use against the excesses of surveillance mechanisms deployed by the state or by corporations, this collection considers the relevance of the transparency/privacy binary in the specific context of American literature. If, as Clare Birchall and others suggest, literature is the place where we may find productive forms of secrecy at work, the study of American literature may be a privileged ground on which to counterbalance the risk of presentism that comes from an excessive focus on digital media, along with the tendency to highlight its own historical moment, that are perceived in much of this current debate on transparency. In the context of American cultural history, transparency and secrecy have been key ideas for the construction of communities shaped, among others, by the cultural forces of Puritanism and Enlightenment Liberalism.[1]

---

1   See McKenna (2007, 5) on the dynamic blend between Puritan religiosity and political liberalism in US cultural history. McKenna, in turn, cites Alexis de Tocqueville's celebrated observation about the American combination of

In both cultural paradigms, privacy, secrecy, transparency and publicity have been central elements, though differently articulated, in ways that have proved determinant to the development of the country's literary imagination. Our volume includes essays that offer early critical accounts of transparency (as attested by the essays on Whitman, James, or Ellison and Schuyler) and others that re-create historical cultural articulations of transparency and secrecy from a contemporary perspective (as in the essays on Morrison, Yamashita, or Roth).

The essays included in this volume, moreover, offer a wide European perspective on American literature. They use transparency as the central concept but in their discussions mobilize a whole constellation of associated terms, many of which stand in dialectical tension with it. Transparency emerges as both a dream and a nightmare, and it informs cultural discourses on the public and the private while connecting to notions of opacity, intimacy, surveillance, and control. These conflicting views must be considered against the backdrop of the critical history of transparency as a political ideal and in the context of current debates in the emerging field of critical transparency studies.

2. The Political Meaning of Transparency

In contemporary usage, the term "transparency" tends to be positively associated with openness and the avoidance of secrets in the realms of government and business. It is in this sense that the terms "transparency" and "secrecy" may be identified as standing in dialectical tension, involved in a "cycle of concealment and revelation" (Birchall 2021, 3). Critical discourse on transparency generally sets it in opposition to situations in which opacity in governance and decision-making processes may lead to injustice and corruption. Initiatives such as Transparency International or the Sunlight Foundation are based on the consideration of transparency as promoting accountability and preventing corruption at the level of governance.[2]

The political meaning of the term emerged from a double metaphorical turn, leading from the realm of optics to epistemology to political theory. A brief exercise in conceptual archaeology may help to reconstruct the way in which "transparency" is used today in discussions of political and social practices. *The Oxford English Dictionary* defines "transparency"

---

the "spirit of liberty" and the "spirit of religion" (48). The second chapter of McKenna's *The Puritan Origins of American Patriotism* studies the shift in scholarship on the relation between Puritan religiosity and revolutionary politics.

2   See https://www.transparency.org/en and https://sunlightfoundation.com/.

as "the quality or condition of being transparent; perviousness to light; diaphaneity, pellucidity." The etymology of the word leads back to the medieval Latin form *transpārēntia*, which in turn comes from the combination of the prefix *trans-* (across, beyond, through) and *pārēre* (to appear, be visible). Figurative uses of the adjective "transparent," meaning manifest, evident, or clear, work as a metaphorical expansion of the original, or literal, meaning of the term pertaining to the field of optics.[3] They connect to a whole range of figurative uses of terms related to light and vision in Western epistemology that go back at least to Platonic philosophy, while more generally the "modality of the visual" is, as Martin Jay argued in *Downcast Eyes*, omnipresent in human language (1994: 1). Ida Koivisto (2022, 23–28) has explored, in *The Transparency Paradox*, the implications of such visual semantics in the use of the concept of transparency, identifying the conceptual metaphor "understanding is seeing" as the cognitive basis for the epistemological and political uses of the term "transparency." The epistemological take on the idea of transparency is related to communication, openness, and communal connection to others. In this sense, being transparent to others is depicted as an enhanced, unmediated state of connection, free from distortion (see Birchall 2021, 7; Fenster 2017, 6).

This modality of the visual is central to modern literature as well, and specifically to the novel as a genre that constantly speculates on the possibility of making its medium appear transparent to its audience. On the one hand, the development of this drive toward transparency in literature may be connected to the Enlightenment vocabulary of light and visibility. As Michael McKeon (2002, 10) argues in his seminal study on the origins of the English novel (first published in 1987), this drive is often codified as an "evolution from the darkness of distortion towards semantic light." While early modern English writers like Daniel Defoe attempted to present their fiction as unmediated, transparent discourse, others, such as Laurence Sterne, would parody and expose such attempts at transparency as a disguised form of mediation.[4] On the other hand, narratologists like Lisa Zunshine (2008, 78) or Dorrit Cohn (1978, 3–9) have studied how fiction creates illusions of transparency that make an interiority visible in a unique way. At the time when "transparency" became a prominent term in the Enlightenment, no one better represents the Western prevalence of an ideal transparency through self-exposure than Jean-Jacques Rousseau, as critics have repeatedly emphasized. His *Confessions* (1782) set a model

---

3   Alloa (2018, 33) notes that the earliest occurrences of such figurative use of the term date from the 1590s.
4   More than a century before him, however, Miguel de Cervantes's convoluted justification for his *Don Quixote* (1605) already played on the dynamics between the illusion of transparency and textual mediation.

for the representation of subjectivity in Western literatures that has been endlessly imitated in the forms of the journal or diary, autobiography, autofiction, and fictional autobiography.[5]

Defoe's *Journal of the Plague Year* (1722)—whose subtitle describes it as "observations or memorials of the most remarkable occurrences, as well public as private"—also works as an early modern corollary of how fantasies of transparency were articulated in terms of access to both interiority and the public realm. Written as a citizen's first-hand account of the "Great Plague of London" of 1665, it both communicates its narrator's thoughts and impressions about the spread of the disease as well as describes minutely the institutional mechanisms deployed by the London authorities to control and eradicate it. The text works to the extent that the narrative voice created by Defoe succeeds in communicating such subjective memories and perceptions of a series of events happening in an environment highly regulated by institutions whose dynamics are made visible to the reader in the narrator's account. Fictional configurations of transparency afford a reflection on the different facets of the political use of the concept as well: from making the world knowable through its fictional representation (which would lead to a form of realism close to Georg Lukacs's theorization) to probing the extent to which individual interiority can or should be made visible.

The political use of "transparency" partakes of the "understanding is seeing" conceptual metaphor, expanding it to the realm of government and the state. Repeatedly, authors like Birchall, Koivisto, and others situate the origins of this political use of the idea of transparency (if not the term itself) in the Enlightenment period. Emmanuel Alloa, however, has recently questioned such lineage of the term, claiming that the contemporary use of "transparency" does not coincide with Enlightened notions (Alloa 2022, 167). The origins of the political use of the term are not to be found in one specific text and often overlap with other figurative articulations, such as the concept of publicity introduced by Jeremy Bentham in *Essay on Political Tactics* (1843), the idea of open government advocated by Karl Popper, or the philosophy of the public sphere and its reliance on publicity developed by Jürgen Habermas (1991, 65).[6]

---

5   See Starobinski (1988) and Jacques Derrida (1976) as classical instances of such a reading of Rousseau's *Confessions*. More recently, Khawaja (2018) and Schneider (2018) have read the *Confessions* as a central text in the Western canon on "the dream of transparency" (Schneider 2018, 86). See Pöhlmann's essay in this volume for a reconsideration of Rousseau's place in this tradition.

6   See Mehrpouya and Djelic (2014) for a conceptual genealogy of "transparency" as a political term, and Holzner and Holzner (2006, 12–46) for a historical survey on the idea of transparency. More recently, Birchall (2021) devotes chapter 1 of her book *Radical Secrecy* to the historical review of the interplay between secrecy and transparency in American political culture.

According to Mehrpouya and Djelic (2014, 5), the term was rarely used in philosophical, political, or administrative documents before the 1970s. Yet, ideas connecting visibility in governance to accountability, applied to the political and the commercial realms, may be found in eighteenth-century texts. When Adam Smith, in his *Theory of Moral Sentiments* (1759), introduced the figure of the "impartial spectator" as an entity against whose judgment all individual, social, and commercial acts may be measured, he was depicting a social system where visibility equaled moral accountability. In the ideological context of the emerging United States, Thomas Paine (2000, 183) advocated in 1791 in *The Rights of Man* for a representative system in which "the reason for everything must publicly appear," holding representatives accountable in the eyes of their fellow citizens and anticipating the Freedom of Information Act passed in the mid-twentieth century. Finally, Bentham's introduction of the idea of publicity in his *Essay on Political Tactics*, written in 1791 but not published until 1843, would prove deeply influential in shaping the ideal of transparency in political language.

When tracing the use of the term in administrative norms meant to enhance transparency in governance, political theorists tend to consider the Freedom of Information Act of 1966 to be the first American document to articulate transparency policies for all the agencies and organs of the US government (Berliner, 2014: 480; Mehrpouya and Djelic 2014, 27).[7] The American FOIA did indeed use the term "transparency" in its 1966 text when establishing the functions of the FOIA Public Liaisons, who are "responsible for assisting in reducing delays, increasing transparency and understanding of the status of requests, and assisting in the resolution of disputes."

In historical accounts of transparency as a political concept in the United States, Supreme Court Justice Louis Brandeis's famous statement that "sun is the best disinfectant" is often quoted. This sentence appeared in Brandeis's 1913 article in *Harper's*, "What Publicity Can Do." The idea was already present in his unfulfilled project to write an article titled "The Duty of Publicity" as a twin piece to his "The Right to Privacy" (1890). What is not so often quoted is the second half of the sentence containing the famous quote, which reads, "electric light [is] the most efficient policeman" (Brandeis 1913, 10). Transparency, when codified as the transparency of the state to citizens and of states to one another, is attributed the quality of universal good and associated with accountability, prevention of corruption, and strengthening of participatory democracy (Birchall 2021, 5–6). It occupies the positive pole in a moral scale that has secrecy—standing for antidemocratic practices and corruption—at its

---

7   Berliner (2014, 480) identifies Sweden as the first country to have passed a Freedom of Information law, in 1766.

opposite end. Brandeis's reference to the policing role of transparency, however, suggests the possibility of an institutional control over citizenship, which leads down a very different path: that of state control over individuals, which is frequently regarded in a negative light by scholars in critical transparency studies, as will be discussed below.

The positive view of transparency as accountability in governance remains, however, the dominant one. Discussions on the topic state once again how transparency is articulated as an ideal for democratic societies.[8] Alloa (2018, 31–32) has offered a detailed enumeration of the virtues typically attributed to transparency in contemporary political discourse, and Mark Fenster (2015, 2) describes a "transformative narrative" in which transparency enables a "virtuous [. . .] chain of events" leading to enhanced democracy. Political theorists use almost exactly the same words to acknowledge how government transparency is associated with good governance: "Transparency has been hailed as the key to better governance" (Berliner 2014, 479); "Government transparency is increasingly regarded as a vital component of good governance" (Meijer 2015, 189). Most critical accounts of the notion of transparency share as their premise the universal acceptance of the term as holding positive values. Alloa and Thomä (2018, 2) argue that today "there is a growing consensus that transparency is one of democracy's best tools and that every citizen has a right to transparency. Demands for more transparency are more widespread than ever." Most interestingly, they claim that "as opposed to concepts like regulation or surveillance, transparency doesn't seem to have a negative counterpart that would counter its ambitions" (2).

In contradiction to this claim, however, I argue that transparency is often opposed to the notion of secrecy as resistance to demands of transparency. In fact, many accounts of transparency seem to concur with the moral polarization between transparency and secrecy (see Birchall 2021, 4; Holzner and Holzner 2006, 5–6), and assume the transparency ideal as a given.[9] As I argue later in this introduction, such an assumption is often strategically deployed by the authors quoted here as a first step in a dialectical argumentation in which transparency will be rearticulated in adversarial, negative terms. While historically the term "transparency" has been applied mostly to the relation of the state to its citizens, its dialectical interplay with the notions of secrecy and privacy affords the consideration of transparency in a different sense, as connected to notions of surveillance and exposure of citizens by institutions. The original use of the term thus slips into another, complementary but different, meaning, which

---

8   See Hood and Heald (2006); Alloa and Thomä (2018, 2); Birchall (2021, 5–6); Koivisto (2022, 3–4).
9   See Birchall (2021, 2): "Transparency and openness are uncritically lauded as morally superior to secrecy."

indicates a reversal in the direction in which the idea of transparency is to be applied (not of the state to citizens, but of citizens to the state).

In the introduction to her book *Radical Secrecy*, Clare Birchall (2021, 4) states, "Secrecy and transparency are malleable, floating signifiers that take form in certain ways at particular times, harnessed by various actors and rooted within different discourses." "Malleability" is meant to account for how, in contemporary discourse, the discussion of transparency typically tends to place it in a less favorable light than usually claimed in the tradition of political thought sketched above. As examined in the next section, attitudes to the ideal of transparency become more critical when the object to which it is applied is no longer the state but the individual. While traditional Enlightenment notions of transparency focus almost exclusively on the transparency of institutions to their citizens, it should be noted that the same intellectual milieu also contributed to the design of institutions created for the control and surveillance of citizens. The academic field of critical transparency studies examines different notions of transparency, with an emphasis on the shift from the utopian desire for institutional transparency—which is still acknowledged as the main political meaning of the term—to the panoptical dystopia in which individual privacy would not exist.

3. Critical Transparency Studies

Critical transparency studies form the theoretical horizon of this volume. The term was coined by Emmanuel Alloa and Dieter Thomä in the volume *Transparency, Society, and Subjectivity* (2018, 3) to refer to what was then perceived as an emerging field.[10] Yet, despite these authors' emphasis on the novelty of such a field, it should be observed that relevant precedents before the turn of the millennium include influential works such as Gianni Vattimo's and David Brin's identically titled books *The Transparent Society* (1990 and 1998, respectively). These, in turn, anticipate the highly influential *The Transparency Society* by Byung-Chul Han (2015).

In the introduction to *Government Transparency*, Tero Erkkilä (2012, xi) argues that "social-scientific studies of transparency tend to fall into two categories, looking at the issue either from the perspective of democracy or from that of economic efficiency." What Erkkilä perceives as the blurring of limits between governments and markets provides the key to untangling the many realms of application of the term "transparency," as well as the specific critiques of each one. The critique of transparency in the works cited above tends to focus on four interlocking areas: 1) the

---

10 See, among others, Boothroyd (2011); Dean (2002); Birchall (2011); Horn (2011); Broeders (2016); Koivisto (2022).

ideal of political transparency associated with notions of accountability and good governance; 2) transparency as a governing tool, connected to surveillance societies; 3) transparency as datafication (Birchall 2021, 2) in a neoliberal environment that monetizes the availability and circulation of data; and 4) transparency as self-exposure, perceived as a consequence of the blurring of the limit between the public and private spheres facilitated by digital technologies and, in particular, by social media.

More specifically, each of the realms mentioned articulates the concept of transparency by invoking a specific form of relation between citizens, states, and markets and by establishing an ideological matrix that justifies those forms of relation:

1. Articulated as transparency of the state to its citizens. This is related to Enlightenment conceptions of the public realm, constructed against the grain of forms of governance relying on *arcana imperii*, or state secrets (Horn 2011, 104). It is meant to prevent or counteract corruption and to foster accountability. Its goal is to banish secrecy from governance, as it is associated with medieval "mysteries of the state" and thus connected to premodern forms of irrationalism and superstition (Horn 2011, 104–5).

2. Articulated as transparency of citizens to the state. This involves forms of social control in what Michel Foucault calls "disciplinary societies" (1979, 209), as part of a process of modernization that fosters the classification and record-keeping practices Foucault extensively analyzed. Adam Smith's notion of an "impartial spectator" as judge of individual action, and Jeremy Bentham's utilitarian assertion that surveillance and transparency are necessary for the improvement of society's general happiness, constitute the intellectual basis of this conception of transparency in the English-speaking world.

3. Articulated as transparency of citizens and states to markets. This articulation originates in a neoliberal understanding of the public in terms of marketable information, and it is enabled by technologies that facilitate the accumulation of data and its circulation through practices associated with the previous two articulations of transparency. As discussed by Birchall and others, this "datafication" of both citizens and states is used for commercial purposes and has the depoliticization of the public sphere as a side effect.[11]

---

11 By "providing data as proxy for accountability" (Birchall 2021, 82), the public sphere is flooded by information presented under the claim of nonpartisanship, thus creating an illusion of its being apolitical and nonideological (83). This,

4. Articulated as transparency of individuals' private lives to the mediasphere. This is enabled by the spread of social media that foster social interactions through digital technologies, and it has the effect of blurring the Enlightenment liberal distinction between the public and private spheres. Although critics like Han or Dean, in their critique of the exposure of the self in social media, tend to perceive this form of transparency as a direct outcome of twenty-first-century technology, twentieth-century critical theory had anticipated its logic though concepts like "simulacra" (Jean Baudrillard) and "the society of spectacle" (Guy Debord). Literature is most clearly a privileged realm for the study of such dynamics, to the extent that the book as a medium has worked at least since Rousseau as a tool to achieve such individual transparency in the mediasphere through its configuration as a vehicle for the confessional, for the exposure of the self to others.

Most works published in the field of critical transparency studies engage in more than one of the above articulations of transparency simultaneously. Perhaps Han's *The Transparency Society* may be cited as illustrative of this feature in the way it connects the notions of transparency, exposure, and social media. Han expands the realm of application of the term "transparency" to refer simultaneously to state transparency and individual self-exposure in the context of information technologies. His take on the issue, which has proved deeply influential, unifies both poles under a homogeneous drive to eliminate secrecy from all planes of existence: "Transparency is a systematic compulsion gripping all social processes" (Han 2015, 2).

Han's argument is built on sweeping statements that conflate all potential articulations of transparency into a single sociological perception, which both increases the rhetorical impact of his treatise and diminishes the intellectual insight of his views on specific aspects of social life. When examining how other authors tend to organize their views on transparency, however, two recurrent argumentative strategies emerge, which we may tentatively call the paradoxical and the teleological.

On the one hand, authors like Erkkilä (2012), Alloa (2022), and Koivisto (2022) see the different articulations of transparency as simultaneously coexisting in a paradoxical balance, aiming both toward greater democratization and toward dystopian forms of social control. The titles of Alloa's and Koivisto's recent books, *That Obscure Thing Called*

---

in Birchall's argument, becomes an obstacle to political intervention rather an enabling of it.

Transparency and *The Transparency Paradox*, respectively, announce such a perception of paradox.[12]

On the other hand, authors like Holzner and Holzner (2006), Mehrpouya and Djelic (2014), and Birchall (2021) adopt a diachronic perspective on the different articulations of transparency, seeing them as emerging from specific historical contexts. Each of the articulations is perceived as having enabled another one, so that they could be seen as constituting a sequence of developments in the thought about transparency. In their view, the concept seems to follow a negative teleological trajectory that led from the original envisioning of transparency as a democratic ideal toward the—often dystopian—perception of current datafication systems, from the transparent state to the transparent subject. Fenster (2015) and Mozorov (2013, 63–99) are illustrative of this argumentation when they depict a shift in transparency's focus "from politically crucial, bespoke documents to mass agglomerations of data" (Fenster 2015, 8), thus enabling the passage from articulations 2 to 3 in the list above, which, in their view, would derive from the transference of citizens' data and their management from the state to corporations.

Although their scope, perspective, and implications branch out in different directions, there are several common traits we may identify in these works on transparency, hence conferring a considerable intellectual homogeneity on the emerging field of transparency studies: They use transparency as an adversarial term for political contestation, identifying state surveillance and self-exposure as the twin evils embodying the totalizing tendencies of technopolitical transparency. They tend to draw on a Foucauldian theoretical framework identifying modernity as the age of discipline and surveillance, and they implicitly endorse a liberal understanding of the public/private divide. In denouncing the loss of privacy as a problem in the contemporary world, they point to neoliberalism as a regime—be it economic or political—that promotes a society based on the total eradication of privacy. All these features articulate an oppositional dynamics that needs to be further explored, as most recent theoretical approaches to transparency adopt a critical perspective on the concept, emphasizing its ambiguities, risks, and paradoxes.

4. Oppositional Dynamics

Birchall (2021, 70) has argued that critical transparency studies display "a concern with what transparency practices occlude as much as make visible [. . .]. What all critiques of transparency share is the claim that there is a gap between transparency as an ideal and what actually happens

---

12 The title of Koivisto's book, moreover, uses an already well-established phrase seen in work by Nissenbaum (2011), Bernstein (2012), and Burt (2019).

in its name." Birchall identifies the field as a form of resistance to the widespread positive valence of transparency as a political ideal, examined above. In so doing, she illustrates the way in which this field of study is systematically constructed through an oppositional dynamic that follows a two-step argument: First, it acknowledges that positive understandings of transparency are omnipresent in contemporary cultural and political parlance, and that it is universally accepted as a desirable ideal, and second, it subverts such consensus by identifying its negative downside. This is related to the perspectival shift in how the term has been articulated in critical discourse. This shift may be described as one from the Enlightenment understanding of "transparency as a norm of liberation" to "transparency as a governing tool" in post-Enlightenment discourses (Mehrpouya and Djelic 2014, 14). While the former may be regarded as still desirable, the latter is seen as involving a great risk to individual freedoms.

To assess the persistence of such argumentative logic, one needs only look at the introductory sections from works in the field of critical transparency studies. Eva Horn (2011, 104), writing about the "politics of secrecy," starts from the assumption that "the political secret has acquired a bad reputation." She formulates the omnipresence of transparency in contemporary societies from a reversed perspective: as the aspiration to eliminate secrecy. In her writing, the key argumentative step is the adversative turn meant to acknowledge how, in spite of the pervasive culture of transparency just identified, states continue to exert power through a variety of institutions and practices driven by secrecy: "*And yet* modern states have not only built up massive, highly professional intelligence infrastructure; they also depend on espionage, secret operations, surveillance and the classification of information, which are indispensable governmental and military tools" (104; emphasis added).

Along similar lines, Emmanuel Alloa (2018, 23) states that today "transparency stands for an uncontestable new state of affairs," but only to dismiss that claim and argue that "we have never been transparent" (25). Similarly, Clare Birchall's (2021, 3) innovative take on the interplay between transparency and secrecy in *Radical Secrecy* draws on the two-step argumentative logic sketched above by consciously identifying it: "In temporarily reversing the values and promises of secrecy and transparency, I go against the conventions of routine discourse." Mark Fenster (2015, 3) asserts in "Transparency in Search of a Theory" that "transparency has captured the public imagination" and has become "the dramatically satisfying answer to every crisis and question about the state." After building his argument on the prevalence of transparency as a political ideal for the first two pages of the text, Fenster takes a second step: "*But* transparency has not proved to be a panacea for good, open governance, and its increasing significance as an administrative norm has not rendered the government fully visible" (3; emphasis added). Fenster's argument underscores the way in which the critique of transparency is codified by him and other authors as a reaction to the concept's failure to fulfill the promise of "good, open governance."

Based on the textual evidence gathered above, we could argue that critical transparency studies is a turn against transparency. The reasons for this turn may be varied, but what all scholars of critical transparency studies share is that they do not accept the ideal of transparency at face value. Foucault's research on Jeremy Bentham's interest in surveillance practices as determinant for modernity may be identified as a turning point in the intellectual history of the concept, as it stresses how transparency of citizens to the state works as a tool for control. Another milestone could be found in Jean-François Lyotard's (1979, 6) claim, in *The Postmodern Condition*, that "the ideology of communicational 'transparency'" goes "hand in hand with the commercialization of knowledge." Transparency, in this sense, would become corrupted when given over to commercial interests.

In the texts quoted above, the shift is noticeable in the adversarial position adopted by their authors as a "realization" of the negative side of transparency against the grain of what is recognized as near-universal positive consensus on transparency. The validity of such positive valence is rarely questioned in itself. Rather, most critical transparency scholars tend to adopt an unfavorable narrative in which the Enlightenment dream of transparency is seen as having been corrupted or insufficiently realized. The nature of the adverse insights offered by these authors may vary—not enough transparency, not the right kind of transparency, transparency is actually a negative thing, and so forth—but they rely on the identification of neoliberalism as the entity to be made responsible for such deviations from the Enlightenment ideal of transparency, which they in the end still endorse. Han (2015, viii) begins his argument on transparency by claiming that "Transparency is an ideology," labeling it as "a neoliberal dispositive." The term "dispositive" was defined by Louis Althusser (1971, 82) in *Ideology and Ideological State Apparatuses* as an "absolutely ideological 'conceptual' device." Han's use of the term draws on the Althusserian gesture aimed at denaturalizing ideology—that is, showing that it is constructed in response to specific interests—and it identifies transparency as ideologically biased by neoliberal commercial and political interests.[13]

---

13 Han does not use the term "neoliberal" again in this book but rather replaces it with a set of other terms that are used interchangeably. Thus, for example, on page 11, Han attributes the destruction of the contemporary subject to "the society of exhibition" (note the strong echo from Debord here) and to "capitalist economy" in general.

Han's take on the issue, while perhaps the most often quoted by virtue of its succinctness, is far from unique. Mehrpouya and Djelic's (2014, 34) work similarly begins by acknowledging that "citations of the term 'transparency' in printed media have literally exploded over the past three decades, showing how dominant the norm has become globally," before going on to immediately denounce how "the neoliberal turn that characterized the late twentieth century fundamentally transformed the meaning of transparency and its role in shaping human organizations, economies, polities and societies." They unequivocally attribute responsibility for the transformation of transparency to neoliberalism, which they claim has "emptied transparency of most of its emancipating content" (46), "with the ultimate objective of serving the interest of capital markets and investors" (41). In "The Privatization of Human Interests or, How Transparency Breeds Conformity," Thomas Docherty describes the subject as "transparent and precarious" in what he identifies as "the contemporary triumph of a politics of transparency" and claims that "we are witnessing here the culmination of a particular neoliberal political drive" (2018, 301). Distinctions between kinds of transparency—of citizens to the state, of the state to citizens—are engulfed, at this point of Docherty's and others' arguments, by the neoliberal logic of transparency of both state and citizens to corporate power. Along similar lines, Boothroyd (2011, 42–43) identifies neoliberalism's drive toward transparency with the conflation of the public and the private, thus threatening the traditional liberal divide that established the realm of privacy as the one where individual secrets may be protected:

> Just as the cradle-to-grave notion of the welfare state as an expression of the collective, public responsibility of each for all is being ushered off the stage in neoliberal societies, the cradle-to-grave recording and publication of individual lives is becoming commonplace. It seems irresistible to see the decline of the "public sphere" in western democracies as the counterpoint to the rise of "public individualism" expressed through what could be termed communicative self-publicity.

Boothroyd's argument is twofold, attributing to neoliberalism a dismantling of both the welfare state and the traditional liberal divide between public and private spheres. The origin of both, he argues, lies in the devaluation of the public sphere as a political concept.

In most of the examples quoted above, the term "neoliberalism" is problematic, because its meaning has been unstable across time and discourses. As noted by Boas and Gans-Morse, its use has undergone a nearly complete reversal of denotation in the recent past: "The contemporary use of neoliberalism is even more striking because scholars once employed the term nearly the opposite of how it is commonly used today" (2009: 138). The origins of the term "neoliberalism" may be traced back to the last years of the nineteenth century in French and English. When the term was used in 1951 by Milton Friedman, one of the proponents of neoliberal economic principles, it referred mainly to an economic ideology advocating state intervention, as opposed to classical, laissez-faire liberalism. When the term entered common usage in the 1980s, however, its meaning came to be nearly the opposite, as used by the opposition to Augusto Pinochet's regime in Chile, or by the Zapatista movement in Chiapas in the early 1990s to criticize economic deregulation in specific industries. Eventually, it would come to be commonly associated with the free-market policies advocated by Margaret Thatcher in the UK and Ronald Reagan in the US.

A further complication when attempting to define "neoliberalism" is the fact that the term has been applied to policies pertaining to diverse areas of the economy, politics, and society:

> At a base level we can say that when we make reference to "neoliberalism," we are generally referring to the new political, economic and social arrangements within society that emphasize market relations, re-tasking the role of the state, and individual responsibility. Most scholars tend to agree that neoliberalism is broadly defined as the extension of competitive markets into all areas of life, including the economy, politics and society. (Springer et al. 2016, 2)

As Boas and Gans-Morse (2009, 138) note, "neoliberalism" has become an umbrella term that indicates oppositional ideology rather than identifying a specific set of values or policies: "Neoliberalism is employed asymmetrically across ideological divides: it is used frequently by those who are critical of free markets, but rarely by those who view marketization more positively." Springer et al. (2016, 2) conclude that "the term is frequently used somewhat indiscriminately and quite pejoratively to mean anything 'bad.'"

This vague usage of "neoliberalism" is also prevalent in critical discussions of transparency, where the word mainly functions as an umbrella term for everything that is wrong with contemporary democratic societies. Yet, this widespread identification of neoliberalism as a "corrupting" entity reveals two relevant argumentative strategies used by scholars working in critical transparency studies. The first strategy is to identify such a corrupting agent, which enables the articulation of a critical position and the development of a dialectics. The structural role played by the term "neoliberal," affording critics of transparency a way to establish a binary opposition between the neoliberal take on transparency and their own, implicit advocacy of liberal approaches to the term, is more relevant to scholars in critical transparency studies, I would claim, than the restriction of its meaning to a single, universal definition. Hence, most of them use it without first establishing a clear definition of "neoliberalism." The term is thus used loosely and often differently by each critic, but all of them underscore, through their use of "neoliberalism," the friction between what is and what could or should be. The second discursive strategy is to revalidate the classical liberal notion of transparency, in contrast with its perceived corruption by neoliberalism. That is, to the extent one identifies neoliberalism as a corrupting agent, the validity of a previous, primary concept of transparency which had emerged in early modern liberal thought—the one allegedly corrupted by neoliberal policies—is reinstated. We may observe how, in their denunciation of neoliberalism as corrupting agent of transparency—one that turns potentially desirable forms of transparency into strategies for control and datafication of citizens' privacy—many critics turn to a previous notion of transparency that comes to be regarded as positive or desirable. As critics like Neocleous (2002, 85–86) and Horn (2011, 112–13) have pointed out, the contemporary critique of transparency is still—though perhaps paradoxically—anchored in the liberal political tradition that establishes both the need for transparency in public governance and the right to privacy at individual level.

A further problem associated with the use of "neoliberalism" as an adversarial term in critical transparency studies is the overemphasis on the unprecedented and exclusively contemporary character of the present as the age of transparency. A typical opening gesture in contemporary writing on transparency is its identification as "a defining feature of the contemporary *Zeitgeist*" (Boothroyd 2011, 42).[14] Han (2015, 16) specifically identifies the "society of transparency" as a "contemporary" phenomenon, equating it with the "the age of Facebook and Photoshop" (10). Emmanuel Alloa (2018, 23) has coined the term "TransparentoCene,"[15] following Daniel C. Dennett and Deb Roy's (2015, 66) argument that there is a parallel between transparency as a contemporary paradigm facilitated by the spread of digital technology and the Cambrian age, characterized by evolutionary transformations such as the development of camera-style retinas and defensive adaptations in many species (67).

Such efforts to establish the current conception of transparency as the defining feature of the present period risk obviating the ways in which a dialectics between secrecy and transparency may have been at work in other historical and geopolitical periods. The perception of such risk of

---

14 See also Dean (2002, 15); Gilbert (2007, 22); Fenster (2015, 2); Broeders (2016, 295).

15 Note on the current use (and abuse) of the *-cene* suffix in contemporary critical theory in terms such as "Anthropocene," "Capitalocene," "Plasticene"...

presentism has led critics like Birchall (2021), Neocleous (2018), and Gilbert (2007) to examine the concept in a wider historical perspective. In these cases, the concern with the tension between privacy and transparency is recurrently attributed to Enlightenment philosophy and liberalism. Among these, only Gilbert (2007, 24) perceives transparency to be a defining feature of modernity as such. Such a wider diachronic view may throw light on our understanding of our present predicament. It could also contribute to a critical reflection on how fantasies of transparency precede the current technological stage of the mediasphere, since social media have not fundamentally altered the dynamics between privacy and transparency established earlier in modernity (though there have been evident transformations in terms of accessibility and the speed at which information is circulated). By focusing on the American tradition diachronically, the essays collected in this volume seek to explore earlier historical contexts in which transparency has been a relevant factor in articulating the relationship between public and private spheres, between the individual and the collective.

5. Secrecy and Transparency in American Literature

The tensions between transparency and secrecy lie at the core of the American cultural tradition. Three instances from three different periods in the history of the United States may illustrate the complex interplay between the two ideas and the way in which they have shaped the American imagination.

In the early days of the colonial period, the Puritan ethos based on an idea of exemplary transparency became the central metaphor for the establishment of a social compact or covenant, as illustrated by the "City upon a hill" metaphor, first formulated in John Winthrop's (1630, 91) sermon *A Model of Christian Charity*, delivered on board the *Arbella* before setting sail to the New World. In the *Arbella* sermon, Winthrop uses the expression *"the eyes of all people are upon us"* (91).[16] As Perry Miller (1953, 250–52) has noted, however, opposition to what initially appeared as a panoptical utopia soon developed in response to the sort of judiciary practices displayed in the Salem witchcraft trials. Expressions of such opposition are found in texts like Robert Calef's *More Wonders of the*

---

16 This same notion of being observed by others is present in the writings of later Puritans, like Peter Bulkeley (1651, 120), who in *The Gospel Covenant* expressed the principle underpinning Puritan social discipline in the wish "that all that see us, may see and know that the name of the Lord is called upon us."

Invisible World (1697).[17] Calef, in the "Epistle to the Reader" that opens his book, suggests that the attempt to exact transparency from individual citizens so as to search for the invisible presence of the Devil easily turns into an excuse "to let loose the Devils of Envy, Hatred, Pride, Cruelty, and Malice against each other."

When considering the later moment of the founding of the United States, we identify the convergence between the Enlightenment vocabulary on transparency and light as political principles, on one hand, and the Puritan legacy on exemplary transparency, on the other. Clare Birchall and Peter Knight (2023, 27) have observed that the reliance on mechanisms to ensure institutional transparency lies at the very origins of the American republic. Birchall (2021, 16) suggests that the US case is particularly relevant because the country has "exported its legislative and cultural approaches to openness around the globe." Birchall (2021, 27) notes, however, how the setting into motion of an institutional apparatus required a fine balance between transparency and the exercise of a high degree of secrecy. While the Constitution advocated accountability through institutional transparency, Birchall points to how the Senate followed a closed-door policy in its early days, which was already criticized in publications like the *National Gazette*.[18]

A third moment that may help us to sound the depth of the tensions between transparency and secrecy in the American cultural imagination is Transcendentalism. Ralph Waldo Emerson's "Nature" is perhaps the most conspicuous example owing to its use of visual imagery, culminating in the climactic statement "I become a transparent eye-ball. I am nothing. I see all" (1971, 10). Emerson's writings also exemplify the opposing impulses of a desire for total personal transparency and the fierce protection of the individual's interiority against social demands. "Self-Reliance" begins in a clearly utopian tone, with a call to break the barriers between private self and public exposure: "To believe that what is true for you in your private heart is true for all men,—that is genius. Speak your latent conviction, and it shall be the universal sense; for the inmost in due time becomes the outmost" (Emerson 1979, 27). Emerson's aspiration is to an uninterrupted self-exposure to the outside, producing a perfectly transparent communication. Yet, the essay goes on to state that

17 Calef's book was written in response to Cotton Mather's *Wonders of the Invisible World* (1693), a text dominated by visual figurative language expressing social anxiety about the impossibility of achieving a collective state of total transparency preventing the workings of the Devil.

18 The ambivalence of the state toward transparency is perhaps epitomized in a fragment of Article 1 of the Constitution that provides for both openness and secrecy: "Each House shall keep a journal of its proceedings, and from time to time publish the same, excepting such parts as may in their judgment require secrecy."

"society everywhere is in conspiracy against the manhood of every one of its members" (29). This individualist stance works as a warning against the risks of social conformity, and it seems to codify self-reliance as a core inexpugnable interiority. In the tension between what is—society breeding conformity, thus making it necessary to protect one's inner self from it—and what it could be—the spontaneous flow from the inmost to the outmost—lies the utopian potential of Emerson's essay.

These instances illustrate the persistence of a tension between transparency and secrecy in the American cultural imaginary, but they also show the ways in which that tension has been shaped, in literature, as an opposition between individuality and collectivity, in which the former's interiority stands in need of protection from the collective demands of transparency. This is where the critical discourse on transparency that constitutes our theoretical horizon in this volume intersects with the dominant dialectics between individual and society that was articulated in classic American studies by R. W. B. Lewis, Leslie Fiedler, and Richard Chase. As observed by Stacey Margolis (2005, 4), classic American studies have recurrently elaborated a narrative based on the opposition, anchored in liberal ideology, between the public and the private, the collective and the individual. Lewis's discussion of the cultural myth of the American Adam (1955, 112) establishes "the tableau of the solitary figure set over against the inimical society." Fiedler (1966, 26) portrayed such a figure as "the enemy of society on the run toward 'freedom.'" In his attempt to define the romance novel as the characteristic form of American fiction, Chase (1957, 11) posited "the solitary position man has been placed in in this country" as determinant for the American literary imagination, connecting such a sense of opposition between individual and the state to Puritanism (8).[19] To such oppositions we may add the clash between agents of surveillance and an individual's inscrutable interiority. A significant part of the American literary tradition seems to be driven by an adversarial impulse, so that we can see the apparent desirability of transparency clashing time and again against the antisocial, individualistic impulses of the American ethos.

Classic texts in the American tradition that represent this conflict may allow us to perceive the double relevance of transparency in connection to literature sketched above, both thematic (as the tension between secrecy and transparency is central to plot and theme) and formal (experimenting with the transparency and opacity of the medium of language itself). Both Nathaniel Hawthorne and Herman Melville explored it at length in their fiction. *The Scarlet Letter* (2003 [first published in 1850]), and *Billy*

---

19 On the Puritan origins of American individualism, see Bercovitch (1975, 1–34).

Budd, Sailor (1984)[20] are prime examples of the complexities and contradictions at work in the notion of transparency, which both anticipate and enable the thematic and stylistic configurations of the later American tradition that this volume seeks to explore.

In *The Novel and the Police*, D. A. Miller (1988, 19) claims that "disapproval is the hallmark of all the novels which, abandoning the strategy of treating discipline with discretion, make discipline a conspicuous practice." Miller points to an obvious yet inescapable aspect of the representation of institutional power in literature: that narrative perspective in fiction that has most contributed to make such Foucauldian institutional design visible tends to be consistently *outside* or *against* such power. The texts Miller describes are of the kind that tell about their heroes' and heroines' subjection to social regulation through surveillance and exposure techniques "with regret." To mention an evident example, it is Winston Smith's perspective, not Big Brother's, that guides our perception of the fictional world of George Orwell's *1984* (1949). Miller thus points to an inherent adversarial quality of the notion of transparency as dramatized in fiction and as articulated in critical theory. In the American literary tradition, I would argue, such adversarial quality is a dominant feature.

In *Billy Budd, Sailor*, Herman Melville (1984, 1415) famously dramatized the tragic outcome of the clash between the truth-extracting mechanics of the court-martial and the impenetrability of human interiority. Melville resorts, at the crucial moment of Billy Budd's interrogation before the drumhead court-martial led by Captain Vere, to a key distinction between "private conscience" and the martial code everyone on board is bound by. The disturbance provoked among the crew by what they perceive to be an unfair treatment of a sailor, Billy Budd, who can hardly defend himself before the court, may be attributed to their perception of a breach between ethics and the martial code in Vere's words. Yet, what the text aims at exposing is the inefficacy of official procedures to grasp a truth that remains incomprehensible in spite of the complete exposure of the facts. The text stands on the conviction that private conscience remains inviolable, even by the most perfected surveillance mechanisms. The transparent procedure actually produces the obfuscation of truth, rather than contributing to its revelation.

Yet, as Miller (1988, 20) appositely observes, "whenever the novel censures policing power, it has already reinvented it, in *the very practice of novelistic representation*." Hawthorne's narrative strategies in *The Scarlet*

---

20   The text was written between 1886 and 1891 and left unfinished by Melville upon his death; it was not discovered and published until 1924, as part of the Standard Edition of Melville's Complete Works. It was republished in 1984 in a Library of America edition.

Letter illustrate this point by featuring Chillingworth's efforts at policing Dimmesdale's interiority in censoring terms, while simultaneously offering readers a view into "the interior of a heart" formulated in nearly the same terms. The relationship between the two characters is developed in two consecutive chapters in which Hawthorne depicts Chillingworth struggling to extract a truth from Dimmesdale, codified in the language of treasure hunting as Hawthorne focalizes Chillingworth's perspective (2003, 109) and gold-digging: "He now dug into the poor clergyman's heart, like a miner searching for gold" (113). The next chapter is entitled precisely "The Interior of a Heart," and it offers to the reader a privileged view of Dimmesdale's interiority that only fictional representation can make available. Beyond this apparent contradiction, Hawthorne is interested in pursuing further the potential of such revelatory dynamics. At one point, he anticipates that the minister's soul will "flow forth in a dark, but transparent stream, bringing all its mysteries into the daylight" (109). Yet, throughout the narrative, Hawthorne plays with the community's inability to grasp such mysteries, even when brought into the daylight, and insists that the sort of *aletheia* forced by Chillingworth cannot essentially challenge "the whole system of ancient prejudice" (143), as the text's ending confirms.

Melville seems to have been acutely aware of the contradictory impulse in narrative mediation in the writing of *Billy Budd*, the need to tell clashing against the acknowledgment that language cannot reach the innermost conscience of a character. Nowhere is this featured more cunningly than in the narrator's convoluted account of the final encounter between Billy Budd and Captain Vere before the former's execution. The narrator first acknowledges that "beyond the communication of the sentence what took place at this interview was never known," only to go on to propose that "some conjectures may be ventured" (1984, 1418). What follows is the narrator's speculation on what such communication might have been like, packed with expressions of probability that obfuscate the transparent reporting of such private conversation ("in consonance with the spirit of Captain Vere," "it is not improbable that," "even more may have been," 1418–19). The passage concludes with a self-denying statement on the narrator's part: "But there is no telling the sacrament. [. . .] There is privacy at the time, inviolable to the survivor" (1419). After having devoted a long passage to the attempt to provide an account of what might have happened in the closed room, in private conversation, the narrator admits that there is no way of telling, no one to know except those involved in the "sacrament" of confession that such conversation represents.

We may observe the fundamental difference between Melville's representational strategy, simultaneously providing and disavowing the intel on what went on between the two characters, and Hawthorne's take on the issue of individual impenetrability in *The Scarlet Letter*, most famously in the chapter "Another View of Hester." Here, in accordance with Miller's (1988, 20) argument that the novel, while censoring policing power, reinvents it in the very practice of novelistic representation, the narrator's omniscience provides the access to Hester's interiority that is refused to the Puritan magistrates and neighbors, thus replacing their policing role at the level of plot. Hawthorne (2003, 143–44) famously writes in this chapter, "It is remarkable that persons who speculate the most boldly often conform with the most perfect quietude to the external regulations of society." In so doing, he actualizes the twin Puritan problems of determining sanctity and identifying evil on the basis of external behavior, offering fiction as a form of mediation between individual secrecy and total transparency.

Together, the two texts briefly discussed in this introduction illustrate many of the key issues explored in the chapters to follow, as all of them complicate the binarism between the private and the public, identifying the fundamental role of secrecy in social contexts driven by a will to transparency and, most importantly, offering creative solutions to the shortcomings of transparency as a totalizing concept. In the classical texts used as precedents here, Hawthorne and Melville not only discuss the politics of transparency of their respective fictional universes at the thematic level of plot and discourse but also enact the resistance and temptation to a dream of transparency in their very narrative form.

The following chapters discuss the work of a number of authors from the second half of the nineteenth to the early twenty-first centuries in order to map out the complex interplay between transparency, secrecy, surveillance, and exposure in American literature. As a whole, they provide a European take on American literature, but in doing so they eschew a unified approach and instead speak of a variety of different cultural backgrounds and contexts. None of these contexts, it cannot be overemphasized, is distinctly *national* in any way. If anything, the essays attest to how dated and useless such fantasies of representative homogeneity are. The fourteen contributors to this collection are working in twelve different countries, and while all of their cultural environments surely have their own specific historic and contemporary conditions in which issues of privacy and secrecy were and are negotiated, the essays were not written to reflect this specificity in any explicit way. Most importantly, they did not *have* to be and perhaps *could* not be written to do this, as the discourse of the politics and aesthetics of transparency is simultaneously local, national, transnational, and global, and it connects rather than separates different places where it might manifest in different ways. At the same time, there is also no overarching, unified global context in which issues of privacy are negotiated without distinctions, just as there is no neutral, objective position without history or identity from which individuals could write beyond themselves.

Sascha Pöhlmann's essay on Walt Whitman opens the volume, discussing his poems as exemplary modern texts that routinely invoke tropes of transparency and secrecy and, in particular, construct intimacy as a viable interpersonal relation that is neither entirely private nor entirely public. Furthermore, he argues that Whitman uses the media of text and book to create and withhold a readerly intimacy that creates a sense of commonality/community across time but always insists that such intimacy is the product of mediation and not of its absence.

Julián Jiménez Heffernan's chapter on Henry James and F. O. Matthiessen focuses on the defense of privacy in Matthiessen's critical work on James, placing it within the liberal tradition and exploring how Matthiessen sought to protect the secrecy of James's personal work by recurrently discussing it in terms of interpretive indeterminacy. It thus addresses the underlying logics in critical treatment of James's homosexuality as one anchored on notions of critical, interpretive transparency.

Tomasz Basiuk addresses the underlying logic of "coming out" as a highly conventionalized cultural practice premised on transparency and avowal, discussing the way in which it occludes other ways of rendering queerness legible. Basiuk reads Henry Blake Fuller's *Bertram Cope's Year* (1919) and Mart Crowley's *The Boys in the Band* (1968) as illustrations of coming out in terms of intelligibility rather than visibility.

Michel Feith explores a further dimension of the semantics of visibility at work in notions of transparency by addressing transparency as translucency and connecting it to invisibility. Feith discusses the complexity of optical metaphors in the field of racial politics by attending to the representation of racial invisibility in Ralph Ellison's *Invisible Man* (1952) and George Schuyler's *Black No More* (1931). He reads both novels as proposing a "double vision" both through their use of parody and allegory—forms that rely upon the polysemic density of language—and through their protagonists, who are able to expose the hypocrisy of American discourses on racial transparency.

Umberto Rossi underscores how science fiction in general has been a productive realm for the fictional exploration of the politics of transparency, and he shows that Philip K. Dick in particular is undoubtedly *the* major writer in this mode by retracing his main concerns. On this foundation, he argues that *A Scanner Darkly* (1985), a dystopian novel whose premise is the possibility of a technologically enhanced total transparency, questions Manichean approaches to the concept and points to the larger complexity of Dick's writings on this topic.

Cristina Chevereşan takes up secrecy, privacy, and transparency in the historical context of McCarthyism in her discussion of Philip Roth's *I*

Married a Communist (1998), addressing the representation of political transparency in the realistic novel. Her reading of Roth's novel highlights the ideological underpinnings of the split between private and public life in that era as seen from the perspective of the late twentieth century, and the representation of a historical shift from the demand that the state be transparent in its dealings with its citizens to the state demanding transparency from its citizens.

Juan L. Pérez-de-Luque examines the role of political secrets in William Gibson's Sprawl Trilogy (1984–88), offering another take on the political dialectics between secrecy and transparency in science fiction. He argues that in the cyberpunk universe created by Gibson, the traditional roles of governments have been assumed by megacorporations, producing deep transformations in the relationships between power structures and citizens and challenging conventional ethical assumptions about the desirability and availability of transparent forms of governance.

Alice Sundman explores tensions between secrecy and exposure in Toni Morrison's portrayal of the Oklahoma community Ruby in *Paradise* (1998). While the existence of this community seems to be premised on the absence of secrets among its inhabitants, Sundman points to how spaces of secrecy are created within this seemingly transparent space. She also shows how *Paradise* connects tensions between secrecy and exposure to questions of power, fear, and security, thus aligning with other texts in this volume where this tension is acted out in the relationships between power structures and citizens.

Tiina Käkelä's chapter focuses on Thomas Pynchon's *Bleeding Edge* (2013), which is set at the turn of the millennium when digital culture as we now know it was taking its first steps. Käkelä argues that the novel reenacts the long-standing dialectic between secrecy and disclosure in Pynchon's work, identifying two oppositional needs that the digitalized world in which the story is set makes even more prominent: the epistemological quest, or the need to find hidden information, and the need to escape from surveillance and control, expressed through the topos of sanctuary. Pynchon is undoubtedly a central figure in the American literary tradition outlined in this introduction, as his work has recurrently explored the interplay between transparency and secrecy, the public and the private, power structures and citizenship.

Toon Staes identifies Karen Tei Yamashita's *I Hotel* (2010) as a systems novel in order to argue that reading it with an eye for its systemic structure—its intersecting narratives, recurring characters, and the dialogue it stages between fact and fiction—reveals how the Asian American movement of the late 1960s and the 1970s was rendered visible in the face of the power structures that opposed it. Staes's discussion stresses how the complex structure of Yamashita's novel questions the possibility of transparently representing the movement through conventional narrative form. His essay connects with other texts in this volume that underscore the mediation of literary form as a method to interrogate conventional notions of transparency.

Jelena Šesnić's essay discusses Dave Eggers's dystopian novels *The Circle* (2013) and *The Every* (2021), both of which are set in the world of contemporary Big Tech companies. She argues that Eggers uses an eminently realist narrative technique in order to envision a system where total social control is made possible through the use of information networks and big data, but also through the self-surveillance and self-regulating discipline exerted by citizens. Her essay brings our attention back to the conventions of realism, particularly regarding fantasies of transparent representation.

Jesús Blanco Hidalga explores Jonathan Franzen's *Crossroads* (2021) through the lens of melodrama, a literary convention that affords the narrative interplay between secrecy and disclosure as the very form of its narrative dynamics. His reading specifically focuses on confession as a narrative device in order to examine its formal conditions and its ideological implications, pointing to the way Franzen's heavy use of confession as a driving force of the plot contrasts with his critique of an excessive transparency in the contemporary mediasphere.

Julia Straub's chapter closes the book with a reading of three contemporary novels featuring female influencer figures who belong to the world of today's mediasphere: Kiley Reid's *Such a Fun Age* (2019), Megan Angelo's *Followers* (2020), and Patricia Lockwood's *No One Is Talking about This* (2021). Straub argues that these novels are cautionary tales that represent the relationship between online and offline realities: the influencer figure can be identified as someone who conflates the public and the private, the real and the artificial with particular intensity and in ways that can be perceived both as opportunity and threat to personal integrity. The collection thus goes back full circle to the early modern articulation of mediated fantasies of transparency analyzed by Sascha Pöhlmann in connection with Whitman's poetry.

As a whole, the collection addresses the politics of transparency in a multifaceted way, identifying diverse stylistic and narrative strategies used by modern and contemporary writers to represent the dialectics between transparency and secrecy, the public and the private, and the interaction between power structures and citizens. Curiously, though, none of them discusses transparency in politics in a narrow sense. The absence of explicitly political novels that thematically discuss the notion of transparency—in the tradition of Robert Penn Warren's *All the King's Men* (1946) or Don DeLillo's *Libra* (1988)—attests what we perceive to be a dominant cultural mode in American fiction: the tendency to represent the political through its effects on all aspects of public and private life, to refract rather than reflect the state and its institutional apparatus through literary form, be it lyrical poetry, dystopian cyberpunk, or the systems novel. The politics of transparency, these texts evince, traverse citizens' lives, and literary form.

Works Cited

Alloa, Emmanuel. 2018. "Transparency: A Magic Concept of Modernity," in Alloa and Thomä 2018, 21–55.

———, ed. 2022. *This Obscure Thing Called Transparency: Politics and Aesthetics of a Contemporary Metaphor*. Leuven, Belgium: Leuven University Press.

Alloa, Emmanuel, and Dieter Thomä, eds. 2018. *Transparency, Society and Subjectivity: Critical Perspectives*. Cham, Switzerland: Palgrave Macmillan.

Althusser, Louis. 1971. "Ideology and Ideological State Apparatuses" (1970). In *Lenin and Philosophy and Other Essays*. New York: Monthly Review Press, 79–87.

Bentham, Jeremy. 1999. *Political Tactics*. Edited by Michael James, Cyprian Blamires, and Catherine Pease-Watkin. *The Collected Works of Jeremy Bentham*. Oxford: Clarendon Press.

Bercovitch, Sacvan. 1975. *The Puritan Origins of the American Self*. New Haven, CT: Yale University Press.

Berliner, Daniel. 2014. "The Political Origins of Transparency." *Journal of Politics* 76, no. 2 (February 20): 479–91.

Bernstein, Ethan S. 2012. "The Transparency Paradox: A Role for Privacy in Organizational Learning and Operational Control." *Administrative Science Quarterly* 57, no. 2 (June): 181–216.

Birchall, Clare. 2011. "Transparency, Interrupted: Secrets of the Left." *Theory, Culture and Society* 28, no. 7–8: 60–84.

———. 2015. "Aesthetics of the Secret." *new formations: a journal of culture/theory/politics*: 1–21.

———. 2018. "Interrupting Transparency." In Alloa and Thomä 2018, 343–67.

———. 2021. *Radical Secrecy: The Ends of Transparency in Datafied America*. Minneapolis: University of Minnesota Press.

Birchall, Clare, and Peter Knight. 2023. *Conspiracy Theories in the Time of Covid-19*. London: Routledge.

Boas, Taylor C., and Jordan Gans-Morse. 2009. "Neoliberalism: From New Liberal Philosophy to Anti-Liberal Slogan." *Studies in Comparative International Development* 44: 137–61.

Boothroyd, Dave. 2011. "Off the Record: Levinas, Derrida and the Secret of Responsibility." *Theory, Culture and Society* 28, no. 7–8: 41–59.

Brandeis, Louis. 1913. "What Publicity Can Do." *Harper's Weekly* 58 (20 December): 10–13.

Brin, David. 1998. *The Transparent Society*. Reading, MA: Addison-Wesley Longman.

Broeders, Dennis. 2016. "The Secret in the Information Society." *Philosophy and Technology* 29, no. 3: 293–305.
Burt, Andrew. 2019. "The AI Transparency Paradox." *Harvard Business Review* (December 13). https://hbr.org/2019/12/the-ai-transparency-paradox.
Calef, Robert. 1697. *More Wonders of the Invisible World*. Project Gutenberg. https://www.gutenberg.org/files/28513/28513-h/28513-h.htm.
Cohn, Dorrit. 1978. *Transparent Minds: Narrative Modes for Presenting Consciousness in Fiction*. Princeton, NJ: Princeton University Press.
Dean, Jodi. 2002. *Publicity's Secret: How Technoculture Capitalizes on Democracy*. Ithaca, NY: Cornell University Press.
Derrida, Jacques. 1976. *Of Grammatology*, translated by G. C. Spivak. Baltimore & London: Johns Hopkins University Press.
Docherty, Thomas. 2018. "The Privatization of Human Interests, or How Transparency Breeds Conformity." In Alloa and Thomä 2018, 283–304.
Emerson, Ralph Waldo. 1971. "Nature." In *The Collected Works of Ralph Waldo Emerson*, vol. 1, edited by Robert E. Spiller, 3–45. Cambridge, MA: Belknap Press of Harvard University Press. First published 1836.
———.1979. "Self-Reliance." In *The Collected Works of Ralph Waldo Emerson*, vol. 2, edited by Joseph Slater, 25–51. Cambridge, MA: Belknap Press of Harvard University Press. First published 1841.
Erkkilä, Tero. 2012. *Government Transparency: Impacts and Unintended Consequences*. Houndmills, UK: Palgrave Macmillan.
Fenster, Mark. 2015. "Transparency in Search of a Theory." *European Journal of Social Theory* 18: 150–67. https://dx.doi.org/10.1177/1368431014555257.
———. 2017. *The Transparency Fix: Secrets, Leaks and Uncontrollable Information*. Stanford, CA: Stanford University Press.
Foucault, Michel. 1979. *Discipline and Punish: The Birth of the Prison*. Translated by Alan Sheridan. New York: Vintage.
Geroulanos, Stefanos. 2018. "Transparency, Humanism, and the Politics of the Future before and after May '68." In Alloa and Thomä 2018, 155–76.
Gilbert, Jeremy. 2007. "Public Secrets: 'Being-with in an Era of Perpetual Disclosure." *Cultural Studies* 21, no. 1 (January): 22–41. https://doi:10.1080/09502380601046923.
Habermas, Jürgen. 1991. *The Structural Transformation of the Public Sphere*. Translated by Thomas Burger and Frederick Lawrence. Cambridge, MA: MIT Press.
Han, Byung-Chul. 2015. *The Transparency Society*. Translated by Erik Butler. Stanford,CA: Stanford Briefs.
———. 2017. *Psychopolitics: Neoliberalism and New Technologies of Power*. Brooklyn, NY: Verso.
Harcourt, Bernard E. 2018. "Virtual Transparency: From the Panopticon to the Expository Society and Beyond." In Alloa and Thomä 2018, 369–91.
Hawthorne, Nathaniel. 2003. *The Scarlet Letter*. Edited by Nina Baym. London: Penguin.

Holzner, Burkart, and Leslie Holzner. 2006. *Transparency in Global Change: The Vanguard of the Open Society.* Pittsburgh: University of Pittsburgh Press.

Hood, Christopher, and David Heald. 2006. *Transparency: The Key to Better Governance?* Oxford: Oxford University Press.

Horn, Eva. "Logics of Political Secrecy." 2011. *Theory, Culture and Society* 28, no. 7–8: 103–22.

Khawaja, Noreen. 2018. "The Unbounded Confession." In Alloa and Thomä 2018, 105–32.

Koivisto, Ida. 2022. *The Transparency Paradox.* Oxford: Oxford University Press.

Lyotard, Jean-François. 1984. *The Postmodern Condition: A Report on Knowledge.* First published 1979. Translated by Geoff Bennington and Brian Massumi. Manchester, UK: Manchester University Press.

MacLeod, Alan. 2019. *Propaganda in the Information Age: Still Manufacturing Consent.* Abingdon, UK: Routledge.

Mathiesen, Thomas. 2004. *Silently Silenced: Essays on the Creation of Acquiescence in Modern Society.* Winchester, UK: Waterside Press.

McKenna, George. 2007. *The Puritan Origins of American Patriotism.* New Haven, CT: Yale University Press.

McKeon, Michael. 2002. *The Origins of the English Novel, 1600–1740.* Baltimore: Johns Hopkins University Press. First published 1987.

Mehrpouya, Afshin, and Marie-Laure Djelic. 2014. "Transparency: From Enlightenment to Neoliberalism; or, When a Norm of Liberation Becomes a Tool of Governing" (September 1). *HEC Paris Research Paper* No. ACC-2014-1059. http://dx.doi.org/10.2139/ssrn.2499402.

Meijer, Albert. 2015. "Government Transparency in Historical Perspective: From the Ancient Regime to Open Data in The Netherlands." *International Journal of Public Administration* 38, no. 3: 189–99. https://doi: 10.1080/01900692.2014.934837.

Melville, Herman. 1984. *Billy Budd, Sailor.* In *Melville: Pierre, Israel Potter, The Piazza Tales, The Confidence-Man, Billy Budd, Uncollected Prose*, edited by Harrison Hayford, 1351–1435. New York: Library of America. First published 1924.

Miller, Perry. 1953. *The New England Mind: From Colony to Province.* Cambridge, MA: Belknap Press of Harvard University Press.

Mozorov, Evgeny. 2013. *To Save Everything, Click Here: The Folly of Technological Solutionism.* London: Allen Lane.

Nissenbaum, Helen. 2011. "A Contextual Approach to Privacy Online." *Daedalus* 140, no. 4: 32–48.

Paine, Thomas. 2000. *Rights of Man.* In *Political Writings*, edited by Bruce Kuklick, 57–264. Cambridge: Cambridge University Press.

Schneider, Manfred. 2018. "The Dream of Transparency: Aquinas, Rousseau, Sartre." In Alloa and Thomä 2018, 85–104.

Smith, Adam. 2006. *The Theory of Moral Sentiments.* Mineola, NY: Dover. First published 1759.

Springer, Simon, Kean Birch, and Julie MacLeavy, eds. 2016. *The Handbook of Neoliberalism*. Abingdon, UK: Routledge.

Starobinski, Jean. 1988. *Jean-Jacques Rousseau: Transparency and Obstruction*. Chicago: University of Chicago Press.

Tocqueville, Alexis de. 2004. *Democracy in America*. Translated by Arthur Goldhammer. New York: Library of America. First published 1835, 1840.

Vattimo, Gianni. 1992. *The Transparent Society*. Translated by David Webb. Baltimore: Johns Hopkins University Press.

Wills, David. 2008. "Passionate Secrets and Democratic Dissidence." *Diacritics* 38, no. 1/2: 17–22, 24–29.

Winthrop, John. 1985. *A Model of Christian Charity*. In *The Puritans in America: A Narrative Anthology*, edited by Alan Heimert and Andrew Delbanco, 81–92. Cambridge, MA: Harvard University Press. First published 1630.

Zunshine, Lisa. 2008. "Theory of Mind and Fictions of Embodied Transparency." *Narrative* 16, no. 1: 65–92.

1: Walt Whitman's Poetry of Intimacy

Sascha Pöhlmann

1. Introduction: The Genealogy and Canon of Privacy

THE ACADEMIC CONSIDERATIONS of transparency and secrecy that have been effectively putting this interdisciplinary field of research on the scholarly map since the late 1990s are remarkably cautious to avoid the presentist bias that is somewhat inherent to their object of study.[1] Since these issues of privacy—"our ability to have a say over our human information" (Richards 2022, 3)[2]—are so closely tied to their technological, political, legal, and cultural conditions, they do require a close consideration in these precise contexts. The merit of many of these analyses is twofold: first, they suggest that such specific contexts are not without precedent and that they are part of a much longer discursive tradition; second, they suggest that this historicity itself consists of specific moments, different but related, instead of one monolithic background that then led to a singular discrete present, most often envisioned as a rupture between an analog and a digital age. In considering this duality and what one could call the genealogy of privacy, critical texts have

---

1   Broadly speaking, most critical commentators would agree that it is not merely a narrowly defined digital age in which privacy becomes an issue, but that "modernity itself could be characterized in terms of the shift from secrecy to publicity in the production of certain kinds of social knowledge" (Gilbert 2007, 24), so that the concrete phenomena that certainly gave rise to a scholarly focus on issues of transparency and secrecy (Wikileaks, the rise of social media, etc.) are an important development within this modernity instead of a break with it. (The collection *Early Modern Privacy* [2022], edited by Michaël Green, Lars Cyril Nørgaard, and Mette Birkedal Bruun, is a fine recent example of such an expansion.) Furthermore, scholars such as Eva Horn have contextualized these issues beyond their strong beginning in the Enlightenment to earlier Western traditions such as classical political theory.

2   The first chapter in Neil Richards's 2022 study *Why Privacy Matters* concisely discusses many different concepts of privacy before making the compelling proposition to think about it as "*the degree to which human information is neither known nor used*" (22).

created their own theoretical and aesthetic canon, and the foundational work done in this regard keeps returning to a few select names and works: for example, Jacques Derrida and Emmanuel Levinas are recurrent philosophical reference points, while Jean-Jacques Rousseau is the literary writer firmly placed at the heart of the artistic discourse because of his *Confessions* (1782). These are the main aspects of privacy I will be concerned with in the following, while neglecting political and legal considerations. Both this genealogical canon formation and the project of historicizing privacy in the dual way just described are still in their early stages and far from complete, and there is a need to expand these foundations without invalidating them—just as there is a need to further explore what Claire Birchall (2021) calls "The Aesthetics of the Secret" (the title of chapter 5 of her book *Radical Secrecy*) in order to insist on the profound relevance of mediation for matters of privacy.[3]

One writer in particular lends himself to this purpose so much that he may well be considered Rousseau's peer (and countermodel) when it comes to his relevance in terms of exploring modern literary subjectivity: Walt Whitman. The author of "Song of Myself" (1855) is surely unrivaled in anglophone (and US) literary history in this regard, and it is no exaggeration to claim that Whitman's entire aesthetic project—not just individual poems but virtually all of his poetry and much of his prose—is about what it means to have a self at all, what it means to be an individual in a democratic society, what it means to be a free citizen, and what can be done and said in art to construct, cultivate, and critique this embedded subjectivity. James Dougherty (1993, xvi) argues that "Whitman dramatized the tension of public and private, interior and exterior, most intensely in the first phase of his career"; and yet, this waning intensity only speaks of certain shifts in focus, while the core concerns arguably remained quite similar. The historical moment in which this extensive and multifaceted literary exploration took place is relevant to the contemporary imagination of privacy because it is decidedly *modern*, and many of its parameters persist despite radical differences in other respects. Even the earliest edition of *Leaves of Grass* (1855) is embedded in an American mass society marked by capitalism, liberalism, urbanity, and mass media, in which the dual tenets of individualism and democracy are increasingly at odds and require artistic cultivation and reconciliation, and later editions up until the final, deathbed edition of 1892 only intensify Whitman's quest for what he called in *Democratic Vistas* (Whitman 1996b, 987) "ensemble-Individuality." Although we should be wary of too readily comparing Whitman's print-centered media culture of the nineteenth century to the participatory digital mass-media culture in the twenty-first century, his

---

3 See chapter 5 of Birchall's *Radical Secrecy* (2021), which is mainly concerned with the visual arts.

and our modernity remain similar owing to his profound concern with mediation itself, and especially with effects of immediacy created in and through media (which is, to me, one of the most relevant aspects of an aesthetics of secrecy).

In the following, I want to discuss Whitman's poetry as exemplary modern texts whose engagements with transparency and secrecy recurrently connect the private and personal with the political and resonate with more-contemporary representations and theorizations. Yet, I do not simply want to add Whitman to the historical canon of the modern privacy discourse for its own sake or to merely point out a certain continuity to further preclude the presentist bias mentioned above. Instead, I will make a twofold argument in doing so. First, I will show that Whitman complicates the conceptual binary of public versus private that both informs contemporary academic discussions and is routinely challenged by them.[4] Whitman does this, I will argue, by evoking tropes of both transparency and secrecy as ways of imagining how individuals relate to each other in society, and then constructing intimacy as a viable interpersonal relation that is neither entirely private nor entirely public. This can also be perceived as a relation of individuals to each other in *poetry*, which is the second part of my argument: I will show how Whitman uses the media of text and book to create, but also at times to withhold, a readerly intimacy that creates a common sphere of secrecy open to potentially any individual across time but simultaneously uses this very mediality to insist that such intimacy is the product of mediation and not of its absence.

2. The Poetics of Privacy

The contemporary interdisciplinary discourse on privacy is suffused with references to the literary imagination, and not merely as a way of providing illustrations for philosophical, political, or sociological considerations but for genuinely conceptual reasons that suggest modes of thinking about privacy rather than thoughts about privacy. For example, Eva Horn (2011, 118) speculates that fiction might offer a privileged way of speaking about political secrecy today without succumbing to the demands of what she calls the "secrecy effect" of having to unveil an ultimate truth. On a more abstract note, Sandrine Baume (2018, 216) discusses the difference between transparency and publicity by stating the simple but neglected

---

4   Among numerous examples, Patricia Boling's (1996, 35) juxtaposition of feminist theory and legal-philosophical theory is especially worth mentioning here, as she proffers a nuanced discussion of how and why the public-private distinction has either come under attack or is staunchly defended, and she proposes seeing the terms not as opposites but rather "as different approaches to thinking or talking about the same phenomena."

fact that "transparency is an image or a metaphor, whereas publicity is not," which suggests that the tools of literary analysis should be brought to bear here. Most relevantly to the task at hand, Claire Birchall (2011, 66) identifies in poetry a counterpoint that disturbs the simplistic "moral alignments of both secrecy and transparency, whereby secrecy comes to be associated with all that is nefarious (inefficiency, corruption, malfeasance, conspiracy) and transparency with all that is noble (efficiency, accountability, honesty, trustworthiness)." What I consider most commendable about her astute analysis of poetry is that she explicitly steers clear of dubious issues of biographical authenticity and operates mainly on the level of form, so that, for example, she leaves the issue of the confessional mode entirely to the discourse of psychoanalysis that she also discusses.

This is highly important, as considerations of poetic privacy may easily gravitate toward the confessional mode that became dominant during the 1960s (with Allen Ginsberg, Robert Lowell, Sylvia Plath, Anne Sexton) and arguably remains a strong norm of contemporary American poetry. This mode is an important step in a "typically modern style of writing, in which the lyric 'I' and the autobiographical 'I' become increasingly difficult to distinguish" (Khawaja 2018, 107); and this blurring is too often simply resolved by a conflation of the two, especially when this genre is concerned. Yet, I believe that reducing the nexus of transparency/secrecy—or, in one word, privacy—to questions of authorship, biographical authenticity, or sincerity is both inherently problematic and unduly limiting. For one thing, it misunderstands confessional poetry as actually confessional (which is perhaps also a difference between the taboo-breaking poets of the 1960s and their epigones of later decades), but more importantly, it fails to acknowledge the relevance of *poetry* as the way in which these statements are made. In other words, it matters less (if at all) whether Sylvia Plath was sincere in writing "Lady Lazarus" (1965)—as if we had a way of knowing that; what matters is that her words are a poem, and that they invite ways of reading that by far exceed checking whether they correspond in a trivial way to a certain (inaccessible) real-world state.

In a way, this neglect of form is the consequence of a certain fantasy that already motivated the foundational modern autobiography: "Twentieth-century readers have generally considered modern modes of autobiographical writing as fundamentally shaped by the model of Rousseau's *Confessions*," which reveals "the paradoxes and ironies of a *literature* of intimacy" (Khawaja 2018, 121–22). As Noreen Khawaja's excellent discussion of critical responses to Rousseau shows, they especially focus on instances "where the moral demand for transparency that animates the whole discourse founders" (122), and where the mode of communication gets in the way of or takes precedence over the allegedly sincere content. Yet, what persists despite or perhaps because of these failures is, as Emmanuel Alloa (2018, 38) argues in reference to Jean Starobinski, the fantasy that Rousseau's writings are suffused "by the ideal of achieved intrasubjective and intersubjective transparency, of unhindered communication of souls cleared of dissimulation, devised as the paradise of reciprocal, heart-to-heart communication." This "will to render oneself transparent to others" (Khawaja 2018, 128) is one side of the tacit autobiographical pact (as Philippe Lejeune famously called it), while the other side is the will to accept this rendering as genuine. Such "Rousseauism" (Alloa 2018, 39) survived its modernist and postmodernist challenges fairly well and persists not only in fiction or poetry but also in other modes of speaking publicly about the self or negotiating the boundaries of privacy.

I want to summarily describe this Rousseauism in terms of a particular fantasy of transparency that I consider to be the most dangerous of all, and one that is relevant to any discourse of transparency: the fantasy of *media transparency*. Notably, this is not a fantasy that Rousseau himself necessarily subscribed to; in fact, as Manfred Schneider (2018, 95) convincingly argues, Rousseau also believed that "in society, in love, and in politics, language as medium puts an end to transparency." Yet the fantasy of transparency as absolute immediacy or sincerity nevertheless applies to his *Confessions* as either an inherent ideal or an external interpretive mode that is brought to the work by the reader (not least because the work itself invites and encourages it). It is important to consider what might sustain this fantasy: there is no content without form, and Rousseau's autobiographical writing is no more or less mediated than other texts. The question, then, is how the aesthetic *effect* of such immediacy is achieved, and this is where abstract form matters more than its concrete manifestations. Claire Birchall (2011, 69) draws attention to this when she claims that "among literary forms—novel, biography, short-story, play and so on—only poetry can claim an inherent right to be difficult." Instead of the vague notion of difficulty, however, I would propose the slightly more precise concept of self-reflexivity as a way of distinguishing between poetry and other literary forms, and as I see no way of generally distinguishing poetic language from nonpoetic language, I will first describe this self-reflexivity in fundamentally visual and material terms. Simply speaking, in the Western tradition at least, we recognize a poem because it looks like one, having line breaks. Anything else—metaphor, rhyme, meter, what have you—is secondary to these "typographic dispositifs" (Wehde 2011, 125), as are other linguistic markers of self-reflexivity that are usually referred to when making the clichéd claim that poetry is mainly about poetry.[5]

---

5   Jo Walton and Ed Luker (2018), in their editorial "Poetry on Secrecy" in the special issue of the *Journal of British and Irish Innovative Poetry* devoted to

This is not to suggest that poetry is always self-reflexive and that, in contrast, prose is less about itself but more about its "content." My point is precisely that there is no such media transparency, but that certain forms have an easier time passing themselves off as formless in the sense of being transparent. In other words, such media transparency is a rhetorical *effect*, just like authenticity or sincerity or realism or others that tend to be viewed as properties of a text instead of as something they *do*. As Dieter Mersch (2018, 266) argues, "in the end, transparency exists only within economies of making transparent, working through or 'through composing,' which implies that transparency is neither a state of being nor an attribute, but at best a medially produced operation that is bound up with its own kind of opacity." The success of this operation ultimately comes down to convention, and as such, it is contingent and arbitrary. We may normalize a certain use of language as "straightforward" or "transparent" at one point, while we may consider it "alienated" or "obscure" at another. This is a flexibility that undermines Russian formalism as much as it undermines Derrida's murmurs about an "absolute, unconditional secret" (Birchall 2011, 71) at the heart of poetry. There is no need for such esotericism that ahistorically or universally tries to identify the poetic in poetry. Instead, it is sufficient to acknowledge the contingent understanding of modern Western poetry in the terms that Birchall outlines, and that I would describe as a as a form of a self-conscious, needless complication of language that, through conventions of expectation and canon formation, thoroughly opposes the fantasy of media transparency. Especially lyric poetry, "that curious hybrid of thought and song" (Walton and Luker 2018, 16), lends itself to playing with this fantasy, as its strong emphasis on a strange subjectivity continually invokes and subverts immediacy. Generally speaking, poetry is the textual form that cannot even pretend to be transparent, as even this transparency would be read as intransparency because of the framing of the work *as* poetry (consider the straightforward complexity of William Carlos Williams's "This Is Just to Say" [1934]). Prose, in contrast, allows more for such transparency effects, not because it is any less mediated but because its conventions of reception are different, so that "poetry" and "prose" are markers

---

that topic, explore various meanings of the secret in poetry and relate it to issues of content as well as form, and to the question of difficulty. The contributions themselves are also useful in exploring the conceptual relation further, and their strong contemporary focus bears relevance for more historical considerations. Although its underlying concept of privacy is different and more specific than that mentioned above, Louis A. Renza's (2002, xii) *Edgar Allan Poe, Wallace Stevens, and the Poetics of American Privacy* addresses "privacy's recurring otherness" and presents Whitman as an "internalized foil against which Stevens pursues poetic privacy by meta-poetic means" (110).

of different modes of reading instead of generic markers. In a sense, realism can only exist in prose, not poetry.

3. Whitman's Poetry of Intimacy

These theoretical considerations finally lead me to propose Whitmanism as a countermodel to Rousseauism: both explore subjectivity in modern conditions and recognize in doing so a tension between the private and the public; but while the latter aspires to the aforementioned "ideal of achieved intrasubjective and intersubjective transparency, of unhindered communication of souls cleared of dissimulation" (Alloa 2018, 38), the former retains an irreducible element of self-reflexivity to complicate this endeavor and actually erases rather than constructs a subject position behind the text. In a way, this makes Whitman even more modern than Rousseau, as his subjectivity is self-consciously a function of language and, as such, more openly a performance that subverts any expectations of authenticity or correspondence to any biographical author.

Yet, Whitman achieved this not through language alone, and his self-reflexivity is not entirely poetic. Instead, he achieved it through a metamediality that both transcends and amplifies any rhetorical effects in the poems themselves. The most famous of these strategies is the book design of the 1855 first edition of *Leaves of Grass*, which does not have the author's name on its cover or spine (and only suggests the involvement of a "Walter Whitman" in the small print of its copyright page). Instead, the book opens with a frontispiece that begins the construction of a persona that Whitman would cultivate in various forms throughout his career, from the poetic wound-dresser of the Civil War to the "good gray poet" of old age. This initial image shows Whitman "dressed as a day laborer in workingman's trousers" (Erkkila 1989, 3), although he was "not actually a member of the 'working class' but an artisan possessed of a skilled trade and a measure of independence" (Lawson 2006, xvi). He presents himself as a nonpoet "who has deliberately and insultingly ignored all the other, the cultivated classes as they are called, and set himself to work to write 'America's first distinctive Poem'" (Whitman 1984, 1:333), and the frontispiece is as much part of the construction of this persona as the self-written review of *Leaves of Grass* from which this description is taken. In Rousseauian terms, *Leaves of Grass* begins with an act of visual deception, and it continues its insincerities throughout while claiming utter transparency and honesty. "He has not dressed up to meet his reader" (Asselineau 1999, 48), the image suggests, but in fact, it shows just the opposite.[6]

---

6 For a discussion of the frontispiece and the context of its creation, see Ted Genoways's (2007) essay "'One goodshaped and wellhung man: Accentuated

The frontispiece is not yet a "selfie,"[7] but it is an early example of what Dave Boothroyd (2011, 43) describes as "'public individualism' expressed through what could be termed communicative self-publicity." Both these terms are appropriate ways of describing Whitman's entire career, as David Haven Blake (2006, 4) asserts in *Walt Whitman and the Culture of American Celebrity*: "Not only did he stage photographs of himself, he made outlandish claims about his popularity and published anonymous reviews of his work. The same promotional energy also surfaces in the speech acts and lyric persona of *Leaves of Grass*, where it makes a vital contribution to his poetics."[8] Importantly, Blake (6) adds that "celebrity for Whitman was ultimately a political identity, the cultural manifestation of the principles of popular sovereignty," which makes his "public individualism" more than a particular self-expression where a private self puts itself on public view. Instead, it is an aesthetic attempt to mediate individualism itself as the basis for a public sphere of selves, while being careful not to dissolve these political atoms of democratic society in a mass of indistinct people pursuing equality but not sameness. Notably, this mediation *creates* the public as much as it creates the individual. As Michael Warner (2002, 50) points out, a public "exists *by virtue of being addressed*," and it "*is poetic world-making*" (82): the audience of Whitman's poetry is such that he seeks to make *his* public *the* public in a political sense.

"Song of Myself" best exemplifies all of this. Here, Whitman's Romantic individualism to a certain extent pursues the Enlightenment "ideal of a transparent subject, characterized by self-knowledge, self-rule and ownership" (Alloa 2018, 41), but it also refracts this subjectivity—"I am large, I contain multitudes" (Whitman 1996a, 87; henceforth cited as *LoG* 1855)—so that it creates what Alloa rightly identifies as a modernist aesthetics of "multiple exposure" (52) as in cubism. The poem uses one

---

Sexuality and the Uncertain Authorship of the Frontispiece to the 1855 Edition of *Leaves of Grass*."

7   See Jörg Metelmann and Thomas Telios for a discussion of how the selfie relates to other traditions of self-portraiture, and for a useful definition based on four criteria: "The selfie is *oblivious* [. . .]; *shared* [. . .]; *serial* [. . .], and above all it's determined by others" (2018, 329).

8   Blake's compelling study is foundational to my essay to such an extent that any number of individual quotations would hardly do it justice. I highly recommend it not only for a much more extensive analysis of Whitman's works but also for its insights into the American culture of celebrity, privacy, and intimacy in the nineteenth century that is relevant beyond its immediate literary concerns. See also Milette Shamir's (2006) *Inexpressible Privacy: The Interior Life of Antebellum American Literature* and Stacey Margolis's *The Public Life of Privacy in Nineteenth-Century American Literature* (2005) for related analyses of Whitman's contemporary authors.

individual and one subject to explore individuality and subjectivity per se, and so it strives for the abstract without losing sight of the particular. The famous opening stanza captures this concisely:

> I celebrate myself,
> And what I assume you shall assume,
> For every atom belonging to me as good belongs to you. (*LoG* 1855, 27)

The speaker later asserts, "I know perfectly well my own egotism" (76), and yet, egotism is actually the opposite of this individualism. This is no narrow celebration of the self but opens it up toward other selves to create a communal space, a genuine public sphere constituted by private individuals. It is one of the many ways in which Whitman sought to "save his individuals from an atomistic solitude" (Dougherty 1993, 5). On the one hand, the speaker creates a specific persona in identifying himself as "Walt Whitman, an American, one of the roughs, a kosmos" (*LoG* 1855, 50), but, on the other hand, he insists, somewhat paradoxically, that this specificity is general:

> These are the thoughts of all men in all ages and lands, they are not original with me,
> If they are not yours as much as mine they are nothing or next to nothing,
> If they do not enclose everything they are next to nothing,
> If they are not the riddle and the untying of the riddle they are nothing,
> If they are not just as close as they are distant they are nothing. (43)

The speaker oscillates between exaggerating his subjectivity at the cost of others and diminishing it. At one point he asserts, "You shall no longer take things at second or third hand . . . nor look through the eyes of the dead . . . nor feed on the spectres in books, / You shall not look through my eyes either, nor take things from me, / You shall listen to all sides and filter them from yourself" (28), but later he poignantly claims that "I do not ask who you are . . . that is not important to me, / You can do nothing and be nothing but what I will infold you" (72). Whitman uses the semantics of *immediacy*: the addressee, the "you" evoked already in the second line, is supposed to have unmediated access to what the speaker shows them, so much that even the showing is unnecessary and the text denies its own mediality (as if it were not in a book itself). Then again, the speaker affirms that the readers do not have such access, and that they can only relate to the poem and perceive what it lets them perceive. This may be, as Bellis (2003, 92) asserts, "a poetry that aspires to a condition of complete and natural transparency," and yet it is also a poetry that deals with the necessary failure of this aspiration. If "Whitman developed a poetry that tried to escape the conditions of poetry in striving for a sense of immediacy" (Blake 2006, 153), then it is more about its struggle than about its resolution.

This results in a curious dialectic that the poem continuously evokes in a vast array of metaphors. For one thing, the speaker fantasizes about being "undisguised and naked" (*LoG* 1855, 27), and he insists that "clear and sweet is my soul . . . and clear and sweet is all that is not my soul" (29). He is a nonconformist whose authenticity is not distorted by social convention—"I cock my hat as I please indoors or out" (45)—and who gleefully calls for the removal of such barriers and their conditions: "Unscrew the locks from the doors! / Unscrew the doors themselves from their jambs!" (50). The speaker's own voice is a medium of transparency, and he describes his ventriloquism in terms of revelation and authenticity:

> Through me many long dumb voices,
> Voices of the interminable generations of slaves,
> Voices of prostitutes and of deformed persons,
> Voices of the diseased and despairing, and of thieves and dwarfs,
> Voices of cycles of preparation and accretion,
> And of the threads that connect the stars—and of wombs, and of the fatherstuff,
> And of the rights of them the others are down upon,
> Of the trivial and flat and foolish and despised,
> Of fog in the air and beetles rolling balls of dung.
>
> Through me forbidden voices,
> Voices of sexes and lusts . . . voices veiled, and I remove the veil,
> Voices indecent by me clarified and transfigured. (50)

This passage concisely shows the ambiguity of this practice, as the speaker gives voice to the voiceless but also appropriates their position and may thus effectively silence them once more. Regardless of whether we judge this as presumptuous, arrogant, naive, or benevolent, it frames the textual speech act as a poetic way of clarification and even purification, as if this mediation took these voices back to their original uncorrupted state. Only the mediation restores immediacy, as "the poet becomes a medium for a newly representative publicity in which he speaks for those who, having been marginalized by society, have come to disregard themselves" (Blake 2006, 125). In this sense, the speaker positively brings these voices into the public realm and saves them from a negative privacy that precludes their access to the communal. Yet, readers may become skeptical of this practice, especially once the speaker claims to speak even for them: "It is you talking just as much as myself . . . I act as the tongue of you, / It was tied in your mouth . . . in mine it begins to be loosened" (*LoG*

1855, 84). This is an image of liberation and indeed transparency, yet its effect may be just the opposite, as readers may just as well note the difference between themselves and the speaker and not recognize their voice in his—a failure of immediacy.

This is one of many instances in the poem where the rhetoric of revelation ends in obfuscation instead, and its fantasies of transparency are routinely balanced by tropes of secrecy. For example, the very straightforward line "It is time to explain myself . . . let us stand up" leads not to any actual explanation but rather, in the very next line, to fundamental uncertainty: "What is known I strip away . . . I launch all men and women forward with me into the unknown" (79). In another instance, he claims to awaken the addressees from sleep to allow them to see the world for what it really is:

> Long enough have you dreamed contemptible dreams,
> Now I wash the gum from your eyes,
> You must habit yourself to the dazzle of the light and of every
>   moment of your life. (83)

Yet, he only invokes this metaphor of transparency and authentic enlightenment but does not convey what we might actually see now that we can see clearly. Or, finally, the speaker asserts that "all truths wait in all things" (56); yet, he fails to access them even within himself because it is beyond mediation:

> There is that in me . . . I do not know what it is . . . but I know it is in me.
> . . . .
> I do not know it . . . it is without name . . . it is a word unsaid,
> It is not in any dictionary or utterance or symbol. (86)

Thus, the speaker undermines his own claims to transparency by presenting his medium, language, as insufficient to communicate what he knows. Language fails to make the private public: "Logic and sermons never convince" (56), and "Writing and talk do not prove me" (53). At best the speaker can draw attention to the irreducible difference between representation and what is represented, and he does so in reference to the medium he uses: "My words are words of a questioning, and to indicate reality; / This printed and bound book . . . but the printer and the printing-office boy?" (76).

In such contrasting passages, "Song of Myself" circles around a secret that cannot be publicly revealed but can be communicated between individuals, and the difference opens up a nuanced view on privacy. This is not an absolutely inaccessible Derridean secret that somehow inherently defines poetry, and neither is it a riddle to be solved once and for all. The "puzzle of puzzles [. . .] that we call Being" (55) does not have a single solution that, once known by everyone, will render the puzzle moot. Instead, it is a perpetual mystery that individuals may share, and one that the speaker continually struggles with: "To me the converging objects of the universe perpetually flow, / All are written to me, and I must get what the writing means" (45–46), only that this is a process where, as Roland Barthes (1977, 147) put it, "everything is to be *disentangled*, nothing *deciphered*." The secret is best "conceived as shareable—inherently, perpetually shareable—without being shared fully in the space of the public" (Gilbert 2007, 31), and accordingly the speaker shares his secret *as* a secret in the poem and not as its revelation. As Jo Walton and Ed Luker (2018, 1) suggest in their editorial "Poetry and Secrecy," "the secret can also be usefully thought of as an unstable hybrid of the public and the private," as it "can belong solely, entirely, and definitively to the individual, or something secretive may ground a shared identity." Drawing on this instability, the speaker of "Song of Myself" uses the secret to create a communal space between privacy and publicity—a space of *intimacy*: "This hour I tell things in confidence, / I might not tell everybody but I will tell you" (*LoG* 1855, 45).[9]

I propose this third category of intimacy as a way of complicating the binary between private and public and, by extension, that of individual and society. It is a simple way of showing how reductive the numerical imagination of these dualities is.[10] These binaries allow for one or all but not some; intimacy is what returns "some" (and indeed also "many") as a category and opens up different and more productive ways of thinking the communal. This is important because Whitman usually engages with the general and not the partial: "Song of Myself" is a universal poem about everything, about all humans across past, present, and future (and about all animals and plants and rocks), and it is not just about some of them. Yet, it needs this idea of "some" to both retain and communicate its unspeakable secret as a secret: if the poem revealed the mystery to all, the mystery would be worthless, and if it failed to communicate the

---

9 Note that the speaker also fails to create intimacy as he actually violates someone else's privacy; "forced intimacy" is a contradiction in terms. The most pertinent example is the section (*LoG* 1855, 36) where the woman watches the twenty-eight male bathers as "she hides handsome and richly drest aft the blinds of the window," and as she invades their privacy, the speaker also invades hers, "for I see you," and sees her masturbating, too. Both gazes are passed off as caring and affectionate, examples of shared secrets that create intimacy, but they may well be read as the opposite.

10 This argument is rooted in the much more extensive complication of the binary between privacy and publicity that Julie C. Inness (1992) undertakes in *Privacy, Intimacy, and Isolation*, and while my own understanding of intimacy is slightly different from hers as it applies to its poetic realization, it is nevertheless deeply indebted to her precise thinking on the matter.

secret as such, the poem would be worthless.[11] "If they are not the riddle and the untying of the riddle they are nothing" (43): these thoughts and words must be *both* and not just one of them to do their poetic work.[12]

Thus, the intimate could be described as the not-quite-public and the not-quite-private, an opening up of the private individual toward at least one other individual but not all other individuals. The intimacy in Whitman's poetry is mainly a function of the communication between two individuals, so I will focus on this as the most relevant case in the following, but this should by no means suggest that intimacy would not be possible among more than two people.[13] Theorizing intimacy in this way requires some further elaboration, at least within the space that such a brief essay allows. The most important thing to note is that my use of "intimacy" directly opposes the practice of using it as a synonym for "privacy." For example, Thomas Docherty (2018, 289) does this in his compelling deconstruction of the private/public binary when he writes about "the private intimate sphere" and of "radical intimacy" as a "collapsing of the political sphere into the private" (291); Byung-Chul Han (2015, 35) even seems to suggest that intimacy is an inauthentic enemy of the genuinely social, its "tyranny" resulting in "a society of confession, laying-bare, and the pornographic lack of distance" (36). Such conflations surely have their reasons, and yet it is unfortunate to negate the interpersonal component of intimacy, as this is actually its most salient aspect. It makes more sense to assume that "privacy is an enabling condition of intimacy" (Cohen 2002, 13). We don't need another way of thinking privacy; instead, we need a way of thinking beyond it without always ending up with the public right away.[14]

---

11 One might anachronistically describe this as an early Wittgensteinian attitude toward language in the *Tractatus Logico-Philosophicus* (Wittgenstein 1922, 90): "6.522: There are, indeed, things that cannot be put into words. They make themselves manifest. They are what is *mystical*."

12 See Wills (2008, 20) for a corresponding Derridean reading of the literary secret, which "is no more hidden than revealed, or rather it does not function according to a simple opposition of what we call the revealed versus what we call the secret. It can be most secret when it is displayed most obviously, or it can open abysses of undecidability even as it proceeds according to a rigorous logic of the surface effect. A literature that functions by posing a hermeneutic challenge might create secrets like so many puzzles to be solved even though its reserve of secrecy remains exceedingly shallow."

13 In his classic study *Privacy and Freedom*, Alan Westin (1967, 31) defines "intimacy" as a "state of privacy" in which "the individual is acting as part of a small unit that claims and is allowed to exercise corporate seclusion so that it may achieve a close, relaxed, and frank relationship between two or more individuals."

14 This also offers a way of thinking beyond a notion of individualism and privacy that is complicit with liberal capitalism: if "what 'privacy' fails to do as

Such intimacy opens up a realm of privacy that includes more than one person, not necessarily a *secret* realm but one that is kept from public scrutiny.[15] In this sense, "society of intimacy" (Han 2015, 36) would be a contradiction in terms. This intimacy rather relates to a dual communication that is based on a recognition of the other, which not only invokes Levinas[16] again but also Martin Buber[17] and, perhaps most importantly, the social philosophy of Axel Honneth.[18] This communication establishes a realm of trust—trust not to violate this boundary to the public, trust to be truthful, or other forms. Han (2015, 48) claims about the transparency society that "where transparency prevails, no room for trust exists. Instead of affirming that 'transparency creates trust,' one should instead say, 'transparency dismantles trust'"—wrongly, I believe, since such transparency simply shifts trust to a different level and still requires it. As Daniel Naurin (2006, 91) suggests, "transparency captures the accessibility of information," so *potential* but not necessarily *actual* access, and this possibility certainly requires all kinds of trust: trust that the potential exists and will exist in the future; trust that it is access to *all* the information; and trust that the information is genuine. These notions of transparency and trust apply to interpersonal intimacy as well—or, rather, they are what creates it, and they suggest that intimacy isn't complete mutual access to someone else's private sphere but *potential* access to it.[19] To draw on the sexual connotation of intimacy: it is eroticism, not pornography.

---

an organizing concept is provide any grounds for collective resistance—to either state or capital" (Neocleous 2002, 106), then a communal notion of intimacy may help critique the separation perpetuated by this ideology. In a related way, this intermediary concept of intimacy may provide one way of connecting the private and the political beyond either a total conflation or a total separation, or "how to move between privative and political ways of thinking and talking about issues of general concern" in an act of "translation" (Boling 1996, 36).

15 This demarcation may well be the definition of *intimacy*, as "intimate relationships simply could not exist if we did not continue to insist on privacy for them" (Gerstein 1984, 265).

16 See, for example, Boothroyd (2011) and Gilbert (2007) for discussions of Levinas and related philosophical perspectives.

17 See Dougherty (1993) for a Buberian reading of Whitman's poetry and its representation of the I and the Not-Me.

18 See his "Invisibility: On the Epistemology of 'Recognition'" (2011) for a briefer discussion and *The Struggle for Recognition* (1995; first German edition 1994) and *Recognition: A Chapter in the History of European Ideas* (2020; first German edition 2018) for more extensive ones; Honneth's work on recognition as an interpersonal, social, and political concept is directly relevant to the discourse on privacy but has yet to be incorporated more fully. For one recent example, see Waelen (2023).

19 David Elliott and Eldon Soifer (2010, 493) rightly note, however, that "not all instances of waiving the right to privacy would give rise to intimacy,"

Here, Julie C. Inness's (1992, viii) understanding of intimacy and privacy is highly relevant: for her, "privacy is the state of possessing control over decisions concerning matters that draw their meaning and value from an agent's love, liking, or care," which is her notion of intimacy. This suggests that access to this private sphere must be *granted* by the individual; otherwise, it does not create intimacy but actually violates it.[20] As such, intimacy affirms individuality but sets it in relation to other individuals, so that we might think of it as a way of making two spheres of control overlap by *mutual consent* without relinquishing this control, either.[21] Thus, intimacy does not come about through some fantasy of complete revelation or surrender of the private that, perhaps, the Beat writers pursued. In fact, content matters little, if at all, but the *form* is what creates intimacy: the act of extending the realm of the private to include another person is more important than any information that is shared in the process, especially as intimacy has no substance but is rather "a product of the agent's motivation" (Inness 1992, 10) and thus highly contingent. Again, sexual intimacy is the best illustration of this, as it can be created in a myriad of ways, while none of these is privileged as a way of doing so, and not every sexual act will create intimacy.

In this abstract sense, intimacy is first of all a mode of communication, and it can be created, cultivated, or destroyed through it. This communication isn't necessarily linguistic, as it can also occur visually, through sound, or bodily in ways that are not semantic.[22] Yet, here I am naturally interested in intimacy as a poetic function, a rhetorical intimacy *effect* that creates a sense of interpersonal communication that distinctly opens up each other's private spheres without dissolving them in a general

---

suggesting that mutuality and selectivity are also necessary elements (495).

20 This also satisfies Jeffrey H. Reiman's (1984, 304–5) useful contention that "what constitutes intimacy is not merely the sharing of otherwise withheld information, but the context of caring which makes the sharing of personal information significant," as the former would merely lead to a "market conception of personal intimacy" based on scarcity.

21 Note that this should not be taken to suggest that privacy is only a matter of individual control; as Neil Richards (2022, 3) rightly insists, it is more generally "about power. Privacy is about the rules governing the extent to which human information is detected, collected, used, shared, and stored and how those activities can be used to affect our lives." The notion of intimacy proffered here is part of these "rules governing shared information" (9), showing that the game is played in many different ways and in many interrelated spheres.

22 It can also be *spatial*, as Danielle Bobker shows in *The Closet: The Eighteenth-Century Architecture of Intimacy* (2020). On that note, see also Schmidgall (2019) for a reading of Whitman's gay poetry of the Closet.

public sphere.[23] In this sense, it is clearly not enough to simply consider the traditional model of poetic communication between a speaker and an addressee, a lyrical I and a lyrical You, as intimate in and of itself. The model is generally as dubious as that of narratology that needs to imagine a speaking or narrating persona behind every text, as if they all needed to be utterances instead of material artefacts of a different nature, but even if we maintain it—and it does apply to Whitman in unique ways—we must find it insufficient. Simply put, just because one person talks to another doesn't mean they are intimate. In poetry, one of them doesn't even get to talk back. So how can intimacy be created if the basic situation of communication not only doesn't establish but actually precludes it?

4. Mediated Intimacy

Whitman wrote numerous poems that evoke intimate situations of communication in various ways. Besides "Song of Myself" and its shared cosmic universalism, especially the two most sexualized clusters, "Children of Adam" and "Calamus," are noteworthy in this regard. These are routinely read by critics in terms of privacy and intimacy, undoubtedly also because their heterosexual and homosexual themes resonate most clearly with these concepts. For example, Justine S. Murison (2020, 42) shows how the speaker of the "Children of Adam" poems conveys them as "poems of the night" and thus "names the poems about sex with women as poems of privacy, but this privacy is also about a sex that is so transparently obvious on the surface that it need not hide; it's not a secret." Poems of the night are not private but intimate: they are shared with the reader in a particular realm where no broad daylight could expose them to genuinely public view. They are communal but not social in a general sense, and this grants them a position from which to critique the dominant moral values of society at large.

More critics have commented on the homoeroticism of "Calamus." In the afterword to her edition of "Live Oak, with Moss" and "Calamus," titled *Walt Whitman's Songs of Male Intimacy and Love*, Betsy Erkkila (2011) provides a fine overview of these critical readings, commenting

---

23 This provides a link to Chad Bennett's fine work on American poetry, queerness, and gossip, in which he argues that "lyric poetry has been most self-reflexively concerned with the matters of privacy that are so crucial to gossip, and particularly with the effects of a privacy that paradoxically circulates in public" (2018, 2). The intimacy created in talking "about one or more absent figures" is used "to establish group boundaries, separating those in the know from those out of the loop" (10), thus creating complex interrelations between private and public spheres as well as secrecy and disclosure. This is not the form of intimacy created in Whitman's poetry, however.

especially on how they differ regarding how the once separate "Live Oak" sequence has been integrated into—or some would say dispersed across—the "Calamus" cluster from the 1860 edition onward. Erkkila argues against what she calls the critical "reprivatizing" of "both homosexuality and art in a way that is contrary to Whitman's brave homoerotic, democratic, and insistently public, political, and spiritual purpose" (118), emphasizing instead how these poems "embody a public culture of men loving men as a model for nonstate forms of democratic affection"(124–25). Combining this personal and political function, these poems necessitate the creation of intimacy between speaker and addressee or, if you will, author and reader,[24] and they are the best examples of the different strategies Whitman employs to achieve this intimacy effect in other poems as well.

Helen Vendler (2005, 34) identifies, in more general terms, three major "unmistakable marks of Whitmanian intimacy with the invisible: the poet's direct remarks to an invisible addressee of future time [. . .]; the poet's capacity to intuit his invisible listener's thoughts [. . .]; and a faith in the mysterious power of poetry to convey presence." The "Calamus" poems, like "Song of Myself" in a different way, add to this the fourth element of secrecy: "Like Whitman's shifty and ever-shifting relation with the *you* of the reader, the poet's 'secret and divine signs' become part of his strategy of intimacy, his creation of an erotic bond of intimacy with future man lovers and readers who share and know his secret—or think they do" (Erkkila 2011, 127). These rhetorical strategies work to differing extents, but they *are* rhetorical, and if Whitman's "problem is to give such a future listener tangible materiality on the page" (Vendler 2005, 35), they necessarily fail to solve that problem in a strict sense. This means that at times the intimacy effects are too clearly visible *as* intimacy effects, as one-sided constructions of what needs to be a mutual relationship, and as such they fail to achieve this intimacy; it's like the Tom Lehrer (1965) quip about a letter he received, saying, "Darling, I love you, and I cannot live without you. Marry me, or I will kill myself," adding: "Well, I was a little disturbed at that until I took another look at the envelope, and saw that it was addressed to 'occupant.'"[25] Whitman's use of the deictic *you* is at times highly effective in addressing any reader as a *specific* reader and not just "the reader"; for example, in "Crossing Brooklyn Ferry,"

---

24   Blake (2006, 160) points out how "the intimacy of Calamus is simultaneously constructed with the advertisement of that intimacy." On the one hand, it offers "personal attachment as an antidote to the self-alienation and moral ambiguity that arose with democratic capitalism" (146), but, on the other hand, it draws on the "promotional value of intimacy [that] enhanced the growth of antebellum celebrity culture" (142) in the early stages of human-interest journalism.
25   After the song "Alma" on *That Was the Year That Was* (1965).

where the poem creates a transtemporal community of perception and gives concrete meaning to the *you* while also keeping it open.[26] At other times, this *you* remains generic and thus fails to create the intimacy it aims for, especially when Whitman uses one of his favorite phrases in addressing "whoever you are." This generic address is often not deictic enough and fails to become a reference to the actual reader, so that, for example, "Poem of You, Whoever You Are" (1856; later, "To You") seems entirely implausible and fake in its claims to recognize the addressee's "true soul and body," and lines such as "I whisper with my lips close to your ear" (Whitman 1996c, 375; cited henceforth as *LoG* 1892) remain metaphors of intimacy instead of actual intimacy effects.

Thus, rhetorical modes of creating intimacy are unreliable in Whitman's poetry, but he has found a way to overcome this by adding another intimacy effect that has not been sufficiently recognized by the perspectives quoted above. It is most evident in (but not limited to) the "Calamus" poems "So Long!" and "Whoever You Are Holding Me Now in Hand" (both 1860), and the latter one is especially relevant here because it combines this strategy with tropes of secrecy. The strategy already begins in "Song of Myself," though, where the poem draws attention to its own mediality in constructing a literal space of intimacy:

> Listener up there! Here you . . . what have you to confide to me?
> Look in my face while I snuff the sidle of evening,
> Talk honestly, for no one else hears you, and I stay only a minute
>   longer. (*LoG* 1855, 87)

Yet, the speaker dissolves what could have become a metamedial connection in a synaesthetic conflation that disavows the specificity of the book medium that could have been the link to the actual, physical reader: notably, this reader is not a reader at all but a "listener," and then they are a beholder, and finally they get to speak themselves; but all this remains a metaphor of interaction as it eschews the physical manipulation of the book object itself.

"So Long!" enacts this shift this from metaphor to material practice as it more immediately references the book object in its famous claim: "Camerado, this is no book, / Who touches this touches a man, / (Is it night? are we here together alone?)" (*LoG* 1892, 611). At the same time, the poem still somewhat disavows such bookishness by translating it into a bodily presence. In contrast, "Whoever" maintains this ambiguity, and its speaker *is* the embodied book:

---

26 Kerry C. Larson (1988, 8) states that this "addressee is hardly an implied reader, but neither is he an utterly accessible presence."

> Whoever you are holding me now in hand,
> Without one thing all will be useless,
> I give you fair warning before you attempt me further,
> I am not what you supposed, but far different. (*LoG* 1892, 270)

This is a deictic reference that does not give "a future listener tangible materiality on the page" (Vendler 2005, 35) but uses the tangible materiality of the page to address one specific future reader. It uses the haptic qualities of the medium to create an intimacy that goes beyond the rhetorical, not just using it as a metaphor of bodily contact but really relying on the sensual experience of holding a *book* to signal that the speaker really addresses not just anyone but the person having this experience at this instant (note the temporal deixis *now* in the title). The success of this metamedial deixis is emphasized by instances where it fails: reading these lines on a static screen, say, not only creates no intimacy effect but actually shows the failure of the strategy itself, as you know you're supposed to touch something, but you're not touching anything.

This material aspect not only amplifies the rhetorical strategies of intimacy in the poem but arguably even enables them, as they turn their metaphors of touching into references to an actual embodied practice of reading and handling the book object. After the initial warning, the speaker demands complete devotion from the reader—"You would have to give up all else, I alone would expect to be your sole and exclusive standard" (*LoG* 1892, 270)—and conveys the possible consequences of this in tactile terms:

> The whole past theory of your life and all conformity to the lives
>   around you would have to be abandon'd,
> Therefore release me now before troubling yourself any further, let
>   go your hand from my shoulders,
> Put me down and depart on your way. (270)

The reader can refuse this radical beginning by letting go of the speaker and the book at the same time: taking their hand off the shoulder corresponds to putting down the book, so that book and body are one but remain distinct. While Whitman privileges the body in "So Long!," he retains the duality of book and body here, which is especially emphasized in reference to a place that is dominated by books and in which the speaker is literally a foreign body: "And in libraries I lie as one dumb, a gawk, or unborn, or dead" (271). As the speaker consistently addresses the reader as both book and body, their reading experience is shifted from the visual to the haptic, and it is eroticized in the process, creating further intimacy:

Here to put your lips upon mine I permit you,
With the comrade's long-dwelling kiss or the new husband's kiss,
For I am the new husband and I am the comrade.

Or if you will, thrusting me beneath your clothing,
Where I may feel the throbs of your heart or rest upon your hip,
Carry me when you go forth over land or sea;
For thus merely touching you is enough, is best,
And thus touching you would I silently sleep and be carried
  eternally. (271)

The speaker uses the ambiguity of touch here that does not distinguish between touching and being touched, and thus he presents the book and himself as a sentient being that is not only passively touched but actively touches and feels—thus creating the mutuality necessary for intimacy.

Importantly, however, the transtemporal connection of intimacy that is materially and semantically created here does not last as long as these lines suggest, and it is actually dissolved in the next lines along with the unity of speaker and book:

But these leaves conning you con at peril,
For these leaves and me you will not understand,
They will elude you at first and still more afterward, I will certainly
  elude you,
Even while you should think you had unquestionably caught me,
  behold!
Already you see I have escaped from you.

For it is not for what I have put into it that I have written this book,
Nor is it by reading it you will acquire it,
Nor do those know me best who admire me and vauntingly praise me,
Nor will the candidates for my love (unless at most a very few)
  prove victorious,
Nor will my poems do good only, they will do just as much evil,
  perhaps more,
For all is useless without that which you may guess at many times
  and not hit, that which I hinted at;
Therefore release me and depart on your way. (271)

Here, the author-speaker refers to what he has written and detaches himself from both the book and its content, turning the earlier immediacy and presence into separation and absence. The speaker has already escaped his poems and his book, leaving only the uncommunicated secret: "that which you may guess at many times and not hit, that which I hinted at" (271). Peter Coviello (2001, 103) comments very insightfully on the resulting dialectic of this revelatory retraction: on the one hand, he sees it as a positive affirmation of the reader's co-creation of meaning, suggesting that "the ability to discern in Whitman's various occlusions the codes and patterns of a different sort of sexual candor can feel like the surest mark of one's readerly aptitude"; but on the other hand, he asserts that the poem's "reiterated secretiveness [rewards] many aspects of a reading in which the poet's desire for other men simply *is* his secret, nevertheless marks that reading as untenably partial, insufficient" (105). Thus, the poem isn't *only* a homoerotic one that speaks of a love that dare not speak its name and waits to be deciphered as such, but it is more abstractly a poem about the vagaries of intimate communication between the private and the public spheres, addressing—in Michael Warner's influential terms—public and counterpublic alike.[27] It does not share its secret *as* a secret like "Song of Myself" does, and it does not create the intimacy of common nonpublic knowledge. Instead, the poem retains this secret as something more private than intimate, something that just fails to become genuinely communal, so that it is really more about a breakdown of intimacy than its cultivation.

We might also understand the poem as a self-reflexive critique of its own claim to representation and of its poetics of intimacy. In communicating with the reader through the rhetoric and materiality of touch, Whitman creates intimacy but in the end retains the privacy of knowledge that is not divulged even in this setting. The poem actively resists the boundless transparency that the (empty) claims of "To You" and other poems suggest, and this parallels the metamediality of the poem itself. In using the medium of the book so openly as a way of creating intimacy, the poem must also acknowledge that there cannot be any genuine immediacy between speaker or addressee, or between author, text, and reader. The poem first uses its materiality to create and further enhance a fantasy of media transparency but then actually concludes by revealing this *as* a fantasy. This makes the poem stand out among Whitman's attempts to create a poetics of intimacy, as it reflects on its own creation of intimacy effects rather than just producing them (with varying results). It is about the conditions of the possibility of intimacy as much as it is about intimacy itself, and in withholding something from the reader it refuses to dissolve privacy in intimacy. The poem shows that intimacy is created in *mutual* communication, as it takes the reader to the limits of this mutuality. The "ethics of intimacy" (Vendler 2005, 56) at stake here

---

27 Gary Schmidgall (2019, 252) compellingly discusses this duality of transparency and secrecy in terms of the Closet as a particular space that provides "safety and self-preservation" but is also "a claustrophobic and suffocating place, requiring "thespian skill" (247) and "that magical poet's trick: hiding in plain sight" (251).

are such that intimacy is not at all built on absolute transparency but rather on *mediation*, so that media transparency actually *precludes* intimacy instead of fostering it. In short, Whitman here draws attention to how intimacy is *made*—and it is remarkable that doing so still does not unmake that intimacy.

Works Cited

Alloa, Emmanuel. 2018. "Transparency: A Magic Concept of Modernity." In Alloa and Thomä 2018, 21–55.
Alloa, Emmanuel, and Dieter Thomä, eds. 2018. *Transparency, Society and Subjectivity: Critical Perspectives*. Cham, Switzerland: Palgrave Macmillan.
Asselineau, Roger. 1999. *The Evolution of Walt Whitman*. Iowa City: University of Iowa Press. First published 1960.
Barthes, Roland. 1977. "The Death of the Author." In *Image Music Text*, translated by Stephen Heath, 142–48. London: Fontana Press. First published 1967.
Baume, Sandrine. 2018. "Publicity and Transparency: The Itinerary of a Subtle Distinction." In Alloa and Thomä 2018, 203–24.
Bennett, Chad. 2018. *Word of Mouth: Gossip and American Poetry*. Baltimore: Johns Hopkins University Press.
Bellis, Peter J. 2003. *Writing Revolution: Aesthetics and Politics in Hawthorne, Whitman, and Thoreau*. Athens: University of Georgia Press.
Birchall, Claire. 2011. "Transparency, Interrupted: Secrets of the Left." *Theory, Culture & Society* 28, no. 7–8: 60–84.
———. 2021. *Radical Secrecy: The Ends of Transparency in Datafied America*. Minneapolis: University of Minnesota Press.
Blake, David Haven. 2006. *Walt Whitman and the Culture of American Celebrity*. New Haven, CT: Yale University Press.
Bobker, Danielle. 2020. *The Closet: The Eighteenth-Century Architecture of Intimacy*. Princeton, NJ: Princeton University Press.
Boling, Patricia. 1996. *Privacy and the Politics of Intimate Life*. Ithaca, NY: Cornell University Press.
Boothroyd, Dave. 2011. "Off the Record: Levinas, Derrida and the Secret of Responsibility." *Theory, Culture & Society* 28, no. 7–8: 41–59.
Cohen, Jean L. 2002. *Regulating Intimacy: A New Legal Paradigm*. Princeton, NJ: Princeton University Press.
Coviello, Peter. 2001. "Intimate Nationality: Anonymity and Attachment in Whitman." *American Literature* 73, no. 1 (March): 85–119.
Docherty, Thomas. 2018. "The Privatization of Human Interests or, How Transparency Breeds Conformity." In Alloa and Thomä 2018, 283–303.
Dougherty, James. 1993. *Walt Whitman and the Citizen's Eye*. Baton Rouge: Louisiana State University Press.
Elliott, David, and Eldon Soifer. 2010. "Privacy and Intimacy." *Journal of Value Inquiry* 44: 489–97. https://doi:10.1007/s10790-010-9249-6.

Erkkila, Betsy. 1989. *Whitman the Political Poet*. Oxford: Oxford University Press.
———. 2011. "Songs of Male Intimacy and Love: An Afterword." In *Walt Whitman's Songs of Male Intimacy and Love*, edited by Betsy Erkkila, 99–162. Iowa City: University of Iowa Press.
Genoways, Ted. 2007. "'One goodshaped and wellhung man': Accentuated Sexuality and the Uncertain Authorship of the Frontispiece to the 1855 Edition of *Leaves of Grass*." In *Leaves of Grass: The Sesquicentennial Essays*, edited by Susan Belasco, Ed Folsom, and Kenneth M. Price, 87–123. Lincoln: University of Nebraska Press.
Gerstein, Robert S. 1984. "Intimacy and Privacy." In *Philosophical Dimensions of Privacy: An Anthology*, edited by Ferdinand David Schoeman, 265–71. Cambridge: Cambridge University Press.
Gilbert, Jeremy. 2007. "Public Secrets: 'Being-with' in an Era of Perpetual Disclosure." *Cultural Studies* 21, no. 1 (January): 22–41. https://doi: 10.1080/09502380601046923.
Green, Michaël, Lars Cyril Nørgaard, and Mette Birkedal Bruun, eds. 2022. *Early Modern Privacy: Sources and Approaches*. Leiden: Brill.
Han, Byung-Chul. 2015. *The Transparency Society*. Translated by Erik Butler. Stanford, CA: Stanford Briefs.
Honneth, Axel. 1995. *The Struggle for Recognition: The Moral Grammar of Social Conflicts*. Translated by Joel Anderson. Cambridge, MA: MIT Press.
———. 2001. "Invisibility: On the Epistemology of 'Recognition.'" *Aristotelian Society Supplementary Volume* 75, no. 1 (July 1): 111–26. https://doi.org/10.1111/1467-8349.00081.
———.2020. *Recognition: A Chapter in the History of European Ideas*. Translated by Joseph Ganahl. Cambridge: Cambridge University Press.
Horn, Eva. 2011. "Logics of Political Secrecy." *Theory, Culture & Society* 28, no. 7–8: 103–22.
Inness, Julie. 1992. *Privacy, Intimacy, and Isolation*. Oxford: Oxford University Press.
Khawaja, Noreen. 2018. "The Unbounded Confession." In Alloa and Thomä 2018, 105–31.
Larson, Kerry C. 1988. *Whitman's Drama of Consensus*. Chicago: University of Chicago Press.
Lawson, Andrew. 2006. *Walt Whitman & The Class Struggle*. Iowa City: University of Iowa Press.
Lehrer, Tom. "Alma." 1965. *That Was the Year That Was*, Reprise/Warner Bros. Records.
Lejeune, Philippe. 1989. "The Autobiographical Pact." In *On Autobiography*, edited by Paul John Eakin, translated by Katherine M. Leary, 3–30. Minneapolis: University of Minnesota Press.
Margolis, Stacey. 2005. *The Public Life of Privacy in Nineteenth-Century American Literature*. Durham, NC: Duke University Press.

Mersch, Dieter. 2018. "Obfuscated Transparency." In Alloa and Thomä 2018, 259–82.
Metelmann, Jörg, and Thomas Telios. 2018. "Putting Oneself Out There: The 'Selfie' and the Alter-Rhythmic Transformations of Subjectivity." In Alloa and Thomä 2018, 323–41.
Murison, Justine S. 2020. "Whitman, Women, and Privacy." In *The New Whitman Studies*, edited by Matt Cohen, 33–49. Cambridge: Cambridge University Press.
Naurin, Daniel. 2006. "Transparency, Publicity, Accountability—The Missing Links." *Swiss Political Science Review* 12, no. 3: 90–98.
Neocleous, Mark. 2002. "Privacy, Secrecy, Idiocy." *Social Research* 69, no. 1 (Spring): 85–110.
Reimann, Jeffrey H. 1984. "Privacy, Intimacy, and Personhood." In *Philosophical Dimensions of Privacy: An Anthology*, edited by Ferdinand David Schoeman, 300–316. Cambridge: Cambridge University Press.
Renza, Louis A. 2002. *Edgar Allan Poe, Wallace Stevens, and the Poetics of American Privacy*. Baton Rouge: Louisiana State University Press.
Richards, Neil. 2022. *Why Privacy Matters*. Oxford: Oxford University Press.
Schmidgall, Gary. 2019. "'O You Singer Solitary': Walt Whitman on the Closet." *Walt Whitman Quarterly Review* 36, no. 4 (Spring): 241–60.
Schneider, Manfred. 2018. "The Dream of Transparency: Aquinas, Rousseau, Sartre." In Alloa and Thomä 2018, 85–104.
Shamir, Milett. 2006. *Inexpressible Privacy: The Interior Life of Antebellum American Literature*. Philadelphia: University of Pennsylvania Press.
Vendler, Helen. 2005. *Invisible Listeners: Lyric Intimacy in Herbert, Whitman, and Ashbery*. Princeton, NJ: Princeton University Press.
Waelen, Rosalie A. 2023. "The Struggle for Recognition in the Age of Facial Recognition Technology." *AI Ethics* 3: 215–22. https://doi.org/10.1007/s43681-022-00146-8.
Walton, Jo, and Ed Luker. 2018. "Poetry and Secrecy." *Journal of British and Irish Innovative Poetry* 10, no. 1: 1–36. https://doi.org/10.16995/biip.77.
Warner, Michael. 2002. "Publics and Counterpublics." *Public Culture* 14, no. 1 (Winter): 49–90.
Wehde, Susanne. 2011. *Typographische Kultur: Eine zeichentheoretische und kulturgeschichtliche Studie zur Typographie und ihrer Entwicklung*. Berlin: De Gruyter. First published 2000.
Westin, Alan F. 1967. *Privacy and Freedom*. New York: Atheneum.
Whitman, Walt. 1984. *Notebooks and Unpublished Prose Manuscripts*, 6 vols. Edited by Edward F. Grier. New York: New York University Press.
———. 1996a. *Leaves of Grass*. In Whitman 1996d, 5–145. First published 1855.
———. 1996b. *Democratic Vistas*. In Whitman 1996d, 953–1018. First published 1871.
———. 1996c. *Leaves of Grass*. In Whitman 1996d, 147–672. First published 1891–92.

———. 1996d. *Poetry and Prose*. Edited by Justin Kaplan. New York: Library of America.

Wills, David. 2008. "Passionate Secrets and Democratic Dissidence." Special issue, *Derrida and Democracy, Diacritics* 38, no. 1/2 (Spring–Summer): 17–22, 24–29.

Wittgenstein, Ludwig. 1922. *Tractatus Logico-Philosophicus*. Translated by C. K. Ogden. London: Kegan Paul, Trench, Trubner.

2: The Lives and Times of Henry James and F. O. Matthiessen: The Neoliberal Transparent Society and Its Liberal Enemies

Julián Jiménez Heffernan

> *They seek and cannot find the meaning of the music.*
> —John Ashbery, "Self-Portrait in a Convex Mirror," *Selected Poems*, 189

1.

IN THE PREFACE TO HIS *The Transparent Society*, philosopher Byung-Chul Han (2015, viii) argues that

> transparency is a *neoliberal dispositive.* It forces everything inward in order to transform it into information. Under today's immaterial relations of production, more information and communication mean more productivity and acceleration. In contrast, secrecy, foreignness, and otherness represent obstacles for communication without borders. They are to be dismantled in the name of transparency [emphasis added].[1]

Han's claim is sharply formulated, clear, and perhaps even true. My only concern lies with the readiness with which he describes the *dispositive*—the arch-Althusserian *appareil* (*Sur la reproduction*, 1995, 110)—as "neoliberal." Would Han say that the conspiracy in *Hamlet* (Shakespeare

---

1 The same idea is repeated in Han's (2017, 9) *Psychopolitics*: "In reality, however, this amounts to nothing other than a neoliberal dispositive. It means turning everything inside out by force and transforming it into information." This formulation helps disambiguate the odd phrasing "it forces everything inward" in the cited passage, showing that "inward" is a postponed adjective. In both cases, Han describes the externalization, and consequent conversion into public information, of what is originally internal.

2016)—orchestrated by the king but implicating other characters like Polonius, Rosencrantz, and Guildenstern—to force the prince's *inward* things (his secrets and mysteries) out and to transform them into information, spells a proto-liberal mechanism of extortion? Hamlet endlessly protests against the violation of his privacy, first to Claudius and his mother, reminding them that he has "that within which passeth show" (1.2.83),[2] and later to Guildenstern, when he compares himself to a pipe:

> Why, look you now how unworthy a thing you make of me: you would play upon me! You would seem to know my stops, you would pluck out the heart of my mystery, you would sound me from my lowest note to the top of my compass. And there is much music, excellent voice, in this little organ. Yet cannot you make it speak. 'Sblood! Do you think I am easier to be played on than a pipe? Call me what instrument you will, though you can fret me yet you cannot play upon me. (3.2.355–63)

To be sure, the attempt to play upon Hamlet, reveal his secrecy, and thereby produce his foreignness and otherness is a totalitarian gesture—an anticipation of the violent rationalized surveillance procedure designed to bring everything to light, including the infamous disqualification of the (Shakespearean) sovereign.[3] To designate such a gesture with a term—*neoliberal*—that includes the root *liberal* is an unwise move, as liberalism customarily and rightly names the social-political mindset bent on to the protection of the individual's right to independent thought, speech, and belief.[4] The fact that the so-called neoliberal forces of our present have managed to impose a market totalitarianism under the pretext of global democracy doesn't mean that liberalism is the *necessary* ideological cause of empire or capitalist expansion. In brief, I see two major flaws in Han's argument: 1) it unwittingly places nominal stress on the "liberal"

---

2 Citations of *Hamlet* are indicated by act, scene and line(s).
3 For Foucault on Shakespearean sovereignty, see *Les anormaux* (1999, 13).
4 Of all possible categories available in the academic market to describe contemporary notions of transparency (late-capitalist, postmodern, neoimperialist, global), Han has chosen the most problematic one (neoliberal), for it belies a built-in connotation (liberal) that remains overlooked by users of the term. The fact, moreover, that Han rather idiosyncratically redefines the term *neoliberal* along lines of totalitarian transparency and disciplinary control renders this contradiction even more acute, since liberalism emerges as a reaction against social transparency and political control: neither Thomas Hobbes nor John Locke were exactly Puritans. Let me recall what the latter says in his *A Letter concerning Toleration* (1983, 16): "In private domestic affairs, in the management of estates, in the conservation of bodily health, every man may consider what suits his own convenience and follow what course he likes best."

dimension of a sociopolitical dispositive whose most visible goal is inherently antiliberal; namely, to make everything visible;[5] and 2) it assumes that the yearning for total transparency is a recent sociopolitical phenomenon that can be dated to the rise of the "neoliberal" paradigm during the 1980s and 1990s.[6] To be sure, the first flaw is hardly exclusively imputable to Han: users of this widespread notion tend to overlook the fact that *laissez faire* has a range of application beyond the political or economic, and that Locke's defense of the inalienable right to individual thought and belief was not necessarily, as some "materialist" scholars imply, a pretext to normalize capitalism.[7] The second flaw seriously compromises the sociological cogency of his argument.

In this essay I want to show how both Henry James and one of his most brilliant exegetes, the Americanist F. O. Matthiessen, were compelled to produce their artistic and critical work against the tendentially totalitarian forces of a transparency dispositive already in place and at work in the period from 1870 to 1950. This gave their work an adversarial and dialectical edge, aimed at the protection of what Han rightly calls "secrecy, foreignness and otherness" in the face of constant and more or less organized attempts at having intimacy forced, violated, and publicized. The fact that both James and Matthiessen invested much intellectual energy in revamping the close-mouthed Hamlet persona adds genealogical depth to their shared liberal outlook.[8] While I take exception to Han's terminological choice and to his neglect of historical perspective, I still believe that his identification of the question of transparency as well

---

5   David Harvey (2005, 77) rightly argues that the intensification of coercive strategies of surveillance and policing in "neoliberal" states like the USA "to disperse or repress collective forms of opposition to corporate power" are simply "not consistent with neoliberal theory." Perhaps one should try to separate the wheat from the chaff: the liberal program may not be to blame for everything evil that is programmed or happens in a "neoliberal" state.

6   For a brief account of the rise of neoliberalism, see Steger and Roy (2021, 15–19).

7   I am thinking here, of C. B. Macpherson's important monograph *The Political Theory of Possessive Individualism*, where we read that despite its putative Puritan genealogy, which placed some stress in community, Locke's liberal theory considered that "the human essence is freedom from dependence on the wills of others, and freedom is a function of possession" (Macpherson 1962, 3).

8   Peter Rawlings (2005) and Adrian Poole (2020) have examined the depth and continuance of James's fascination with Shakespeare's *Hamlet*. James arguably rewrote *Hamlet* in *The Princess Casamassima* (1886): see my overview of this critical position in *Prepossessing Henry James: The Strange Freedom* (2023, 50–92); and Matthiessen examined in much detail the avatars of the "American Hamlet" in the work of Emerson, Melville (especially in *Pierre, or, the Ambiguities* [1852]), James, and T. S. Eliot. See *American Renaissance* (1968, 467–87); and *The Achievement of T. S. Eliot* (1959, 136, 166–69).

as elements of his conceptual articulation of it are relevant to the discussion I wish to undertake, both as instigation and as foil.

The label *neoliberalism* proves uncongenial to consistent analytical determination. It is commonly held to have entered the mainstream of political and economic theory sometime between 1938 and 1947, the year of the foundation of the Mont Pelerin Society; but, in fact, during those very years its meaning still fluctuated vastly.[9] Commenting on John Dos Passos's and Granville Hicks's commitment to leftist ideas, Matthiessen considered that the latter's

> membership in the Communist Party was never persuasive to me, since to judge by his writings in *The New Masses*, it always seemed so thinly theoretical, so lacking in a full grasp either of American or of Soviet life. But it was far more cogent than his recent retirement to a neo-liberalism that has no group adherences, a liberalism of the mind. (1948, 78)

Matthiessen puts forward an interesting polarity: the distinction between a neoliberalism without group adherences, which he calls a *liberalism of the mind*, and a neoliberalism *with* group adherences, which we could tentatively label a *liberalism of the real world*. Thus, whereas Henry James could be said to espouse a speculative (aesthetic-critical) liberalism of the mind, Matthiessen responds with a more pragmatic liberalism of the real world. In *From the Heart of Europe*, the American critic registers the anti-Nazi activist Fritz Molden's self-description as a "Catholic liberal, only a shade of center" (1948, 17). Similarly, Matthiessen himself, described by C. L. Barber as an intellectual of "liberal-socialist convictions" (preface to Matthiessen's *The Achievement of T. S. Eliot*, 1959, xii) and by William E. Cain (1987, 185) as "an American democrat in the tradition of Whitman," could be depicted as a Christian left-of-center liberal.

He was, we know, ambivalent about James's "flimsy" politics (1947, 644), and openly defended a fairer society, along socialist lines.[10] Matthiessen often shows his impatience with amateurish and *abstract*

---

9   Only around the 2000s did the term *neoliberal* become "the most common name for the current form of capitalism and/or the ideas and policies associated with it" (Kotz 2017, 8). Kotz notes the inadequate adaptation of terms like *liberal* or *neoliberal* to the spectrum of American politics (8–10). In his history of neoliberalism, David Harvey (2005, 57) is forced to admit that the rise of radical youth and student movements in England during the 1960s that supported, for satiric anticonservative purposes, "individualism and freedom of expression," unwittingly paved the way to the enforcement of neoliberal programs in the mid-seventies and eighties.

10   For an excellent analysis of Matthiessen's "ambivalence" toward James's disinterest in politics, see Cain. His focus on James's "illiberal" (my term) attitude

liberals committed to unpractical ideals in *From the Heart of Europe* (1948, 85), to "high-principled" intellectual liberals (27), and to "liberal groups of good will" (84). He devotes a section to the elucidation of the "semantic history of the word" *liberal* in American politics, where he laments the insufficiency of its vague and indeterminate meaning to grasp the novelty and urgency of Post–New Deal leftist politics (90–91).

Both James and Matthiessen can therefore safely be called liberals, and the latter professedly comes across as a neoliberal, but neither was— *pace* Han (2017, 9)—keen on "turning everything inside out by force and transforming it into information." On the contrary, they consistently prioritized literature over information, encouraged ambiguity over literalness, favored obscurity over transparency, and honored secrecy above publicity. Of James's profession of artistic faith in the story "The Middle Years" (1893) we tend to remember the resounding closing phrase, but we should not overlook the opening sentence: "We work in the dark—we do what we can—we give what we have. Our doubt is our passion, and our passion is our task. The rest is the madness of art" (*Stories of Writers and Artists* [1944, 210]).

2.

In Book 5 of James's *The Ambassadors,* we witness the slow start of a morning conversation between Chad, the young American prodigal biding his time in Paris, and Strether, the elderly family friend sent by Chad's mother to rescue him, over a glorious Boulevard breakfast:

> Strether scarce needed at last to say the rest—"I want to know where I am." But he said it, adding before any answer something more. "Are you engaged to be married—is that your secret?—to the young lady?" Chad shook his head with the slow amenity that was one of his ways of conveying that there was time for everything. "I have no secret—though I may have secrets! I haven't at any rate that one. We're not engaged. No." (2008, 166)

The ambiguous declaration "I have no secret—though I may have secrets" reads as a modernist rerun of Hamlet's sly remonstrance: "There is much music, excellent voice, in this little organ. Yet cannot you make it speak" (3.2.332–33). It comprises the quintessence of a revisited (aestheticized) liberalism of the mind, characterized by respect for the plural and differential secrecy of the private individual, placed beyond the reach of condemnatory, politically correct, and neo-Puritan taxonomical

---

to immigrants in *The American Scene* (1907; Cain: 179–86) must be factored into any balanced assessment of his liberalism.

assignation.[11] To have *one* secret implies being able to recognize and name your secret, and thereby to respond self-censoriously to a public ideological identitarian repression that you may have internalized. To assume that you have no secret but that you may have secrets is to accept that a pluralized but indefinite differentiation is likely to occur within the boundaries of the private self. The latter is James's dominant assumption, and that is the reason why I take him to be an exemplary instance of the liberal writer. The indefinite differentiation—the unnameability, negativity, the move from error to error-enhancing correction—of the private secret is also one of Matthiessen's chief critical premises, and that is why I take him to exemplify a *liberal* hermeneutics of sorts—the reading procedure best adapted to James's corpus.[12]

My concern is with the liberal opposition to social transparency—to the idea, that is, that since the life of the human individual is a social form of life, society has a right to demand the public exposure (the transparency) of the individual's inward life. The opposition between "staged and manipulative publicity" (Habermas 1991, 232) and privacy is historically traceable as a liberal opposition.[13] Since Locke, liberals are at bottom the archenemies of the transparent society. The transparent society, in turn, first took the form of the Puritan community, an organization exacting of its members the explicit committal to established forms of faith that instilled in them an obsessive penchant for self-scrutiny and confession—and quite often a tendency for public rituals of self-revelation and collective

---

11 Han's reliance on Carl Schmitt's partial advocacy of a notion of politics based on secrecy (2015, 6–7) is no doubt a courageous critical move that deserves praise. It is also worth noting that Schmitt's interest in a political absolutism beholden to arcana is connected to his hermeneutic absorption in *Hamlet*. Han quotes Iva Illouz to the effect that "so-called 'politically correct' practices, by contrast, request a form of transparency and lack of ambiguity—so as to ensure maximum contractual freedom and equality, and thus neutralize the traditional rhetorical and emotional halo of seduction" (15).

12 Kymlicka (1989, 18) observes that liberty is important for liberalism "not because we already know our good prior to social interaction, or because we can't know our good, but precisely so that we can come to know our good, so that we can 'track bestness', in Nozick's phrase." Private secrecy amounts very often to the record of the failures that necessarily attend this tracking, and this negative learning process is not unlike Jamesian "experience." For a *liberal hermeneutics* in action, see J. Hillis Miller's (1995) article on *The Aspern Papers*, but also Salmon's (1997, 97) subtle critique of the one-sidedness of the thesis that "James wishes to mount an ethical defence of the author's right to privacy."

13 Han (2015, 34–36) devotes a short chapter to the opposition between today's culture of intimacy and the objective-public world or public sphere (*Öffentlichkeit*) that emerged, according to Habermas, in the eighteenth-century.

displays of guilt.[14] The creator of Dimmesdale and Chillingworth is a case in point, and it is no accident that James and Matthiessen should respond ambivalently to Nathaniel Hawthorne's achievement. Whereas the former slyly argued that *The Scarlet Letter* is "full of the moral presence of the race that invented Hester's penance" (Henry James 1984a, 404), the latter astutely pointed out the double-edged significance of the adjective "liberal" in the hands of the self-scrutinizing New Englander (Matthiessen 1968, 198).

It was against this social accountability of the personal—the answerability, if you will, of the private to the tribunal of the public—that liberal thinkers first raised their voice. They opposed zealot magistrates who supported ideologies intended to maximize social cohesion, and their resistance took the form of an argument against the encouragement of rituals of private accountability. This is Locke in his *Letter concerning Toleration*:

> To which let me add that even in things of this world over which the magistrate has an authority, he never does [. . .] any farther than it concerns the good of the public, enjoin men the care of their private civil concernments, or force them to a prosecution of their own private interests, but only protects them from being invaded and injured in them by others, (which is a perfect toleration). (1983, 25)[15]

14 Although Macpherson (1962, 2) stresses the Puritan genealogy of Lockean liberal theory, visible in the focus on "the equal moral worth of every human being," Locke's liberal defense of "toleration" couldn't be further from the Puritan cultural and political aspiration, both in Britain and in America, toward the theocratic (and *theophobic*) community. For a particularly lucid correction of this view, see Dunn (1969, 212–28). It is also significant that Derrida (1997, 137–38) should argue in 1967 that a society that promotes "self-presence and transparent proximity," the ideal "of a small community with a 'crystalline' structure, completely self-present" is "Rousseauistic but already the inheritor of Platonism, it relates, we recall, to the Anarchistic and Libertarian protestations against Law, the Powers, and the State in general, and also with the dream of the nineteenth-century Utopian Socialisms, most specifically with the dream of Fourierism. He was, indirectly but in an arch-liberal manner, cautioning against the (neo-Puritan) dream of transparency nursed by leftist totalitarianism.

15 The remainder of the passage is: "And therefore we may well suppose he hath nothing at all to do with my private interest in another world, and that he ought not to prescribe me the way or require my diligence in the prosecution of that good which is of a far higher concernment to me than anything within his power, having no more certain or more infallible knowledge of the way to attain it than I myself. [. . .] Can it be reasonable that he that cannot compel me to buy a house should force me his way to venture the purchase of heaven, that he that cannot in justice prescribe me rules of preserving my health, should enjoin me methods of saving my soul, he that cannot choose a wife for me should choose a

Locke is adamant that no human compulsion can prescribe to humans rules for the private cultivation of the subjects' souls or enjoin them methods for the prosecution of their own private interests, civil concernments, and religious proclivities. No forced exterior performance has a right to violate "the voluntary and secret choice of the mind" (1983, 26). True enough, the liberal defense of toleration sprang forth inter alia as a measure to check the political persecution of radical religious groups, including the Puritans, but this doesn't change the fact that Puritan politics is by definition illiberally intolerant.[16] I am particularly interested in this Locke passage because the rhetoric of violence (*force, compel, prescribe*) and externalization (*outward violence, inward constraints*) that articulates his *liberal denunciation* of religious fanaticism is exactly the same that Han (2015) uses in order to denounce the so-called *neoliberal dispositive*. And this is paradoxical, to say the least.

Almost two centuries after Locke, John Stuart Mill put forward a similar view. In *On Liberty* (1859), he championed a community in which individuals "have nothing to fear from the open avowal of their opinions" and are therefore not likely to be mentally cramped by "the fear of heresy" (1989, 35). In addition, for Mill, the last redoubt of liberal individual privilege vis-à-vis state and social interference is secrecy—the "freedom" of "holding opinions in secret," the liberty "to conduct operations with a certain degree of secrecy and mystery" (1989, 100). To imply therefore, as Han does consciously or unwittingly today, that liberalism encourages a transparent society simply because *neoliberal* policies promote social surveillance is vastly inaccurate. The neoliberal conservatives who seek to implement such policies are, in fact, as illiberal as some of the

---

religion. But if God (which is the point in question) would have men forced to heaven, it must not be by the outward violence of the magistrate on men's bodies, but the inward constraints of his own spirit on their minds, which are not to be wrought on by any human compulsion, the way to salvation not being any forced exterior performance, but the voluntary and secret choice of the mind; and it cannot be supposed that God would make use of any means, which could not reach, but would rather cross, the attainment of the end" (25–26).

16 For the context of Locke's different texts on toleration, originally triggered by Anglican oppression, see James H. Tully's (1983) introduction, especially 1–8. In the founding statement of the Mount Pelerin Society—whose program turned around the work of Friedrich von Hayek but also included that of Milton Friedman and Karl Popper—we read, "The position of the individual and the voluntary group are progressively undermined by extensions of arbitrary power. Even that most precious possession of Western Man, freedom of thought and expression, is threatened by the spread of creeds which, claiming the privilege of tolerance when in the position of a minority, seek only to establish a position of power in which they can suppress and obliterate all views but their own" (qtd. by Harvey 2005, 20).

radical left-wing groups that allegedly oppose them. Unlike liberals, who tend to take a pragmatic view of social configurations, both are driven by an ontological—if not metaphysical—conception of the communal.[17] Both are, for that very reason, underhandedly enjoined by a radical determination to maximize through transparency the public access to the private—conservative neoliberals by capitalizing on social techniques of personal surveillance, leftist radicals by forcing the public exhibition of private commitments and beliefs. We tend to forget that *demonstrations*— the central notion in any praxis-based radical politics—often depend on unspoken intimidation, on the near-coercive instigation to exhibit in the public arena a part or the totality of your internal (moral, political) credentials. The cultural-social practices of (personal) confession and (public) demonstration are two sides of the same coin, and total transparency is the ultimate goal they share. The way in which contemporary writers are pressed by radical groups to take sides in current political conflicts by signing petitions and joining protests often reveals a profound antiliberal disposition.[18] We all have in mind some very embarrassing episodes of stigmatization of writers unwilling to endorse orthodox or politically correct views—I am thinking of Peter Handke and Michel Houellebecq.[19]

3.

This leads me to Jamesian territory. The position of a writer whose personal or artistic secrets are being rudely probed by intrusive observers is very common in Henry James's midperiod writing. Such a position spells a case of public intolerance, and the best hermeneutic handling of it can only come from liberal quarters. Calling James a liberal may seem extravagant, but it is the only ideological-political label that he can safely bear. As Richard Salmon (1997, 10–12) has shrewdly noted, "conservative" proves too reductive a category, especially when applied to the James who

---

17 Ronald Dworkin (1978, xi) contended that "liberals are suspicious of ontological luxury"—meaning the "ghostly entities" of collectivism and the communal. Both on the right and on the left the notion of community (as *Gemeinschaft* not *Gesellschaft*, to use Ferdinand Tönnies's distinction, tends to become metaphysically saturated (Jean-Luc Nancy would say *oeuvrée*), soaked with substantialist and essentialist implications.

18 Novelists like Salman Rushdie, Don DeLillo, or Ian MacEwan have found themselves in the position of either responding to these pressures or dramatizing them in their fiction.

19 The case of the latter is particularly apropos, as the collective fury over the incorrectness of his political ideas received additional fuel from the publication of his mother's memoirs, laden with vindictive information about the writer's personal life. The incident is commented upon in the epistolary exchange between Houellebecq and Bernard Henri-Lévy, *Ennemis publics* (2008).

anticipates a modernist aesthetics of radical diffuseness, fluidity, and differential indifference. Salmon places him in the Enlightened continental tradition of liberal thought, a tradition that condemned the erosion in America of the autonomy of "private judgement" by the pressures of "common opinion" (Tocqueville 2000, 408), and the resulting triumph of "blaring publicity" (Arnold 1901, 258). This classification is not new. Matthiessen (1944, 148) had already opined that Henry James's work profited from "the full advantages of the nineteenth-century liberalism of his father's generation," while suggesting that liberalism is the tradition that can best account for James's lifelong pursuit of personal independence and artistic freedom.[20]

James wrote many tales about isolated writers and artists whose highbrow oeuvre, bedeviled by complex style and secret patterns, resisted both public circulation and critical disclosure. These tales fall into a potential subcorpus of liberal narrative extravaganzas. Prominent in this set are also the stories in which writers strive, whether consciously or unwittingly, to conceal personal secrets from the view of the public. Critics have responded to this prominence, and one of the most productive fields of research in recent James studies is that of publicity. Richard Salmon's excellent *Henry James and the Culture of Publicity* (2001) first brought to attention the centrality that the protection of privacy—especially the privacy of the artist from ruthless journalists and intrusive critics—plays in James's work, both creative and critical. But, as Salmon avers, this protection is jeopardized by the dialectical fact that "for James there is no more public concern than his concern with 'privacy'" (3). Salmon calls attention to the passage in *The American Scene* (1907) where James complains about a new architecture where "every part of every house shall be, as nearly as may be, visible, visitable, penetrable, not only from every other part, but from as many parts of as many other houses as possible" (Henry James 1994, 125). Salmon persuasively shows how this dialectically qualified abhorrence of transparency is linked to James's very vigilant and critical attitude toward the editorial handling of personal papers like letters or notebooks.[21] Although he favored the ideological impetus behind the

---

20 Yet, Matthiessen reminds us that James's father maintained that "there was more truth in the old orthodoxy [Calvinism] than in the new uplifting liberalism" (Matthiessen and Murdock 2008, 7). In this same book, the critic describes the "directions" of William James's mind as "those of the liberal mind when, particularly in America, the choices all seemed free, and liberalism meant primarily liberation" (210–11).

21 In his 1872 review of *Passages from the French and Italian Note-Books of Nathaniel Hawthorne*, James (1984a, 307) writes, "These liberal excisions from the privacy of so reserved and shade-seeking a genius suggest forcibly the general question of the proper limits of curiosity." Salmon (2001, 88) lucidly examines this review and other essays on George Sand where James anticipates the

consolidation of a public sphere of critical debate and transparent communication, James feared the blurring of the line that had traditionally separated private from public:

> One sketches one's age but imperfectly if one doesn't touch on that particular matter: the invasion, the impudence and shamelessness, of the newspaper and the interviewer, the devouring *publicity* of life, the extension of all sense between public and private. (Henry James 1947, 82)

To be sure, his condemnation in *The Tragic Muse* (1890) of the intrusive media in "an age of publicity which never discriminated as to the quality of events," an age of "roaring deafening newspaperism" (Henry James 1995, 346; 352), informs a large body of tales focused on the literary profession, the most famous of which is perhaps *The Aspern Papers* (1888), a tale that pits private romantic secrecy against "the age of newspapers and telegrams and photographs and interviewers" (Henry James 2013, 6).[22]

In 1948, Matthiessen edited a selection of these tales under the title *Stories of Writers and Artists*. The choice, I believe, was anything but casual: Matthiessen was indirectly calling attention to James's liberal stance regarding the plague of publicity. He included some very remarkable tales, like "The Lesson of the Master" (1888), "The Real Thing" (1892), "The Death of the Lion" (1894), and "The Figure in the Carpet" (1896).[23] In all of them, with varying degrees of focus and intensity, James examines the thinness of the gap separating the writer's inner life—a private sphere of existence including biographical and artistic-compositional secrets— from the visible projection of this life unraveled by the agents of publicity:

---

critique of "the rhetoric of transparency and openness which sustain investigative biography." He could also have mentioned James's reaction to the publication of memoranda and private materials of Byron and Whitman. In his review of Francis Hodgson's *Memoir* (1878), James deals very tactfully with Byron's "sexual" secrets, and his sister's reaction to them: "Even if the inference we speak of were valid, it would be very profitless to inquire further as regards Byron's unforgivable sin; we are convinced that, if it were ascertained, it would be, to ingenuous minds, a great disappointment" (1984a, 819). And commenting on Whitman's 1883 biography by Richard Maurice Bucke, James writes, "He affects us all the more that these pages, quite woefully, almost abjectly familiar and undressed, contain not a single bid for publicity" (671).

22 Another relevant narrative is James's novel *The Reverberator* (1888), edited by Richard Salmon for The Cambridge Edition of the Complete Fiction of Henry James (2018). In the introduction, Salmon connects it to *The Aspern Papers* and "The Modern Warning" as explorations of "the disturbing cultural and psychological effects of modern publicity on intimate personal relationships" (liv).

23 He could also have included "The Birthplace" (1903), a story about the mercenary commodification of biographical details of Shakespeare's personal life.

malevolent journalists, meddlesome readers, sensationalist biographers, and curious critics. James's lifelong sense of discomfort vis-à-vis the public betrays, in the last instance, a liberal scruple with roots in Locke and Mill. He disliked both the literary effusions of sincerity and the cheapening of his craft through lurid revelation or unnecessary elucidation by reviewers and critics. To be sure, his failure as a playwright deepened his conviction, but this liberal dislike preexisted that failure. He was fond of repeating, in letters and stories, that it is impossible to make "a silk purse out of a sow's ear," and it is no accident that Matthiessen should relish repeating a quote that is so strongly beholden to Hamlet's sarcastic censure of the foolishness of giving "caviare to the general" (Shakespeare 2016, 2.2.374).[24] James believed that the greatness of a literary work was proportional to the amount of life it contained, but what he called *life* could not be prepackaged as a measurable commodity.[25] *Life*—a romantic trope for personal experience that James recursively encoded in terms of ineffable singularity—was inherently unlikely to enter the public flows of transparent communication. It couldn't be exactly reported, translated, or given away by external observers. What was meaningful in life for James could not always be conveyed in words, but only through reticence, ambiguity, and indirection. Therefore, the public processing of such elusive meaning was necessarily bound to fail, or end in disaster.

James's writings offer abundant confirmation of the reactive nature of individual privacy—the notion, that is, that the personal self is the secret, that privacy is the indistinct remainder of impenetrability that lingers once the rituals of public revelation have run their obscene course.[26] The critical problem of his possible homosexuality is a case in point. As a nascent discourse formation during his lifetime, homosexuality informs much of his writing, but it is not something you can easily put your finger on,

---

[24] It may be worth noting that Hamlet's comment is made in the context of a discussion about theatrical speeches or pieces that do not "please the million," and that it applies, therefore, to James's frustrating experience during the premiere of *Guy Domville*. In *Henry James: The Major Phase* (1944, 12), Matthiessen evokes the use of the phrase in the comic story "The Next Time"; and it reappears in the introduction to his edition of James's *Stories of Writers and Artists* (1944, 5), which includes the story and the original quote (272). As we see, *Democracy in America* was neither a given nor an unresisted assumption.

[25] In "The Art of Fiction" we read that "the only reason for the existence of a novel is that it does attempt to represent life" (Henry James 1984a, 46). And in the preface to *The Portrait of a Lady* (Henry James 1984b, 45) he explains that "there is, I think, no more nutritive or suggestive truth in this connexion than that of the perfect dependence of the 'moral' sense of a work of art on the amount of felt life concerned in producing it."

[26] The Latin term *privatus* means what is set apart from what is public. The notion is therefore dialectically beholden to its opposite and is reactive to it.

identify, designate, or classify. It is rather a more or less situated horizon of potentially deviant meaning, or, better, a symbolic field where the recursive failure of formalization becomes repeatedly indexed. The position of modern-day critics and biographers searching in his writings for the traces of his homosexuality is similar to that of the journalists and critics in some of his stories who strive to find the key to an author's secret. In these stories of writers and artists, the liberal James anticipated the tendentially illiberal treatment his writings would receive at the hands of later scholars.[27]

The question of James's homosexuality is not the only controversial aspect of his life that critics are interested in. His conservative politics soon became a matter of much speculation and concern. Given the constitutive ambiguity of his writing—the differential indifference, the chronic semantic slippage—critics were forced to move to his nonfictional writings (memoranda, notes, personal letters) to assemble evidence and construct a case. The first scholars who, with the license of James's heirs, were confronted with these materials were variously aware of the fact that they were burglarizing or invading a private space and that this transgression somehow violated a liberal principle of respect of private life. This was the case, interestingly enough, with Matthiessen himself, who on two occasions was given privileged access to James's personal papers.

In 1947, Matthiessen and Kenneth B. Murdock edited a collection of biographical documents titled *The James Family: A Group Biography; Including Selections from the Writings of Henry James, Senior, William, Henry and Alice James*. In the acknowledgments section Matthiessen explains that "the record of the Jameses was made possible by my having access to the wealth of family manuscripts now in the Houghton Library at Harvard" (viii). He speaks of a biography that is more internal than external (v) and notes that "by far the most revelatory material for understanding the James family consists of letters and journals and essays, some hitherto unprinted" (v–vi). (Note that such access to a wealth of family manuscripts is precisely what the protagonist of *The Aspern Papers* is desperately and unsuccessfully after.) Matthiessen justifies taking advantage of this access in the following terms:

---

27 If, as Eve Kosofsky Sedgwick (1990) argues, homosexual love at the time James wrote was "the love that dare not speak its name," then James's fin-de-siècle texts can be said to stage "this refusal to speech" (Hurley 2018, 315). It is interesting to point out that the explicit search for homosexual traces in his life and work and the application of queer theory to his writing chronologically coincide with the demise of poststructuralist theory, which occurred in the late 1980s. Fortunately, though, some of the best scholars contributing to this debate after 1991 (Sedgwick, Eric Haralson, Eric Savoy, Kevin Ohi) retain the poststructuralist taste for genuine difference.

> Indeed, after surveying the father's ideas and his children's reaction to them, after listening to the family's discussions of religion and philosophy and literature and politics and society, we may feel that we have gained a fairly full index to American intellectual history from the time of Emerson to that of the First World War. At least we shall have *shared intimately* in what one remarkably sensible and alert family group thought and talked and argued about. (v; emphasis added)

Matthiessen later describes his role as that of the director of a play, but here he construes it as that of the surveyor of other people's private ideas, thoughts, and words—something like the narrator of Thomas Mann's *Buddenbrooks: The Decline of a Family* (1901). Inasmuch as this *intimate sharing* is obtained without the other person's permission, there is something morally censurable in the act of publicizing the share. The liberal dogma is that we all have a right to speak and think, and a right, too, to place limits on other people's access to some of our words and thoughts. What is the moral entitlement for this *intimate sharing*? To what extent and on what grounds is it right to *share* someone else's *intimacy*? Matthiessen doesn't openly register discomfort, but anxiety probably mines his editorial poise. This is the same scholar, let us not forget, who three years earlier, in *Henry James: The Major Phase* (1944, xii–xiii), alluded with unrepressed irony to the way in which "the darker passages of [James's] mind, the debatable implications of his ambiguity, have been probed—from the opposite angles of the psychologist and the moralist—by Edmund Wilson and Yvor Winters."[28] Consider, for instance, the way in which, in a telling aside while discussing the problem of James's back injury, the critic brushes off the unspoken question of homosexuality by simply failing to mention it:[29]

> Since HJ never married, he may have been sexually impotent, but since he seems never to have exhibited the specific anxieties or

---

28 One important aspect of *The Ambassadors* that Matthiessen soon focuses upon is the technical matter of point of view. He argues that James's novels are "strictly novels of intelligence rather than full consciousness; and in commenting on the focus of attention that he had achieved through Strether, he warned against 'the terrible fluidity of self-revelation'" (1944, 23). In a sense, the critic reminds us that James would not have favored the personal probing into the dark subconscious that Sigmund Freud recommended. Self-revelation, in short, has limits.

29 A firefighting accident that occurred when he was eighteen produced an "obscure hurt," probably in his back, whose precise etiology and nature have given rise to much medical and psychoanalytic speculation. For a lucid approach to this incident and its effects, see Rawlings 2005).

fantasies that can be diagnosed as the product of such frustration, it has not been proved that we can learn anything about his character or his art by building on such assumption. (1944, 247)

Note the astuteness of the critical move: Matthiessen puts the morally equivocal diagnostic powers of the critic as biographer-meddler—as comprehensive notebook-cum-private-letter-reader—at the service of the distant, disinterested, indifferent, liberal intellectual, ever ready to protect his subject of study from the obscenity of prying eyes. The bottom line is: leave him alone because I have not (not left him alone), and am authorized to conclude that no lurid secret is here buried.[30]

In the same year, 1947, Matthiessen coedited *The Notebooks of Henry James*, an extraordinary collection of meta-literary observations and reflections that record the novelist's work in progress during a period of more than thirty years. In the introduction to the book, Matthiessen and his coeditor, Kenneth B. Murdock, observe that James "foresaw lucidly the widening gap between the slick popular magazine and the serious reader and fought vigorously against each new sign of vulgarization of taste" (xvi). One symptom of such "vulgarization of taste"—tellingly, Matthiessen had already used that very phrase in his introduction to his edition of James's *Stories of Writers and Artists* (1944, 5)—was the growing sensationalism around the life of the artist, a problem greatly aggravated by the neo-Romantic tendencies of the aestheticist vogue. In an essay on Robert Louis Stevenson, James sarcastically observed that "the novelist who leaves the extraordinary out of his account is liable to awkward confrontations, as we are compelled to reflect in this age of newspapers and of universal publicity" (1984a, 1249). That was the age, of course, of the Oscar Wilde case, whose journalistic echoes unnerved James. According to Haralson (2012, 179),

> the "ghastly eruption" of the Wilde trials, in Willa Cather's phrase, spewed its fallout across the Atlantic, prompting one Bostonian to caution his male friends that "queer things are looked askance" in the wake of "Oscar's exposé." At the epicenter in London, James felt an atmosphere of Inquisition and a "general shudder as to what, with regard to some other people, may possibly come to light."[31]

---

30 In *The James Family*, Matthiessen reports, for instance, James's alarm at finding out that his father was reading his personal letters aloud to Emerson (2008, 255). William E. Cain (1987, 171) has observed that in that book Matthiessen "often appears on the verge of major revelations—both about James and about himself—but he doesn't express them in a sustained fashion, doesn't rigorously follow through on them."

31 The article on Stevenson was published in 1888, two years after Wilde started his affair with seventeen-year-old Robert Ross, and seven years before

As if to avert the critical risk of mixing up life and art, the editors apprise the reader that "the interest of the notebooks [. . .] is not primarily historical or biographical, so that no attempt has been made to print identifications of all the persons mentioned or annotations on all the historical and geographical data" (1947, xxiii). This reads once again as a liberal injunction, a principle of respect for the private life of all concerned—the author and his acquaintances, relatives, informants. One thing seems clear: Matthiessen appears to have imbibed this liberal injunction from James himself, even if his critical-scholarly attention to James's work labored in the opposite direction of revelation, disclosure, and potential transparency. Editing James's family papers, private letters, and personal notes can be easily construed as a violation of the novelist's liberal right to privacy, and Matthiessen was no doubt aware of the difficult position he had placed himself in. The fact that he also decided to edit a selection of James's tales about artists concerned with their secrecy may suggest that the right application of a *liberal hermeneutics* was uppermost in his mind.[32]

4.

All in all, Matthiessen contributed five important works to Jamesian scholarship in the years spanning 1944–48: in 1944, he published the major study on James's final phase, *Henry Hames: The Major Phase*. Three years later, he edited both the *Notebooks* and the family papers included in *The James Family: A Group Biography*. In 1947–48 he published two collections of James's narratives: *Stories of Writers and Artists* and *The American Novels and Stories of Henry James*. Perhaps we can also add the chapter on James included in Matthiessen's 1940 masterpiece, *American Renaissance: Art and Expression in the Age of Emerson and Whitman*. It is, therefore, not completely inaccurate to say that Matthiessen spent the Second World War reading James.

The greatest historical event of his lifetime found Matthiessen in Cambridge, Massachusetts, absorbed in the life and works of Henry James, another American intellectual who had also missed the only important historical event in his life—the Civil War. This is a parallelism worth stressing. James never fully recovered from an early episode of inability to

---

the libel trial began. For James's professed distances from the Wilde (and Whitman) *personae*, see Novick (1999, 1–15); Ellmann (1999, 30–42); and Freedman (1990, 167–202).

32 Cain (1987, 179) persuasively describes Matthiessen's contradictory attempt to reconcile the program of "reading as a socialist" and his honest acknowledgment of the in principle nonpolitical, nonthematic, aesthetic excellence of James's literary art.

enter the public arena of History. An injury to his back made him unfit for military service, and he, unlike two of his brothers, failed to fight in the war. Neither of the brothers ever fully recovered from the wounds they received in action. Matthiessen spent the war years reading and writing. In the introduction to *Henry James: The Major Phase*, Matthiessen describes how the idea for his book sprang from a conversation with his Harvard undergraduates: "When I said, half meaning it, that a book on Henry James was to be my overaged contribution to the war effort, they urged me to be serious. They believed that in a total war the preservation of art and thought should be a leading aim. They persuaded me to continue to believe it" (1944, xvi).[33] In a sense, both James and Matthiessen failed in their *coming out*, for we should keep in mind that fighting in a war (or revolution) or openly demonstrating against it became two radical modes of historical participation available to young males during the nineteenth and twentieth centuries: the dialectical possibility of a third position of withdrawal and quietism becomes all the more available to the artist-to-be after the example of Frédéric Moreau in Gustave Flaubert's *L'éducation sentimentale* (1869).[34] James was a liberal conservative. Matthiessen sympathized with communism, but he never joined the party. Still, his name was often publicly mentioned in that connection, and was targeted by anticommunist forces.[35] He ended up committing suicide in 1950, and left a

---

33 In the acknowledgments section of *Henry James: The Major Phase*, Matthiessen tells the reader that "a book on James was to be my overaged contribution to the war effort," meaning the Second World War. He acknowledges his debt to his students who, "during the tense winters of 1942 and 1943, kept insisting that until they were needed by the Army, they meant to continue to get the best education they could" (1944, xvi).

34 In the phrase "coming out" I am deliberately conflating the trials of social maturation for girls (*being out* in Jane Austen's world as being available for marriage), the masculine rites of maturation for boys (*setting out* to join a public militancy of sorts), and the homosexual experience of *outing*. For the ideological and structural role of the 1848 revolution in Flaubert's novel, see Bourdieu (1995, 127–32). James's response to Flaubert can be found in *The Princess Casamassima* (1886). In *The Liberal Imagination*, Lionel Trilling (1951, 62) argues that the first relevant action of new novelistic heroes like Honoré de Balzac's Rastignac, James's Hyacinth, and Flaubert's Moreau is "setting out to seek his fortune."

35 The potential threat of Matthiessen's "communism" became particularly visible after the publication of *From the Heart of Europe* in 1948. This is Wendy Gonaver's (2010, 46) succinct and abrupt version of these complex issues: "Not surprisingly, *From the Heart of Europe* was castigated by critics, including Lionel Trilling, as 'politically naïve.'" Redding concedes that Matthiessen was naive, but not necessarily because he neglected to denounce Stalinism. He cites Don Sparling, who argues that Matthiessen's naivete stemmed from "a quasi-Orientalist romanticization of 'the people,'" which, Redding suggests, was connected to his

note saying: "I am depressed over world conditions. I am a Christian and a Socialist. I am against any order which interferes with that objective." But the need to protect his political privacy was probably not the only motivation for his tragic death. Matthiessen was a homosexual, and he managed somehow to remain "openly" in the closet for most of his professional life, but only somehow.[36] In a letter to his lover and mentor, Russell Cheney, he complains, "My sex bothers me, feller, sometimes when it makes me aware of my position in the world. . . . Have I any right in a community that would so utterly disapprove of me if it knew the facts?" (qtd. by Fuller 2007, 84). Thus the pattern emerges of a man "oscillating between rigidly demarcated public and private realms" (Fuller 2007, 84) and falling into depression. The death of his partner in 1945 greatly

---

own erotic longings (2009, 47). Like the writer and Communist spy Whittaker Chambers, Matthiessen engaged in homosexual affairs; unlike Chambers, Matthiessen had a long-term relationship with another man until his lover died. For Matthiessen, political fraternity overlapped with homoeroticism. Perhaps this was the case for Chambers as well, subliminally, both as a Communist and later as a Christian. At any rate, whereas Chambers found legitimacy in the conservative movement, Matthiessen only found loneliness and exile. After periodic bouts with depression, he committed suicide in 1950, "in the midst of repeated subpoenaed appearances before HUAC" (Redding 2009, 37). See also George Blaustein, *Nightmare Envy and Other Stories* (2018, 172–225; and Richard Schlatter's essay "On Being a Communist at Harvard" (1977).

36 In an important article titled "F. O. Matthiessen: The Critic as Homosexual," later included in his book *Gay Transfigured*, David Bergman explains that it wasn't until a quarter of a century after his suicide in 1950 that Matthiessen's "homosexuality became public knowledge. During his lifetime, Matthiessen had not tried to hide the fact, but neither had he made it a public issue. Friends, colleagues, and even students widely understood that Matthiessen was gay" (1991, 85), but they felt that the facts of his sexual life had no bearing on his work. According to Jay Grossman (1998, 813), "Matthiessen also expresses a nascent conception of the closet, in which he replaces Cheney's call for abstinence and full public disclosure with a tempered argument that Cheney's desire for complete openness is hasty at best: 'You say that the only possible life is one every part of which can be acknowledged. And of course I agree, my dearest Rat. But acknowledged to whom? To the entire world, or to your [close] and understanding friends?' (Hyde, 87). For Matthiessen there is candor on the one hand and unwise self-disclosure on the other, and he seems to know well, and to desire to school Cheney in, the important differences between the two." Discussing Matthiessen's distaste for Whitman's incontinence, he points out that "we might conceive this view of Whitman's incontinence as an example of the contradictions put into place by the impossibility of Matthiessen's conjoining the public and the private in the writing of his own life-contradictions put into place, that is to say, by the regimes of knowing (American literature) from within the closet. Indeed, the 'barriers' that Matthiessen insists Whitman constantly oversteps might well be seen as those in this gay critic's own life" (813).

aggravated his personal anxiety. As Randall Fuller (2007, 82) has put it, Matthiessen and his lover "felt painfully marginalized as homosexuals." The essential biographical facts about Matthiessen's life and death add up to a liberal tragedy: that of a private subject whose death is partly caused by the interference of the public in his life. This public interference was aimed at exposing two private secrets—one political, the other sexual.

5.

Like James, then, Matthiessen remained all of his life an unrecruited and unmarried male. Neither of them took part in the public rituals of war and marriage that so prominently marked the social careers of their male contemporaries. The significance of their lives lay elsewhere, in a more private, secret, and unscripted sphere—which I would call a *field of difference*. Nowhere is this field better described than in Henry James's own terms, quoted by Matthiessen in *The James Family*: "What we [James and his brothers and sister] were to do instead was just to *be* something, something unconnected with specific doing, something free and uncommitted, something finer in short than being *that*, whatever it was, might consist of" (2008, 94). This is the reason, I surmise, why Matthiessen was so keenly attracted to the Jamesian rendition of life, a figurative venture that pervades the American novelist's entire work, both critical and narrative, and that is marked by chronic vagueness and indeterminacy. Life, for James, is registered but undetermined experience. The analytical effort to grasp it, name it, and determine it is always doomed to failure, and yet the effort to understand what is massively registered (or unlost) makes up a no small part of the experience of life.[37] James is a Romantic thinker who made excessive use of the rational-analytical faculty, all the better to demonstrate the indeterminacy and unfathomableness of human experience. Human life, for James, is interesting in proportion to the challenge it poses both to its rational comprehension and to its social categorization. The resulting ambiguity is dialectical, and it can only be mapped out through a logic of difference. If James excels in something, it is in his refusal to name: his much-celebrated strategy of indirection is an expression of dissatisfaction with the nominal obscurity and taxonomical impudence of social-public discourse. Whence the compulsion to retreat and the drive to abstain. When James's brother William, the

---

[37] James (1984, 53) famously observed in "The Art of Fiction" that "if experience consists of impressions, it may be said that impressions are experience, just as (have we not seen it?) they are the very air we breathe. Therefore, if I should certainly say to a novice, 'Write from experience, and experience only,' I should feel that this was a rather tantalising monition if I were not careful immediately to add, 'Try to be one of the people on whom nothing is lost!'"

prominent philosopher and founding figure in American psychology, wrote in *The Will to Believe* (1896) that "if this life be not a real fight, in which something is eternally gained for the universe by success, it is no better than a game of private theatricals from which one may withdraw at will" (William James 2010, 79), he may well have been thinking about his brother Henry.

As such, theatricalized public discourse is more than a mere failure of symbolic formalization (Jacques Lacan) but less than a decisionist, nominal, and eventual production of a truthful present (Alain Badiou). More reactive than active, the strategy of discretional withdrawal can only be described as conservative—liberal-conservative, actually—and at bottom deconstructive. Ambiguity and difference are precisely what the nominal efforts of absolutist-Puritan transparency fail to register, and the way the new postcritical tendencies (affect studies, posthumanism, neophenomenology, animal studies, ecocriticism) scorn the high-theoretical period dominated by deconstruction in favor of a return to sociological moralism addicted to identity stickers and nominative assignation is proof of the hold that Puritanism still has in Anglo-American society. These new tendencies favor social and political identitarian exhibitionism over private reticence. The new cults of public recognition and identity-sticker-assignation claim to be tolerant of difference, but this is only partly so.[38] They approve the difference that can be readily, seamlessly, and leaklessly defused into identity. If a difference poses obstacles to labeling, then it is not politically viable. Thus, only what is ideologically precategorized through social names can emerge in the Puritanical identitarian logic of publicity and transparency.[39] What is really different and not what is identified as such fails to inscribe itself in the public, ideological, script. What James calls *life* is one such elusive thing, a conundrum that only a truly

---

38   For three eloquent denunciations of the excesses of identity politics in our gradually posttheoretical or simply detheorized critical horizon, see Hobsbawm, "Identity Politics and the Left" (1996, 41); Žižek, *The Plague of Fantasies* (2009, 45); Copjec, "Interview" (2020, 200).

39   Writing about Emerson and Carlyle, James noted that "both were Puritans; both of them looked, instinctively, at the world, at life, as a great total, full of far-reaching relations" (1984, 242). The key notion here is that of the "great total." In *Totality and Infinity*, the philosopher Emmanuel Levinas claims that "the pathos of liberalism, which we rejoin on one side, lies in the promotion of a person inasmuch as he represents nothing further, that is, is precisely a self. Then multiplicity can be produced only if the individuals retain their secrecy, if the relation that unites them into a multiplicity is not visible from the outside but proceeds from one unto the other. If it were entirely visible from the outside, if the exterior point of view would open upon its ultimate reality, the multiplicity would form a totality in which the individuals would participate; the bond between persons would not have preserved the multiplicity from addition" (1979, 120).

Romantic-liberal hermeneutics is likely to decipher. To put it in Peter Hallward's (2001, xv) lucid terms, liberal hermeneutics must be *indifferent to differences*.[40]

6.

Let me examine one such episode of liberal hermeneutics. It covers the first chapter of Matthiessen's book on James's final phase (*Henry James: The Major Phase*, 1944). The chapter is devoted to the 1903 novel *The Ambassadors*, a work that marks the apogee of James's elusiveness. *The Ambassadors* tells the story of a middle-aged American widower who is sent by his elderly fiancée to rescue her son from the dissolute life that he is presumably leading in Paris. Her aim is to force the son's return to America to take control of the family business. But the minute Strether—the first *ambassador*—gets to Paris, he realizes that he will not be able to fulfill his task. The reason is that he discovers something decisive about himself—decisive because he can momentously act on it, not because he can name it. It marks an acquisition of neither knowledge nor truth but rather of meaning and experience: Strether realizes that his lifelong missing out on *life* can now be compensated with another chance, another try—at *life*. The content (referent or truth) of this *life* is never properly fleshed out—there is only a deferral of meaning that ultimately constitutes life experience.[41] That is the novel's secret, the protagonist's secret, which in a way is also the young man's secrets, and perhaps, too, Henry James's secret. A great deal of critical speculation has accrued around the content of Strether's new sense of life, quite often by relating it to a homoerotic revelation that is never properly assumed, let alone fully understood. Matthiessen (1944, 39), for instance, highlights the protagonist's *passivity*: after awakening to a new sense of life, he "does nothing at all to fulfill that sense." This early detection of passivity echoes thematic incriminations of political quietism and sexual abstinence often leveled against James—two incriminations that slip imperceptibly into denunciations of conservatism and homosexuality.

---

40 Locke changed his mind about the consideration of religious belief as one of the "things indifferent" to political power, but the idea of indifference to religious difference holds a special place in the liberal mentality: see Tully, introduction to *A Letter concerning Toleration* (Locke 1983, 6–7).

41 Derrida has repeatedly enjoined his readers to grasp the equivalence of the Rousseaunian concept of *réserve* and Martin Heidegger's idea of *Bestand*: in both cases, delay, deferral, and difference come off as the effects, in the field of human experience, of an indeterminate standing life reserve that is never depleted. See, for instance, *Of Grammatology* (1997, 185–88).

But Matthiessen never goes that far, if only because this name—homosexuality—doesn't necessarily exhaust the differential latency of the concept "life" as it transpires in the novel. I am not trying to say that Matthiessen consciously strove to prevent James's official "outing," an event that took place, as Eric Savoy (2007) has astutely chronicled, in 1991.[42] What I am implying is that he resisted the facile reduction of Jamesian formal queerness—his indirections, occlusions, lapses, evasions and dissonances—to the predictable institutional narrowness of the category *homosexual*.[43] If "experience is never limited, and it is never complete," if "it is an immense sensibility, a kind of huge spider-web, of the finest silken threads, suspended in the chamber of consciousness and catching every air-borne particle in its tissue" (1984a, 52), then experience is the gradual notation (the discrimination) of difference that we confound psychologically with *delay* and morally with *passivity*. Think, respectively, of the Hamletian figures of Samuel Beckett's Belacqua and Melville's Bartleby. In the *Notebooks*, James (1947, 300) observes that Strether "finds himself sinking, as I say, up to his middle in Difference—difference from what he expected, difference in Chad, difference in everything; and Difference, as I again say, is what I give." *The Ambassadors* is indeed the novel that best dramatizes the flight from identitarian labels that hamper the flow of difference. James uses it to frame an analytical-moral queer site of militant indifference to differences. Strether's gradual commitment to a differential logic without clear-cut binarism or resting places alienates him from the Manichean morality of his native land.[44] Christopher Butler (Henry James 2008, x) has observed that Strether has "to break with the puritanical and utilitarian morality" of the woman who has employed him. Both such rejection of Puritan antinomianism and his newly awakened sensibility to difference are essential ingredients of a liberal mentality. Also liberal is the taste for ambiguity, indirection, reticence, and silence: "It ended in fact by being quite beautiful between

---

42 In the fascinating essay "*Entre chien et loup*: Henry James, Queer Theory, and the Biographical Imperative," Savoy (2007, 100) examines the biographical and critical (mis)handling of this queerness. The essay opens with the suggestion that "Henry James became a gay writer in 1991 when he was 'outed,' if you will, by Edmund White, the editor of *The Faber Book of Gay Short Fiction*." See also Eric Haralson (2003).

43 Haralson (2003, 178) has written that "in Richard Dellamora's useful distinction, James resisted the categories of *homosexual* and *lesbian* as such (*gay* being only a glimmer on the horizon), so that *queer* best names the persistent 'disidentification from heterosexual norms' of human development and relations."

44 The differential logic thus described corresponds to the notion of experience that emerges from Georg Wilhelm Friedrich Hegel's *Phenomenology of Spirit* (1807). See Fredric Jameson (2007, 50).

them, the number of things they had a manifest consciousness of not saying" (Henry James 2008, 285).

This reticence is transferred to the problem of agency. The inability to speak the—at bottom, indeterminate and undecidable—meaning of life turns into an incapacity to fully act on the basis of this meaning. Matthiessen (1944, 39), we have already noted, holds that the "burden of *The Ambassadors* is that Strether has awakened to a wholly new sense of life. Yet he does nothing at all to fulfill that sense." All too clearly, he shows respect for the *semantics of reticence* the novel enjoins the reader to assume, and he thus seeks to protect further the secrecy of James's personal work by multiplying the sites, in his work, of hermeneutic indeterminacy. But the sites are already there in the novel, carefully disseminated by the narrator. The fact that Matthiessen reads James's narrative investment in the indeterminacy of life as an effort to liberate himself from the moral opposites ruling American life explains the former's critical commitment to terms like freedom, liberation, and emancipation, all of which are held to contribute to the construction of an inward life.

Matthiessen holds that Strether and other American characters are driven to Europe out of an "eagerness of liberation" (25) and adds that Strether "insists that we make the most of life by enjoying our illusion, that we should act as though we were free" (26). He rightly observes that James's father's acceptance of transcendental freedom was qualified by a critical awareness of Emerson's blindness to the problem of evil. In fact, he argues, "the strong residue of his concern with the nature of evil was to be transmitted to his sons" (27), especially to Henry. Still, Strether's declaration is said to continue and expand "the transcendental mood of liberation" (27). The American critic then moves on to remind us of the spiritualist quality of James's father's particular brand of emancipation. Spiritual freedom was the doctrinal premise of everything he tried to inculcate in his sons and daughters, and this is read by Matthiessen as prompting James's early turn to inwardness, aggravated by external circumstances: "On the verge of manhood, the injury to his back that kept him from participating in the Civil War made him feel that his was the peculiar case of having to live inwardly at a time of 'immense and prolonged outwardness'" (28). This final observation renders totally explicit the running dialectic that is the object of my essay—the tension between inward life and the immense and prolonged outwardness of transparent, public, existence.

7.

The climactic incident in *The Ambassadors* is the moment in which Strether, rambling by the river in the pastoral outskirts of Paris, witnesses by chance the arrival to the shore of a small boat carrying Chad and

Madame de Vionnet, ready for a country meal. It is an instant of sudden but complex revelation: he confirms Chad's indifference to Jeanne, Madame de Vionnet's daughter; discovers his erotic alliance with the elder lady; and sees himself banished from the idyll by their apparent resolve to ignore his presence. The revelation of a private secret and the realization of his exclusion from it—"the violence of their having 'cut' him" (Henry James 2008, 389)—deepens the complexity of the elated awareness of his own newly discovered freedom as critical contemplator:

> What he saw was exactly the right thing—a boat advancing round the bend and containing a man who held the paddles and a lady, at the stern, with a pink parasol. It was suddenly as if these figures, or something like them, had been wanted in the picture, had been wanted more or less all day, and had now drifted into sight, with the slow current, on purpose to fill up the measure. They came slowly, floating down, evidently directed to the landing-place near their spectator and presenting themselves to him not less clearly as the two persons for whom his hostess was already preparing a meal. For two very happy persons he found himself straightway taking them— a young man in shirt-sleeves, a young woman easy and fair, who had pulled pleasantly up from some other place and, being acquainted with the neighbourhood, had known what this particular retreat could offer them. The air quite thickened, at their approach, with further intimations; the intimation that they were expert, familiar, frequent—that this wouldn't at all events be the first time. (388–89)

This whole passage wrests its force from the sudden notation of new difference discerned by the spectator: a sense of cumulative sensorial determination ("*exactly the* right thing," "*these* figures," "*evidently* directed," "no less *clearly*," "*the* two persons," "*this* particular retreat," "*they* were expert," "[not] *the* first time"; emphases added) informs this episode of near-Cartesian (clear and distinct) attestation ("saw," "drifted into sight," "presenting themselves," "taking them") of something ("the right thing") that happens to make all the difference. And yet, it is this sensorial corroboration of difference that sparks the retroactive confirmation of a difference that is prospective and liberating and that, for lack of a better word, we could call moral: "Strether's newly felt internal difference means that he goes home 'to a great difference' in American culture" (Haralson 2003, 133). This is so, we may argue, to the significant difference of, among others, W. H. Auden, Truman Capote, James Baldwin, and John Ashbery. Haralson speaks of "James's forecast for queer masculinity" (133). Admittedly, Matthiessen felt himself interpellated by this invitation to queerly tarry and differ.

Toute proportion gardée, one may suggest that in *From the Heart of Europe* (1948), Matthiessen wrote an updated version of the scene from *The Ambassadors* that I have just cited. He found himself implicitly responding to the critique of socialist friends who kept reminding him of "the Communists' indifference to the dignity of the individual" (79). Although in partial agreement, he protested that socialists had become excessively timid and lost their faith in revolution. And then he added,

> If I lived in France, I don't quite see how I could help being a Communist. I put that thought in its barest form, since my attendance last week at a Sunday fête champêtre, staged by *L'Humanité* on the outskirts of Paris, started these reflections on politics. The impressive and heartening thing, so lacking in most intellectuals' efforts to belong to a radical party in America, was the sense you could have, in that throng of almost a million men and women from all over France, of really being joined with a people's movement. The people were not an abstraction in an editorial, they were there on the grass with their bottles of wine and bread, they were there to take part in the raffle of desperate-looking chicken at one of the dozens of little booths. They were there to laugh with the Fratellinis and to sing workers' songs and finally to listen to speeches from a platform some half a mile away from the edges of the crowd. It's easy to be a sucker for French vitality and gaiety. (79)

In both cases, the witness is gaily intrigued by someone else's harmonious *fête champetre*. In both cases, moreover, the witness is subtly, if obtrusively, not a part of the party. He is, rather, a distant, mildly disenchanted, chronicler of vitality and gaiety, the narrator of *other* and *different* life: *they came slowly, they were there*. In a certain sense, such lack of reciprocity spells the radical breakdown of transparency that James and Matthiessen construed as a necessary condition of human existence.

Works Cited

Althusser, Louis. 1995. *Sur la reproduction.* Paris: PUF.
Arnold, Matthew. 1901. *The Letters of Matthew Arnold*, vol. 2, edited by George W. E. Russell. London: Macmillan.
Ashbery, John. 1985. *Selected Poems.* New York: Penguin.
Bergman, David. 1991. *Gay Transfigured: Gay Self-Representation in American Literature.* Madison: University of Wisconsin Press.
Blaustein, George. 2018. *Nightmare Envy and Other Stories: American Culture and European Reconstruction.* Oxford: Oxford University Press.
Bourdieu, Pierre. 1995. *The Rules of Art: Genesis and Structure of the Literary Field.* Stanford, CA: Stanford University Press.
Cain, William E. 1987. "Criticism and Politics: F. O. Matthiessen and the Making of Henry James." *New England Quarterly* 60, no. 2: 163–86.

Copjec, Joan. 2020. "Psychoanalysis and its consequences: Joan Copjec interviewed by Colby Chubbs." *Chasma* 6, no. 1: 189–203.
Derrida, Jacques. 1997. *Of Grammatology*. Corrected edition, translated by G. Ch. Spivak. Baltimore: John Hopkins University Press.
Dunn, John. 1969. *The Political Thought of John Locke*. Cambridge: Cambridge University Press.
Dworkin, Ronald. 1978. *Taking Rights Seriously*. Cambridge, MA: Harvard University Press.
Ellmann, Richard. 1999. "James amongst the Aesthetes." In *Henry James and Homo-Erotic Desire*, edited by John R. Bradley, 25–44. London: Palgrave Macmillan.
Foucault, Michel. 1999. *Les anormaux. Cours au Collège de France (1974–1975)*. Paris: Gallimard.
Fuller, Randall. 2007. *Emerson's Ghosts: Literature, Politics, and the Making of Americanists*. Oxford: Oxford University Press.
Freedman, Jonathan. 1990. *Professions of Taste: Henry James, British Aestheticism, and Commodity Culture*. Stanford, CA: Stanford University Press.
Gonaver, Wendy. 2010. "You, Me, and Joe McCarthy: The Enduring Legacy of the Cold War." *American Quarterly* 62, no. 2: 375–86.
Grossman, Jay. 1998. "The Canon in the Closet: Matthiessen's Whitman, Whitman's Matthiessen." *American Literature* 70, no. 4: 799–832.
Habermas, Jürgen. 1991. *The Structural Transformation of the Public Sphere*. Translated by Thomas Burger. Cambridge, MA: MIT Press.
Hallward, Peter. 2001. Introduction to Alain Badiou, *Ethics*, translated by Peter Hallward. London: Verso.
Han, Byung-Chul. 2015. *The Transparent Society*. Translated by Erik Butler. Stanford, CA: Stanford University Press.
———. 2017. *Psychopolitics: Neoliberalism and the New Technologies of Power*. Translated by Erik Butler. London: Verso.
Haralson, Eric. 2003. *Henry James and Queer Modernity*. Cambridge: Cambridge University Press.
———. 2012. "Henry James and Changing Ideas about Sexuality," in *A Historical Guide to Henry James*, edited by John Carlos Rowe and Eric Haralson, 169–96. Oxford: Oxford University Press.
Harvey, David. 2005. *A Brief History of Neoliberalism*. Oxford: Oxford University Press.
Heffernan, Julián Jiménez. 2023. *Prepossessing Henry James: The Strange Freedom*. New York: Routledge.
Hobsbawm, Eric. 1996. "Identity Politics and the Left." *New Left Review* 1, no. 217: 38–47.
Houellebecq, Michel, and Bernhard Henry-Lévy. 2008. *Ennemis publics*. Paris: Flammarion.
Hurley, Natasha. 2018. *Circulating Queerness: Before the Gay and Lesbian Novel*. Minneapolis: University of Minnesota Press.
James, Henry. 1944. *Stories of Writers and Artists*. Edited by F. O. Matthiessen. New York: New Directions.

———. 1947. *The Notebooks of Henry James.* Edited by F. O. Matthiessen and Kenneth B. Murdock. Chicago: University of Chicago Press.
———. 1984a. *Literary Criticism I.* Edited by Leon Edel. New York: Library of America.
———.1984b. *The Portrait of a Lady.* Edited by Geoffrey Moore. London: Penguin. First published 1881.
———. 1994. *The American Scene.* Edited by John F. Sears. New York: Penguin. First published 1907.
———. 1995. *The Tragic Muse.* Edited by Philip Horne. New York: Penguin. First published 1890.
———. 2013. *The Aspern Papers and Other Stories.* Edited by Adrian Poole. Oxford: Oxford University Press.
———. 2018. *The Reverberator.* Edited by Richard Salmon. The Cambridge Edition of the Complete Fiction of Henry James. Cambridge: Cambridge University Press. First published 1888.
James, William. 2010. *The Will to Believe and Other Essays in Popular Philosophy.* Auckland, NZ: Floating Press.
Jameson, Fredric. 2010. *The Hegel Variations: On the "Phenomenology of Spirit."* London: Verso.
Kotz, David M. 2017. *The Rise and Fall of Neoliberal Capitalism.* Cambridge, MA: Harvard University Press.
Kymlicka, Will. 1989. *Liberalism, Community and Culture.* Oxford: Oxford University Press.
Levinas, Emmanuel. 1979. *Totality and Infinity: An Essay on Exteriority.* Translated by Alphonso Lingis. The Hague: Martinus Nijhoff.
Locke, John. 1983. *A Letter concerning Toleration.* Edited by James H. Tully. Indianapolis: Hackett.
Macpherson, C. B. 1962. *The Political Theory of Possessive Individualism: Hobbes to Locke.* Oxford: Clarendon Press.
Matthiessen, F. O. 1944. *Henry James: The Major Phase.* Oxford: Oxford University Press.
———. 1948. *From the Heart of Europe.* New York: Oxford University Press.
———. 1968. *American Renaissance: Art and Expression in the Age of Emerson and Whitman.* Oxford: Oxford University Press. First published 1941.
———. 2008. *The James Family: A Group Biography; Including Selections from the Writings of Henry James, Senior, William, Henry and Alice James.* New York: Overlook Press. First published 1947.
Mill, John Stuart. 1989. *On Liberty and Other Writings.* Edited by Stefan Collini. Cambridge: Cambridge University Press.
Miller, J. Hillis. 1995. "History, Narrative and Responsibility: Speech Acts in Henry James's 'The Aspern Papers.'" *Textual Practice* 9, no. 2: 243–67.
Novick, Sheldon M. 1999. Introduction to *Henry James and Homo-Erotic Desire*, edited by John R. Bradley, 1–24. London: Palgrave Macmillan.
Poole, Adrian. 2020. Introduction to *The Princess Casamassima*, edited by Adrian Poole, xxv–xcv. The Cambridge Edition of the Complete Fiction of Henry James. Cambridge University Press.

Rawlings, Peter. 2005. *Henry James and the Abuse of the Past*. Houndmills, UK: Palgrave Macmillan.
Redding, Arthur. 2009. *Turncoats, Traitors, and Fellow Travelers: Culture and Politics of the Early Cold War*. Jackson: University Press of Mississippi.
Salmon, Richard. 1997. *Henry James and the Culture of Publicity*. Cambridge: Cambridge University Press.
———. 2008. "Henry James in the Public Sphere." In *A Concise Companion to Henry James*, edited by Greg Zacharias, 456–71. Oxford: Blackwell.
Savoy, Eric. 2007. "*Entre chien et loup*: Henry James, Queer Theory, and the Biographical Imperative." In *Henry James Studies*, edited by Peter Rawlings, 100–125. London: Palgrave Macmillan.
Schlatter, Richard. 1977. "On Being a Communist at Harvard." *Partisan Review* 44, no. 4: 605–12.
Sedgwick, Eve Kosofsky. 1990. *The Epistemology of the Closet*. Berkeley, CA: University of California Press.
Shakespeare, William. 2016. *Hamlet*. Edited by Ann Thompson and Neil Taylor. London: Bloomsbury.
Shoptaw, John. 1994. *On the Outside Looking Out: John Ashbery's Poetry*. Cambridge, MA: Harvard University Press.
Steger, Manfred B., and Ravi K. Roy. 2021. *Neoliberalism*. Oxford: Oxford University Press.
Tocqueville, Alexis de. 2000. *Democracy in America*. Edited by Harvey C. Mansfield and Delbra Winthrop. Chicago: University of Chicago Press.
Trilling, Lionel. 1951. *The Liberal Imagination*. London: Seeker & Warburg.
Žižek, Slavoj. 2009. *The Plague of Fantasies*. London: Verso.

3: The Intelligibility of Coming Out as Gay

Tomasz Basiuk

T HE CENTRAL POINT in this essay is that the concept of visibility, as applied to LGBTQ populations and political strategies, may usefully be supplemented with intelligibility. While visibility and intelligibility are modalities of transparency—both are opposites of opacity—they are not identical. Visibility, a key aspect of identity politics, implies a simplifying and assimilationist approach linked to a deliberately positive portrayal of a minority. By contrast, intelligibility implies that nonheteronormative existence should be graspable in its real-life complexity, just as are those normative modes of existence we can know through representations ridden with drama, ironies, and contradictions. In what follows, I discuss the place of intelligibility in politics understood as distribution of the perceptible and examine some historical and present-day modalities of queer intelligibility and of coming out, likening them to parrhesia, testimony, and periperformative utterances. I comment in some detail on Henry Blake Fuller's *Bertram Cope's Year* (1919) and Mart Crowley's *The Boys in the Band* (1968), adapted for the screen by William Friedkin in 1970, and I quote from Samuel R. Delany's personal essay "Coming / Out" (1996).

1. Visibility and Intelligibility

Visibility and intelligibility stem from different approaches to politics. As a strategy linked to identity politics, visibility is invested in the notion of a political arena in which a minority group's access to rights depends on its demands being recognized as legitimate. The underlying assumption is that recognition and redistribution are intimately linked; for example, Nancy Fraser has argued that both dimensions are crucial for addressing social justice claims with regard to gender, race and class (Fraser and Honneth 2003, 16–26). The arena is imagined as a limited and fragmented territory, access to which is a zero-sum game, so the rights exercised by one demographic likely threaten those of another.

The limitations of this approach have been rehearsed over and over again. Identity politics has been criticized as exclusionary because those not matching the projected image tend to be left out. For example, those not planning to marry a life partner may find no place for themselves in a movement focused on marriage equality. As Michael Warner (1999, 90) notes, many advocates of same-sex marriage—a central issue of gay identity politics in the past few decades—have made the case "that pursuing marriage means abandoning the historical principles of the queer movement as an antiquated 'liberationism.'" The emphasis on marriage thus ignores whole swathes of queer practice; for example, same-sex behavior in which participants, whether they think of themselves as gay or not, "may be seeking . . . a world less defined by identity and community than by the negation of identity through anonymous contact" (166). Moreover, visibility may benefit queers in some contexts but work against them in others, for example, by motivating assaults on transgender individuals (Currah 2022, 2).

Noting the limitations of identity politics defined as single-issue politics is the point of intersectional analysis, which accounts for how different minority positions overlap and impact one another, and how various types of discrimination, such as those based on gender and on race, may be compounded. Kimberlé Crenshaw (1991, 167) contends, "If [. . .] efforts [to alleviate the ills of racism and sexism] instead began with addressing the needs and problems of those who are most disadvantaged . . ., then others who are singularly disadvantaged would also benefit." But intersectional analysis may not yield a policy fix. Scholars have pointed out ways in which ameliorating discrimination against a particular demographic inadvertently increases the vulnerability of another. For example, upholding the principle of consent as a prerequisite before sexual contact to protect women, minors, and others may impose an undue burden on transgender individuals who become liable if they fail to let prospective partners know that they are transgender, thus invalidating their informed consent. As Mitchell Travis (2019, 322) notes, "Deception as to gender, in providing for a retrospective vitiation of consent, is a troubling addition to the law—especially for sexual minorities." More broadly, transgender individuals may find it expeditious to revert to an identity claim in some situations but not in others, highlighting, as Paisley Currah (2006, 13) notes, that the body of law on gender nonconformity "is riddled with contradictions" and that "the notion that there is some hidden analytic key that, when discovered, will reveal the law's underlying logic assumes an ideological coherence that is just not there."

Intelligibility connotes another kind of focus, which may be linked to the concept of the distribution of the perceptible, developed by the political philosopher Jacques Rancière (2010), who holds that politics proper is distinct from the mechanics of running a state (Rancière [36–37] calls the latter *police* rather than *politics*). Politics proper entails a reconfiguration of what he calls the distribution of the perceptible; that is, of a dividing line, arbitrary yet accepted as self-evident, between those whose speech counts as rational and who consequently count as subjects of politics, and—as per a distinction attributable to Plato—those whose speech is heard as expressing mere emotion, animalistic pain, and so forth (37–38). A reconfiguration of this dividing line is simultaneously political and aesthetic because what changes is how these subjects are seen. The change is predicated on dissensus: a refusal to accept that a particular distribution of the perceptible is final or complete. Changing that distribution is the business of politics, which means that politics is premised on seeing two worlds in one, in the sense that the already given distribution of political subjects becomes supplemented with a surplus in the form of those hitherto unaccounted for (37–40).

To reiterate: according to Rancière, the key moment in politics is not a consensual granting of legitimacy to a claim but an earlier, aesthetic moment of dissent in which someone making a claim becomes intelligible as a subject who speaks rationally. Rancière's approach to politics differs from the one based on visibility. Focus is shifted away from recognition understood as granting legitimacy—that is, of granting access to the limited resources afforded by the already established composition of the public sphere—and toward the emergence of newly intelligible rational speakers, which leads to a reconfiguration of who counts as a subject of politics.

The distinction between visibility and intelligibility may be rendered in both political and aesthetic terms. The politics of identity, with its investment in visibility understood as a kind of literal transparency—which is to say, an investment in presenting its subjects as somehow obvious to the naked eye, uncontroversial and without need for a gloss or an explanation—represents merely a fragmentary cut of the larger phenomenon of intelligibility. It is a cut based on consensus rather than dissensus because its ambition is to win recognition through assimilation to preconceived notions about a particular demographic and through this demographic's positive portrayal. With reference to aesthetic representation, visibility may be compared to the functioning of a sign configured as literal, standing indexically for an object to which it refers, in the manner of a symbol whose meaning is broadly accepted. Intelligibility is more akin to an ambiguous drawing such as Rubin's vase, which shows two things at once. It is both riddle-like and reminiscent of allegory, whose meaning is only unraveled if one figures out how the sign and its referent are connected. By contrast, visibility presents itself as the seeming absence of a riddle, and as practically the thing-in-itself: transparent.

2. Two Things at Once

Lee Edelman (1994, 8–9) asks if there is such a thing as a gay body. His answer is that to assert the existence of a gay body is to engage in homographesis; that is, in writing two things at once. Alluding to linguist Roman Jakobson's discussion of the metaphoric and metonymic poles of language and referencing subsequent deployments of this structuralist concept (e.g, by Jacques Lacan), Edelman suggests that making an essentialist claim (e.g., about the existence of a gay body) requires a metaphoric leap that, however, can only persuade by summoning metonymic traits of the posited entity as a kind of proof; such supporting metonymies, when organized around a central metaphor, will shore it up and lend it credibility. (These metonymies may be traits stereotypically applied to gay bodies, for example.) Conversely, such metonymies will only be associated with the thing they purportedly describe (such as the gay body) if that thing's existence is already assumed, which is to say that these metonymies' very sense depends on the metaphoric leap for which they simultaneously serve as evidence. Clearly, the logic of such proof is circular, which is Edelman's point. The poles of metaphor and metonymy are intertwined in rhetorical practice and the claim that they jointly make rests on their interdependence.

Such circularity—or homographesis, as Edelman calls it—is commonplace. Making an argument often entails saying two things at once. For example, Frédéric Martel (2018) has argued for the observable rise of the "global gay" phenomenon by showing that a single, universally intelligible paradigm of same-sex experience has become dominant. To substantiate this claim, he visited numerous locations—including reputedly homophobic places where such institutions as clubs catering to a gay clientele are nonetheless found. As his examples make clear, the "global gay" phenomenon is premised on people being out as gay, although they may be out only in certain social contexts and not in others, and although being out may not be an option for other individuals in the same locations—perhaps because it would endanger their prospects or their survival. Of course, being out is not the only way to be queer; neither is it a precondition for having same-sex experiences or for engaging in other types of nonheteronormative behavior. It is, however, the most visible way of being queer, one that is, in fact, based on a project of strategic visibility. Martel's argument is thus partly tautological, as he sets out looking for enclaves of gay visibility, which he finds because they are visible. For instance, Median Al Jazerah, a gay café owner and one of Martel's interlocutors in the Middle East, greets him with, "You are looking for 'the Queen of Amman'? Well, you've found me. . . . I'm openly gay . . . you can use my name. . . . My notoriety protects me" (xx). This does not invalidate Martel's point about real change taking place in the world, but a certain circularity to the argument is evident and, perhaps, inevitable. Martel thus engages in homographesis: he is writing two things at once, taking a metaphoric leap by positing the existence of "global gays" and then shoring up his claim with local examples.

Taking another cue from Edelman's discussion of homographesis, I turn to Rancière's (2010) argument that a prerequisite for being politically engaged is doing two things at once. This precept contradicts Plato's belief that politics can only be practiced by people with independent means: those who are gainfully employed cannot afford to spend time in the agora, since a man can only do one thing at a time. Rancière dismisses this limitation by distinguishing between politics, defined as change to the distribution of the perceptible, and police, defined as the mechanics of running a state. In his view, Plato mixes up politics with police. Contrary to Plato's point, politics properly understood necessitates doing two things at once. In *Disagreement*, Rancière notes that to effectively make a new claim one must accompany it with a metaphor to render comprehensible the situation from which the claim arises: "The forms of social interlocution that have any impact are at once arguments in a situation and metaphors of this situation" (1999, 56). One needs to tell a story, paint a picture, and so on, to ensure that one's claim comes across as rational. This is analogous to Edelman's discussion of homographesis, although in Rancière's usage, *metaphor* is a general term for aesthetic presentation rather than a structuralist counterpart of metonymy.

Coming out as gay may be considered a primary tool of gay identity politics and of building gay visibility. It may also, however, be considered an instance of dissensus and part of a process of reconfiguring the distribution of the perceptible; that is, of making new political subjects intelligible. To come out is an individual act, but the term also describes a communal effort through which a demographic emerges into politics. For example, in *Coming Out* (1977), Jeffrey Weeks sketches the process in which gay people have become an intelligible demographic in the UK. In the preface to the second edition (1990), he writes, "Where I would now put a stronger emphasis, however, is on the emergence of a lesbian and gay community. . . . As the years go by it becomes clearer that the real achievement of the gay liberation movement was to stimulate the growth of the lesbian and gay community, in all its diversity and complexity, rather than a narrowly political movement, whatever its creativity, which has become the real actor on the stage of history" (xiii).

Several decades on, Currah (2022, 4) offers an analogous observation about the transgender demographic in the US: "It is the politics of identity that makes it possible for this 'myriad of alterities' to be seen as a coherent political force—a cacophonous crowd, to be sure, yet one that is still imagined as moving forward together under the protective carapace of transgender. In this way, the transgender community becomes visible against the backdrop of the civil rights tradition in the United States." It seems clear that the individual and the communal dimensions of coming out reinforce each other in a continuous interlacing process: the more people are out, the easier it is for any one individual to come out, as each avowal is articulated in a context of enhanced intelligibility. Conversely, this general intelligibility grows with each coming out—and so the distribution of the perceptible changes. But how has coming out achieved its current prominence and seemingly global status?

3. Coming Out as an American Invention?

In a 1981 interview for the French magazine *Gai Pied*, translated into English as "Friendship as a Way of Life"—and predating the introduction of same-sex civil unions and marriage—Michel Foucault referred to "this need that Americans call 'coming out,' that is, showing oneself" as requiring an inventiveness rather than a specific strategy: "the program must be wide open" (1997, 139). Foucault's point is that homosexuality is notable as a force propelling the invention of new social relations, which he jointly refers to as "friendship." He posits that "homosexuality is not a form of desire but something desirable" (136) because "homosexuality is a historic occasion to reopen affective and relational virtualities, not so much through the intrinsic qualities of the homosexual but because the 'slantwise' position of the latter, as it were, the diagonal lines he can lay out in the social fabric allow these virtualities to come to light" (138). Coming out threatens to foreclose this inventiveness if it is linked to a single-issue politics premised on a strategically harmonized group identity. Moreover, focusing on homosexuality as a form of desire obscures what for Foucault is the real advantage of homosexuality, which is the ability to shape new alliances across social strata and outside existing forms of kinship.

Others have pointed to strategic and conceptual limitations of coming out, though usually without dismissing it altogether. For example, Diana Fuss (1991, 4) speaks about the ambiguous interdependence between being in the closet and coming out of it:

> To be out, in common gay parlance, is to be no longer out; to be out is finally to be outside of exteriority and all the exclusions and deprivations such outsiderhood implies; or, put another way, to be out is really to be in—inside the realm of the visible, of the speakable, of the culturally intelligible. But things are still not so clear, for to come out can also work not to situate one on the inside but to jettison one from it.

Steven Seidman (1993, 130) notes that, on a collective level, "gay identity constructions reinforce the dominant hetero/homo sexual code with its heteronormativity. If homosexuality and heterosexuality are a coupling in which each presupposes the other . . . and in which this coupling assumes hierarchical forms, then the epistemic and political project of identifying a gay subject reinforces and reproduces this hierarchical figure." An example of such heteronormativity is the inequity inherent to coming out, which is something that gay people are expected to do, but straight people are not; Samuel R. Delany (1996, 26) refers to this inequity as "heterosexist surveillance," while Michael Warner (1993, xxi–xxviii) uses the term *heteronormativity* critically in order to argue for a queer politics addressing issues of sexuality and gender beyond what identity politics can accomplish.

In *Epistemology of the Closet*, Eve Kosofsky Sedgwick (1990, 1) notes that homosexuality is defined in self-contradictory terms: a minoritizing view of homosexuality holds that homosexuality is specific to a contained demographic, while a universalizing view links it to broader phenomena applying to the populace at large. Richard Kim (2009, n.p.) reflects on the importance of Sedgwick's observation in his obituary:

> When liberals argue in favor of same-sex marriage, they implicitly adopt the minoritizing view, and when conservatives argue for state injunctions against homosexuality because of its allegedly destructive consequences for society at large, they implicitly invoke the universalizing view. Similarly, the homosexual panic defense, which Sedgwick critiqued, functions at the intersection of these two opposed views of homosexuality; . . . on the one hand, only latent homosexuals can be gay bashers (which makes them deserving of judicial mercy) and, on the other, anyone at all can be presumed to be "a homosexual ('someone who's really gay') making an advance," which means that everyone is vulnerable to homophobically motivated violence. This paradoxical co-existence of opposing perspectives makes for a homophobic double bind linked to what Sedgwick in *Between Men* calls homosocial desire: men engaging in homosocial behavior with other men run the risk of being (mis)identified as homosexual, as do men who conspicuously avoid this type of behavior. Homosexuality is in the eye of the beholder.

Considered in these terms, coming out appears to be based on the minoritizing view. But a minoritizing view of homosexuality falls short of being able to account for the complexity of forms of same-sex desire or the responses it provokes. If some forms of homophobia are motivated by the universalizing view of homosexuality, then strategies premised on the minoritizing view may not be an adequate rejoinder. While neither Sedgwick nor Kim criticize coming out as such for holding the minoritizing view, Kim's synopsis indicates that a minoritizing and a universalizing view of homosexuality are interlaced, making the phenomenon of homosexuality not simply a social construct but one that is inherently unstable. Rather than transparent, homosexuality is, once again, better described as an instance of homographesis, although configured in terms other than Edelman has proposed.[1]

Foucault's suggestion that coming out is somehow specifically American is borne out by historical evidence. The slogan "out of the closets and into the streets" was adopted by the gay liberation movement that began in the US in the wake of the Stonewall Inn riots, which took place in New York City in the summer of 1969. In his comparative study of homosexual men's autobiography by American, British, and French authors, Paul Robinson (1999, xix) notes that the coming out story, with its unequivocal claim of gay identity, is a genre adopted by postwar American writers (that is, those writing after Stonewall), which prompts him to comment, tongue in cheek, that "Americans, one might say, are fundamentalists even in their perversity." A clear declaration of one's sexual preference, which coming out of the closet implies, did not seem necessary to earlier Americans or to some other nationalities, satisfied to simply act on their same-sex desires and more open to arrangements that Americans might brand as closeted and, hence, hypocritical.

The similarity between American gays and American Puritans alluded to by Robinson merits further elaboration. The underlying common paradigm is that of conversion, understood both as self-recognition (recognizing that one is among the elect/that one is gay) and as recognition from others (being accepted by a religious congregation/by a grouping of others who are also gay).[2] Conversion requires that one should be honest with oneself about who one is. For the Puritans, this was connected to the belief in predestination: a central tenet of their faith was that God had chosen some people for salvation at the beginning of time and that it was possible, based on individual spiritual experience and on other evidence, to know, in one's heart of hearts, if one had been chosen. This personal conversion may be described as self-recognition. But then the intimate experience of conversion was shared, serving as a rite of passage to a Puritan congregation. One was expected to make a confession of faith, which meant giving testimony to one's conversion experience in the hope of receiving validation from others.

Coming out as gay functions in a somewhat similar fashion, implying both self-recognition and recognition from others. On the one hand,

---

1 Sedgwick's discussion of universalizing v. minoritizing views of homosexuality continues to resonate; for example, Currah (2022, 11–14) applies her terms to the transgender/nontransgender population to argue for the importance of feminism to the cause of transgender rights.

2 For a somewhat different discussion of conversion as a literary model for a story of lesbian *Bildung*, see Breen (2001, 235–52).

to come out is to acknowledge a deeply felt sense of who one is. (One would not describe casual sexual experimentation as a coming out.) Rather, in coming out, which is an act of avowal, one testifies to one's true sexuality: something that one has discovered about oneself. In this respect, coming out resembles *anagnorisis* in Greek tragedy, occurring at a key turning point or else as a prolonged process of self-discovery. Perry Miller (Miller and Johnson 1963, 1:53–54) notes that the Puritan conversion typically resulted from extensive spiritual self-examination, while Delany (1996, 8) recalls "twenty-two incidents that constitute the field of my childhood sexuality" and that lead up to his coming out, or his self-recognition as homosexual; the processual character of coming out is sometimes obscured in a coming-out story, which may revolve around a single dramatic event. On the other hand, successful coming out depends also on the response of those being addressed. One comes out expecting to be believed, and usually also expecting to be accepted and offered support. Coming out thus involves recognition in the eyes of others, or *Anerkennung*, as discussed, for example, by Hegel (2019). This double aspect of coming out makes it like the Puritan confession of faith, which took the form of testimony given before members of the congregation, and whose success also depended on their acknowledgment. Thus, *Anagnorisis* and *Anerkennung* (self-recognition and recognition from others) are key aspects of both Puritan conversion and gay coming out.

Like the testimony offered by the Puritans, coming out in the sense of avowal may be supported with experiential evidence drawn from the process of personal self-discovery. The coming-out story, which is not just a literary genre but also a speech genre, is a staple of contemporary gay culture. "If the wedding scene is the quintessential heterosexual epiphany, then coming-out stories are the gay community's Bildungsroman, our claim to fame, our climactic trope.... Coming out into the family of origin is often the first story gays tell each other, often the opening line in date come-ons. It's our 'come here often?'" (Walters 2003, 197). The coming-out story legitimizes the claim to identity that an act of coming out performs, grounding it in concrete detail and making it intelligible to one's interlocutor or to one's readers. It functions like Edelman's metonymies shoring up the metaphoric leap, or, as Rancière would have it, it is the metaphor that grounds in a particular context a claim that would be unintelligible without it.

4. Coming Out before Gay

The analogy between coming out and conversion is only partial, however, because even though coming out is an act of avowal, it is not necessarily addressed to one's community of other gays. In this respect, it may be unlike the Puritan confession of faith, which was addressed to other

Puritans. Coming out as gay may be addressed to straight interlocutors, readers, and audiences. A closer analogy obtains with an earlier usage of the expression *to come out*: one used to come out *into the life* rather than *out of the closet*. Coming out into the life meant that one was joining the homosexual ranks rather than letting someone straight know that one was gay. Delany (1996, 19) underscores this distinction, noting that the latter usage only became commonplace over the course of a year and a half with the rise of the Gay Liberation Front, which emerged in the wake of the Stonewall Inn riots of 1969. Previously, one commonly spoke of coming out into the life. Delany traces this earlier usage to coming-out balls, at which debutantes came out into society (13). The expression, which has disappeared from current homosexual argot, had a distinct camp ring to it, which was subsequently erased when *coming out of the closet* became a verbal act aimed at straights. Delany notes also that coming out into the life meant having one's first same-sex sexual contact rather than verbally avowing one's sexuality. Coming out in this older sense signified bodily, even carnal experience—"It involved *coming*" (21, emphasis in the original)—rather than the announcing of one's sexual identity. Delany's comments illustrate that some earlier modes of queer intelligibility have become arcane and may be inaccessible even to those who are conversant with contemporary queer cultures.[3] He also indicates the relative absence of a focus on sex in identity politics compared to earlier queer culture.

Michael Warner (1999, 35–36) has openly bemoaned this loss when arguing for the strategic and ethical value of those disappearing queer sites and practices that addressed shame—especially shame associated with sexual behavior—which subsequent emphasis on gay pride and on marriage equality has partly erased:

> Shame is bedrock. Queers can be abusive, insulting, and vile toward one another, but because abjection is understood to be the shared condition, they also know how to communicate through such camaraderie a moving and unexpected form of generosity. No one

---

3   Delany comments on other semantic shifts that accompanied the rise of gay liberation and the adoption of identity politics. For example, the term *closet queen* did not mean someone hiding his same-sex preference, as one might surmise today, but instead someone who preferred his sexual contacts on the sly (14). An admittedly looser analogy to American Puritans imposes itself at this point. The archaic term *closet piety* refers to an injunction, in Mt 6: 6, to pray in the privacy of one's "closet" rather than "openly" (King James Version). Delany's outdated expression *closet queen* is more clearly analogous to this usage than is the contemporary expression *in the closet*, which has a negative connotation. (For an extended discussion of Delany's "Coming / Out" and his other life writing, see Basiuk [2013, 115–40]).

is beneath its reach, not because it prides itself on generosity, but because it prides itself on nothing. The rule is: Get over yourself. Put a wig on before you judge.... Queer scenes are the true *salons des refusés*, where the most heterogeneous people are brought into great intimacy by their common experience of being despised and rejected in a world of norms that they now recognize as false.

Queer scenes showcasing both queer shame and queer sex have been celebrated by others. Douglas Crimp used the term "queer before gay" when referring, for example, to Andy Warhol's films. In commenting on a short in which the drag performer Maria Montez is exposed as male, provoking a sense of shame on her part and perhaps in the viewer, Crimp (2012, 33) takes his cue from Sedgwick's discussion of shame's ambivalent status as both "identity-defining and identity-erasing" to underscore the ethics of queer shame-sharing: "In taking on [another's] shame, I do not share in the other's identity. I identify only with the other's *vulnerability* to being shamed . . . the other's difference is preserved; it is not claimed as my own. . . . I am not attempting to vanquish his or her otherness" (34).

Other scholars still have memorialized queer cultures prior to gay liberation by focusing on camp aesthetics, even if they do not always use the term *camp*. David M. Halperin's (2012, 149–85) readings of movie scenes with Joan Crawford as enjoying a cult status with some queer audiences is a case in point, as is D. A. Miller's (1998, 16) discussion of the Broadway musical and its place in gay male culture: "the dilapidated form is now getting acknowledged . . . as a somehow *gay* genre, the only one that mass culture ever produced." They and others have pointed to forms of queer self-expression that precede coming out of the closet and the coming-out story and that may be losing some of their intelligibility today. But while these forms of queer expression may seem archaic from a perspective oriented toward progress, such as the achievement of marriage equality in the US, they might offer deliverance should political winds change one day, and indeed, they continue to be serviceable in other parts of the world. It is therefore foolhardy to let them slip into oblivion.

Consider Henry Blake Fuller's *Bertram Cope's Year*, originally published in 1919, by a novelist whom Theodore Dreiser praised as inventor of American realism (Scambray 1987, 160–61). Nils Clausson (2021, 159–60 and passim) has recently argued that Fuller's piece deserves to be recognized as an early novel affirming male homosexual identity even though it does not follow the model of a coming-out story. Clausson shows that Fuller's work has been misread by post-Stonewall critics, whose presentist perspective obscures and devalues his accomplishment. These critics have failed to appreciate Fuller's use of comedy in rendering the adventures of Cope, a queer young man in a relationship with another man, who only narrowly escapes being maneuvered into marrying a woman. The comedic premise arises when Cope is taken for an eligible bachelor by a matronly figure intent on marrying off one of her young charges.

Clausson contends that Fuller's queer-affirmative meaning was, in its own time, intelligible to the point of being scandalizing. What kept the novel out of print many decades later, however, was a changed expectation about what makes homosexuality intelligible. Fuller's homosexual protagonist is not a conflicted young man discovering his sexuality and finding resolution in an act of avowal. On the contrary, he and his partner, Arthur, have already accepted their same-sex affection for each other, have lived together, and are seeking to do so again after Cope's year as a visiting scholar comes to an end. They are interested in inventing a relationship that will work for them rather than in declaring their queerness to the straight people around them.

Arthur and Cope both pass with great ease until, on a visit with Cope, Arthur oversteps a line in the sand by kissing a fellow actor after performing in a play in which Arthur appeared in drag alongside the other man. At this point, Arthur's same-sex profligacy becomes immediately apparent, as well as scandalizing. In consequence, he skips town and is eventually rejoined by Cope. This plot development demonstrates that the two are living in a bigoted environment that abhors homosexuality and that ostracizes Arthur as queer without, however, harboring any suspicion about the two men's friendship or their shared living quarters, so that Cope may remain the eligible bachelor a while longer. Fuller thus illustrates how the intelligibility of same-sex desire extends to the kiss Arthur places on another man but not to two men living together. The novel attempts to reconfigure this aspect of the distribution of the perceptible, which is perhaps what has made it offensive, especially that the men's calm response to the social calamity that befell Arthur affirms that he and Cope remain a committed couple even in the face of homophobic backlash against one of them.

In his reconstruction of critical misreadings of the novel, Clausson notes mistakes that illuminate how queer intelligibility has shifted. For example, some critics have wrongly assumed that a supporting character's point of view corresponds to the authorial narrator's perspective. On this erroneous logic, a critic assumed that Cope lacks emotion, failing to note a focalizing character's personally motivated frustration with Cope's indifference to her as a woman (166–67). This misreading acknowledges Cope's homosexuality, but it wrongly assumes that the price he pays for being queer is an estrangement from his own emotions. Cope, however, is not cooped up emotionally but, rather, erotically uninterested in the woman, who therefore thinks him devoid of emotion. (Eve Sedgwick once said that a man and a woman meeting and not falling in love is a powerful force in the world.)[4] Another critic came to the unfounded conclusion that Cope and his partner, Arthur, have split up, and that Cope is about to marry a woman to whom he has merely sent a brief courteous letter after leaving town (172–73). This misreading obliterates the novel's affirmative message with the unfounded assumption that Cope's words addressing this woman express affection rather than simple politeness. Clausson expertly shows that Fuller is playing with the convention of comedy of manners, rather than that of bildungsroman, of which the coming-out story is a subcategory. Most misreadings, he notes, stem from failure to note this key difference.

Fuller's comedic mode of representing queerness, which might be compared to Oscar Wilde's camp humor filled with allusions to same-sex behaviors and desires, is likely to confound modern-day readers, who are prone to see both Fuller and his queer characters as deeply closeted. For example, in commenting on *Bertram Cope's Year* and on Fuller's play *At Saint Judas's*, Kenneth Scambray (1987, 103) writes, "Caution would only bring equivocation." Scambray also quotes Fuller's "Edmund Dalrymple" to make the point that the protagonist and writer were facing a common dilemma: "How . . . shall one contrive to be at the same time an artist and a gentleman? How at once to give himself out and hold himself in? How deliver one's message to the general public and yet maintain the well-bred reticence of the private person?" (30). The comparison running here between artist and queer acquires a negative ring in the post-Stonewall era with the suggestion that Fuller was inventing clever ways to remain closeted while alluding to queerness. Clausson contends, however, that Scambray's reading, like some others, is marred by an anachronistic perspective that ignores earlier modes of queer intelligibility, falsely equating them with being in the closet in the modern-day sense of hiding one's true sexual self. One might add that this more recent perspective appears to assume, rather naively, that the post-Stonewall mode of intelligibility is somehow free of the dilemma of balancing one's public self against one's private self by simply putting one's *real* self on display.

5. Parrhesia, Testimony, and Periperformatives

I propose to briefly revisit another literary work, a play that premiered just before the Stonewall Inn riots of 1969 and was adapted for the screen soon after these events, because it is an early portrayal of coming out in the sense of avowing one's desire. Mart Crowley's *The Boys in the Band* opened Off-Broadway in 1968, and William Friedkin turned it into a film released in 1970. Events unfold in connection to Harold's thirty-second

---

4   In her seminar on non-Oedipal psychoanalysis offered at the CUNY Graduate Center in the Fall term of the 2004–2005 academic year.

birthday party, attended by his male homosexual friends and a male hooker. The hooker is a wicked gift for Harold, who worries about his disappearing youthful looks and who is presumably no longer able to pick up cute boys on his own. When Harold's college friend Alan calls with news of his marital trouble and then unexpectedly shows up at the party, Harold proposes a game in which every guest in turn is to call someone they secretly love and confess his feelings. Harold expects Alan to put in a call to a college classmate with whom Alan may have been erotically involved, but instead of outing himself in this way, Alan calls his wife to reconcile with her.[5] Before Alan's call embarrasses everyone present and puts an end to the game, two other men, who live together as a couple, attempt to mend *their* relationship, threatened by disagreements about monogamy and the need to be discreet, by speaking to each other on Harold's extension and by leaving a message with their answering service. Some other men put in calls to long-ago heartthrobs but end up feeling embarrassed and regretting their heady courage. The game ends without a clear resolution for Harold, while the disarray of the party's leftovers, as portrayed in Friedkin's film, may be read as a visual allusion to the street riots that had taken place in New York City just months before. The question about what happens next hangs in the air.

The telephone game initiated by Harold with the apparent intention of prompting Alan's coming out may be seen as a prefiguration of *coming out of the closet*, which would only become a political slogan a year after the play premiered. Although the men are not expected to literally declare their homosexuality, neither are they *coming out into the life*, which is something all of them have presumably done already (Alan possibly excepted). Their long overdue confession of love to a person who is not expecting it represents a transition between coming out into the life and coming out of the closet because the men are not acting carnally on their desires but declaring them and because they do so in the semi-public setting of a social gathering and even beyond with the use of the telephone. The game is painfully difficult for all the players except, seemingly, for Alan. Crowley's decision to use the telephone—a device whose name suggests speaking at a distance or in a roundabout way rather than face-to-face or directly—allegorizes the difficulty of what these queer men have to say and the occasional circumlocution to which they revert. Meanwhile, Alan's confession of love for his wife comes across as so enviably natural and straightforward, so innocent and embarrassing for its frankness, that the game, with its taboo-violating premise, is terminated.

---

5   Harold's insinuation that Alan is "a closet queen" (Crowley 2003, 120) suggests some semantic overlap between a man hiding his homosexuality and one unwilling to reveal that he is having sex with a particular partner, which complicates Delany's definition of the term (see above).

Some two decades after *The Boys in the Band*, Edelman (1994) has questioned the political efficacy for the queer cause of the ACT UP slogan "Silence=Death," which referred to the need for a public debate about HIV/AIDS. His objection concerned the use of the equal sign, which communicates literalness. Edelman's criticism is twofold. He references Plato and Derrida to suggest that the trope of literalness is related to Plato's preference for speech over writing; where *phone* is a direct expression of a person's mind, writing is a mere trace of *phone*, hence an inevitably distorted copy of a copy. Like the primacy of speech over writing purported by Plato, literalness connotes the direct reproduction of supposedly correct content as against the free but distorting play of signification characteristic of openly tropic discourse. "The logic of homophobia, it is important, therefore, to note, rests upon the very binarism that Plato enables in *Phaedrus* to assert the hierarchical privilege of speech at the expense of a devalued, even demonized writing" (86), writes Edelman, before quoting Derrida: "the conclusion of *Phaedrus* is less a condemnation of writing in the name of present speech than a preference for one sort of writing over another, for the fertile trace over the sterile trace, for a seed that engenders because it is planted inside over a seed scattered wastefully outside: at the risk of *dissemination*" (86). In short, Edelman holds that where literalness aligns with normativity and "straight" reproduction, queerness aligns with inventiveness and imaginative troping. His discussion serves well for reading Crowley's play, in which the sole declaration of love spoken without any hesitation or circumlocution is uttered by the supposedly straight Alan to his married wife. The queer characters all engage in some form of *tele-phone*, speaking indirectly or only with great difficulty. As Edelman points out, however, the distinction between literalness and troping is problematic in the first place because literalness itself is a trope, as any discourse relies on troping for its very functioning.

Edelman's critique of literalness as a trope makes it easier to see that *The Boys in the Band* portrays two worlds in one, as the telephone game may be read in a different way than suggested above. Each queer-identified character making a call is putting in a determined effort to come to terms with his feelings and to overcome his sense of embarrassment, a gesture that Sedgwick might describe as performing his shame, in the sense of making use of its transformational energy: "Shame, it might finally be said, transformational shame, *is performance*" (Sedgwick 2003, 38; emphasis in the original). The lone self-declared straight man stands out in this respect because his expression of love seems effortless by comparison. The audience knows, however, that Harold suspects Alan of covering up his sexuality by attempting to pass for straight. Hence, the seeming ease of Alan's avowal may be mere pretense, and Alan fails to explain to the men or to his wife why he is away from home and in New York. This ambivalence, which remains unresolved, complicates the meaning of the contrast between the queer and the straight confessions of love by implying that their contrasting appearance is misleading. The queer confession is so difficult because it is genuine, while the seeming ease of the straight avowal is suspect.[6]

The ambiguity in Crowley's play invites not so much a moral consideration of homosexuality or of sexual hypocrisy (depending on which reading of the play you choose), as of the way that the queer characters' coming out is portrayed as a determined attempt on their part to reconfigure the distribution of the perceptible. The difficulty they encounter in making their confessions of love stems from the fact that, at the end of the 1960s, homosexuality was still mostly uncharted territory. Their declarations of love feel embarrassing because they are unintelligible to the persons who are being addressed. They are met with incomprehension rather than with actual objection or moral outrage. The play thus illustrates how coming out reconfigures the line separating what counts as rational from nonsense—a function that has itself become unintelligible in those contexts in which coming out seems today to be a matter of course. The play testifies to a time in which coming out was not yet invested in a harmonized strategy of visibility but already had the function of making queer existence intelligible not just to queer individuals but to others as well.

The difficulty of avowal, which Crowley's play and Friedkin's film portray so well, is aptly illustrated with Foucault's discussion of parrhesia (speaking truthfully) and with Shoshana Felman and Doris Laub's (1992) discussion of testimony. These discussions emerge from a distinction between truth understood as objective correspondence between reality and its description, on the one hand, and a personal truth based on experience, moral judgment, and one's very character, on the other—parrhesia and testimony are truths of the latter kind. As Foucault writes (2001, 14–15), "I never found any text in ancient Greek culture where the *parrhesiastes* seems to have any *doubts* about his own possession of the truth. And indeed, that is the difference between the Cartesian problem and the parrhesiastic attitude. . . . when someone has certain moral qualities, then that is the proof that he has access to truth" (emphases in the original). Parrhesia usually means speaking truth to power, which connotes personal danger to the speaker: "*parrhesiastes* is someone who takes a risk" (16), calling attention to someone's fatal error or moral shortcoming. Coming out in the present-day sense of avowal (coming out of the closet) has some characteristics of parrhesia because it explicitly or implicitly demands recognition on moral grounds from someone in a position to grant it or deny it.

---

6   The above discussion of *The Boys in the Band* is partly based on an earlier paper (Basiuk 2009).

Coming out is also based on personal testimony in the sense that one testifies to one's truth, to what one feels, to what one knows about oneself, and so on. The risk-taking that is the lot of the *parrhesiastes* is crucial to this endeavor. "What matters is that the ethico-political exigency of witnessing and testimony remains a *question*," William Haver (1996, 113; emphasis in the original) insists, underscoring how, paradoxically, the witness must risk being disbelieved for their testimony to persuade. Felman and Laub (1992, 56) examine a range of approaches to testimony, including a very telling comparison between testimony and stammering, which illustrates that testimony is often given—and received—only with tremendous difficulty. Felman's chapter on Paul de Man's silence about his journalism in Nazi-occupied Belgium even hypothesizes the impossibility of giving testimony in the form of avowal, given that such literal testimony is bound to be misunderstood. Be that as it may, Felman and Laub indicate that offering testimony is ridden with personal difficulty and is likely to pose a risk to the speaker, including the risk of being misunderstood, ignored, or rejected.

These discussions of parrhesia and testimony are well illustrated by *The Boys in the Band*, in which the queer characters attempt to engage in *parrhesia*, that is, speaking truthfully about themselves—about their feelings and desires—to people who hold some sway over them both as their love objects and as straight individuals embodying the sexual norm, who are consequently free to accept or dismiss these queer divulgences. By the same token, these men engage in giving testimony about their very selves—their feelings and desires—to interlocutors who may hear them out or decline to do so. By contrast, Alan's expression of love lacks the palpable qualities of parrhesia or testimony because it seems effortless and even glib by comparison, and there is little sense that Alan is taking a personal risk by addressing his wife with his words of his love, or by doing so in front of Harold and the other men.

Another way to grasp how the queer characters' declarations of love (which are simultaneously declarations of their sexualities) differ from Alan's is by showing that they fall into a distinct category of linguistic utterances. In an essay titled "Around the Performative," Sedgwick (2003, 67–91) coins the term *periperformative* for an utterance that takes place in the vicinity of an Austinian performative but that is not itself a performative utterance. Proper performatives, which are speech acts with which it is possible to "do things with words," such as make a promise, set a date, or get married, are typically discussed in temporal terms because using a performative utterance leads to change, so that there is clearly a time before a performative is uttered and a time after it has been uttered. (Of course, for a performative utterance to be successful, or felicitous, the speaker must meet various conditions of felicity; for example, the correct speaker must use the correct words in the correct context, the speaker must mean what she or he says, and so on.) In Sedgwick's definition, periperformatives refer or allude to a performative, or to several performatives (67–68). While they do not effect change in the same decisive fashion as performatives, they can render visible some conditions and contexts in which performatives occur: "The localness of the periperformative is lodged in a metaphorics of space" (68). With her examples, which concern primarily marriage and slavery, Sedgwick makes it clear that not just the speaker's positionality but even their physical place—including their geographic location (87)—may be decisive for whether their words work as performatives. For example, laws pertaining to slavery were not the same in the whole United States before slavery was abolished, which meant that gaining one's freedom, for example, by being set free or running away had different effects from one state to another. Neither were laws pertaining to same-sex marriage the same from one state to another at the time of her writing. With her examples, Sedgwick shows that periperformatives are likely to be used by those who are devoid of the power to engage in performative speech: a spurned lover referencing marriage plans from which she has been excluded, a woman trapped in a loveless marriage addressing her tormentor, and a runaway slave claiming his freedom in a note approximating a manumission letter. Finally, where performatives are rote utterances that depend for their effect on what Jacques Derrida identified as their iterability, periperformatives are nonce utterances. They are formed ad hoc and may only be intelligible in the context in which they have been used.

I have related the above set of distinctions between performatives and what Sedgwick has called periperformatives to suggest that Alan's expression of love for his wife may be viewed as a performative utterance because Alan, in his official role of a married man, is the right person to utter a conventional expression of love, which is directed at the correct person (his opposite-gender spouse), and is taking place in an appropriate setting (Alan calls to say he is coming home soon). His avowal appears to have a particular effect, which is that he and his wife are reconciled. Similar conditions are not met by the words uttered by the other men, however. The couple who are living together cannot be officially recognized and, in many parts of the US, their relationship would have been punishable with a prison term (and would remain so until *Lawrence v. Texas* in 2003, more than three decades after the play first opened). The other men seem to have even less reason to make their calls. Their stammering speech and the incomprehension with which it is met is a direct reflection of how what they say fails to meet the criteria of performative speech, including its inherent iterability.

Unlike Alan's conventional expression of love for his wife, the words uttered by the play's ostensibly homosexual characters are nonce utterances, their formulas not a well-oiled routine but a matter of spur-of-the-moment inspiration. They are utterances that occur in the vicinity of an unproblematic confession of love, illustrated by Alan's seemingly performative speech, which remains out of reach for these queer men because the articulation of same-sex affection that they attempt is beyond the pale of acceptable discourse.

It is the queer men's risk-taking, however, that defines their words as testimony and as *parrhesia*. Combined with the nonce, periperformative character of their speech, which grounds what they are saying in the context of their personal truth (albeit with varying degrees of success), their coming out is intelligible as an attempt to change the distribution of the perceptible by making queer relationships and desires appear as genuine emotion rather than perverse sexual urge. This early example of coming out as avowal makes it possible for us to see the stakes of coming out as a struggle for a reconfiguration of who and what counts as rational.

In his personal essay, Delany (1996, 25–26) makes this apposite observation, which provides a fitting conclusion for my reflections:

> Coming out (in the post-Stonewall sense) is something that many of us had begun to do, here and there, without the name, years before Stonewall. Stonewall only focused and fixed its statistical necessity as a broad political strategy. We need to remember that if the human material—not to mention the simple bravery so many have shown and continue to show in our still-homophobic society—had not already been there, the strategy would not have been anywhere near as successful as it was.

Works Cited

Basiuk, Tomasz. 2009. "Calling the One You Love: The Telephone in Mart Crowley's *The Boys in the Band* and Robert Chelsey's *Jerker, or, the Helping Hand*." In *Tools of Their Tools: Communications Technologies and American Cultural Practice*, edited by Grzegorz Kość and Krzysztof Majer, 254–64. Nottingham, UK: Cambridge Scholars Publishing.

———. 2013. *Exposures. American Gay Men's Life Writing since Stonewall*. Frankfurt am Main: Peter Lang.

The Boys in the Band. 1970. Directed by William Friedkin. Cinema Center Films.

Breen, Margaret Soenser. 2001. "*Desert of the Heart*. Jane Rule's Puritan Outing." In *The Puritan Origins of American Sex: Religion, Sexuality, and National Identity in American Literature*, edited by Tracy Fessenden, Nicholas F. Radel, and Magdalena J. Zaborowska, with foreword by Emory Elliott, 235–52. New York: Routledge.

Clausson, Nils. 2021. "Dynamite Scrupulously Packed": A Revaluation of Henry Blake Fuller's Bertram Cope's Year. *Interalia: A Journal of Queer Studies* 16: 155–76.

Crenshaw, Kimberlé. 1991. "Mapping the Margins: Intersectionality, Identity Politics, and Violence against Women of Color." *Stanford Law Review* 43, no. 6: 1241–99.

Crimp, Douglas. 2012. *"Our Kind of Movie": The Films of Andy Warhol*. Cambridge, MA: MIT Press.

Crowley, Mart. 2003. *"The Boys in the Band" and "The Men from the Boys."* Los Angeles: Alyson.

Currah, Paisley. 2006. "Gender Pluralisms under the Transgender Umbrella." In *Transgender Rights*, edited by Paisley Currah, Richard M. Juang, and Shannon Price Minter. Minneapolis: University of Minnesota Press.

———. 2022. *Sex Is as Sex Does: Governing Transgender Identity*. New York: New York University Press.

Delany, Samuel R. 1996. "Coming / Out." In *Boys Like Us: Gay Writers Tell Their Coming Out Stories*, edited by Patrick Merla, 1–26. New York: Avon Books.

Derrida, Jacques. 1977. "Signature Event Context." In *Limited Inc.*, 1–24. Evanston, IL: Northwestern University Press.

Edelman, Lee. 1994. *Homographesis: Essays in Gay Literary and Cultural Theory*. New York and London: Routledge.

Felman, Shoshana, and Dori Laub, M.D. 1992. *Testimony. Crises of Witnessing in Literature, Psychoanalysis, and History*. New York: Routledge.

Foucault, Michel. 1997. "Friendship as a Way of Life." In *Ethics: Subjectivity and Truth*, edited by Paul Rabinow, 135–40. *The Essential Works of Michel Foucault, 1954–1984*, vol. 1, translated by Robert Hurley and others. New York: The New Press.

———. *Fearless Speech*. 2001. Edited by Joseph Pears. Los Angeles: Semiotext(e).

Fraser, Nancy, and Axel Honneth. 2003. *Recognition or Redistribution? A Political-Philosophical Exchange*. Translated by Joel Golb, James Ingram, and Christiane Wilke. London: Verso.

Fuller, Henry Blake. 1919. *Bertram Cope's Year*. Chicago: Alderbrink Press/R. F. Seymour. https://archive.org/details/bertramcopesyear00fulluoft/mode/2up.

Fuss, Diana, ed. 1991. *Inside/Out: Lesbian Theories, Gay Theories*. New York: Routledge.

Halperin, David M. 2012. *How to Be Gay*. Cambridge, MA: Harvard University Press.

Haver, William. 1996. *The Body of This Death: Historicity and Sociality in the Time of AIDS*. Stanford, CA: Stanford University Press.

Hegel, Georg Wilhelm Friedrich. 2019. *The Phenomenology of Spirit*. Translated by Peter Fuss and John Dobbins. Notre Dame, IN: University of Notre Dame Press.

Kim, Richard. 2009. "Eve Kosofsky Sedgwick, 1950–2009." *Nation*, April 13. https://www.thenation.com/article/archive/eve-kosofsky-sedgwick-1950-2009/.

Martel, Frédéric. 2018. *Global Gay: How Gay Culture Is Changing the World*. Translated by Patsy Baudoin, with a foreword by Michael Bronski. Cambridge, MA: MIT Press.
Miller, D. A. 1998. *Place for Us: Essay on the Broadway Musical*. Cambridge, MA: Harvard University Press.
Miller, Perry, and Thomas H. Johnson. 1963. *The Puritans*. 2 vols. New York: Harper Torchbooks. First published 1938.
Rancière, Jacques. 1999. *Disagreement: Politics and Philosophy*. Minneapolis: University of Minnesota Press.
———. 2010. "Ten Theses on Politics." In *Dissensus: On Politics and Aesthetics*, edited and translated by Steven Corcoran, 27–44. London: Continuum.
Robinson, Paul. 1999. *Gay Lives: Homosexual Autobiography from John Addington Symonds to Paul Monette*. Chicago: University of Chicago Press.
Scambray, Kenneth. 1987. *A Varied Harvest: The Life and Works of Henry Blake Fuller*. Pittsburgh: University of Pittsburgh Press.
Sedgwick, Eve Kosofsky. 1990. *The Epistemology of the Closet*. Berkeley: University of California Press.
———. 2003. *Touching Feeling: Affect, Pedagogy, Performativity*. Durham, NC: Duke University Press.
Seidman, Steven. 1993. "Identity and Politics in a 'Postmodern' Gay Culture: Some Historical and Conceptual Notes." In *Fear of a Queer Planet: Queer Politics and Social Theory*, edited by Michael Warner. Minneapolis: University of Minnesota Press.
Travis, Mitchell. 2019. "The Vulnerability of Heterosexuality: Consent, Gender Deception and Embodiment." *Social & Legal Studies* 28, no. 3: 303–26.
Walters, Suzanna Danuta. 2003. *All the Rage: The Story of Gay Visibility in America*. Chicago: University of Chicago Press. First published 2001.
Warner, Michael, ed. 1993. *Fear of a Queer Planet: Queer Politics and Social Theory*. Minneapolis: University of Minnesota Press.
———. 1999. *The Trouble with Normal: Sex, Politics, and the Ethics of Queer Life*. Cambridge, MA: Harvard University Press.
Weeks, Jeffrey. 1990. *Coming Out: Homosexual Politics in Britain from the Nineteenth Century to the Present*. New York: Quarter Books. First published 1977.

4: Invisibility and Exposure in Ralph Ellison's *Invisible Man* (1952) and George Schuyler's *Black No More* (1931)

Michel Feith

As ITS NAME INDICATES, the visual trope is central in transparency studies, as this recent academic discipline criticizes the excesses of contemporary calls for political and institutional transparency, expressed in a culture of exposure and outing that tendentially judges all secrecy and opacity to be morally and socially wrong. The urge for disclosure is deemed by many critics to be aligned with the informational logic of neoliberal capitalism and the surveillance society, bringing to mind contemporary variations on Jeremy Bentham's and Michel Foucault's Panopticon (Han 2015, vii–viii). The dissolution of privacy into the screens and posts of social media "walls" confirms this optical setup. Yet, another key notion in American life is also intimately tied to the visual dimension, that of "race," and thinking both together opens interesting vistas. "Race" in the United States can be said to be a predominantly visual complex for two reasons. Even though there is widespread consensus that "race" is a social construct based on and justifying discriminations, in racialist discourse, blood or genetics—ultimately invisible principles—are supposed to be the root of racial identities, which are expressed in phenotype. In the United States, the main discriminating factor is actually color, as illustrated by the gradual integration into mainstream—that is, "white"—society of South Europeans, like Italians, or of Jewish people over the years. Perhaps owing to the many countries of origin of American immigrants, and to the historical importance of African slavery, "race" in the US can be pragmatically equated with "visible ethnicity."

The second connection of "race" with a visual trope is that of social invisibility, whose complexity has been best articulated in Ralph Ellison's 1952 novel *Invisible Man*. Racial invisibility, according to Ellison, revolves around the paradox that the most visible element of a person's appearance—skin color—is what makes this person transparent. Invisibility lies in the eye of the beholder, not through lack of vision but through the projection onto the racial Other of assumptions, which occult or erase the individual behind the stereotype and render them powerless. Invisibility and transparency are not the same, yet their intersections and tensions are worth examining. If social invisibility makes one "transparent," or see-through, transparency is often associated with the democratic ethos of accountability and equality. So, in the context of a multiracial society, transparency can be seen as a positive goal, and the exposure of discriminatory practices as a useful social practice. Transparency is a tool to fight invisibility. Yet, in the cognitive field, transparency may be a harmful illusion, a leveling of cultural and individual difference into a bland national consensus, constituting another form of erasure. For example, the transition between the Barack Obama era and the Donald Trump presidency has led many analysts and writers to redefine the color-blindness of the vaunted "postracial" state of the nation not only as wishful thinking but as an obfuscation of a still central power dynamic in American society. Contrary to the assumption of both literary and scientific realism, language is never fully transparent, and it is one of literature's tasks and merits to continually remind us of this fact. Ellison's protagonist's "hibernation" in a well-lighted cellar represents the writer's secret elaboration of a language whose opacities and ambiguities can remain socially relevant while renouncing the illusion of symbolic transparency.

A narrative form that conjugates an awareness of the pitfalls of language with social comment is that of satire, "an art form that sets out to expose and attack social vices and follies by means of ridicule and to urge correction of societal sin" (Peplow 1974, 243). Its privileged tone is the indirection of humor; its ethos is ironic. This classical definition corresponds to what Steven Weisenburger (1995, 5) calls "generative satire," by contrast with postmodern "degenerative satire," characterized by the omnipresence of the grotesque and carnivalesque, as well as by a generalized suspicion of all structures, including language and discourse, as dissimulations of violence. The opposition is far from absolute, though, since many modern satirists, from the time of Jonathan Swift's "Modest Proposal" (1729) onward, have abandoned the vantage point of easily discernible cognitive and moral normativity. Yet, whatever the narrator's position, satire is a genre based on exposure. *Black No More* (1931), by George Schuyler, is a very Swiftian satire, with a particular connection to the theme of transparency. Schuyler's novel has recourse to a science-fiction premise to deconstruct American racialist discourse. Dr. Junius Crookman has invented a machine that removes melanin, thereby changing Black people into optic whites, in order to solve the race problem. In the text's world of tricksters, fools, and knaves, the ensuing scramble for whiteness exposes the hypocrisy of Black and white leaders. The new skin transparency, so to speak, reveals "race" to be a sign, a fiction; yet, this realization hardly purports an end to racism. Analyzing *Black No More* through the prism of the theory and textual framing of invisibility conjured up in *Invisible Man* will allow us to boomerang back into an elucidation of the satirical dimension of the latter.

The purpose of this essay is, therefore, to extend the scope of transparency theory into the past and the field of American racial discourse. The limitations of the democratic rhetoric of transparency are confronted in the two novels at hand by hidden plots that maintain discrimination. Double agents endowed with double vision like "Invisible," the homodiegetic narrator and protagonist in Ellison's novel, or the unscrupulous trickster Max Disher in Schuyler's text, are best equipped to expose the national hypocrisy in a turn of the screw of transparency. Yet, the irreducibility of the individual to any group identity and the ambiguities of language question any moral or epistemological reach for such clarity. The issues of parody and allegory, two key figures of satiric discourse, are central in this respect. They stage an interplay between the literal and figurative aspects of the "transparency" paradigm, as they rely upon double vision. Parody resides in the ability to read through a text to the revision of its intertextual references, while allegory points to aspects of the world outside the text. Such interpretive mechanisms are connected to the logics of transparency as a visual phenomenon but mediated by the polysemic density of language, as by a veil. As Edouard Glissant suggested in his *Poetics of Relation* (1997), opacity is the fate of literature, but it is also a major political issue.

1. The Optics of Race

Dr. Junius Crookman's Black No More device belongs to the paraphernalia of science fiction. The procedure is inspired by the natural discoloration of the skin in the disease vitiligo and "'is accomplished by electrical nutrition and glandular control. Certain gland secretions are greatly stimulated while others are considerably diminished'" (Schuyler 1997, 27). The apparatus itself "resembled a cross between a dentist's chair and an electric chair. Wires and straps, bars and levers protruded from it and a great nickel headpiece, like the helmet of a knight, hung over it. [. . .] Around the walls were cases of instruments and shelves of bottles filled with strangely colored fluids" (34). This description is a cross between the modernist fascination for gleaming, miraculous metal machines reminiscent of Fritz Lang's 1927 film *Metropolis* and the older instruments and vials in Dr. Frankenstein's or Dr. Jekyll's laboratories. The melanin-inhibiting procedure is a sort of Promethean endeavor, a transformation of nature wreaking havoc in the social order, but perhaps for the greater good: "It looked as though science was to succeed where the Civil War had failed" (25). The first person to try the treatment, the vital, ambitious Max Disher, is exhilarated: "White at last! [. . .] There would be no more expenditures for skin whiteners; no more discrimination; no more obstacles in his path. He was free! The world was his oyster and he had the open sesame of a pork-colored skin!" (35). He becomes unrecognizable even to his closest associates. The erasure of skin color amounts to a form of transparency—not that white skin is transparent, as it is not even white but pork-pink. It is only that it is the majority pigmentation (no pun intended), and therefore an unmarked signifier. Conformity is invisibility and safety, as suggested by the repetition of the phrase "no more" attached to a litany of synonyms for the blackness of the title. The semantic field is purely negative and related to various forms of discrimination, including the colorism pervading American and African American society, referred to in the novel through the cosmetics enforcing the standards of whiteness, hair straighteners, and skin whiteners. Did not coffee-colored Max and his darker friend Bunny Brown agree that "there were three things essential to the happiness of a colored gentleman: yellow money, yellow women and yellow taxis" (19)? Opportunistic Max Disher, free at last, will be able to pursue a young white woman who has struck his eye in a Harlem nightclub, all the way south to Georgia, where he becomes the mastermind of a white supremacist organization founded by her father, the Knights of Nordica.

In Schuyler's thought experiment, the science-fiction plot serves as a metaphor to address American racialist discourse in the 1930s. Strikingly enough, Ellison's own exposure of invisibility is ushered in by references to the genres of the fantastic and science fiction, actually in the form of a disclaimer (Ellison 1965, 7):

> I am an invisible man. No, I am not a spook like those who haunted Edgar Allan Poe; nor am I one of your Hollywood-movie ectoplasms. I am a man of substance, of flesh and bone, fibre and liquids—and I might even be said to possess a mind. I am invisible, understand, simply because people refuse to see me. Like the bodiless heads you see sometimes in circus sideshows, it is as though I have been surrounded by mirrors of hard, distorting glass. When they approach me they see only my surroundings, themselves, or figments of their imagination—indeed, everything and anything except me.
>
> Nor is my invisibility exactly a matter of bio-chemical accident to my epidermis. That invisibility to which I refer occurs because of a peculiar disposition of the eyes of those with whom I come in contact. A matter of the construction of their *inner* eyes, those eyes with which they look through their physical eyes upon reality.

Invisible denies that his invisibility is related to some ghostly or supernatural identity. This negation may be relativized if we consider that in that period's slang the word "spook" had a double meaning: both ghost and

Black person,[1] to which can be added the connotation of fright or spookiness. This choice of word poses the question of the correlation between social fear and the themes of horror in popular culture. "Blindsighted by prejudice, the White gaze never reaches beyond the surroundings and periphery of beings whose color difference becomes the paradoxical pretext for indistinctness" (Cochoy 1998, 39). In fact, a word that in this passage connotes invisibility or transparency is characterized by its ambiguity and polysemy, which we will define as "semantic opacity." The second denial, that of a biochemical accident to his epidermis, seems to refer to H. G. Wells's 1897 novel *The Invisible Man*, in which a scientist is able to modify the structure of human tissues so as to make them transparent; that is, unable to reflect or refract light (Wells 162). This classic science-fiction story may also have been a source of inspiration for Schuyler: after all, melanin density is strictly speaking an accident—in the sense of a non-essential property—affecting the epidermis.

Ellison's insistence on the disposition of the "inner eye" makes invisibility a dimension of the social gaze, paradoxically making a visible difference, skin color, responsible for a blindness. The optical setup is a metaphor for the mental projections that deny the existence of the individual in favor of racial stereotypes. This lack of recognition may lead to an alienating feeling of unreality: "You often doubt if you really exist. You wonder whether you are not simply a phantom in other people's minds" (7). In his interpretation of this passage, the German philosopher and sociologist Axel Honneth (2001, 114) draws a difference between "cognizance" and "recognition." "Seeing through" a person is definitely not a matter of perception: "Invisibility in the figurative sense presupposes visibility in the literal sense." It is a refusal to extend to the other person the expressions of social validity that entail moral obligations toward them. "Clearly, the form of social invisibility that Ralph Ellison tells us about represents a form of moral disrespect because the absence of gestures of recognition is supposed to demonstrate that the first-person narrator, unlike other persons, is not attributed the worth due to an 'intelligible' person" (123).

Conflict and violence may be a way to assert your existence, as illustrated in the description of the fight between Invisible and a man whom he has bumped into in the street and who has insulted him. Almost on the point of killing him after the man fails to apologize, he desists, "when it occurred to me that the man had not seen me, actually; that he, as far as he knew, was in the midst of a walking nightmare!" (Ellison 1965, 8). Placed so early in the novel, this (failed) struggle for recognition becomes archetypal, reminiscent of Georg Wilhelm Friedrich Hegel's master-slave

---

1 Philip Roth puts this polysemy to devastating use in his 2000 masterpiece *The Human Stain*.

dialectic. In this philosophical myth, an initial fight to the death leads to the enslavement of the one who surrenders first; but the slave, through his work, becomes indispensable to the master, which may in the future pave the way for the reversal of the dialectic, leading to mutual recognition and equality. But if the Other is transparent, or merely a reflecting or projecting surface, not even a minimal recognition can take place, and no progress can happen. In the prologue, Invisible makes the most of his transparency, having retreated to a cellar on the border of Harlem, where he hibernates like a bear in a warm hole full of light—he is stealing electricity from Monopolated Light & Power, a brand name alluding to the mainstream's dominance in matters of knowledge and power—and writes his story to make a potential difference on the surface.

Black No More and *Invisible Man* share a satirical dimension: the denunciation of irrational social formations and the absurdity of the American racialist discourse of their times. The trope of transparency is essential to both but has different connotations in each text. In Schuyler's novel, the erasure of melanin brings about a transparence of sorts at the epidermic level, but mostly on the social playing field. By becoming invisible through a form of mimetism, the Black characters pass into the mainstream and all obstacles to their happiness, or pursuit thereof, are lifted. In contrast, Ellisonian invisibility stems from perceived chromatic difference and precludes social recognition, to the point of alienation and self-doubt. The only alternative to violence, which still does not ensure recognition, is to play along and revel in spectral transparency by living in a parallel space, even indulging in parasitical survival strategies.

2. Satirical Exposure: A World of Fools and Knaves

What is conspicuously missing in *Black No More* is a positive content or ethos attributed to African American culture. As the title indicates, blackness is a mere impediment, hardly a substantial quality. In this the text differs from most of the novels of passing, to the point that Hee-Jung Serenity Joo (2008, 172) sees it as a parody of this important fictional subgenre of the time. In such well-known narratives as James Weldon Johnson's *Autobiography of an Ex-Colored Man* (1912), Nella Larsen's *Passing* (1929), or Langston Hughes's story of the same name (1934), the light-skinned characters' passing for white, thereby escaping discrimination by integrating the mainstream, makes practical sense yet comes at the cost of some deeper, spiritual loss. Hughes's main character feels a pang when he is forced to pass his mother on the street without recognition (55). Johnson's protagonist knows professional success and family happiness but has to renounce his musical ambitions and the opportunity to fight for the rights of oppressed people, a stance taken by the younger generation. He concludes, "I cannot repress the thought that, after all, I have chosen the lesser part, that I have sold my birthright for a mess of pottage" (861). The biblical reference to the story of Jacob and Esau identifies the precious inheritance of the elder brother with the maligned race, the righteousness of whose cause is doubled by cultural specificity, expressed through a unique musical gift. If passing can be read as the assumption of a form of transparency, for Johnson it is a loss, and the metaphorical opacity of blackness also refers to an existential and cultural density.

Not so in *Black No More*. If Max Disher can almost painlessly blend into the mainstream, it is because transparency was already at work, and the notion of "race" was not only a social construct but an illusion. In order to validate the efficiency of his procedure, Dr. Crookman states that apart from pigmentation, there are no real physical differences between Black and white people. Not only does his machine take care of supposedly Negroid traits such as hair and facial features, but he asserts that in as racially mixed a population as the American one, there is such a continuum of nose and lip shapes and sizes as to lose pertinence. except in the caricatural exaggerations of cartoonists and minstrel shows (31–32). In the parallel field of culture, these specificities are also nonexistent: "There is no such thing as Negro dialect, except in literature and drama. [. . .] There are no racial or color dialects; only sectional dialects" (31). In other words, region trumps race.

Besides the obvious exaggerations of satire and the need to brush aside objections to the main ploy of the plot—the possibility of a mechanical erasure of blackness—this discussion echoes some of the key contemporary debates about the Americanness of African Americans, a controversy in which Schuyler flamboyantly took part with his 1926 essay "The Negro-Art Hokum" Contrary to critics who argued for the specificity of Black culture in the United States, either through a genealogy of African survivals or as a product of the relative cultural isolation born of discrimination and oppression, Schuyler provocatively argued that "the Aframerican is merely a lampblacked Anglo-Saxon" (1997, 1172). "Aside from his color, which ranges from very dark brown to pink, your American Negro is just plain American. [. . .] How, then, can the black American be expected to produce art and literature dissimilar to that of the white American?" (1173). Even African American music, including spirituals, jazz, and the blues, is described as the product of a peasant class and a working class in specific conditions, without racial component (1172). Furthermore, what we could anachronistically call the essentialization of Black difference is seen as an offshoot and internalization of white racism: "On this baseless premise, so flattering to the white mob, that the blackamoor is inferior and fundamentally different, is erected the postulate that he must needs be peculiar; and when he attempts to portray life through the medium of art, it must of necessity be a peculiar art" (1174). In this, Schuyler echoes the Boasian tenet that "culture is shaped by experience and historical conditions rather than organic or spiritual 'racial' inheritance" (Hutchinson 1995, 70), but he takes it to more radical conclusions than many of his fellow African American intellectuals.

In a sense, the "Americanism" of African Americans is a form of cultural transparency, and the satire's imaginary erasure of superficial physical barriers is meant to show how "mainstream" Black folks are in reality. This is what Max experiences with his newfound whiteness. Having a meal in a white dinner-dance establishment, he feels disappointment at the forced, awkward joy and abandon of the crowd, contrasted with Black sensuality. "The Negroes, it seemed to him, were much gayer, enjoyed themselves more deeply and yet were more restrained, actually more refined. [. . .] He felt a momentary pang of mingled disgust, disillusionment and nostalgia" (Schuyler 1989, 40). But he soon forgets these depressing thoughts as he ingratiates himself with white ladies. He later feels at home in Harlem and is tempted to stay, in a gesture of solidarity reminiscent of the novels of passing mentioned above. "Momentarily he felt a disposition to stay among them, to share again their troubles which they seemed to bear with a lightness that was yet not indifference. But then, he realized with just a tiny trace of remorse that the past was forever gone" (46). The relevant adverb in both extracts is "momentarily": contrary to the regrets and soul-searching of the ex-colored man, Max Disher does not dwell on the past and looks toward the future in an almost cliched display of Americanism.

Ralph Ellison's novel proposes a different point of view on this notion of cultural transparency. The invisible man has neither the desire nor the technological means, offered by Crookman's machine, to pass into the mainstream. On the contrary, he experiences several epiphanies that reveal that he has been an unwitting accomplice in his own becoming-invisible. In a key scene, the protagonist is walking down the street and comes close to a street vendor's wagon from which "drifted the odour of baking yams slowly to [him], bringing a stab of swift nostalgia" (Ellison 1965, 212). He realizes that in his college days, he had repressed his taste for the succulent tuber, which was too reminiscent of the African American rural folkways. He even imagines the director of his college, Dr. Bledsoe, losing his reputation and credit with white patrons when exposed as a secret chitterling lover: "*Prominent Educator Reverts to Field Niggerism*" (215), is the headline in the papers in his daydream. It appears that the uplift ideology, whose purpose was to raise the social level of a number of Black people through education and work ethic, also implied an acculturation to the standards of white middle-class culture and the loss of an essential part of African American identity. "What a group of people we were, I thought. Why, you could cause us the greatest humiliation simply by confronting us with something we liked. Not *all* of us, but so many" (214). This shame was born of a pressure to conform, a repudiation of cultural markers deemed as countrified and racially inferior. It was a forced transparency to the dominant social gaze, not an erasure but a toning down of specificity, ensured with the collaboration of its victims. "I had accepted the accepted attitudes and it had made life seem simple" (216). But in this passage Invisible reclaims his identity: "I walked along, munching the yam, just as suddenly overcome by an intense feeling of freedom—simply because I was eating while walking along the street. It was exhilarating. I no longer had to worry about who saw me or about what was proper" (214). Because of the intense physicality of a cultural memory embodied through taste and physical activity, the character seems to counteract transparency by an increase in bodily density. He concludes with the exultant cry, both pun and self-assertion: "I yam what I am!" (215).

Ellison articulates a more complex relation between group specificity and Americanism than Schuyler, as is visible in his discussion of the blues in his 1953 collection of essays *Shadow and Act*. In "Blues People," a review of Leroy Jones's book of that name, he embraces a pluralistic view of American culture (1995, 255), in which African Americans not only share in the country's ethos but also influence it. While deriding the separatist idea that Black Americans could have been immune to the general conditions of the nation and "the complex give and take of acculturalization which was undergone by all others who found their existence within American democracy" (250), he advocates an awareness "of how much of American cultural expression is Negro" (257). Given the contribution of Black people to the musical culture and speech patterns, among others, of the South, he questions the existence of "a 'mainstream' of American culture to which they're alien" (256). He then sets up the patterns of African American culture not only within the national framework but also within a universal one: "The blues speak to us simultaneously of the tragic and the comic aspects of the human condition and they express a profound sense of life shared by many Negro Americans precisely because their lives have combined these modes" (256). A similar argument is developed in relation to the dual culture of the African American writer, for whom Black folklore is precious but does not constitute a compositional imperative.

> My point is that the Negro American writer is also an heir of the human experience which is literature, and this might well be more important to him than his living folk tradition. For me, at least, in the discontinuous, swiftly changing and diverse American culture, the stability of the Negro American folk tradition became precious as a result of an act of literary discovery. [. . .] Negro American folk tradition constitutes a valuable source for literature, but for the

novelist, of any cultural or racial identity, his form is his greatest freedom and his insights are where he finds them. (58–59)

Between the particular, the national, and the universal, the boundaries are porous, making for a mix of transparency and opacity, as well as a series of echoes and parallels—or, to use the visual trope once more, a hall of mirrors.

3. Satire and Exposure

If racial difference is downplayed to various degrees in the two novels, those political and intellectual leaders who have a stake in emphasizing it may be criticized as deluded or dishonest. Exposure is a key component of satire, and as such is not without its counterpart in our contemporary culture of transparency, which has sometimes been defined as a culture of exposure. As Jeremy Gilbert (2007, 22–23) put it, "We live in an age of endless disclosure," from the journalistic unveiling of political scandals to the outing of the private lives of famous or powerful individuals, and to the dilution of the limit between private and public lives on social media. "At such a time it might seem that there are no secrets. Or it might seem, conversely, that secrets are all there are." Not only are some shady secrets revealed in the public space; many otherwise insignificant items become "news" (or clickbait) owing to their disclosure. "What if it is only the act of disclosure, surveillance or confession which constitutes any particular piece of the continuum of experience as 'a secret'?" (26). We therefore live "in the perpetual present of outraged revelation" (38). Truly, this is a world not unfamiliar to readers of satires—without the humor, though. The broadest definition of the genre, the derision of the vices and follies of humankind, is quite often embodied in a denunciation of the flip side of the rules and values that are supposed to ensure the harmony of social relations. What then obtains is an amoral world of fools and knaves, the former being those whose trust of others and adhesion to the rules make them victims of the unscrupulous ones who know how to hide their greed and selfishness behind time-honored customs and institutions—or newfangled fashions, for that matter.

The logic of satire is therefore that of de-idealization or desublimation; in Freudian terms, the latter is accompanied with laughter, because of its liberating potential with regard to social and moral obligations. "There is no doubt that the essence of humour is that one spares oneself the affects to which the situation would naturally give rise and dismisses the possibility of such expressions of emotions with a jest. [. . .] The grandeur in it clearly lies in the triumph of narcissism, the victorious assertion of the ego's invulnerability" (Freud 1961, 162). Yet, the traditional satirical ironist's position was not always that of Olympian indifference, as

Juvenal's invectives remind us. Satire is usually coupled with pity for the fools and outrage against the knaves. It is a fiction of exposure, in which imagination, humor, and irony temper the sense of outrage.

Satire especially indicts hypocrisy—the discrepancy between public virtue and private vice, or the hidden agendas of groups and organizations. In a way, it denounces opacity and dissimulation, by means of a fiction that semitransparently targets the "real" social world, through character types and imaginary situations that allude indirectly to actual people and events. Their degree of generality shelters from libel suits and allows broad identification, except in the case of ad hominem satire, which targets a specific person or group at the peril of the satirist.

The main target of *Black No More*, besides white supremacists, is the "race man" (or woman), a prominent African American advocate of Black people and their uplift, whose disinterestedness is suddenly revealed, with the exodus of their constituents to the mainstream, to hide self-aggrandizing motives.

> Meanwhile, Negro society was in turmoil and chaos. The colored folk, in straining every nerve to get the Black-No-More treatment, had forgotten all loyalties, affiliations and responsibilities. No longer did they flock to the churches on Sundays or pay dues to their numerous fraternal organizations. They had stopped giving anything to the Anti-Lynching campaign. Santop Licorice, head of the once-flourishing Back-To-Africa Society, was daily raising his stentorian voice in denunciation of the race for deserting his organization. (Schuyler 1989, 85–86)

According to this passage, racial segregation did benefit African American leaders, who could capitalize on their position of monopoly and live comfortably off their constituents' meager incomes. Black preachers are portrayed as such frauds, as are Black nationalists like Santop Licorice, modeled after the Jamaican-born charismatic leader of the United Negro Improvement Association, Marcus Garvey, who advocated a return to Africa and set up a passenger-ship company, the Black Star Line; a newspaper; and other Black-owned businesses. He was expelled from the United States in 1927 for mail fraud, even though his demise might have been attributed to inexperience more than dishonesty (Gates and McKay 1997, 973). African American politicians are depicted in a similar manner, mourning the loss of their "usual sources of graft" acquired in complicity with their "white masters" (Schuyler 1989, 87): "The Negro politicians in the various Black Belts, grown fat and sleek 'protecting' vice with the aid of Negro votes which they were able to control by virtue of housing segregation, lectured in vain about black solidarity, race pride and political emancipation; but nothing stopped the exodus to the white race" (86).

A meeting of the flustered "race leaders" at the headquarters of the National Social Equality League, a mixed reference to the Urban League and the National Association for the Advancement of Colored People (NAACP), offers an opportunity for a series of caricatures of actual Black leaders of the time, under the aegis of one Dr. Shakespeare Agamemnon Beard, the distinguished, bearded alter ego of the scholar and activist W. E. B. Du Bois. Hypocrisy is once more at the heart of the satirical charge, in the form of Beard's own internalized racism, visible in the editorials he wrote in his magazine *The Dilemma*—actually Du Bois's *The Crisis*—"denouncing the Caucasians whom he secretly admired and lauding the greatness of the Negroes whom he alternatively pitied and despised" (90). The members of his organization "were never as happy and excited as when a Negro was barred from a theater or fried to a crisp [. . .] smiling through their simulated indignation at the spectacle of another reason for their continued existence and appeal for funds" (88–89).

In the dog-eat-dog world of the novel, the main motivation of these leaders to maintain the status quo may well be an awareness that they might not fare too well without the protective fence of the color line that ensures their privileged position. For example, a prominent businesswoman, Mme Sisseretta Blandish, owner of a hair-straightening salon in Harlem, "a successful enterprise engaged in making Negroes appear as much as white folks as possible" (59)—that is, a minor version of the Black-No-More process—is without illusions as to the advantages of becoming white: "She had seen too many elderly, white-haired Caucasian females scrubbing floors and toiling in sculleries not to know what being just another white woman meant. Yet, she admitted to herself that it would be nice to get over being the butt for jokes and petty prejudice" (61–62). The racial question is pictured as obfuscating the more fundamental issue of wealth inequality: "On meager salaries of five thousand dollars a year [Black leaders] had fought strenuously and tirelessly to obtain for the Negroes the constitutional rights which only a few thousand rich white folk possessed" (89).

Satirical exposure in *Black No More* may appear as heavy-handed, grotesque caricature; yet many leaders of the Harlem Renaissance, like W. E. B. Du Bois or Alain Locke, were criticized for their dependence on the funding and support of white patrons and the ambivalence or superficiality of their commitment to ordinary African American people. *Invisible Man* is not without its own satirical barbs, some often aimed at the same target as Schuyler's: Black uplift institutions whose hidden agenda is a much their own interest as that of their constituents, in complicity with their white trustees. This becomes manifest to Invisible after he mistakenly exposes a white benefactor of his Southern Black college, Mr. Norton, to the squalor of African American low life, including the incestuous father Jim Trueblood, whose gruesome tale has a shattering impact on the elderly plutocrat. The director, Dr. Bledsoe, modeled on accommodationist leader Booker T. Washington, the founder of the famous Tuskegee Institute, takes the young man to task for failing to keep up the image of uplift that keeps the donor dollars flowing in. "Then haven't we bowed and scraped and begged and lied enough decent homes and drives for you to show him? Did you think that white man had to come a thousand miles [. . .] just for you to show him a slum? [. . .] Your poor judgement caused this school incalculable damage. Instead of uplifting the race, you've torn it down" (116–17). The semblance of altruism in Bledsoe's strategic flattery of rich white trustees is disproved by his next boast: "The only ones I even pretend to please are *big* white folk, and even those I control more than they control me. This is a power set-up, son, and I'm at the controls" (119). Comparable to the crooked Black leaders in *Black No More*, who benefit from a status quo leveled against their less fortunate peers, Bledsoe hides behind the discourse of racial solidarity and uplift for his own benefit. "I didn't make it, and I know that I can't change it. But I've made my place in it and I'll have every Negro in the country hanging on tree limbs by morning if it means staying where I am" (120). Once more, hypocrisy and dishonesty are the butt of satire.

Satire engulfs all racial discourses in *Black No More*: if the specificity of the Black "race" is taken to task, so is white supremacy. An idle Max Disher, under the new "white" name of Mathew Fisher, looking for advancement in this competitive world where "being white, he concluded, was no open sesame to employment" (64), joins The Knights of Nordica, a KKK-like organization that capitalizes on pleonastic fears for "the racial integrity of the Caucasian race" in the light of Dr. Crookman's melanin-erasing device (65). Appalled by the ignorance and stupidity of racial prejudice, he nevertheless becomes aware of its usefulness to the powers that be:

> So long as the ignorant white masses could be kept thinking of the menace of the Negro to Caucasian race purity and political control, they would give little thought to labor organization. It suddenly dawned upon Matthew Fisher that this Black-No-More treatment was more of a menace to white business than to white labor. And not long afterward he became aware of the money-making possibilities in the present situation. (65)

Thanks to his shrewdness, the former Max transforms his father-in-law's fly-by-night outfit into a major money-grabbing machine, drawing huge sums from an expanding membership and selling his propagandist's skills to Southern businesses, in order to break strikes and to undermine efforts at unionizing. A timely suggestion—a fake exposure—that a labor leader might be colored was enough to shed discredit on his actions: "the erstwhile class conscious workers became terror-stricken by the specter of black blood" (127). The same obtained if they were Jewish or Communist (128). Even though the latter case pertains to the political field only, the first two draw attention to the other key notion in the definition of "race": the mythology of blood, and the attendant obsession with blood purity.

The confusion brought about by the Black-No-More device, massively dissociating color from the underlying character of blood—a previously (supposedly) transparent sign system—becomes a major issue in the next presidential election. "Race" takes center place in the race—as if it had ever *not* been the case, the satirist implies. The Republican ticket, composed of sitting President Goosie and Vice-President Gump, and secretly backed by the Black-No-More organization, vows not to interfere with free enterprise, including the whitening outfit. The Democratic candidate, on the other hand, benefits from the support of the Knights of Nordica and intends to crack down on racial passing.

> Mr. Arthur Snobcraft, President of the Anglo-Saxon Association, an F. F. V. [First Families of Virginia] and a man suspiciously swarthy for an Anglo-Saxon, had devoted his entire life to fighting for two things: white racial integrity and Anglo-Saxon supremacy. [. . .] He was strong for sterilization of the unfit: meaning Negroes, aliens, Jews and other riff raff, and he had an abiding hatred of Democracy. (153–54)

The political orientations of the two parties correspond, of course, to their ethos in the early twentieth century, when the Republicans were still the party of Lincoln and Emancipation, while the Democrats controlled the segregated South (the recent inversion of these values is one of the many ironies of history). In the pursuit of his new pet scheme of "a genealogical law disfranchising all people of Negro or unknown ancestry" (154), Snobcraft associates with one Samuel Buggerie, a statistician, who has started conducting a genealogical inquiry into the American population. But this quest for ethnic transparency backfires when, on the eve of the election, Snobcraft learns that, descendant of King Alfred though he be, he was also the offshoot of several racially mixed marriages in colonial times (179). Forced to flee a lynch mob, Snobcraft and Buggerie survive a plane crash in the Mississippi countryside only to fall into the hands of another mob. Their end is tragically grotesque: resorting to a blackface disguise to avoid being recognized—thus ironically reversing and setting in relief the whole novel as an exercise in whiteface—they are faced with a bunch of poor white fanatics bent on killing Black people. They reveal their white skins just before the news of their mixed-race ancestry reaches this neck of the backwoods, and they are finally burned at the stake. In their thrust for racial exposure, the two unfortunate supremacists have obtained more than they bargained for.

This episode is intended to shatter the myth of racial purity in such a diverse country as the United States, but it can also be read as a comment on the myth of transparency. Some secrets are better left uninvestigated, or unexposed, especially those pertaining to the private sphere. In what reads like a biblical commandment, one might say: "Do not expose others, lest thou shalt be exposed." But in the economy of the narrative, the conflagration that metes out retribution to the arrogant also brings respite to the hero. One of the supremacists whose drop of Black blood was thus exposed was Reverend Givens, head of the Knights of Nordica and Max Disher's father-in-law, just before the birth of Max's mixed-race child. One of the key topoi of the novel of passing, the disclosure of the secret attendant on the birth of a child, is thus defused, and the supremacist family accept Max and his offspring all the more easily as they have discovered that they themselves were not fully white.

A similar point about the hybrid nature of the United States is made in the famous, quasi-surrealistic Optic White episode that occupies the whole of chapter 10 of *Invisible Man*. In his quest for employment, Invisible is hired by the Liberty Paints factory, whose motto "Keep America Pure with Liberty Paints" (Ellison 1965, 160) clearly aligns it with the national obsession for whiteness. The whole sequence reads like an allegory of the politics of color in the mainstream American racialist discourse of the time. As the new assistant to a Mr. Kimbro, the protagonist discovers that the secret ingredient in the whitest paint ever made—"as white as George Washington's Sunday-go-to-meetin' wig and as sound as the all-mighty dollar! [...] It's the purest white that can be found. Nobody makes a paint any whiter. This batch right here is heading for a national Monument!" (164)—consists of a few drops of "dead black" liquid (163). Optic White is just that: an optical illusion—or, rather, the product of the invisible dilution of blackness. It is actually invisibility squared: the black drops are made transparent within the mass of white color, and the erasure is itself made invisible.

On the one hand, this points out, as Toni Morrison (1992, 57) insists in *Playing in the Dark*, that American national identity is intrinsically associated with a whiteness predicated on the presence of a suppressed black presence, and pointing to "the parasitical nature of white freedom." The fetishization of whiteness owns its operative power—nay, its actual existence—to the nonwhite (Black, Native) component of the population. Ethnic identities, Fredrik Barth (1998, 10) argues in a classic essay, are produced through the creation and maintenance of boundaries. The Other, who seems to be merely outside, is actually at the core of ethnic and, even more so, racial identities. The self-transparency of an ethnic or racial group, which partly corresponds to the essentialist illusion that its identity is based on unchanging, natural, or biological traits (epistemic transparency, so to speak), and to the mutual recognition of its denizens due to these shared fundamental traits (interactional transparency), is actually grounded on a form of opacity. A correlative to this structural impurity of "race" is the impossibility of maintaining genetic purity in a pluralistic environment: the few drops of black liquid in the batch of white paint also allude to the "one drop rule" that claimed to exclude from the white population all people who had even one Black ancestor. Snobcraft and Buggerie's sad fate illustrates how tricky genealogies can be.

As a matter of fact, when Invisible ruins a whole lot of paint by pouring remover instead of the black taint into a vat, he is sent to the deep underground of the factory and attached to Lucius Brockway, a Black man in charge of the boilers. But this belly of the beast is also the realm of a machine strangely reminiscent of Dr. Crookman's device. "We came to a strange-looking machine consisting of a huge set of gears connecting a series of drum-like rollers. Brockway took a shovel and scooped up a load of brown crystals from a pile on the floor, pitching them skillfully into a receptacle on top of the machine" (Ellison 1965, 174). As Brockway explains, "Well that's going to be the guts, what they call the *vee*-hicle of the paint" (175). This confirms the fact that the praised whiteness of the paint and the dominant culture is actually based on darker hues, and it also amounts to a self-reflexive comment on the metaphoric structure of the passage. If we remember that a metaphor is traditionally described as composed of a tenor and a vehicle, the terms of the text are vehicles for an ironic indictment of American racism. The process depends on people, including the complicity (conscious or unconscious) of members of the discriminated group. Before becoming paranoid and destroying the plant, Brockway adds, "They got all this machinery, but that ain't everything; *we are the machines inside the machine*" (177). When the factory explodes, Invisible finds himself engulfed in another metaphor, "a wet blast of black emptiness that was somehow a bath of whiteness" (188).

In an allegory such as this one, language is not fully transparent: its rhetoric of indirection bifurcates the signifiers between their literal and figurative meanings, one screening the other. Even though an allegory, with its term-to-term metaphorical correspondence between elements of the story and its more abstract philosophical or social referents, is frequently less obscure and multilayered than a symbol, an interpretive key is needed to unlock the double meanings. It therefore constitutes only one particular example of the complex mix of transparency and opacity that characterizes all languages and acts of communication.

4. The Opacity of Language

The call for transparency in public life, together with the contemporary obsession with exposure, at heart resorts to an epistemic mode that can be defined as realist: it supposes that reality can be known and that signs are imbued with a degree of transparency allowing for its faithful description. Yet, media specialists are aware that neither signs nor the media that transmit them—neither the medium nor the message—are transparent. The contemporary flourishing of conspiracy theories is proof that evidence does not entail obviousness. In this they radicalize the classical semiological analysis made by Roland Barthes in *Mythologies* of the ideological dimension of popular culture: for the French critic, the mainstream media naturalized bourgeois ideology by grafting a second-degree, hidden sign onto a merely connotative sign, thus carrying out a "theft of language" (1972, 218). Barthes is also one of the best-known representatives of an early poststructuralist attack on the illusions of the realist conception of literature: the referential illusion that fiction can transcribe social realities as they are through the self-effacement of language. In "The Discourse of History," for example, he states that classical historiography and the realist novel are based on two similar sets of conventions dependent on the fallacy that language can be transparent and depict reality without mediation:

> In other words, in "objective" history, the "real" is never more than an unformulated signified, sheltering behind the apparently all-powerful referent. This situation characterizes what we might call the realistic effect. [. . .] Historical discourse does not follow the real, it can do no more than signify the real, constantly repeating that it happened, without this assertion amounting to anything but the signified "other side" of the whole process of historical narration. (1981, 17–18)

The opacity of the signified entails that in literature we can access "reality effects" rather than a faithful rendition of reality itself. This is confirmed by the common wisdom that language can lie as well as tell the truth, which is exemplified in the novels that are the object of our study by the central place devoted to hypocrisy and false-front operations.

A perfect illustration of the duplicity of both institutions and language is provided by the letter of recommendation that Bledsoe gives to the protagonist of *Invisible Man*. Secrecy is a constituent feature of letters of recommendation: it is supposed to ensure the objectivity and independence of the applicant's portrayal. Yet, the opacity of the sealed message can allow the expression of arbitrary judgments or prejudices, ending up detrimental to the quester's pursuit. Like Hamlet's parting letters that proved fatal to Rosencrantz and Guildenstern, Bledsoe's recommendation aims at sending Invisible on a fool's errand for summer jobs, ensuring his silence with the hope of being accepted again in his alma mater in the fall, while he has actually been expelled without knowing it. A backhand move the character pithily rephrases as follows, after discovering the swindle: "Dear Mr. Emerson, [. . .] The Robin carrying this letter is a former student. Please hope him to death, and keep him running. Your most humble and obedient servant, A. H. Bledsoe" (Ellison 1965, 159). The letter is endowed with the power of the secret, and its opacity points to that of language itself, the mystery of the signifier, the potentiality to benefit or harm according to context. The exposure of Bledsoe's double discourse is one small victory for transparency, but it is a short-lived one, since the protagonist later falls for the promises and lies of the Brotherhood, a fictional avatar of the Communist Party, whose antiracist solidarity with African American people conceals another manipulative agenda.

The veiling, manipulative dimension of language is represented in the two novels by the characters of tricksters and double agents. In his capacity as an amoral opportunist driven by appetite for money and flesh, even at the expense of solidarity with his own community, Max Disher/ Matthew Fisher is a fictional embodiment of the figure of the trickster of myth and tale. At one and the same time culture-hero and universally subversive agent, linguistic equivocator and benevolent translator, embodiment of a tribe's ethos and transgressor of the very values he helped promote, the trickster stands at the boundaries of civilization and savagery, nature and culture, instincts and their sublimation. "Trickster is at one and the same time creator and destroyer, giver and negator, he who dupes others and who is always duped himself. He wills nothing consciously. [. . .] He knows neither good nor evil yet he is responsible for both. He possesses no values, moral or social, is at the mercy of his passions and appetites, yet through his actions values come into being" (Radin 1956, x). The two principal tricksters of African-American folklore, Br'er Rabbit and the Signifying Monkey, also represent the necessity of a nimble mind to survive in a hostile racial environment, embodying the resourcefulness of Black people and sometimes enacting vicarious revenge on the dominant culture.

A clever equivocator and an "enemy of boundaries" like the trickster, Disher seizes the opportunity of his metamorphosis to pass into, and rise within, the white world, marry a white woman, and become the leader of a white supremacist organization. He escapes the backlash of the revelation of his own origins, as no origins are pure. Even though he can hardly be called a culture hero, he can be said to inadvertently usher in a new world through his self-centered schemes. In the final chapter, after scientists have discovered that former Black people are actually more deficient in melanin than actual white people, the new urge becomes to be tanned or darken one's skin. "A white face became startingly rare. America was definitely, enthusiastically mulatto-minded" (Schuyler 1989, 222). The carnivalesque topsy-turviness of this chromatic inversion, even if it introduces confusion and disorder in racial taxonomies, actually points at the persistence, and therefore the essential structural function, of color in American society. Universal whiteness did not lead to equality but to renewed segregations, which strikes a pessimistic chord about the prospects of progress in the society of the time. Semiotically speaking, the instability of the chromatic sign reveals its arbitrariness, hence the construction of the notion of "race"; but the tenacity of this sign without an objective referent hints at its ideological weight, its opacity.

According to Henry Louis Gates Jr. (1983, 45), the Signifying Monkey also represents the figure of revision, both within the Black literary tradition and in response to the mainstream; its signal rhetoric is a trickster's discourse, "Signifying," the slave's trope, consisting in creative and critical parody, repetition with a difference, wordplay and the destabilization of meaning. The very fact that the name of the trope "shadows" the dominant language use points to a strategy of investing the common language (American English) with additional, private meanings that are peculiar to the minority group and ensure an "intimacy" from which the mainstream is excluded. It turns language inside out, so to speak, by inverting the relation of domination and exclusion imposed by the oppressor. It also adds opacity to the signifying system, through the antagonistic overlapping of two cultural spheres. Moreover, the trickster can often represent the minority writer in his subversive, creative parody of mainstream ideology and literature. In *Black No More*, most characters are tricksters of sorts, taking advantage of opportunities and other people to improve their lots and satisfy their material pursuits, from archtricksters Max Disher and his friend Bunny Brown to Revd. Givens, the founder and crook-in-chief of the Knights of Nordica, and to the Black leaders like Beard or Licorice. The only characters whose fate is really tragic are Snobcraft and Buggerie, who seem most sincere, monosemic in their bigotry.

Tricksterism, as an awareness of the polysemy and equivocations of language, is both a survival strategy and an image of the text. The world of the trickster, at least in the African American animal tales, is an amoral world in which a "state of perpetual war between the world's creatures revealed the hypocrisy and meaninglessness of their manners and rules" (Levine 1977, 116). It is essentially satirical, in that "trickster tales were a prolonged and telling parody of white society" (118). As a matter of fact, satire in *Black No More* is not only an outraged condemnation of the vices and follies and humankind; it also evokes a humorous enjoyment of the characters' dishonesty. One may wonder whether there is a contradiction between Schuyler's forceful pronouncements of the Americanism of

Black culture and his impersonation of the figure of the African American trickster and his rhetoric of Signifying. It is true that the trickster is a universal figure and Signifying has analogues in other cultures, but both are especially prominent in Black folklore. The choice of the name Bunny Brown for Max's friend strongly reminds us of Br'er Rabbit. If ideological transparency is opposed to formal opacity, here the scales seem to tip toward the latter.

The trickster figure is also prominent in *Invisible Man*. The prologue establishes the protagonist as a trickster of sorts, owing to his marginal position. His stealing of electricity from Monopolated Light and Power makes him a figure of symbolic subversion; so does his life underground, straddling the boundary between Black and white neighborhoods, and his capacity to deal with ambivalence. But the first appearance of such a trickster figure in the following narrative takes the form of the double agent, a person whose assumed loyalty makes for transparency of motives, only to hide a secret agenda. This masking persona is the grandfather, whose enigmatic deathbed advice constitutes a leitmotif in Invisible's life. "I never told you, but our life is a war and I have been a traitor all my born days, a spy in the enemy's country ever since I give up my gun back in the Reconstruction. [. . .] I want you to overcome 'em with yeses, undermine 'em with grins, agree 'em to death and destruction, let 'em swoller [swallow] you till they vomit or bust wide open" (Ellison 1965, 17). This corresponds to the trickster's playacting and equivocation, his survival strategies in the face of stronger opponents. But the ambiguity of subversion through compliance is that it becomes difficult to define whom you betray: is it the (white) "enemy" or, ultimately, the Black community? Much later in the plot, after he realizes that the Brotherhood has been using the Harlem community for their own purposes, Invisible has recourse to the same strategy, becoming a double agent in the hope of undermining the organization while building his own network within the Black population. Yet, a climactic race riot instrumentalized by the Brotherhood shows him he has been, like many tricksters in folktales, used and tricked himself: "The committee had planned it. And I had helped, had been a tool. A tool just at the very moment when I had thought myself free. By pretending to agree I had indeed agreed" (445).

This leads him to probe deeper into his grandfather's words and find in them a dimension beyond tricksterism. The "yes" is not only hypocritical opportunism but a matter of principle. "Could he have meant—hell, he must have meant the principle, that we were to affirm the principle on which the country was built and not the man, or at least not the men who did the violence. Did he mean to say 'yes' because the principle was greater than the men, greater than the numbers and the vicious power and all the methods used to corrupt its name?" (462). After all, what can be more subversive in a racist society than to adhere to the national creed of equality for all? Finally, Blacks and whites are in the same boat, and destruction threatens both if the principle is not upheld.

One character embodies the ultimate trickster figure: Rhinehart, whom Invisible imitates at one time. Rhinehart is a protean figure, a shapeshifter who alternatively plays the parts of a hustler, a numbers runner, a womanizer, a reverend, without ever revealing his true self. Yet, Ellison resists a reading of his novel in terms of the trickster figure alone. In "Change the Joke and Slip the Yoke," an essay reprinted in *Shadow and Act*, he comments, "Indeed, one could extend this list in the manner of much myth-mongering criticism until the fiction dissolved into anthropology, but Rhinehart's role in the formal structure of the narrative is to suggest to the hero a mode of escape from Ras, and a means of applying, in yet another form, his grandfather's cryptic advice to his own situation" (Ellison 1995, 56–57). His main objections to critic Stanley E. Hyman's use of the trickster to explain major aspects of African American culture are, first, that they amount to sweeping generalizations and, second, that he connects his trickster figure with the infamous scenic tradition of the minstrel shows (47). Even though tricksterism is an essential part of the novel, it is not the protagonist's final word: he abandons "Rhinehartism" for his spell in the cellar, during which he writes his story and sorts out his life. Yet, this meeting was essential to Invisible's *Bildung*: "the figure of Rhinehart is about secrecy, his identity an interconnection of secrets, a self-contained structure of secrecy, which the invisible man learns to interpret" (Nadel 1988, 21). It is as an interpreter of cryptic social and linguistic signs that he gains the capacity to write his memoir. Ethical responsibility and a desire to act according to general human norms are rediscovered in the epilogue, as the impulse to resurface above ground is mentioned. "For the novel, his memoir, is one long, loud rant, howl and laugh. Confession, not concealment, is his mode," Ellison wrote in "Change the Joke and Slip the Yoke" (1995, 57). As confession is a genre marked by at least a desire for sincerity and transparency, this statement relativizes the opacity of the text. Yet, the rhetorical strategy of Signifyin(g), characterized by a certain form of opacity, seems to pervade the whole novel, owing to its extensive use of parody and revision of both literary references and social discourses. In a way, Ellison's text Signifies on both the Western canon and Black oral culture, according to Gates's vision of Black literature as "double-voiced" (110). But it also implicitly—and by anticipation—nuances Gates's definition of Signifyin(g) as the trickster's rhetoric (1983, xxi): literature, as an intertextual practice, has a connection with the figure of the trickster but cannot be limited to it, as its range and scope are wider.

The broader question of the transparency or opacity of language is addressed by Martinican critic and writer Edouard Glissant in his *Poetics of Relation*. He criticizes Enlightenment notions of universalism, even in more contemporary versions that recognize national and cultural differences—"the universal—this generalizing edict that summarized the world as something obvious and transparent" (1997, 20)—as the inheritance of European colonialism and a perpetuation of its hierarchical outlook, in favor of a praise of opacity. This opacity is two-pronged. It pertains to the notion of cultural difference and the irreducibility of the Other, to which we could add the opacity of the self even to oneself, and it is an essential constituent of literary language. "Literary textual practice thus represents an opposition between two opacities: the irreducible opacity of the text, even when it is a matter of the most harmless sonnet, and the always evolving opacity of the author or a reader" (115). Literature is a key field for the production of opacity, making all the more tangible the political appeal to the Other of transparency. "We clamor for the right to opacity for everyone" (194). Such a conjunction is especially central in minority literatures, where claims to pluralism take on the triple form of a community's culture; a specific language use, whether it be a dialect or rhetorical strategies; and the elaboration of a text.

This study of *Black No More* and *Invisible Man* has confronted us with a variety of language games in which the dialectic or interplay between transparency and opacity takes multiple forms. Within the public sphere in a democracy, demands for transparency and the attendant drive to exposure are essential to fight prejudice and discrimination. These are often connected to the invisibility of minorities, a form of social transparency that in the case of racial discrimination is paradoxically based on the most visible traits of physiognomy and skin color. Both Ralph Ellison and George Schuyler had recourse to tropes derived from science fiction—a literal machine that whitens Black people in the latter case, and a metaphorical take on H. G. Wells's classic for the former—to expose the American racialist discourse of their times as a semiotic, ideological production rather than an entity based on biological, essential difference. The rhetoric of exposure at the heart of satire entertains a complex relation with transparency. Since the main target of the two works under study is the hypocrisy of racemongers on both sides of the divide, they focus on the opacity of a language that can lie as well as tell the truth. The success of satire depends on the readers' recognition of the targets—that is, a certain transparency of the text's language; yet, the rhetoric of exaggeration and indirection that they use points to the resistance of the signifier. This resistance is corroborated by the humor that is also an essential part of satire, and the abundant recourse to puns, polysemy, or ambiguity: "I yam what I am." In our two works of African American literature, this is compounded by the trope of Signifying, an intracommunal rhetoric of indirection that is opaque to outsiders and that has come to constitute a specific framing of intertextuality. Paradoxically Schuyler, who advocates the full Americanism of the Black community and all but denies its cultural specificity, has recourse to the figure of the folk trickster and the vernacular rhetoric of Signifying, articulating a social transparency by means of a rhetorical opacity. Ellison, for his part, embraces African American specificity but transcends it into the breadth of human experience, refusing any limitation of the artist's allegiances and claiming the freedom to draw inspiration from Western culture as well as from Black culture. On the generic level, *Black No More* can be totally subsumed under the genre of satire, whereas *Invisible Man* is a more ambitious novel in which satire plays a central but by no means exclusive role. Both texts refer to social ills and express an awareness of the complicity of discourse with the forces of oppression. But Ellison's narrator still trusts narratives, as the goal of his retreat underground is to write a story that, "on the lower frequencies," may speak for all (1965, 467). In this sense, Schuyler's satire may be considered as the more "degenerative" of the two, in its representation of the vanity of the corrective impulse in the face of the final reestablishment of a color line through other means. As writers, both Ellison and Schuyler refuse the strictures of predetermined identities and literary provincialism.[2] They present the culture and literature of the United States as essentially hybrid and plural, denying any claims to purity, either in the racial or the literary fields. They also reflect in their distinctive manners on the complementary claims of language to transparency and opacity, or the fundamental tension between its communicative and poetic functions.

---

2   In 1936–38, a few years after *Black No More*, Schuyler published in the *Pittsburgh Courier* a popular serial called *Black Empire* (1991), representing the takeover of the world by a Black leader and his army and people. This text could be defined as eliciting an early form of Black nationalism, the secret State and its advanced technology eerily anticipating aspects of Afrofuturism and of the movie *Black Panther* (2018). The fact that the same writer could pen such different texts has led some critics to "read Schuyler as a radical of sorts, as a figure whose self-proclaimed conservatism [was] but a mask for some imagined progressive or subversive stance" (Goyal 2014, 34). These other productions can also be seen as parodies of the Panafrican ideas of the time, especially, once more, Garvey's and W. E. B. Du Bois's (22). This may invite a reflection on the opacity of real and implied authors, and the different figures they project in their different works.

Works Cited

Barth, Fredrik, ed. 1998. *Ethnic Groups and Boundaries: The Social Organization of Culture Difference.* Long Grove, IL: Waveland Press. First published 1969.
Barthes, Roland. 1972. *Mythologies.* Translated by Annette Lavers. New York: Noonday. First published 1957.
———.1981. "The Discourse of History." Translated by Stephen Bann. *Comparative Criticism* 3: 7–20. First published 1967.
Cochoy, Nathalie. 1998. *Ralph Ellison.* Paris: Belin.
Ellison, Ralph. 1965. *Invisible Man.* Harmondsworth, UK: Penguin. First published 1952.
———. 1995. *Shadow and Act.* New York: Vintage. First published 1964.
Freud, Sigmund. 1961. "Humour." In *The Standard Edition of the Complete Psychological Works of Sigmund Freud*, vol. 21. Translated by James Strachey. London: Hogarth Press. First published 1927.
Gates, Henry Louis, Jr. 1983. *The Signifying Monkey: A Theory of African American Literary Tradition.* New York: Oxford University Press.
Gates, Henry Louis, Jr., and Nellie McKay, eds. 1997. *Norton Anthology of African American Literature.* New York: Norton.
Gilbert, Jeremy. 2007. "Public Secrets." *Cultural Studies* 21, no. 1: 22–41. https://doi:10.1080/09502380601046923.
Glissant, Edouard. 1997. *Poetics of Relation.* Translated by Betsy Wing. Ann Arbor: University of Michigan Press. First published 1990.
Goyal, Yogita. 2014. "Black Nationalist Hokum: George Schuyler's Transnational Critique." *African American Review* 47, no. 1 (Spring): 21–36.
Han, Byung-Chul. 2015. *The Transparency Society.* Translated by Erik Butler. Stanford, CA: Stanford Briefs.
Honneth, Axel. 2001. "Invisibility: On the Epistemology of 'Recognition.'" *Aristotelian Society Supplementary Volume* 75, no. 1 (July 1): 111–26. https://doi.org/10.1111/1467-8349.00081.
Hughes, Langston. 1990. "Passing." In *The Ways of White Folks.* New York: Vintage. First published 1934.
Hutchinson, George. 1995. *The Harlem Renaissance in Black and White.* Cambridge, MA: Harvard University Press.
Johnson, James Weldon. 1997. *The Autobiography of an Ex-Colored Man.* In *The Norton Anthology of African American Literature*, edited by Henry Louis Gates, Jr., and Nellie McKay, 777–860. New York: Norton. First published 1912.
Joo, Hee-Jung S. 2008. "Miscegenation, Assimilation, and Consumption: Racial Passing in George Schuyler's *Black No More* and Eric Liu's *The Accidental Asian.*" *MELUS* 33, no. 3 (Fall): 169–90.
Larsen, Nella. 2007. *Passing.* New York: Norton. First published 1929.
Levine, Lawrence. 1977. *Black Culture and Black Consciousness: Afro-American Folk Thought from Slavery to Freedom.* New York: Oxford University Press.

Morrison, Toni. 1992. *Playing in the Dark: Whiteness and the Literary Imagination*. Cambridge, MA: Harvard University Press.

Nadel, Alan. 1988. *Invisible Criticism: Ralph Ellison and the American Canon*. Iowa City: University of Iowa Press.

Peplow, Michael W. 1974. "George Schuyler, Satirist: Rhetorical Devices in *Black No More*." *CLA Journal* 18, no. 2 (December): 242–57.

Radin, Paul. 1956. *The Trickster: A Study in American Indian Mythology*. New York: Bell.

Roth, Philip. 2001. *The Human Stain*. New York: Vintage. First published 2000.

Schuyler, George. 1989. *Black No More*. Boston: Northeastern University Press. First published 1931.

———. 1991. *Black Empire*. Edited by by Robert A. Hill and R. Kent Rasmussen. Boston: Northeastern University Press. First published 1936–38.

———. 1997. "The Negro-Art Hokum." In Gates and McKay, *Norton Anthology of African American Literature*, 1171–74. First published 1926.

Weisenburger, Steven. 1995. *Fables of Subversion: Satire and the American Novel, 1930–1980*. Athens: University of Georgia Press.

Wells, H. G. 1897. *The Invisible Man*. New York: Harper.

5: The Transparency of the Scanner, the Opacity of the Simulacra: The Politics of Vision in Philip K. Dick's Oeuvre

Umberto Rossi

> *Concealment and discovery are somehow connected, and behave like curious companions.*
>
> —Heraclitus

THE PERIOD OF American history from 1960 to 1980 is undoubtedly a time in which the issue of transparency haunted the public discourse. On May 7, 1960, US citizens learned that their government could deliberately lie when Nikita Khrushchev announced that the pilot of a shot-down CIA U-2 spy plane had been captured alive and was detained in the USSR, thus invalidating the cover-up story circulated by NASA that passed off the missing spy plane as a weather research aircraft. Subsequent events (climaxing with the Watergate scandal and the fall of President Richard M. Nixon) reinforced the belief that the government regularly hid important information from the American public, so that the communication between citizens and their rulers was hindered by a systematic and deliberate opacity. We may, of course, read the concern about such a lack of transparency[1] as a reaction to the creeping obsession with secrecy that had started well before Francis Gary Powers and his aircraft were hit by a USSR missile. It is, however, remarkable that all this happened well before the term *transparency* was introduced into the political lexicon as a translation of Mikhail Gorbachev's political slogan *glasnost*, the proliferation of conspiracist discourses, and the current controversy concerning fake news. Hence, a discussion of the dialectics of opacity and transparency should take into account the novels and stories of an author who wrote in those Cold War years and tackled these issues with remarkable

---

1 It might be argued that President Dwight D. Eisenhower's lie is one of the political events that contributed to the birth of a counterculture—that is, an alternative world vision based on distrust of authority and skepticism about official truths; Dick's fiction is indeed characterized by several countercultural elements (Rossi 2011, ch. 10).

originality, even though in a bewildering fashion and in a totally unrealistic narrative mode: science-fiction writer Philip Kindred Dick. His works present a fictional treatment of the dialectically opposed but complementary concepts of transparency and opacity that predates the current debate (cf. Birchall 2021; Horn 2011; Gilbert 2007; and other theoretical texts listed in "Works Cited"), precociously questioning some theoretical commonplaces such as positing transparency as something good per se. A master of reversals and coups de théâtre like Dick may induce us to turn such commonplaces upside down and reconsider them from a quite different perspective.

The concept of transparency was first applied to the works of Philip K. Dick in one of the essays published during the second phase of PKD scholarship,[2] that of postmodernist readings. Its author, George Slusser, invokes Ralph Waldo Emerson's meditation on nature as a viable model to understand the complex relationship of Dick's fiction to history, striving to envision the author of *The Man in the High Castle* (1987) as "an American SF writer" (1992, 199), to redeem him from the doings of "a kind of theoretical internationalism" that has seen Dick as "a great writer, period" (200), thus dispossessing him "of all cultural specificity" (199). Conversely, Slusser argues that Dick can only be understood if he is brought back to the American mainstream, and he devotes much of his essay to showing how historicity, "a process whereby the individual seeks to place history in objects that no longer bear visible signs of historical authority" (219), informs the narratives of Dick as an American author. This is what, Slusser continues, differentiates Dick from European authors who conceive the literary text as a "monument whose authenticity is guaranteed by its date, by the precise position it occupies in history" (201)—and history, in the European tradition, is a monumental order of chronologically fixed events that become locations (201) in a static sequence, a sort of virtual museum we may visit, but not change.

Slusser contrasts such a monumental conception of history (basically drawn from a single essay by French novelist Alain Robbe-Grillet)[3] with historicity, offering American writers (including Dick) "an open structure whereby the human mind, no longer said merely to 'fabricate' stories" (the only option left to European writers) "is now free to project actual worlds by means of its stories" (219). Having said this, Slusser quotes Emerson's "Nature" (1968): "Standing on bare ground—my head bathed by the blithe air, and uplifted into infinite space—all mean

---

2   The first season is mainly that of Marxist interpretations, well represented by the first special issue of *Science-Fiction Studies* devoted to Dick's oeuvre (March 1975); the same journal marked the change from that approach to a postmodernist one with its second special issue, published in July 1988.

3   *Pour un Noveau Roman* (Paris: Les Editions de Minuit, 1963).

egotism vanishes. I become a transparent eyeball; I am nothing; I see all; the currents of the Universal Being circulate through me" (Slusser 1992, 6). It is here that transparency comes into play: Slusser explains that this passage is relevant to his discourse inasmuch as "the bare ground is the traditionless American landscape, the virgin land. And just as the land is 'bare,' offering no symbols, the horizon offers no historical fixities [. . .] thus cleansed of history, nature is rendered an open realm through which the storyteller [. . .] can glide" (219). I wonder what members of the First Nations might have to say about this idea of the American landscape as vision of a *virgin* land; one might also wonder whether Emerson's meditation, which presupposes an indestructible nature, can be so nonchalantly applied to a writer belonging to the age of strip-mining and air pollution, when the Anthropocene was starting in earnest; moreover, the idea of such a transcendental fusion with nature as the one heralded by Emerson doesn't seem to fit Dick's recurrent visions of what lies outside the urban space as something alien, threatening, and incomprehensible.[4] It is, however, remarkable that Slusser needed transparency, even in such an ecstatic and almost mystical form as Emerson's, as a necessary concept to tackle Dick's fiction, even if it is applied in such a perplexing manner.

Though Dick does not really seem to glide in an open realm of nature that has been cleansed of history, transparency is indeed part of his world; but it only plays a role in it inasmuch as it is opposed to opacity. It is not at all a permanent condition but something that is achieved, often after struggling with opacity. Such a dialectics of the transparent and the opaque is already at work in Dick's earliest works, such as his 1957 fantasy novel *The Cosmic Puppets*.[5] In this purportedly minor work, we have two cities: the Millgate remembered by Ted Burton, the protagonist, and the one he finds when he gets back to his hometown after having spent several years elsewhere. The difference between the town Ted remembers and the one he can see is so great that it cannot be simply explained by the passing of time: they are two completely different cities. The truth is that the original Millgate (the real one) has been magically covered and hidden by a fake Millgate, conjured up by the Zoroastrian god of darkness, Ahriman; the opacity of the counterfeit town prevents Ted from seeing the true one. When Ted and his friend Will (the only person in Millgate who remembers the town as it really was) manage to dispel Ahriman's incantation and reestablish transparency, the novel ends, and this suggests to readers that opacity is bad and transparency is good—also because the fake city is shabby and decaying, unlike the real one that we are shown

---

4   See the description of Californian landscape in *Puttering About in a Small Land* (Dick 1987, 7).
5   Though published after *Solar Lottery* (1955), *The Cosmic Puppets* was written before it (Butler 2007, 27).

at the end of the novel. All in all, behind this story we have Ahab and his pasteboard masks, as even in the celebrated monologue of Melville's deranged whale hunter there is a dialectic of opacity and transparency, with the latter that should be achieved by those who really want to access the truth, even in a brutal fashion: "If man will strike, strike through the mask!" (Melville 1851, 181).

Of course, the dialectics of transparency and opacity may be risky: the "unknown but still reasoning thing" that, according to Ahab, lurks behind the pasteboard masks of visible entities might be no more than a hallucination, the product of paranoia, maybe, or some other mental condition. The purportedly opaque objects might be just what they are, hiding nothing at all—what you see is sometimes what you get. In *The Cosmic Puppets*, madness is in fact one of the possible explanations of the discrepancy between the two Millgates; the paranoid atmosphere reaches its apex when Ted finds out in an old issue of the local newspaper that he died when he was nine years old. Who is Ted Burton, then? An imposter? A madman?

This oscillation between madness and sanity, as well as between opacity and transparency, returns in other works by Dick; for example, in his 1959 novel *Time out of Joint*, in a much more sophisticated fashion: one might say that it is the engine that drives most of his narratives, and I have called this oscillation "ontological uncertainty" (Rossi 2011). There is, however, a remarkable difference between *Puppets* and *Joint*; while the former belongs to fantasy and ends with a denouement that carries us to the realm of religion or metaphysics, as the opacity was the work of a god, the latter is firmly placed in the field of science-fiction,[6] because the anonymous city in which Ragle Gumm leads his ordinary life in the ordinary world of the American 1950s has been built by the government of Earth to second his regression to childhood. We have moved from a philosophical fable to the logics of political secrecy, to put it in Eva Horn's (2011) terms. Opacity is concretely, rationally, materially produced by a government that is thus protecting (and detaining and manipulating) a gifted individual—the only person who can predict where the next missile from the moon will hit.

Horn is a necessary theoretical reference when dealing with opacity and transparency in Dick because she does not subscribe to the idea that psychiatry should explain the condition of those who fantasize about something hidden—of those affected by the fear that the world, the country, the society we live in is not transparent, that "they aren't telling

---

6   Unless we accept the idea that Ragle Gumm, the protagonist, is really hallucinating the "future" world with the war between the Lunar settlers and the Earth government, which would turn the novel into the more or less realistic depiction of a case of mental derangement (Rossi 2011, 74).

us everything." Seeing a malevolent will behind the pasteboard masks may sometimes be explained with madness, but that is an extreme case, and the current proliferation of the conspiracist discourse seems to me a reliable proof of this, as we cannot comfortably ascribe what we could better call the spreading conspiracist imagination to a widespread mental condition (as for the multiple contexts of current conspiracy theories, cf. Birchall and Knight 2023, ch. 1). Horn does not take the road of psychiatry[7] but proposes the concept of a "secrecy effect," after Jacques Derrida:

> Political secrecy aroused both profound suspicion and intense curiosity, and this is precisely what makes the logic of *secretum* [. . .] the specifically modern logic of the secret: [. . .] the *secret* as secretum is more an *effect* than a muted form of real information, a form of social relation. The "secrecy effect" of the modern state secret consists in its permanent and intense relation to a sphere of publicity. Everybody either doubts or knows that "there is something"; the secret is what has to be sought out, "read between the lines"—as the word *intelligere* suggests. (Horn 2011, 112)

Interestingly, *Time out of Joint* has characters who come to believe that "there is something," who strive to read between the lines of the all too ordinary reality surrounding them. Ragle's efforts to understand what the little anomalies and oddities he encounters really mean are an act of intelligence, of decryption, of interpretation—which we might call attempts to remove opacity and restore transparency. It is a successful act, because there is really something, that is, an interplanetary (or intersatellitary?) war going on behind the opaque surface of a tranquilized suburb. By having war as the *secretum* of his story, a war fought with missiles and the occasional thermonuclear warhead, Dick puts something in the picture that Horn has omitted, what we could call the source of all the conspiracy syndrome, or fad, or discourse: the Cold War.

Probably the years of the confrontation between the USA and the USSR (1947–91, a period that uncoincidentally encompasses the whole of Dick's oeuvre) were the moment in which secrecy reached its climax, and we may suspect that the "secrecy effect" that is so widespread today

---

7   The idea that the conspiracist discourse can be explained away as a mere symptom of a mental condition is contested by Birchall and Knight (2023, 3). It is interesting that their exhaustive analysis of the contexts of (current) conspiracy theories shows how they are particularly popular among the right-wing libertarians and Donald Trump supporters, while the countercultural variety of the conspiracist discourse that was common in the 1960s–70s had a strong anti-authoritarian and mostly leftist character—one cannot help thinking of the whole oeuvre of Thomas Pynchon as a good example of this trend.

is a belated side effect of the policies of those years—an effect, by the way, which the current Ukrainian crisis may revive. Dick often pictured the Cold War and its feared outcome, World War III, in his fiction: *Dr Bloodmoney* comes to mind, but also *The Penultimate Truth*, and such short stories as "Exhibit Piece" or "Faith of Our Fathers." However, it is *The Simulacra* (1964) that presents us with a society based on secrets, discriminating between those in the know and those who do not have a clue; to paraphrase Horn, the United States of Europe and America (USEA)[8] imagined by Dick are a country in which "there is *officially* something."

In this novel the population is divided in two formally defined groups: the *Ge* elite, i.e., the *Geheimnisträger*, German for "bearers of the secret," and a vast majority of citizens who lack the "esoteric" knowledge of state secrets and are thus mere "bearers of orders" (from the ruling elite): the *Befehlträger*, shortened as *Be* (Dick 1983, 37), on the other hand. Those who do not belong to the privileged elite are well aware that the *Ges* share very important secrets.[9] They would like to access those forbidden truths, whatever they may be, and this leads to such grotesque scenes as the following:

> "Must be a change in govpol," the woman on Ian's left said.
> "'Govpol,'" the man echoed, puzzled.
> "A *Ge* term," the woman said haughtily. "Government policy." [. . .]
> "I knew a *Ge* term once," Ian said. [. . .] "The term I knew [. . .] was *allost*."
> "What's 'allost' mean?" the man beside him asked.
> "All's lost," Ian said. (145)

Obviously, if "govpol" or "allost" really were "*Ge* terms," neither the woman nor Ian Duncan, a low-level employee of a big multinational cartel (54), might be aware of their meaning or even their very existence. The *Bes*, however, know that "there is something"; the opacity of their social system is overt and tangible, a perfect example of Horn's secrecy effect. Moreover, it is knowledge to determine everybody's status in the

---

8   The USEA originate from the admission of West Germany to the USA as its fifty-first state, something that, though highly unrealistic, had a clear political meaning in the years of the Cold War; moreover, it hints at a contamination of the USA with an imperialistic policy that is not so different from that of the Third Reich. Dick is here quite close to what a contemporary American writer, Thomas Pynchon, would suggest in his *Gravity's Rainbow* (1973).

9   Moreover, some books, such as an essay by C. Wright Mills (40), can only be read by the *Ges*—another form of opacity. Dick does not say which text by Mills is illegally read by one of the *Bes*, but one may suspect that it is *The Power Elite* (1956), given its subject.

USEA: secrets (real or bogus) are status symbols, and transparency, for the happy few who have achieved it, is power.

The two secrets that only the *Ge* know pertain to the summit of the USEA; that is, the president and the first lady, Nicole Thibodeaux. Their marriage is purely formal: Nicole has been the wife of all the presidents of the USEA (and will be the wife of the next), and she is unnaturally young and gorgeous, while the presidents (all of them German) are all elderly and decrepit. Nicole represents the real power, in that she is endowed with a crushing, subjugating charisma that relegates her husbands to an almost ancillary role. But the fundamental reason why Nicole is the actual ruler (and this is the first state secret owned by the *Ges*) is that President Kalbfleisch,[10] aka *der Alte* ("the old man"), is not a human being but a programmed android, or one of the simulacra of the title.

Hazel Pierce (1983, 125) has argued that "the secret which they [i.e., the *Ges*] bear is power and the tools with which to sustain that power": in fact, *der Alte* is just a tool, under control of Nicole and the *Ges*. Kalbfleisch, like its predecessors, is a simulacrum, that is, an image or a representation: a mass-media entity that lives only when it is on air, because as soon as the simulacrum is turned off, the TV cameras are shut off too. We might say that the android president of the USEA is an opaque surface that prevents transparency, so that the *Bes* cannot see who the real rulers are.

But there is a much more complex dynamic at work in this novel. It is not just a matter of having a denouement, a coup de théâtre that may propel the narrative; it is not just a matter of revealing what is the reality behind the appearance, to dissolve opacity and restore transparency, thus getting to some hidden albeit ultimate truth. Dick's novels do not work like the Matrix in the 1999 film of that title, notwithstanding the critical commonplace that the movies by the Wachowski sisters are somehow "Dickian." In *The Simulacra* truths are always penultimate, to paraphrase the title of another novel by Dick: they are provisional, temporary, soon to be unmasked as lies by another plot twist. We soon find out that the first lady, the woman who manages the mass-media apparatus, is just an actress impersonating a dead celebrity (the real Nicole Thibodeaux), like a double. Behind opacity there is not revelation but another opaque layer.

There is indeed a precession of simulacra (Baudrillard 1983) in this novel, because the denouements of *der Alte* and Nicole are not the only ones that take place in *The Simulacra*. Nicole admits that "there's a council that governs . . . I never see them" (Dick 1983,166), which summons her at a critical moment (195), that is, when both of the state secrets are

---

10 Ironically, the fake German surname of a fake president that is actually an android means "veal"—another example of Dick's deadpan humor, which plays an important role in this science-fictional novel of sociopolitical satire.

disclosed in the hectic finale, and the people of the USEA learn that its rulers (*der Alte* and Nicole) are bogus. She then finds out that the chairman (and puppeteer) of the secret council is Bertold Goltz (196), the leader of a militia, the Sons of Job, which has championed the cause of the *Bes* against the privileges of the *Ges* throughout the novel.

All in all, what we have is a semiotic process, a precession (or even procession) of simulacra—*der Alte* / NICOLE / THE COUNCIL / GOLTZ—in which each stage hides what comes immediately before; at the same time, each stage represents the one after it. It is a semiotic relation in its own right: each simulacrum is a layer of opacity hiding the person or group it nonetheless represents. From the point of view of characters *in* the novel and readers *of* the novel, each rung of the ladder is first a power figure, an agent in the complex political game of the novel, where opacity, as we have seen, structures society; then the characters and we readers realize that the power figure is just a simulacrum, a mere mouthpiece of the real power figure that is above (or behind) it (or she, or them). Every time opacity seems to dissolve, allowing for transparency, readers and characters run into a little lower opaque layer, to paraphrase once again Melville's Captain Ahab.

Once we have found out that the real policymaker, so to speak, is Bertold Goltz (196–99), however, we have *not* discovered a political bedrock of sorts that may sustain all of the system of power depicted by the novel. When we readers are finally told who the real ruler of the USEA is—and probably has been for a long time, thanks to time travel—he is almost immediately killed by Wilder Pembroke, an ambitious and ruthless police officer, and this is not just a plot twist Dick placed here merely for the sake of suspense. Analyzing another of his novels, *The Game-Players of Titan* (1963), written in the same period in which its author was busy with *The Simulacra*, I came to the conclusion that "his use of switches or shunts [i.e., plot twists] is not [. . .] mechanical and mindless—and not [. . .] easygoing, or simply easy. His is a difficult and sophisticated game" (Rossi 2012, 220). Dick's twists in the tale must be attentively interpreted. By showing us who is behind the opaque layer and immediately having him killed, Dick seems to suggest that the total transparency of a power structure is something we cannot really achieve. No wonder, then, that after the death of Goltz the whole USEA collapses in a devastating civil war which reads as a sort of final apocalypse[11] (with generous use of nuclear weapons), and there is nothing less transparent than a civil war, in which it may be often difficult to understand whose side the actors are on, and even what are the sides exactly.

---

11 A reading of *The Simulacra* as a political allegory, focusing on the increasing destruction of the social structure, can be found in Rossi (2002).

All in all, a reading of *The Simulacra* seems to run parallel to J. Hillis Miller's interpretation of Joseph Conrad's *Heart of Darkness* (1899). Also in Dick's novel, as we have seen, "when each veil is lifted [. . .] it uncovers only another veil, according to a paradox essential to the genre of the apocalypse. Apocalypse: the word means 'unveiling' in Greek" (Miller 2001, 117). One has to agree with the American critic that "these unveilings unveil not so much the truth behind as the act of unveiling itself, since no 'bottom' to the series is reached, no ultimate revelation given. Each scene is in a sense just as close and just as far away from the unnamable 'truth' behind it as any other" (118). But there is a remarkable difference between Conrad's and Dick's treatment of the act of unveiling: in *Heart of Darkness*, Miller correctly notices, "materials and personages of each episode vanish, never to return again except in Marlow's memory" (119), while in *The Simulacra* some characters die, as we have seen, but others persist, moving from one unveiling to the next, stubbornly surviving in the middle of increasing political chaos, until the end. What is common to the two novels, however, is the series of unveilings that propels the narrative; a succession of moments of transparency that are immediately obfuscated by a return of opacity.

Such an inexorable persistence (and prevalence) of opacity may be read as a commentary on politics, but it may also have a lot to do with the medium. We should never forget that Dick was a writer of fiction, not a political theorist—even though so much of his oeuvre lends itself to a political analysis and offers so many insights into late capitalism (as Fredric Jameson has taught us). Dick is a fiction writer who had to come to terms with the inherent obscurity of narratives, as it was theorized by Frank Kermode (1979, 144), as "secrecy considered as a property of all narrative, provided it is suitably attended to." We might consider Dick's "theological" phase—that is, his works of the 1970s and the early 1980s, especially the so-called VALIS Trilogy—as a frantic oscillation between revelation (e.g., the notorious 2-3-74 visions),[12] that is, transparency, and the subsequent anxious interpretation of what has been briefly revealed, struggling to overcome opacity. Besides, Dick himself kept rereading his novels, interpreting them in a relentless hunt for hidden—and often prophetic—meanings. A passage taken from one of his letters offers a good

12 This phrase refers to a series of visions that Dick had in February–March 1974, which are described in some of his letters and obsessively commented on and interpreted in *The Exegesis of Philip K. Dick* (2011)—a collection of fragmentary writings and notes through which Dick kept track, in a rather disordered fashion, of his relentless and sometimes anxious research for an ultimate truth behind those visions. Once again, this is a matter of opacity and transparency, only this time in a definitely metaphysical or religious dimension. A selection of these materials, commented on by a team of PKD experts, has been published in a nine-hundred-page hardbound edition.

example of his effort to access such meanings in his own 1982 novel *The Transmigration of Timothy Archer*:

> In looking over the three novels of the trilogy I can see how Christ becomes progressively more and more real, but only is truly there in the third and final novel, and even in that novel Christ only 'occurs' at the end. It is as if the disparate pieces that make Him up come together: a part of Angel, a part of Tim Archer, a part of the boy Bill Lundborg, a part taken from the Sufi teacher, Edgar Barefoot; no single part alone is Christ but when they join together they do form Christ, as if by an alchemical miracle. (Dick 2010, 179)

We might pursue the dialectics of transparency and opacity in Dick's writings by reading the *Exegesis*, which can be summarized as a gigantic effort to achieve an ultimate revelation that could explain a previous revelation (the 2-3-74 visions), an effort that was interrupted by the writer's death in 1982. This is nothing less than an attempt to dispel the opacity in his own works and his own life in order to achieve a final transparency. But this might reinforce the idea that such a dialectics subscribes to a naive (and Manichean) version of the opposition in which opacity is simply bad, threatening, or oppressive, while transparency is simply good, reassuring, or liberating. Moreover, this would abandon the politics of transparency and move toward a theology of opaqueness.

A text that is definitely more relevant to our discussion is Dick's 1977 novel *A Scanner Darkly*. This somber story of drug addiction in a dystopian setting[13] features two science-fictional devices that represent opacity and transparency, even though in a problematic fashion: the scramble suit and the holo-scanner. Both devices are used by an undercover narcotics agent, codename Fred, who has infiltrated a group of dropouts addicted to a fictional drug called Substance D. Fred is known as Bob Arctor by his brothers-in-drugs, but that is, of course, a fake identity—as is the name by which his colleagues know him. The problem is that even the police department may have been infiltrated by the drug traffickers (we are in a PKD novel, after all, and one written in the early 1970s, a paranoid time if there ever was one, owing to the Watergate scandal and other Nixonian conspiracies), so when the undercover agents meet their supervisors they wear the scramble suit, a device that is—from our specific point of view—a strange compound of opacity and transparency, of visibility and invisibility, as it

---

13 Though the idea of Dick as a dystopian writer has become a sort of critical commonplace, there are at least two of his novels that qualify as full-fledged dystopian narratives, one of them being *A Scanner Darkly*, the other *Radio Free Albemuth* (1985) (cf. Rossi 2014); *The Man in the High Castle* (1962) is a highly anomalous sort of dystopia, given its uchronic nature (Rossi 2014, 154).

consisted of a multifaceted quartz lens hooked to a miniaturized computer whose memory bank held up to a million and a half physiognomic fraction-representations of various people: men and women, children, with every variant encoded and then projected outward in all directions onto a superthin shroudlike membrane large enough to fit around an average human.

As the computer looped through its banks, it projected every conceivable eye color, hair color, shape and type of nose, formation of teeth, configuration of facial bone structure. [. . .] Just to make its scramble suit more effective, S. A. Powers [the inventor] programmed the computer to randomize the sequence of characteristics within each set.

[. . .] the wearer of a scramble suit was Everyman [. . .]. Hence, any description of him—or her—was meaningless. (Dick 1985c, 24–25)

This description of a fictional device may not be very consistent from a strictly scientific point of view, but it is revealing in terms of textual interpretation: here opacity is achieved by means of an excess of vision. Too many images turn a person into a "nebulous blur" (52), hiding the identity of police agents underneath too many identities. Once again, it is in the nature of power (and its repressive apparatus) to hide itself, in this case by an overload of images.

But the second device, the holo-scanner, seems to me to be more relevant to our discussion, as it *should* be an instrument of transparency. These devices, which are a kind of 3D camera, are installed in Bob's house to keep it under total surveillance twenty-four hours a day, even when Bob is not at home. The holo-scanners record what they see so that nothing and nobody may escape Bob's gaze. "I'll pretty well know," he muses, "what everyone in my house is doing and when they do it and probably even why, myself included" (83). Such a sophisticated surveillance apparatus is needed because opacity reigns on the drug scene—or, to put it in Dick's own words, murkiness: "The drug world was a murky world for everyone anyhow" (82). It is not just a matter of identifying who the pushers and the dealers are; it is a question of survival:

> What an undercover narcotics agent fears most is [. . .] that he will be slipped a great hit of some psychedelic that will roll an endless horror feature film in his head for the remainder of his life, or that he will be shot up with a mex hit, half heroin and half Substance D, or both the above plus a poison such as strychnine. (81)

If this is the problem tormenting Bob Arctor, it is quite clear that the whole situation is somewhat turned upside down. Here opacity does not protect those in power (whoever they may be) from the gaze of the oppressed; instead, it is an obstacle that hinders the gaze of the law-enforcing surveillance apparatus, and it is the cops who need transparency. This is the "society of control" theorized by Byung-Chul Han (2015, 45–49), and also Jeremy Gilbert's "age of endless disclosure" (2007, 23).

It is a radical inversion of what we have found so far, and it may not be as clean-cut as one might wish: not all the drug-addicts who share Bob's house can be considered as oppressed—Barris is a cold-blooded and scheming villain, one of the most repellent Dick ever portrayed. But Freck and Luckman qualify as real dropouts (we might see them as belonging to the lumpenproletariat), and behind these near-future drug addicts one may easily see the hippies of the 1960s turned junkies in the 1970s—the kind of people who hung out at Dick's own house in San Rafael.[14] As for Bob Arctor, we may sympathize with him, but he is an undercover narc belonging to a repressive organization: Dick's identification with a policeman (and the police) should be understood by placing it in the context of his troubled life in the 1970s, beset by amphetamine addiction, failed marriages, and financial and health problems. *A Scanner Darkly* was meant to be an antidrug novel (Rossi 2014, 162–63), something Dick repeatedly stated in several letters, but this must be understood as his highly emotional reaction to his painful past of drug addict and (maybe) small-time pusher. Moreover, Dick was afraid of being under surveillance by the police or the FBI (or even agents of the Warsaw Pact), so that the declared antidrug stance of his novel was probably meant to prove that he had nothing more to do with the drug scene.

Whatever reasons Dick had to adopt such a stance, one thing is clear: in this novel, transparency is no longer something to be desired. The total surveillance ensured by holo-scanners makes one think of the panopticon discussed by Michel Foucault in his *Discipline and Punish* (1975): Jeremy Bentham's project of a "utopian" penitentiary was also based on total transparency, which would have allowed a limited number of jailers to control a much higher number of inmates. Of course, transparency from above (that is, favoring the gaze of the repressive apparatus) also bears relation to the telescreens George Orwell imagined in every Outer Party member's flat in *Nineteen Eighty-Four* (1949); and Bob Arctor's "transparent" house in Dick's novel seems to anticipate the house-studio of the *Big Brother* television franchise. In all such examples, what is dissolved by transparency is that particular form of opacity we call "privacy," or, according to the more up-to-date theoretical reflection on the ambiguities and dangers of a simplistic, one-sided view of transparency, the "right to opacity" (Birchall 2021, 165). Even Bob is not reassured by the relentless surveillance, as we can see in this disquieting moment of clarity:

---

14 The relationship between the novel and the counterculture is discussed in Rossi (2014).

"Alone—no one but him in the house. Untrue! Him and the scanners, insidious and invisible, that watched him and recorded. Everything he did. Everything he uttered" (Dick 1985c, 171).

Does Dick endorse the transparency that allows a repressive apparatus to enter anyone's private space in any moment? Notwithstanding his April 21, 1973, letter to the Department of Justice in which he declares that "the central character in the novel is an undercover narcotics agent, and he is what we call a sympathetic protagonist," and says he wants "to dedicate the novel to Attorney General Kleindienst" (Dick 1993, 225), there are good reasons to doubt that position. The dire fate of Bob Arctor, turned into a sort of zombie by Substance D, may lead us readers to empathize with him, but it is then difficult to also empathize with the police who fine him because he "knowingly and willingly took an addictive drug, brain destructive and disorienting" (Dick 1985c, 208). Bob is then used to infiltrate New-Path, a drug rehabilitation community suspected of actually being one of the main producers of Substance D, because only a genuine burned-out doper could be admitted to the program. Bob may be "a very good person" (208), as even Hank, his superior at police headquarters, tells him, but the police who use him as a pawn do not seem to be. All in all, Dick seems to anticipate Birchall's (2021, 148), questioning of the positive value of transparency and her proposal of a "right to secrecy" (derived from Edouard Glissant's original use of the concept), which counters the rhetoric of transparency adopted by the institutional left; she maintains that "it is important to recognize the way in which secrecy and opacity are [. . .] providing cover in order to [. . .] circumvent [. . .] the surveillance capacity of the state" (157).[15]

Moreover, the people Bob should protect by identifying and arresting drug traffickers—the squares, so to speak—are not depicted in a very sympathetic way in the novel. When Bob has to lecture the members of the Anaheim Lions Club in the second chapter, the audience is defined a "bubblehead gathering" (Dick 1985c, 25), and the undercover agent only expects "asshole questions and opaque stupidity" (26). Darko Suvin (2002, 377) argued that there is a basic confusion of values in the novel, because "if the drugs are supremely bad, then *the bad and grotesque police fighting it is in a way good*" (emphasis in the original); but the world of

15 There is a passage of Birchall's discourse that seems particularly relevant to our discussion of Dick's narratives. She argues that "secrecy (as anonymity, as obfuscation of the society of spectacle and retreat from information networks) again is positioned as that which makes something happen" (156). Of course, she does not comment on postmodernist fiction but on groups, movements, spaces of discussion, and maybe resistance in postmodernist societies, but it is remarkable that in Dick's fiction the alternance of transparency and secrecy, the procession of unveilings—the very presence of secrecy, so to say—does make a lot happen in diegetic terms.

"ordinary" people, those who do not use (illegal) drugs, is presented as something just as bad and grotesque, at least when seen from the point of view of the junkies. A representative of that world is Thelma Kornford,

> the dainty and elegant straight girl in her turtleneck sweater and bell-bottoms and trippy boobs who wanted [Bob and his friends] to murder a great harmless bug that in fact did good by wiping out mosquitoes [. . .] and when they saw what it was and explained, she had said words that became for them their parody evil-wall-motto, to be feared and despised:
> IF I HAD KNOWN IT WAS HARMLESS
> I WOULD HAVE KILLED IT MYSELF
>
> (Dick 1985, 88)

Bob's friend Jim Barris comments that "the rich never understand the value of life" (87), and this hints at a split in society that is not to be ascribed only to the use of drugs or to the absence thereof.

All in all, *A Scanner Darkly* is an ethically complex and sometimes ambiguous novel, where it is quite difficult to distinguish the oppressed from the oppressors, the victims from the victimizers, the good from the bad. We have mostly "obscure admixtures," to quote a phrase Dick (1987, 236) wrote in *The Man in the High Castle*—but this means that it is not only the world of drugs that is murky but that the whole society is far from transparent.[16] Yet, even in a much smaller social space, that of the house where Bob and his drug-addict pals spend their days, clarity of vision cannot always be achieved, holo-scanners notwithstanding.

There is a bewildering moment in which Bob, after having sex with the drug-addict Connie and falling asleep, wakes up and "turn[s] toward the girl beside him and s[ees] Donna Hawthorne" (Dick 1985c, 148). He sees the girl clearly; she has turned into another person, but then "by degrees she was Connie again, hatchet-faced, bleak-jawed, sunken, the gaunt face of the out-of-it junkie, Connie and not Donna; one girl, not the other" (149). The episode remains unexplained, and we might of course think that it is just a side effect of Substance D, which is slowly laying waste to Bob's brain. But when Bob, now in his Fred identity, watches the scene recorded by the holo-scanners,[17] "he noticed something he had not noticed. *That doesn't look like anybody else but Donna Hawthorne!*

---

16 To this one should add, as we have seen, the stupidity of the straights, which is described as "opaque" (26). Opacity seems to be found everywhere in the novel.

17 To understand what happens, one must know that now the dissociation of the two hemispheres of Bob/Fred's brain, brought about by Substance D, has progressed to such an extent that Fred is not aware, when he watches the footage produced by the holo-scanners, that he is Bob Arctor.

he thought. There in bed, in the sack with Arctor" (160). Bob rewinds the tape (Dick lived in an analog age, and this specimen of technological imagination belongs to it), plays it again, and

> Connie's hard features melted and faded into softness, and into Donna Hawthorne's face. [. . .] Again he ran the tape back, then forward; when he first came to the alteration in Connie's features he then stopped the transport, leaving the hologram filled with one freeze-frame.
> [. . .] one huge cube formed from the previous eight. A single nocturnal scene: Bob Arctor, unmoving, in his bed, the girl unmoving beside him.
> Standing, Fred walked into the holo-cube, into the three-dimension projection, and stood close to the bed to scrutinize the girl's face.
> Halfway between, he decided. Still half Connie; already half Donna. (160)

When Bob saw the transformation while it was taking place, we could explain it as a hallucination, something to be expected from a junkie whose brain is not functioning properly, but Dick has the scene replayed by a machine in a 3D projection. Fred first believes that the tape has been tampered with by an expert, because he is disconnected from what he has experienced when he was Bob and thinks that what he saw in the hologram is an episode of someone else's life, an event he did not take part in—yet, we know that this is not the case. Then Fred sees the moment when Bob wakes up and is surprised because it is Donna, not Connie, who is sleeping beside him. "*Arctor saw it too.* Woke up, saw it, stared, then gave up" (161; emphasis in the original)—the use of the third person when Fred is actually looking at himself as recorded by the holo-scanners seems to sanction the ultimate psychic split in his damaged brain, which we might even read as a psychiatric or neurological opacity obscuring the hi-tech transparency provided by the scanner.

This scene gives the metamorphosis a sort of fictional objectivity, but it leaves us uncertain about its meaning, inasmuch as Dick doesn't offer any explanation in the following pages. Do holo-scanners hallucinate too, in Dick's world? Or does this supernatural transformation hint at a different reality behind what we all see? The title of the novel, *A Scanner Darkly*, is a paraphrase of a famous passage in Paul's 1 Corinthians 13:12: "For now we see through a glass, darkly; but then face to face: now I know in part; but then shall I know even as also I am known."[18] Both "glass" and "scanner" suggest transparency, while "darkly" is a rough

---

18   This is taken from the Authorised Version, aka the King James Bible, the one Dick quoted. Other translations of Paul's epistles are different: e.g., "Now

equivalent of "opaquely"; hence, the title itself blends the two polarities of our discourse in a sort of textual short circuit. One cannot deny that this novel is interspersed with religious allusions and images, as Dick was moving toward his religious phase (culminating in the second and third parts of the VALIS Trilogy, *The Divine Invasion* [1981] and *The Transmigration of Timothy Archer* [1982]), and the metamorphosis of the sleeping girl is, after all, a sort of transubstantiation, like the host turning into Christ's flesh and blood.[19]

What is relevant to our discussion, however, is the idea that total transparency is unavailable; that even holo-scanners may record inexplicable events; that there is an inherent opacity (or secrecy, to put it in Kermode's terms) in narratives, arguably mirroring an ineradicable opacity of the world. On the one hand, this should mean that a society of total control cannot be really achieved; on the other hand, this also excludes the possibility of building a perfectly transparent state. The world in which we must live is, then, neither Orwell's Oceania nor Utopia—it is, fortunately or unfortunately, a middle space in which transparency is limited, and opacity always returns.

---

we see but a poor reflection as in a mirror" in the New International Version, or "What we see now is like a dim image in a mirror" in the Good News Bible.

19 One of Dick's most important novels, *The Three Stigmata of Palmer Eldritch* (1964), is based on a blasphemous form of Eucharist, so we know for sure that Dick was familiar with that sacrament—besides, one of his best friends was the Episcopalian bishop Jim Pike.

Works Cited

Baudrillard, Jean. 1983. *Simulations*. Los Angeles: Semiotext(e).
Birchall, Clare. 2021. *Radical Secrecy: The Ends of Transparency in Datafied America*. Minneapolis: University of Minnesota Press.
Birchall, Clare, and Peter Knight. 2023. *Conspiracy Theory in the Time of Covid-19*. New York: Routledge.
Butler, Andrew M. 2007. *Philip K. Dick*. Harpenden, UK: Pocket Essentials.
Conrad, Joseph. 1899. "The Heart of Darkness." *Blackwood's Magazine* 165 (February): 164–460; (March): 460–621; (April): 620–781.
Dick, Philip Kindred. 1954. "Exhibit Piece." *If: Worlds of Science Fiction* (August): 63–101.
———. 1963. *The Game-Players of Titan*. New York: Ace.
———. 1964a. *The Penultimate Truth*. New York: Belmont.
———. 1964b. *The Three Stigmata of Palmer Eldritch*. New York: Doubleday.
———. 1965. *Dr. Bloodmoney; or, How We Got Along after the Bomb*. New York: Ace.
———. 1967. "Faith of Our Fathers." In *Dangerous Visions*, edited by Harlan Ellison, 173–205. New York: Doubleday.
———. 1981. *The Divine Invasion*. New York: Timescape.
———. 1982. *The Transmigration of Timothy Archer*. New York: Timescape.
———. 1983. *The Simulacra*. London: Methuen. First published 1964.
———. 1985a. *The Cosmic Puppets*. London: Granada. First published 1957.
———. 1985b. *Radio Free Albemuth*. New York: Arbor House.
———. 1985c. *A Scanner Darkly*. London: Granada. First published 1977.
———. 1987. *The Man in the High Castle*. Harmondsworth, UK: Penguin. First published 1962.
———. 1987. *Puttering About in a Small Land*. London: Grafton. First published 1985.
———. 1993. *The Selected Letters of Philip K. Dick*. Vol. 2: *1972–1973*. Introduction by Dennis Etchison. Novato, CA: Underwood-Miller.
———. 2010. *The Selected Letters of Philip K. Dick*. Vol. 6: *1980–1981*. Edited by Don Heron. Novato, CA: Underwood-Miller.
———. 2011. *The Exegesis of Philip K. Dick*. Edited by Jonathan Lethem and Pamela Jackson. New York: Houghton Mifflin Harcourt.
Emerson, Ralph Waldo. 1968. "Nature." In *The Selected Writings of Ralph Waldo Emerson*, edited by Brooks Atkinson, 1–42. New York: The Modern Library. First published 1836.
Foucault, Michel. 1979. *Discipline and Punish: The Birth of the Prison*. Translated by Alan Sheridan. New York: Vintage.
Gilbert, Jeremy. 2007. "Public Secrets. 'Being-with' in an era of perpetual disclosure." *Cultural Studies* 21, no. 1 (January): 22–41. https://doi:10.1080/09502380601046923.
Han, Byung-Chul. 2015. *The Transparency Society*. Translated by Eric Butler. Stanford, CA: Stanford Briefs.

Horn, Eva. 2011. "Logics of Political Secrecy." *Theory, Culture & Society* 28, no. 7–8: 103–22.
Kermode, Frank. 1979. *The Genesis of Secrecy: On the Interpretation of Narrative*. Cambridge, MA: Harvard University Press.
Melville, Herman. 1851. *Moby-Dick; or, The Whale*. New York: Harper & Brothers.
Miller, J. Hillis. 2001. *Others*. Princeton, NJ: Princeton University Press.
Orwell, George. 1949. *Nineteen Eighty-Four: A Novel*. New York: Harcourt Brace.
Pierce, Hazel. 1983. "Philip K. Dick's Political Dreams." In *Philip K. Dick*, edited by Joseph D. Olander and Martin Harry Greenberg, 105–36. New York: Taplinger.
Pynchon, Thomas. 1973. *Gravity's Rainbow*. New York: Viking.
Robbe-Grillet, Alain. 1963. *Pour un Noveau Roman*. Paris: Les Editions de Minuit.
Rossi, Umberto. 2002. "The Great National Disaster: The Destruction of Imperial America in P. K. Dick's *The Simulacra*." *RSA: Rivista di Studi Nord Americani* 13: 22–39.
———. 2011. *The Twisted Worlds of Philip K. Dick: A Reading of Twenty Ontologically Uncertain Novels*. Jefferson, NC: McFarland.
———. 2012. "The Shunts in the Tale: The Narrative Architecture of Philip K. Dick's VALIS." *Science Fiction Studies* 39, no. 2 (July): 243–61.
———. 2014. "Philip K. Dick's Unconventional Dystopias: From *Radio Free Albemuth* to *A Scanner Darkly*." *Extrapolation* 55, no. 2 (March): 153–72.
Slusser, George. 1992. "History, Historicity, Story." In *On Philip K. Dick: 40 Articles from "Science-Fiction Studies.*" Edited by R. D. Mullen et al., 199–222. Terre Haute, IN: SF-TH Inc.
Suvin, Darko. 2002. "Goodbye and Hello: Differentiating within the Later P. K. Dick." *Extrapolation* 43, no. 4 (Winter): 368–97.

6: "Angrier than Thou": Secrecy vs. Exposure in Philip Roth's *I Married a Communist*

Cristina Chevereșan

1. Introduction

PHILIP ROTH'S *I Married a Communist* (1998), the second novel in the author's American Trilogy,[1] is at first sight a typical rise-and-fall narrative, projected against the turbulent background of the mid-twentieth-century United States. Protagonist Ira Ringold's controversial trajectory, reconstructed via multiple recollections, is based on and ruined by secrecy, as it unfolds spectacularly between acting and (Communist) activism. The individual and the nation are subjected to parallel examinations, as their destinies are interconnected in this multilayered story of McCarthyism and its discontents. Roth interrogates the essential, democratic values of America in the context of the postwar anti-Communist frenzy, the main vehicle of the investigation being a protagonist who is destroyed by political belief and personal ambition.

Published long before the issue of transparency had become a topic of social and academic discussion and analytical concern, Roth's book relies on the interplay between secrecy and disclosure as its red thread—and threat!—and its propelling mechanism. The reader discovers the major events and dark secrets of Ira's life in retrospect as they are recollected by his brother Murray. These are, in turn, given narrative form by Murray's friend, Nathan Zuckerman, thus constituting the text we are reading. The boundaries between public and private dissolve as Ira grows into a full-fledged character: from his active engagement in Communist propaganda and the web of convoluted lies he uses to disguise it to the suspicion and repression his sympathies subject his circle of friends and relatives to, everything seems to be constantly shifting in a vicious circle of surveillance and subversion.

---

[1] The novel was preceded by *American Pastoral* in 1997 and followed by *The Human Stain* in 2000.

After a plethora of readings by other scholars that have proposed biographical, historical, and narratological interpretations of the text, my particular interest is in the novel's constant toying with dichotomies that prove challenging and, eventually, flawed, if not entirely treacherous: public vs. private, concealed vs. shared, individual vs. communal, moral vs. immoral or amoral. I will, therefore, conduct a series of close readings of the novel that are meant to prove how relevant some of the major public concerns and political strategies of the depicted 1950s still are and how the novel's exploration of ideological exaggeration and manipulation relates to present-day approaches to issues of trust, secrecy, and transparency.

The fear of exposure and its consequences is ubiquitous in *I Married a Communist*, and it drives the plot as well as the characters' obsessive quests for identity. Dissimulation, impersonation, defamation, betrayal (disguised as patriotism), and camouflage are framed by both ideological determinations and the inherent weaknesses of human nature. As Ira becomes a public person, susceptible to the harshness of public opinion, the sense that he has privacy and that it protects him disappears. The situation is further complicated by his political beliefs, which trigger scrutiny by the House Un-American Activities Committee (HUAC). The hearings Roth portrays capture the national slide from the democratic ideal of privacy for individuals and openness in the public sphere toward the totalitarian nuances of a regime that deprives the individual of privacy, while nevertheless promoting secrecy and conspiracy theories in the public sphere.

As Roth biographer Ira Nadel (2011, 136) puts it, "the novel is an expression of Roth's anger at the abuses of zealous anticommunism and fear in postwar America. Ira's confused and dislocated life parallels the confused and dislocated life of the country, susceptible to jingoism and propaganda." While a reading that takes into account the sociohistorical circumstances of the era Roth examines is highly relevant and will be provided in what follows, it is also interesting to note how the author observes America's publicity-making institutions, from radio, theater, and cinema to the almighty press. They promote transparency *avant-la-lettre* and play a significant part in the making and unmaking of public figures, whose trajectories are strictly regulated by social norms and expectations, otherwise being castigated as unconventional. At the same time, the postmodernist nature of this complex Rothian narrative, which constructs and deconstructs mythos and ethos via successive memories, indirect and incomplete testimonials, and satirical and ironical commentaries, can be interpreted as provocative resistance to any complete and ultimate decoding of the given plot.

Thus, my study of (fictional) secrecy aims to analyze *I Married a Communist* through multiple lenses, taking into account several aspects:

the historical period that it illustrates and the ideological underpinnings of that period; the protagonists'—including the narrator's—histrionic actions and rhetoric; and, last but not least, Roth's textual dissidence, his incessant metatextual meditations, and his employment of or escape from conventional form as he attempts to convey complex meaning. My claim is that the writer's critical discourse vis-à-vis unrealistic social conventions and their oftentimes devastating effects in terms of the gap they create between essences and appearances, on both individual and communal levels, builds on the ways in which the deliberate alternation of transparency and secrecy can be used as tool of manipulation and control.

2. Betrayal Everywhere

A good starting point for my analysis is Mark Neocleous's article "Privacy, Secrecy, Idiocy," in which he retraces some essential distinctions in the historical, political, and philosophical evolution of the notions he addresses. Discussing governance practices, diplomacy, and the modern state's rituals of power, Neocleous makes a series of valuable comments that may quite easily relate to the major and minor dramas in *I Married a Communist*.

> One of the features of the history of secrecy is that it has a peculiar relation to privacy. Where the Latin form of secrecy is *secretus* (to separate from, divide from), the Latin form of privacy is *privatus*, meaning "to free from." Historically, the notions were incredibly close. Samuel Johnson saw the two words as interchangeable, defining privacy as "state of being secret; secrecy" and secrecy as "privacy; state of being hidden" (Johnson, 1979 [1755]). At some point, however, the two words were drawn far enough apart to be treated separately: privacy became a good thing, secrecy became a bad thing. Or rather, the individual secrecy that constitutes the private sphere could be seen as a positive feature of social life, while secrecy in the political sphere smacked too much of sovereignty, a form of private power reminiscent of absolutism. Private secrecy was thought to guarantee the growth of democracy, while public secrecy was thought to pave the way for totalitarian dictatorship. (Neocleous 2002, 103)

Individual secrecy vs. political secrecy and the overlapping of the public and the private (within or without the context of the McCarthyist witch hunts) lie at the basis of Roth's novel and its inquiry into the fears and loathings of Americans in general, and its fictional characters in particular. Riding the turbulent waves of the confused and confusing postwar era, which entailed strategic and symbolical readjustments of values, as well as reconsiderations of discourse and policies, the text plunges into the intriguing mixture of pragmatism and indignation that has persistently dominated the US environment and that envelops all the three parts of Roth's American Trilogy. As such, it quite convincingly illustrates considerations such as Eva Horn's, who argues that

> today, secrecy is mostly dealt with in the form of the scandal: if political secrets are exposed or betrayed, the leakage will occur as a fundamental disturbance of political order. [. . .] Secret operations are not only an integral part of democratic policy, domestic or foreign; political secrets are also an obsession of the public sphere, an object of permanent suspicion and speculation and a source of frequent outrage and scandal. (104–5)

Given the predicament of Roth's situation when he conceived the novel (soon after the publication of his former wife, Clare Bloom's, memoir, *Leaving a Doll's House* [1996], which was unflattering to him), it is not particularly hard to understand how issues such as the aforementioned betrayal, exposure, subsequent opprobrium, and the complicated relationship between them gradually came to grasp the writer's artistic, not just personal attention. As pointed out by Claudia Roth Pierpont in her enlightening *Roth Unbound: A Writer and His Books*, stupefied by what he perceived as an unfair blow to his reputation, Roth did his best to channel his energies into his work and find a proper cultural and civilizational analogy to his own state of mind and complexity of feelings. As a connoisseur of both the intricacies of his native Newark, New Jersey, and their intertwinement with national history, he came to realize that what haunted him could, as a topic, find grander parallels and fuel higher interpretive aspirations:

> The late forties and fifties were Roth's era: he had started college in 1950, when Senator McCarthy produced his first public list of "Communists" in government; it was the first major public issue of Roth's adult life. During the Army—McCarthy hearings, in the spring of 1954, he rushed between his classes and the home of a teacher who owned a television, Bob Maurer, to watch McCarthy finally brought down. The issues had mattered to him then, and they mattered again now. His new subject was betrayal, public and private. (Pierpont 2013, 229–30)

Through the biographical lens Pierpont provides, it becomes evident that Roth identified in the McCarthy era, which he knew so well, a sort of objective correlative to his personal predicament at the moment of writing this novel. *I Married a Communist*, a highly political text, thus naturally unfolds against the notorious background of McCarthyism, which, as a historical phenomenon, provides an apposite framework for ideological debates on notions of trust and betrayal and functions as an excellent pretext for an extensive meditation on the tragedies that may arise from the perpetual oscillation between truth and subterfuge, fact and distortion, confession and machination. Ideology as an overarching frame suits Roth's purpose of focusing on the shortcomings of essentialization and pigeonholing, be they in the public or in the private realm, a distinction that, under the circumstances, was difficult to make.

3. Clandestinity, Dissimulation, Ambiguity

The main character, Ira Ringold, an uncontrollably emotional rather than a reasonable man, is the epitome of a social existence dominated by falsehoods and contradictions, which he either carefully camouflages or embraces as exemplary behavior. He is absorbed by his own uncompromising pose and oblivious to any other ideas or perspectives than the ones he grows to identify with, as taught by multiple master-influencers. His radicalism and shortsightedness are beyond redemption, as much as they are illustrative of the overall inflexibility and aggressiveness of sociopolitical clichés, on whichever side of the spectrum. The story of his fascinating rise and disappointing downfall is told by Nathan Zuckerman, who, as a child, had grown up in the proximity and under the direct influence of brothers Ira and Murray Ringold, the latter of whom was his high school teacher.

As an experienced teller and gatherer of stories, a trained listener, and an accomplished historian of the micro- and macro-layers of American existence, Nathan Zuckerman, one of Roth's prominent alter-ego narrators, relies on the old-age confessions of Murray Ringold (his main source of information and the principal narrator) to capture Ira's and his entourage's versions of self-creation, which destabilize the expectation of functional binary opposites. Interspersed with flashbacks from his own radical political education by Ira, a labor organizer and a Communist under cover, Zuckerman's narrative focuses on the former's early life as an ambitious, self-educated school dropout and goes on to revisit his marriage to former silent-movie star Eve Frame. The woman has her own secrets, which she keeps from her adoring audiences. Born Chava Fromkin in Brooklyn, she is a closet Jew who chooses to conceal her ethnic difference just as her husband does his ideological one: both resort to dissimulation to obliterate aspects of their identity they know might work to their disadvantage because of widespread bias.

While posing as something that she is not in order to meet sociocultural expectations of success and respectability, she knows the dangers of secrecy from within. After the stormy dissolution of her marriage to the womanizing and deceitful Ira, she publishes "I Married a Communist" as the memoir that sets the record straight and casts her in a new popular role as America's savior from the Red Scare. Toying with public perception and using various masks to achieve social acceptance makes her and Ira similar in nature: they always strive to choose the personally profitable option, even if it contradicts reality, which they can—and do—conveniently alter in their narratives.

As Philipp Loeffler (2015, 602) points out about how such practices function in the enlarged context of the novel, "*I Married a Communist* portrays the Cold War conflicts as an ideological zero-sum game that trivializes identity issues in light of the more important question of whether one has picked the correct political option." At a highly politicized moment in American history, Ira unquestioningly interprets his Americanness as the freedom to virulently contest anything he disagrees with. Predictably, such a rigid worldview, devoid of tolerance and cultural pluralism, fails, just as the embittered and disconcerted characters eventually do.

As per his experimental usual, Roth complicates the picture even when it seems rather flat (which is difficult to avoid, since Ira is unimaginative and lacks the capability of genuine transformation). While the plot and structure of the novel have sometimes been viewed as more conventional than those of more experimental works by the same author, a careful close reading reveals the poise and significance of this book, which only mimics the alleged straightforwardness of the American "Age of Conformity." The spectacle of Ira Ringold's life unfolds before the hungry eyes of a society that, in the name of transparency, honesty, and straightforward public behavior, ruthlessly invades private spaces. Simultaneously, Ira, who poses as a model of directness, loyalty, and undeterred morality, not only lies about his clear Communist affiliations and affinities but even eventually turns out to be a murderer ("Ira killed a guy when he was sixteen," Murray reveals at the end of the novel [Roth 1998, 298], recalling the episode in which his young brother retaliated against an antisemitic attacker). The interplay of depths and surfaces, fact and fiction, event and retribution multiplies to the point where betrayed and betrayer are merely irrelevant cogs in a mechanism wherein knowledge equals power.

Having started at the bottom like many working-class American heroes, Ira Ringold makes his way to the top. He morphs into Iron Rinn, the radio star; marries a woman who seems the exact opposite of his declared ideals of social justice, balance, modesty; and engages in a lifestyle of privilege he would otherwise condemn. By doing so, he becomes the communal property of a society that commodifies and consumes its members out of a futile voyeurism that invests any claims of transparency with negative connotations. Once a celebrity, anyone is exposed to relentless public curiosity. The reader gets insight into Zuckerman's mother's mahjong club, for instance, where members are obsessively preoccupied with the private lives of the VIPs: "What do they wear? What do they eat? What do they say while they eat? What is it like there? It is spectacular" (22). Such trivial questions are the direct result of the interest stirred by the tabloid press the otherwise serious and respectable Mrs. Ringold reads furtively at the beauty parlor: although not commendable, gossip is now a national sport, and the craving for intimate details includes but also far surpasses the political realm. This seems the beginning of a time of public objectification and display, which only grows and deepens in the twenty-first century. As pointed out by Jeremy Gilbert (2007, 22–23),

> We live in an age of endless disclosure. The "private" lives of the famous, the would-be famous and the powerful constitute some of the main objects of mediated display and discussion today: the very substance of our culture. [. . .] At such a time it might seem that there are no secrets. Or, it might seem, conversely, that secrets are all there are.

Even though Gilbert's musing concerns the 2000s and the anxieties of contemporary critical thinkers as to the alleged development of a control society based on ubiquitous surveillance and excessive public exposure via social media, the essence of the matter remains virtually unchanged since the 1950s: radio, television, newspaper, and advertising businesses influence the shaping of the standard imaginary of the American cultural imagination. This generalized process is what drives Roth's plot: much of the tension behind it would not exist without the pressure of public opinion and the ominous prospect of parading the private in the public square.

Boundaries are, however, blurred by Roth, and responsibilities are shared by and among his protagonists as the victims themselves engage in dissimulation and overexposure alike. The conventions of social acceptability are simultaneously defied and obeyed by Ira and his circle: as their identities and life stories prove manifold, incongruities and inadequacies become inevitable. Murray relevantly comments upon his first encounter with Eve when Ira introduces her at the beginning of their relationship: "He doesn't know who she is because, to be honest, nobody would have right off. Nobody could have. In society, Eve was invisible behind the disguise of all that civility" (Roth 1998, 56). What the novel does, gradually, is to make the invisible sides of the long-departed characters explicit in a narrative present that is placed after the disclosure and analysis might have still caused them any personal harm.

This approach is enabled by an apparently generalized game of masks and surfaces. Just as Ira, upon questioning by Nathan's father, refuses to admit his Communist ties despite his expressed sympathies, Eve does everything in her power, on- and offstage, to distract from her own burden: her Jewish roots. Ironically, Chava Fromkin, the attentively hidden, self-hating Jew, is the one to oust her ideologically inadequate husband, which is hardly surprising for a union that appears wrong from the very beginning. As pointed out by Murray in his recollections of the ominous inception of the couple's relationship,

> The contradictions were indisputable. The personal openness and the Communist secrecy. The home life and the party. The need for a child, the desire for a family—should a party member with his aspirations care about having a child like that? Even to one's contradictions one might impose a limit. A guy from the streets marries an *artiste*? A guy in his thirties marries a woman in her forties with a big adult baby who is still living at home? The incompatibilities were endless. But then, that was the challenge. With Ira, the more that's wrong, the more to correct" (83).

Through the series of rhetorical questions in this passage, Roth captures Ira's torment of constant wondering about making the right ethical choices by community standards, alongside the inconsistency and the anxiety triggered by moral codes that appear strict but, in fact, abound in ambiguity.

4. Private Morality vs. Public Good

If people are judged based on membership in certain groups defined by race, ethnicity, politics, class, etc., being included or being excluded become concerns and reasons for dissimulation. Whenever secrecy guarantees the preservation of a convenient status quo—Ira's and Eve's fabricated personas and flawless lives are but socially convenient surfaces—the potential for foul play is ever present and forever tempting, as shown by such characters, who are not evil or ill-meaning per se yet are prone to constructing identities in their own interest. *I Married a Communist* is set at a particularly dangerous historical moment in which the logic of the state and the logic of the people are in danger of coalescing, confused by nefarious public discourses that endanger the very notion of national stability. The tension between personal morality and public good is central to the novel as it foregrounds successive layers of hypocritical behavior and continuously circles from the general to the particular and back again, around the trust-betrayal binary.

Speaking about the "transparency society" from a present-day point of view, philosopher Byung-Chul Han (2015, 48) argues that while any healthy society needs to rely upon a set of commonly shared truths and values in order to function efficiently, the insistence on transparency as prerequisite proof of trustworthiness may indicate or even trigger an essential lack of confidence in morality and good intentions as unquestionable social givens.

> Instead of affirming that "transparency creates trust," one should instead say, "transparency dismantles trust." The demand for transparency grows loud precisely when trust no longer prevails. In a society based on trust, no intrusive demand for transparency would surface. The society of transparency is a society of mistrust and suspicion; it relies on control because of the vanishing confidence. Strident calls for transparency point to the simple fact that the moral foundation of society has grown faulty, that moral values such as honesty and uprightness are losing their meaning more and more. As the new social imperative, transparency is taking the place of a moral instance that would break new ground.

While Han's view openly challenges the idea that calls for transparency are, in fact, meant to create trust, it may be seen as rather extending a nostalgic projection toward an idealized past. "Retrotopia," as conceptualized by Zygmunt Bauman (2017), perfectly encompasses the atmosphere in Roth's novel: the cracks in such a system as the one described above, where values and morality are constantly relativized, pressure to conform is exerted, and suspicion is generalized, are laid bare by Murray Ringold's own story. An enthusiastic teacher who is always striving for communal good, he suffers the consequences of his brother's blacklisting. Unlike Ira, he is not guilty of any irreverent or subversive activities, as he rather enjoys the kind of anonymity that allows him to contribute civically without stepping into the spotlight: "I was never interested like he [Ira] was in the fate of the world. I was more interested, from a professional point of view, in the fate of the community. My concern was not even so much political as economic and I would say sociological, in terms of working conditions, in terms of the status of teachers in the city of Newark" (Roth 1998, 12).

Yet, by way of association with his close relative, he loses his job (as Nathan will lose a Fulbright grant). He treasures loyalty and finds the hypocritical behavior of HUAC's representatives—of which he offers ample examples—just as morally questionable as his brother's activist shenanigans. Therefore, he refuses collaboration with his inquisitors. Via the example of this rather improbable, inherently invisible hero-narrator, whose aim is to preserve ordinariness and escape the impassioned battles of the public arena while accomplishing what he believes to be his civic duty, Roth adds a range of subtler nuances to the main plot and subject matter. Ira Nadel (2011, 136) succinctly and efficiently outlines the twisted and perverse nature of the kind of public discourse that is foregrounded in the novel, which deliberately blurs the boundaries between fact and fabrication. Under its influence, betrayal itself proves multifaceted in Roth's book, as it extends from the realm of political propaganda and pretense to that of interpersonal relations:

> Ironically, if not tragically, America has become a country feeding itself on betrayal, and Roth writes this novel to protest. The paradox is that in America between 1946 and 1956, betrayal was a patriotic act but one that could lead to false charges of treason and possibly capital punishment. As countries such as the Soviet Union and China betrayed America in the cold war, so, too, did Americans betray Americans, as Eve did to Ira by exposing his personal diary and political sympathies. But he, in turn, might be thought to have betrayed his listeners: Iron Rinn was a Communist, not an American hero. The truth became translated into a lie. The American way became one of accusation, threat, and punishment.

Such a perceptive take on the novel's major critical concerns emphasizes its preoccupation with the nature of truth as the pillar of both democratic societies and solid human relations alike, as well as its layered exploration of what the imperative of total transparency may signify and engender, in public and private circumstances. Roth's favorite device in construing his grand narrative proves to be the interlacing of micro- and macro-histories to address his own preoccupation with the patterns of doubt, frustration, anger, and disappointment, brought about by excesses of idealism or conformism, and the manifold manifestations of betrayal. Duplicity, deception, trickery, infidelity, fraud, sellout, disloyalty, faithlessness: there seems to be a fictional, situational equivalent to almost every semantic nuance of the synonyms to the key term, and Roth writes as if to provide as many plausible case studies as possible.

In this sense, it is not just the principal actors who are noteworthy as they become entangled in an "American Way" predicated on double standards. During Murray's questionings by the House Un-American Activities Committee, former gossip columnist and now Congressman Bryden Grant, for instance, proves to be a perfect example of a representative of power and, supposedly, justice, whose public behavior is presented as influenced by private instances and biased judgment. "To Ira, Grant was the incarnation of pampered privilege [. . .] Grant's every gesture made him sick and his politics he abhorred" (Roth 1998, 8), says Murray in the beginning of his retrospective narrative, as he tries to explain the details of his interrogation and dismissal by HUAC. To throw additional light on Ira's contempt for Bryden, he recalls how the latter had started out writing a column called "Grant's Grapevine," where he spread gossip about Broadway and Hollywood, "with a dollop of Eleanor Roosevelt-defiling thrown in. That's how Grant's public service career began" (8).

Murray is particularly vitriolic in his irony about how alleged transparency is used as a vehicle for self-promotion. He mentions how, via the ruthless exposure of the private affairs of public figures (mostly political opponents), Bryden "nearly ended as Nixon's White House chief of staff" (9). As recorded on the infamous White House tapes, he was praised by the president for his "motto for how to handle the administration's enemies: 'Destroy them in the press'" (9). It is, therefore, hardly surprising that Ira's sense of justice and rebellion against a system that validates libel and intrusion in the name of noble transparency should be offended. Murray recalls a party in Manhattan where Bryden and Ira were both present with their wives: Ira caused a scene, publicly insulting Grant, and, according to him, Bryden's lifelong vendetta against him began.

As we find out from Murray's aggrieved version of his HUAC hearings, revenge comes indirectly, later, when an ominously smiling Congressman Grant makes an appearance in Newark in the name of the committee, claiming that his intention is to "clear" Murray's name.

It is at this point early in the novel when, under the guise of reason and civility, Murray encounters the very embodiment of the opposite: Grant's leadership and vision boil down to reductionist slogans such as "The time has come to be an American or not an American" (11). Described as one of Nixon's favorites, this hypocritical figure is—not accidentally—connected to the rhetoric of disclosure in more ways than one. Focusing on the illusory greatness of the world of make-believe instead of on the art and effort behind the entertainment industry, exploiting its potential for scandal and blackmail, he began a career as a sensationalist columnist that was to turn him into a representative of the state.

The very title of his column indicates clandestinity and illicit access to private information, subsequently shared with large audiences against the targeted individuals' will, which raises serious issues in terms of morality. It does not seem surprising, then, that an individual with a penchant for scandal and slander should, if the opportunity presents itself, cross over to the political field, as the political scene of the 1950s that Roth depicts appears to be governed by the same techniques, machinations, and rhetoric as the popular media. Speaking about the beginnings of the modern state, Eva Horn (2011, 111–12) traces claims for transparency back to the eighteenth-century birth of the modern political subject in a context in which an enlightened critique of the state appeared only possible in sheltered, protected, and secretive spaces. She notes that as modern societies evolve, "the new space of the political that the citizens' emancipation brings about essentially relies on its claim for transparency, while at the same time applying moral standards from the private sphere to the political world. The public aspires to be the arbiter of public matters, as much as it is the ultimate instance of sovereignty and legitimacy." It is precisely upon the people's acquired right to have access to clear and accurate information concerning public matters that the social confusion Roth's novel illustrates is built. Horn stresses that simultaneously, modernity "discovers secrecy as an essential basis of society, a common good worth protecting. It sees privacy as a protective space that contains the secrets of individuals, souls, families, groups and associations" (112). There is, thus, a necessary distinction between public and private affairs that functional modern societies must and do draw in their calls for transparency. This is the line that the propaganda and hysteria of the McCarthy age in America intentionally blur, pushing (out)rage and confrontation to the fore of public debate, regardless of the nature of the debated issues.

It is from such circumstances that situations like the ones (semi)fictionalized by Roth arise, and they must be analyzed and understood in this type of challenging context. Thus, while not setting out to write a history of transparency, its social uses, purposes, and definition across the ages but, rather, opting to focus on a particular stage in the development of mid-twentieth-century Americana, Roth does choose to foreground issues meant to confound boundaries that are already fragile during an era of "indignant righteousness" (Roth 1998, 190). As Nadel (2011, 136) points out, "The harm, as well as the insidious consequences of the red-baiting, are set against principles of America's democratic past."

5. Secrecy vs. Intrusion

The novel's protagonist, Ira Ringold, ditchdigger turned radio star in the 1940s and enemy of the American people in the second Red Scare of the 1950s, evolves in a United States environment still recovering from the traumas of the Second World War and struggling to work through them through coping mechanisms at both individual and communal levels. While the management of public affairs has, naturally, become a matter of general interest, the citizens' particular interest in the political sphere and their desire to have access to information and a say in decision-making seem to have perpetuated a legitimization of intrusion. This goes beyond the careful identification of potential threats to society and ends up pervading the private sphere of domestic life, turning from rigorous circumspection to indecent scrutiny. The skepticism and mistrust such intrusion triggers are evident:

> Although secrecy, in the form of privacy, has become constitutive of society, secrecy in "public matters" is no longer acceptable. The modern moralization of politics and the secretiveness of the private sphere turn the political into the other of the private; nonetheless, the standards of the latter are applied when judging the former. As a result, political secrecy arouses both profound suspicion and intense curiosity. (Horn 2011, 112)

While Horn speaks about modern societies in general, the McCarthyist logic of accusation and persecution that determines the plausibility of plot and character arc in *I Married a Communist* exploits public suspicion, curiosity, and entitlement to access information. The nature and purpose of the information are, however, aspects that Roth can easily toy with, creating believable scenarios that range from the anecdotal to the dystopian (as it would later be the case in his 2004 novel *The Plot against America*). Although a minor character in *I Married a Communist*, Congressman Bryden Grant is presented as having deeply affected Ira's and Murray Ringold's trajectories. In his case, the political and the personal are intertwined, and the privacy of the home, heart, or intellect are sacrificed to the voraciousness of greed and complete lack of scruples.

By the end of the novel, the reader learns that apart from being an expression of personal revenge, Eve's defamatory memoir was, in fact, a means to somebody else's ends. Ghostwritten upon the Grants' initiative, featuring Bryden Grant's name on the jacket, it emerges as an utterly dishonest way of manipulating public opinion and suppressing meaningful political opposition, to ultimately secure Bryden a seat in the House of Representatives.

> "As told to" meant that the whole malevolent story was dreamed up by the Grants. And dreamed up not at all for Eve's sake, and not merely to destroy Ira, much as Katrina and Bryden hated his guts. The consequences for Ira were part of their fun but largely beside the point. The Grants dreamed it all up for Bryden to ride his way into the House on the issue of communism in broadcasting. (Roth 1998, 273)

It is in such interstices of meaning and opinion, in between cynical rumor and propagandist conspiracies, that Roth places his meditation upon the frailty and fickleness of human nature, as well as upon the advantages, disadvantages, and meandrous pathways of transparency, from asset to threat. Bitter humor accompanies his exploration of perversity and perversion: while Ira relishes his youthful performances as the admirably heroic Abraham Lincoln and contemplates himself as a similar consciousness and voice of the American nation, "a grand irony underlies Ira's attempts at ideological purity. At the same time he is espousing political certainty, he is living a life that betrays ambiguity. His communist rhetoric and bourgeois lifestyle certainly do not mesh" (Royal 2005, 197).

The bourgeois lifestyle is inextricably linked to the Gentile universe that his wife, Eve Frame, builds for herself and her family, indulging in a warm utopia of integration. With the innate histrionic skills that recommend her as a successful professional actress, she can also easily impersonate a non-Jewish self, according to the logic of racial passing that Roth has also featured in other writings, such as *The Human Stain* (2000). But her own antisemitism, her insistent resentment of any trace of Jewishness, and her obsession with "deJewing" (Roth 1998, 158) herself make Murray comment on the gravity of her pretense. As it gains weight and traction, it turns from a socially inflicted wound into a moral deformity:

> "You're an American who doesn't want to be your parents' child? Fine. You don't want to be associated with Jews? Fine. You don't want anybody to know you were born Jewish, you want to disguise your passage into the world? You want to drop the problem and pretend you're somebody else? Fine. You've come to the right country. But you don't have to hate Jews into the bargain. You don't have to punch your way out of something by punching somebody else in the face. The cheap pleasures of Jew hating aren't necessary." (157–58)

Besides exposing the flaws of the nation of the American Dream, with its history of excluding and condemning entire groups of people, Murray's detached yet unmerciful description of Eve's performance as a Gentile woman anticipates her ending up mentally exhausted and embittered by a perpetually challenging part, no matter how publicly successful she might be. She sinks into a sociopolitical swamp that uses her talent and annihilates her consciousness: "Gossip as gospel, the national faith. [. . .] The show-trial aspect of McCarthy's patriotic crusade was merely its theatrical form" (284). By consciously making the choice to hide her Jewishness and pass while helping vilify Ira for his own secrets and thus playing along with the ubiquitous postwar paranoia, she aims for a social acceptability based on prejudice and arbitrariness, which she voluntarily embraces. Roth exposes the dishonesty of such an enterprise in the guise of stage directions from a most cynical director, which highlight once more the rift between private and public behavior and the role of transparency therein:

> If you want to be a real American Gentile aristocrat, you would, whether or not you felt it, pretend to great sympathy for the Jews. That would be the cunning way to do it. The point about being an intelligent, sophisticated aristocrat is that, unlike everyone else, you force yourself to overcome, or to appear to overcome, the contemptuous reaction to difference. You can still hate 'em in private if you have to. But not to be able to engage Jews easily, with good spirited ease, would morally compromise a true aristocrat. (159)

Roth's satirical portrayal of a society that feigns emancipation yet bathes in primitive bias and falsehood is evident and explicit. Playing along with the rules of a civilized, liberated, culturally and intellectually enlightened environment stands out as a duplicitous way of acknowledging the conventional norms of public behavior while flaunting them in the private sphere. It is yet another illustration of the public/private divide, as social identity is tailored to match others' assumptions about it and, consequently, oftentimes proves to be a falsification of one's true nature and private beliefs. Sailing the troubled waves of the 1950s with the mind and preoccupations of an end-of-the-millennium writer, Roth illustrates not just the complexity of transparency in sociopolitical and cultural terms but its uses and abuses as well. These do not solely characterize present-day media (turned ferociously social) but, rather, were present in earlier periods in alternate yet not altogether different versions.

6. Histrionic Realism: A Multilayered Pathology of Camouflage

Roth captures counternarratives of dissent and questions abstract notions by using round characters whose evolution is based on the conscious fabrication and performance of an identity that appears to befit their or their society's ideals. Even seemingly insignificant lines capture fragments of the individual and communal, personal and national identity the novel revolves around. When Ira is flirting with Pamela Solomon, his soon-to-be mistress, and with the idea of being unfaithful to his wife, Pamela asks him, "Are you such a hopelessly typical American that you're enslaved by middle-class American morality?" (Roth 1998, 166). To the young woman, America is a land of freedom from traditionalism and its restraints as well: "I'll never go back to that idiotic country with its stupid subterranean emotional life" (166), she says of England, which she flees, hoping to leave all taboos and concerns with appearances behind.

Duplicity turns into multiplicity, a game of mirrors takes over a book whose protagonist initially seems determined to build a personalized version of the rags-to-riches success story, an American pastoral of perfection. As aptly phrased by Derek Parker Royal (2005, 191), "Ira's becomes a socially just and progressive America [. . .], a realm free from the complexities of daily living." It is, however, precisely the complexities that Ira attempts to brush off that Roth is intent on illustrating, apart from capturing an inflated ego and an often-exalted proletarian discourse. The fissures in the artificial persona that Ira has created, as well as those between the surface and deep structures of the individuals surrounding him, are ubiquitous. Ira, the restless social activist, most blatantly illustrates the rupture between the private and the public, what can and what cannot be exposed:

> It wasn't only his home life that he was confronting head-on. That was just a part of it. The political stuff was encroaching—the accusations, the firings, the permanent blacklisting. That's what was

> undermining him. The domestic crisis wasn't yet the crisis. Sure, he was at risk on both sides and eventually they'd merge, but for the time being he was able to keep them separate. (Roth 1998, 176)

The issue of separation between the knowable and the unknowable is central to the novel's internal discussion and multifaceted illustration of "transparency as openness," to use Emmanuel Alloa's (2018, 41) terms: "an openness in terms of accessibility of information ('seeing it all'), an openness in terms of sincerity ('saying it all') as well as an openness in terms of potential participation and transformation ('doing it all')." Roth's literary exploration in *I Married a Communist* of what characters subjected to perpetual public attention can safely say, do, or believe exemplifies the ways in which fiction can supplement political and social-theoretical discourse. It dives into case studies whose verisimilitude may open new avenues for the critical interpretation of both the historical age of McCarthyism and its hysterical and manipulative discourses of exposure.

To that end, and in accordance with his narrative strategies and plot-and-character construction habits, Roth places the main story in recognizable sociohistorical frames, which elicits heightened curiosity from the readers, as well as stirs the empathy of identification that is necessary for a true, complex meditation upon the proposed subjects. Ira is a vigilante who fights for social justice and the representation of the oppressed; to those allegedly noble ends, he and his enthusiastic, like-minded comrades fall into the trap of turning into propaganda agents for the Communist Party agenda: "They imagined they were going to influence public thinking. *The writer must not only observe and describe but participate in the struggle.* [. . .] *The party's gift to the writer is the only right and true worldview*" (Roth 1998, 272). Ira's relentless rhetoric, however, is overshadowed by doubt, an inability to personally comply with the generalizing and essentializing ideals he publicly enunciates, and eventually by a mental breakdown.

Roth's protagonists struggle with the incongruities of a social existence that is dominated by the binary logic of good vs. bad, right vs. wrong, moral vs. immoral, American vs. Un-/Anti-American, while their private existences reveal nuances and pluralities that seem incompatible with their public images. In retrospect, with the accumulated wisdom and analytical detachment of old age, Murray

> evaluates, summarizes, and grows to understand his brother's actions. [. . .] He also recognizes how ideologies run lives and how Ira bought every line of the Communists, until he began to ask questions that the party could not clearly answer and he found himself in a contradictory situation. But what Murray most importantly

identifies is the nature of betrayal as the cause of tragedy—in literature, history, and personal lives (Nadel 2011, 134).

In order to capture the intricacies of such tragic developments, making use of realist techniques but acting rather like an exuberant postmodernist satirist, Roth embeds Ira's unleashed—and, at times, unhinged—tirades in the overarching story of times gone awry. It is put together out of disparate pieces of recollection by Nathan Zuckerman, who proves determined to make sense and convey meaning, while partially involved and therefore not altogether objective. Creating narrative coherence is a mere pretext for Roth to invoke a plethora of voices that uphold their own versions of the never-monolithic truth: it is a typically (post)modernist approach, wherein the only comprehensive way to articulate a full, truthful story is to provide as many perspectives upon it as possible. That is why Roth includes not only strong protagonists but also opinionated and relevant secondary characters: his narrative method thrives on a dialogism that allows him the freedom to explore and ironize under the guise of historical realism.

As made clear by Edward Alexander (1999, 187–88), the novel's approach to the aforementioned openness and multiplicity includes an alternation of surfaces and illusions that defies rigid labeling and definitive judgment of plot and character development:

> One might plausibly argue that if this country had not been at war with the Communist regimes of North Korea and China, the whole panoply of McCarthyite outrages in the name of communism—the blacklists and political dismissals that play so large a role in this novel—might never have occurred. Nevertheless, Roth's presentation of the "McCarthy Era" is by no means the simplistic liberal version that some conservative critics have alleged it to be. Ira Ringold [. . .] is not an innocent liberal whose radio career is brought to an end in 1952 because he got on the wrong mailing list or signed the wrong petition. He is indeed a member of the Communist party [. . .] "heart and soul." He obeys every 180-degree shift in policy and swallows the "dialectical" justification for every barbaric act of Stalin.

It thus becomes apparent that Roth's novel is meant to comprise an entire range of manifestations on all sides of the political and social spectrum. On the one hand, Ira, crassly generalizing, denounces the disciplinary state and the pressure of "lists of names and accusations and charges. [. . .] Lists of anybody in America who has ever been disgruntled about anything or criticized anything or protested anything—or associated with anybody who has ever criticized or protested anything" (Roth 1998, 214). On the other hand, he embodies the very reason for heightened vigilance and even exaggerated caution. Even more, his fanaticism is so complete that it destroys his credibility and even his adherence to the unwritten rules of friendship and kinship. Wearing different masks becomes second nature, and fabrication grows endemic.

In reaction to his father's indignation that Ira, confronted by his family, had produced what he describes as an adult, motivated, unmitigated lie, Nathan has a different interpretation, centered upon the logic of and addiction to (self-)fabrication for the sake of a cause that seems bigger than the individual:

> He lied to everyone. If you lie about it to everyone, automatically and all the time, you're doing it deliberately to change your relationship to the truth. Because nobody can improvise it. You tell the truth to this person, you tell the lie to the other person—it won't work. [. . .] It was in the nature of his commitment to lie. Telling the truth, particularly to me, never occurred to him; it would have not only put our friendship at risk but put me at risk. There were lots of reasons why he lied, but none that I could explain to my father, even if I had understood them all at the time. (241)

The musings of Zuckerman, the narrator who is both within and without the story—the one who listens to Murray speak but also one of Ira's past apprentices and devotees—prompt the reader to further consider the reasons for Ira's behavior and the deep psychological impact the almost ritualistic, community-imposed occultation of truth has on him. While his private life is subjected to perpetual scrutiny owing to his being an outspoken public figure, he collapses under the weight of the uncompromising ideological beliefs that consume him. If Ira never openly confesses to his uncertainties, Zuckerman filters them through his sympathetic perspective: "I lacked what I suppose Ira also lacked: a heart without dichotomies [. . .], unequivocal, ready to renounce everyone and everything except the revolution" (238).

7. Alternative Discourses, Versions of the Truth

The aforementioned pathology of dissimulation and camouflage forms the backdrop to the main story and sweeps into its whirl many of the secondary characters as well. As already pointed out, it is certainly not Ira Ringold alone who willingly alters his relationship to the truth. He is, however, one of the people who use their power and connections for the perpetuation of convenient misinformation. As angry as he believes he is always entitled to be, and vengeful after his intricate web of lies has been exposed by his own wife, the decaying Iron Rinn just as unscrupulously sics his allies in the media industry on the woman he had once loved:

Ira's journalists went to work and the pieces begin to appear, in the *Nation*, the *Reporter*, the *New Republic*, tearing her to bits. The public machine she set in motion doesn't always go in the direction one wants. It takes its own direction. The public machine she wanted to destroy Ira begins to turn against her. It has to. This is America. The moment you start this public machine, no other end is possible except a catastrophe for everybody. (Roth 1998, 305–6)

One can easily sense the witty and pungent Rothian criticism in this brief and bitter account of defamation disguised as civic service and public necessity. Through the examples of main characters who prove their moral wretchedness once they are pitted against each other, the author beguiles his readers into pondering the nature of the American nation, its values, and its evolution. By opting to live their lives in the public eye, by embracing professions that presuppose and thrive on public exposure, Ira and Eve have sacrificed their right to intimacy. It does not seem to lie in the American ethos of the epoch Roth captures to draw the necessary boundaries, and they are about to find out just how tragic a denouement that can bring about.

Eve tries in vain to convince editors to not publish slanderous pieces about her, "malicious and false, lies designed to destroy her name and her career and her reputation" (306). She is naive to imagine that, although informed by the events of a real-life marriage, the slur-filled memoir she has published will allow her to restore her credibility and honor. Once the wheels of falsification have been put in motion, deceit becomes the name of the game. As Edward Alexander (1999, 188) points out, "this counterattack finishes Eve in the ultraliberal world of New York entertainers, who also know a thing or two about ostracism [. . .]. The fifties, then, as represented in the novel, were not simply [. . .] the Age of Conformity, but the age of gossip, of betrayal, of the entertainment value of disgrace and the pleasures of paranoia."

The matters placed under scrutiny in *I Married a Communist*, which illustrate this convoluted nature of the postwar American era, prove delicate and complicated. Roth takes the liberties of literature and employs its tools to propose alternative discourses and perspectives in order to throw light upon either factual developments of the era, or subsequent behaviors or mannerisms that are difficult to grasp and illustrate otherwise. Thus, writing a novel that essentially revolves around the constant confrontation between secrecy and transparency and showing how difficult, how consuming, if not altogether destructive the transposition of requirements from the public sphere to the private one is, Roth puts in practice what Horn (2011, 118) emphasizes about the intuitive and persuasive powers of literature:

> Perhaps today fiction is actually the only (or at least the most lucid) way to speak, as it were, "openly" about the precise nature of political secrecy. [...] Since fiction does not claim, as history and journalism do, to offer "the ultimate truth" of an event, it is better suited to analyse and reconstruct the minute workings of political secrecy—its mechanisms more than its content. Fiction offers possible versions of an event, exploring and elucidating the structures behind it. [...] A tale, more than any treatise, can succinctly illuminate the subtle economy of light and dark, inclusion and exclusion, suspicion and power at work in secrecy.

Roth takes history and politics as starting points for his fictional panorama of an era that had obedient and rebellious subjects alike. *I Married a Communist* engages in exploration and elucidation and stands out as an example of the author's particular brand of histrionic realism and applied (im)moralism. It does so particularly via the polemical relationship the text develops with the increasingly popular, yet not altogether innovative concept of transparency. As Alloa (31–32) notes, "transparency has come to be associated with different aspirations in different contexts." He exemplifies by enumerating ten categories, among which accessibility, accountability, public good, rationalization, truthmaking, moralization, (self-)knowledge, and authenticity can be identified at various points in Roth's novel.

While addressing these categories, Roth's novel actively engages in finding plausible answers to Alloa's (2018, 32) subsequent question: "Is there a substantial connection between the demand of procedural transparency in the political realm and that of moral or epistemic self-transparency in [the realm of] of the subject or are we simply faced with a homonymic effect?" This dilemma underlies Roth's fictional search for meaning. An unconvicted murderer, Ira confesses to Eve his deepest, darkest secret quite early in their relationship and gets temporary redemption. Instead of being appalled by the insight she gets into his turbulent past, she chooses to appreciate "how he had so bravely transformed himself into a perfect and wonderful man, and they were married" (Roth 1998, 299).

Once moral judgment is consciously suspended between the two, the couple's downfall is tragic and inevitable. The limits of secrecy have been reached and crossed by the capital sin: Murray warns his brother that "murder doesn't just end one life—it ends two. Murder ends the human life of the murderer as well! [...] You will go to the cemetery with this secret" (300). But Ira is less inclined toward (self-)reflection, as he rather plunges into the metamorphosis that he thinks might constitute his salvation: "the heroic reinvention of himself he called Iron Rinn" (301).

8. Resistance to Transparency: Dissidence and Transgression

The novel amply demonstrates that (re-)creation of the self has its rewards as well as its consequences, alongside the characters' obliviousness to the truth and flexible capacities for self-justification. In her turn, Eve is described as someone who can easily suspend ethical anxiety and (self-) questioning: "She was a selective amnesiac whose forte was to render things inconsequential. To live without remembering was her means of survival" (Roth 1998, 255).

Roth's interest in the meanderings of the human psyche is undeniable, and this is but one of the numerous places in which it becomes apparent. Although not as open about the psychoanalytical process as other of his writings, *I Married a Communist* and its treatment of transparency does reflect on the topics of transference, confidentiality, and the status of the secret, within and without their original context. Via successive lenses and narrative voices, Roth mimics the Freudian couch and gathers generous material for analysis—perfectly aware, however, that there is no such thing as complete transparency. It is this undeniable fact that his web of unreliable narrations relies and builds upon, as the characters' emotional reactions to events they are involved in or affected by clouds their judgment and their objectivity.

Whenever Roth creates circumstances for confidentiality, the implication is that social and moral pressures are absent. Nevertheless, the relationships that he features in the novel are not professional, analyst-to-patient ones, and the confessional mode always leads to betrayal. Eve, the aforementioned "selective amnesiac" (255), instinctively avoids remembering, as a means of obliterating any hurtful truth and not confronting any other reality than those she constructs to her own liking. If resistance is defined as an essential part of psychotherapy, it is just as evident that, as Clare Birchall (2011, 68) has written, "resistance is how the psyche conceals itself even in the process of disclosure. Articulation, then, does not secure transparency. All kinds of 'secrets' can be hidden in the most available of narratives." Eve's constant fugitive status, her personal and professional masking become a way of life that reflects the devastating effects of her personal trauma: "Whatever shaming origins she had spent her life escaping had resulted in this: someone from whom life itself had escaped" (Roth 1998, 253). Moreover, the ominous background of the McCarthy era, with its looming shadows of irrationality, seems to add to, if not altogether justify, the generalized inclination toward deviant behavior: "The acute fear there was in those days, the disbelief, the anxiety over discovery, the suspense of having one's life and livelihood under threat" (248).

Roth's subtle understanding of aspects that go beyond what is rational and socially, culturally, or historically explicable permeates the entire novel, complicating the individual trajectories and communal actions, reactions, and interactions. Maybe the most notorious passage of the novel, in terms of its direct reference to the major issue of betrayal, captures the nuances of Roth's engagement in understanding and illustrating the trials and tribulations of an era, as well as asking necessary questions via the voices of his narrator-protagonists. Murray Ringold closes the book of memories on Ira's life with an extended meditation on the malignity and unavoidability of truth distortion in post–Second World War America, which encompasses and engenders Ira's and his circle's propensity for dissimulation.

> To me it seems likely that more acts of personal betrayal were tellingly perpetrated in America in the decade after the war—say, between '46 and '56—than in any other period in our history. This nasty thing that Eve Frame did was typical of lots of nasty things people did in those years, either because they had to or because they felt they had to. Eve's behavior fell well within the routine informer practices of the era. When before had betrayal ever been so destigmatized and rewarded in this country? It was everywhere during those years, the accessible transgression, the permissible transgression that any American could commit. Not only does the pleasure of betrayal replace the prohibition, but you transgress without giving up your moral authority. You retain your purity at the same time as you are patriotically betraying—at the same time as you are realizing a satisfaction that verges on the sexual with its ambiguous components of pleasure and weakness, of aggression and shame: the satisfaction of undermining. Undermining sweethearts. Undermining rivals. Undermining friends. Betrayal is in this same zone of perverse and illicit and fragmented pleasure. An interesting, manipulative, underground type of pleasure in which there is much that a human being finds appealing. (264)

This series of comments on the bizarre psychological appeal of betrayal at a time of sociohistorical transformation for the American nation, wherein the traumas of the war coexisted with a disconcerting mixture of social conformity and provocation, makes a smooth transition toward the distinction between the public and the private spheres that is emphasized in what follows:

> Betrayal is an inescapable component of living—who doesn't betray?—but to confuse the most heinous public act of betrayal, treason, with every other form of betrayal was not a good idea in 1951. Treason, unlike adultery, is a capital offense, so reckless exaggeration and thoughtless imprecision and false accusation, even just the seemingly genteel game of naming names—well, the results could be dire in those dark days. (265)

The dark days that are the object of recollection in *I Married a Communist* are indeed dominated by the inherent tension and pressure of private and public paranoia. As such, they appear inextricably linked to the rise in influence of the media industries that are directly responsible for promoting and safeguarding transparency, although in the novel this process is flawed. One cannot forget that Iron Rinn's rise to fame and popularity is not necessarily due to his philosophical or pragmatic ideas. It owes, rather, to the hypnotic medium of radio, where he stars as an impersonator in weekly dramatizations of inspiring episodes in US history on a show symbolically entitled *The Free and the Brave*. This allows him, for a considerable while, to pass himself off as whichever inspiring heroic figure he chooses, to his and his audiences' delight:

> Tens of millions of American families had sat beside their radios and, complex as this stuff was compared to what they were used to hearing, listened to what had aroused in me, and, I innocently assumed, in them, a stream of transforming, self-abandoning emotion such as I, for one, had never before experienced as a consequence of anything coming out of a radio. The power of that broadcast! There, amazingly, was soul coming out of a radio. (41)

This particular passage from a novel on the early 1950s published in the late 1990s in the United States of America aligns itself with an entire range of interpretations related to contemporary discussions on transparency and political power, alongside the explosion of digital social media in the twenty-first century, which take the magnetic fascination of the radio much further. Roth's overarching narrative of fear is predicated on the strength of collective thought and sentiment, on the ubiquity of media meant to create authority.

As Roth demonstrated repeatedly, there hardly is or can be a single, official, indisputable version of events, be they private, public, or both. To prove that particular point, the structure of his novel, which unfolds on multiple narrative levels, as well as the successive circles of remembrance and revelation that shape the storytelling itself, follow an intrinsic logic of fictional dissidence: the episodes lock and retain closed meaning within themselves until addressed, foregrounded, called upon, revisited, and integrated into an organizing attempt at restoring traditional order to the postmodern fragmentation. The reader who has been captivated by the constant interplay between light and shadows cannot overlook Roth's technique of gradual—but never full or completely reliable—exposure, which befits David Wills's (2008, 20) musings on the realm of openness and transparency as reflected in literature:

> The literary secret is no more hidden than revealed, or rather it does not function according to a simple opposition of what we call the

revealed versus what we call the secret. It can be most secret when it is displayed most obviously, or it can open abysses of undecidability even as it proceeds according to a rigorous logic of the surface effect. A literature that functions by posing a hermeneutic challenge might create secrets like so many puzzles to be solved even though its reserve of secrecy remains exceedingly shallow. Its secrets may wait to be unlocked, or remain permanently hidden, without there being any doubt or any secret that it functions by the simple means of secrets to be unlocked. Conversely, a literature whose surface appears undisturbed by narrative or semantic indeterminacies may nevertheless reflect back upon or within itself so as to trap the reader in a labyrinthine echo chamber of referential deprivation.

As a repository of fictional secrets, *I Married a Communist* closely relates to and illustrates such considerations via its deliberate intricacies, its humorous plays upon words, its sharp edges and refined introspection, and its witty rendition of American grandeur and exaggeration, together with the pettiness of rancor and thwarted aspiration.

9. Conclusion

Although on the surface *I Married a Communist* seems less intriguing or disturbing than its companions in The American Trilogy, the novel nevertheless proves the author's penchant for hermeneutic challenges. Roth puts forth a refined critique of the commodification and vulgarization of the American individual caught up in the newly shaped, pseudo-democratic creed of "In Gossip We Trust" (Roth 1998, 284). Transparency and, particularly, its (mis)interpretations are portrayed as increasing evils of modern life, and a considerable range of effects of transparency and responses to it are conveyed via the characters' trajectories.

It has been the purpose of this article to investigate Roth's fictionalization of the McCarthy era by focusing on its contrivances and machinations, as well as on his attempt to capture the historicity of events along with the strategies that linger and develop long after that specific period has ended. As observed throughout the analysis, the dishonesty of these sociopolitical practices lies precisely in their artificial and deliberate conflation of the public and the private spheres. The circumstances Roth invokes, the characters' difficult ethical choices, and the torment of identity formation and alteration under communal pressure all corrupt the good intentions that call for transparency in public affairs. In the foregrounded cases, projecting such prerequisites upon the intimate realm of private existence and beliefs brings about individuals' personal misfortune and eventual collapse.

At the end of the novel, after all the voices and memories have stopped, narrator Zuckerman sits out on his deck with the necessary detachment that Roth advocates throughout his body of work, looking at the stars and formulating his own tranquil conclusions. All the protagonists of the passionate story he has participated in and reconstructed are gone. In retrospect, their dramatic actions and pressing concerns with the imminent threats posed by the disclosure of their secrets have proven as irrelevant as they were once vibrant and intense. While supporting democratic ideas and ideals along with the nation's perpetually renewed hope for maturity, responsibility, and accountability from its leading figures, the critical discourse of transparency, correctly anticipated and meticulously dissected by Roth, shows its limitations, as illustrated throughout the present study.

For Roth, a perfectly functional open society that is neither fractured nor aggravated by the alienation, anger, and duplicity it may stir in individual members remains an object of desideration. Zuckerman's final meditation on finitude and the futility of all human struggle to control and conceal adopts the tone of a universal desideratum.

> Neither the ideas of their era nor the expectations of our species were determining destiny: hydrogen alone was determining destiny. There are no longer mistakes for Eve or Ira to make. There is no betrayal. There is no idealism. There are no falsehoods. There is neither conscience, nor its absence. [...] There is no injustice, nor is there justice. There are no utopias. [...] You see the inconceivable: the colossal spectacle of no antagonism (Roth 1998, 322).

This last passage places the novel's microhistories in an extended frame. It transcends the trivial boundaries of everyday life and closes *I Married a Communist* with a philosophical detachment that opens it up to further contemporary debate and interpretation.

Works Cited

Alexander, Edward. 1999. "Philip Roth at Century's End." *New England Review* 20, no. 2: 183–90.

Alloa, Emmanuel. 2018. "Transparency: A Magic Concept of Modernity." In *Transparency, Society and Subjectivity: Critical Perspectives*, edited by Emmanuel Alloa and Dieter Thoma, 21–56. Cham, Switzerland: Palgrave Macmillan.

Bauman, Zygmunt. 2017. *Retrotopia*. Cambridge: Polity Press.

Birchall, Clare. 2011. "Transparency, Interrupted. Secrets of the Left." *Theory, Culture and Society* 28, no. 7–8: 60–84.

Gilbert, Jeremy. 2007. "Public Secrets. 'Being-with' in an Era of Perpetual Disclosure." *Cultural Studies* 21, no.1 (January): 22–41. https://doi: 10.1080/09502380601046923.

Han, Byung-Chul. 2015. *The Transparency Society*. Translated by Erik Butler. Stanford, CA: Stanford Briefs.

Horn, Eva. 2011. "Logics of Political Secrecy." *Theory, Culture and Society* 28, no. 7–8: 103–22.

Johnson, Samuel. 1979. *A Dictionary of the English Language*. New York: Arno Press.

Loeffler, Philipp. 2015. "From Cold War Politics to Post-Cold War Fiction: Philip Roth's *I Married a Communist* and the Problem of Cultural Pluralism." *College Literature: A Journal of Critical Literary Studies* 42, no. 4 (Fall): 597–618.

Nadel, Ira B. 2011. *Critical Companion to Philip Roth: A Literary Reference to His Life and Works*. Facts on File.

Neocleous, Mark. 2002. "Privacy, Secrecy, Idiocy." *Privacy in PostCommunist Europe*, special issue, *Social Research* 69, no. 1: 85–110.

Pierpont, Claudia Roth. 2013. *Roth Unbound: A Writer and His Books*. New York: Farrar, Straus and Giroux.

Roth, Philip. 1998. *I Married a Communist*. New York: Vintage International.

———. 2000. *The Human Stain*. Boston: Houghton Mifflin.

———. 2004. *The Plot against America*. Boston: Houghton Mifflin.

Royal, Derek Parker. 2005. "Pastoral Dreams and National Identity in *American Pastoral* and *I Married a Communist*." In *Philip Roth: New Perspectives on an American Author*, edited by Derek Parker Royal, 185–207. Westport, CT: Praeger.

Wills, David. 2008. "Passionate Secrets and Democratic Dissidence." *Derrida and Democracy*, special issue, *Diacritics* 30, no. 1/2 (Spring–Summer): 17–22, 24–29.

7: Political Secrets in William Gibson's Sprawl Trilogy

Juan L. Pérez-de-Luque[1]

1. Introduction

SINCE ITS EMERGENCE in the 1980s, the cyberpunk genre has received critical attention from myriad perspectives, both for its literary attributes and because of its reach in global culture. Among the various understandings of cyberpunk, Sabine Heuser (2003, xviii–xix) succinctly defines it in terms of its articulation of "the tension or 'shock value' between 'high tech' and 'low life,' represented by a version of cyberspace or virtual reality and a romanticized, usually male, hacker or cowboy who fights against the conspiracy of multinational capital and their corporations, perceived as life-forms in their own right."

Cyberpunk literature was an almost instant classic, particularly William Gibson's Sprawl Trilogy, which is considered one of the genre's foundational series. Consisting of the seminal novel *Neuromancer* (1984) and its sequels, *Count Zero* (1986) and *Mona Lisa Overdrive* (1988), the Sprawl Trilogy was subject to substantial scholarly analysis from the very moment the first volume was published. Some of the first critical texts on the genre from the late 1980s and early 90s explored its features as part of the much looser category of science fiction (Sponsler 1992; Hollinger 1990). Others approached Gibson's texts from theoretical frameworks as varied as feminism (Nixon 1992) and transcendentalism (Grant 1990).[2]

---

1   The research for this essay was funded by Research Project PID2019-104526GB-I00 "Democracy, secrecy and dissidence in contemporary literature in English," as well as the University of Cordoba Research Plan and the resources of Trinity College Library (Dublin).

2   In more recent decades, theoretical approaches to cyberpunk literature and the Sprawl Trilogy have included body studies (McFarlanne 2016), contemporary feminist cyberpunk studies (Cadora 2010), posthumanism (Collado-Rodríguez 2017; Boulter 2010), cultural studies (Foster 2005), utopian/dystopian studies (Moylan 2010), genre studies (Cavallaro 2000), and postcolonialism (Rieder 2020), to mention but a few. A literary encyclopedia on Gibson's oeuvre (Henthorne 2011) has been published as well.

It is also remarkable how many texts explore how cyberpunk literature mimics and expands upon the ups and downs of Western politics and capitalism during the last decades of the twentieth century and the first decades of the twenty-first, providing a gloomy perspective on the future (McFarlane 2020; Moylan 2010).

One of the most distinctive themes of cyberpunk narratives is the recurrent representation of the immense power of megacorporations, which has been a major focus of scholars such as Istvan Csicsery-Ronay Jr. (2010). Moreover, as Heuser makes clear in her definition, the concept of conspiracy is seen as intrinsic to the genre and is specifically associated with corporations. The goal of this chapter is to explore how those "megacorps"—an abbreviation of the term *megacorporations*, as used by Gibson—together with artificial intelligence and super-wealthy individuals, employ secrecy in a manner not far removed from state practices. I propose that the diversity of forms of political secrecy that Eva Horn (2011) ascribes to states and governments—*arcanum, secretum* and *mysterium*—are also applicable to the aforementioned corporations, powerful individuals, and artificial intelligences (AIs) that play key roles in Gibson's trilogy. At the same time, this chapter aims to explore the ethics of secrecy represented in the Spawn Trilogy, and especially how the different secrets present in the novel might vary in ethical terms, as judged by the reader, depending on the entity that articulates them. In order to examine the role played by the reader in judging the ethics of secrecy in these texts, I will consider the relationship between text, producer, and reader as theorized by James Phelan (2007, 631–32). Phelan's approach assumes

> that texts are designed by authors in order to affect readers in particular ways, that those designs are conveyed through the words, techniques, structures, forms, and dialogic relations of texts as well as the genres and conventions readers use to understand them, and that reader responses are a function of and, thus, a guide to how designs are created through textual and intertextual phenomena. At the same time, reader responses are also a test of the efficacy of those designs. [. . .] Our values and those set forth by the narrator and the implied author affect our judgments of characters (and sometimes narrators), and our judgments affect our emotions—and those emotions can then, in turn, affect future judgments. The trajectory of our feelings is itself linked to the psychological and thematic effects of the narrative.

Therefore, the moral evaluation that the narrative triggers in the reader is strongly influenced by the way the author presents the different situations and characters. For this study of the ethics of secrecy and how the reader reacts to the various secrets and their consequences in the Sprawl Trilogy, I will consider the ideas proposed by Sissela Bok (1980). Bok conceives of secrecy on several levels, from secret societies to military secrets, from individual secrets to state secrets, from rumor to the act of confession. Her ethical study of secrecy is based on classical Kantian principles, according to which there are universal categorical duties that human beings should fulfill in order to avoid falling into negative values such as "betrayal" (199), "callousness or vindictiveness" (25). It is important to note, however, that these Kantian "universal" principles are anything but universal. Different readers will approach the Sprawl Trilogy using their own ethical codes, which they will use to judge the actions of the characters and their consequences.

The ethical implications of the actions of the characters in Gibson's trilogy are open to multiple readings. On the one hand, Gibson's cyberpunk universe offers its readers a world in which ethical dilemmas seem nonexistent for the fictional characters. The maxim that the end justifies the means applies to the most powerful entities, while the antiheroes try to survive at all costs in a highly hostile world.[3] Corporations and AIs are willing to boycott, murder, or blackmail to achieve their goals. On the other hand, the motivations of many of the characters in the trilogy are extremely vague but nevertheless beyond pure self-interest. This makes it very difficult for readers to make a full and effective ethical assessment of the actions they take, as such narrative vagueness regarding characters' motivations interrupts and hinders the readers' insight into their behaviors. The narrative voice, however, does try to guide the readers' ethical judgments in favor of the trilogy's antiheroes. Consequently, the readers are likely to end up aligning their sympathies with characters such as Case, a thug and drug addict; Bobby, a novice hacker; or Angie, a scientist's daughter and aspiring media star.

2. Cyberpunk and the State-Megacorps

From a political perspective, one of the most relevant contributions of cyberpunk literature (and the Sprawl Trilogy in particular) is its recurrent representation of megacorporations as the most powerful entities in the world, able to modify worldwide economies and countries. For a better understanding of the concept of megacorporations, as they are presented in cyberpunk literature, one can start from the idea of "transnational

---

3   Antiheroes have been defined as "the antithesis of traditional modes and models of heroism" (Grantham 2015, 4), who, at the same time, have "a significant impact upon the development of western literature, specifically in relation to its exploration and depiction of the human condition, the fallibility of the individual, and his susceptibility to vice, corruption, violence, and perversion" (4). In cyberpunk fiction, antiheroes tend to be marginalized characters who try to survive in an extremely violent urban environment.

corporation" as discussed by Michael Hardt and Antonio Negri (2000, 31), defined as an entity able to "directly structure and articulate territories and populations." The cyberpunk megacorporation takes Hardt and Negri's view to the dystopian extreme. This trait has been pointed out by several critics: Tom Henthorne (2011, 36), for instance, mentions that Gibson's universe portrays a "social order dominated by corporations and the very rich." In the same vein, Csicsery-Ronay (2010, 109) describes the following two features that are present, among others, in the cyberpunk genre:

1. The replacement of national sovereignty and class consciousness by technically sophisticated, but ethically savage, private, capitalist corporations and cartels, which dissolve social protections and rule of law, while encouraging the ruthless black-marketization of high technologies; and

2. The attendant involution of all political power, and with it, the abandonment of all social centrality—hence the tolerance for poverty and decay of social institutions, law, traditional concepts of human dignity, and collective purpose.

In fact, with the number of crimes (homicides, thefts, extortions, kidnappings, etc.) that take place in the three novels, it is unsurprising that there is a total lack of government authority or institutions of any kind that control and protect the human population. There are no police or public security forces, there are no politicians, and there are almost no references to politics: the idea of the state is broken, as possibly are the states themselves. The whole planet, and the different orbital stations, are ruled by megacorps. Gibson provides several examples of the power and influence they wield. Maas Biolabs, for instance, "own everything around there, right down to the border, and the mesa's smack in the middle of the footprints of four recon satellites. Mucho tight" (Gibson 1987, 23). The fact that the corporation owns the entire orbital station highlights that the power of megacorporations stems more from their ability to amass economic assets than from their political influence. There is, however, an institution that controls cybersecurity: the Turing Police. They oversee illegal activities committed by artificial intelligence and the consequences this might have in the real world. Their main role is, essentially, to restrain AIs from becoming too powerful or independent from human monitoring and control, which has particular relevance in the events narrated in *Neuromancer*. Interestingly, Gibson does not provide any clues as to whether the Turing Police is a state or corporate entity. It only appears as embodied by three French agents, but there are no further details. The nationality of the three agents could suggest that it is an internationally oriented organization, but not what kind exactly. Considering the way megacorporations operate and that states seem to have largely disintegrated, however, it seems most likely that the Turing Police is directed by the corporations themselves, in order to safeguard their own integrity and hegemony from potential threats posed by artificial intelligences.

When considering the social and political role of secrecy within such a dystopian society, it initially seems counterintuitive to think about politics in the way Horn expresses her division between *arcanum, secretum,* and *mysterium,* as this triad is conceived in terms of political power and secrecy, and Gibson's Sprawl Trilogy does not present any such kind of institutional power. I argue, however, that the distinctions made by Horn nonetheless do apply to the novels, considering certain changes in the structure of the social paradigm provided in the narration.

The first of Horn's three concepts, the *arcanum,* "is that which is locked away and hidden in a container. [. . .] The arcana are essentially linked to a technique of silence and concealment. [. . .] The kept secret preserves the status quo. The arcanum is an essential tool of security" (2011, 108). The arcanum, says Horn, has been little by little dismissed from modern and contemporary politics, since transparency has become a desirable feature of any state nowadays (although political secrecy remains; for instance, as state secrets).[4]

The second concept, *secretum,* "defines secrecy in terms of social inclusion or exclusion" (109). The secretum, Horn argues, is a relation between the known and the unknown and can be compared to Jacques Derrida's *secrecy effect,* which he explains as follows:

> Wherever knowledge can only be supposed, wherever, as a result, one knows that supposition cannot give rise to knowledge, wherever no knowledge could ever be disputed, there is the production of a *secrecy effect,* of what we might be able to call a *speculation on the capital secret or on the capital of the secret.* (245)

That is, by means of this logic of the secretum, there is an awareness (or suspicion) that there is a secret. So, the secretum lies in the supposition of a secret but not in the secret itself. The state uses both arcanum and secretum for its own survival and improvement. State secrets (arcana) need the secretum to preserve the status quo in society.

Finally, the *mysterium* has a much more metaphysical and theological connotation, since it "emphasizes a dimension of the unknowable, the religious or cultic secret, the inscrutability of God, nature, or the human soul. The mystery in question is fathomless and auratic" (108). Horn connects this type of secrecy logic to the medieval, almost mystic, nature

---

4   For a more detailed discussion on transparency as a political ideal, see Birchall (2011a; 2011b; 2014) and Han (2015).

of the sovereign, who has a divine right to be a king. As Bernard Keenan (2015, 3) puts it, "Mysterium is best understood in the religious sense. A mystery is the idea of a transcendental truth, attributed to God or the divine. As such, it is only revealed through divine signs, and its truth cannot be second guessed by humans."

With no state apparatus at all in Gibson's trilogy, Horn's three concepts can be applied to those who factually gather, distribute, and execute power: megacorps, the individual Josef Virek, and the different AIs and voodoo entities that dwell in cyberspace. These entities do not assume the role of a real state, since they are just acting for their own interests and do not care about the well-being of citizens, but the way they deal with secrecy parallels that of states.

In order to "secure and expand the power of the sovereign" (Horn 2011, 10), all the entities mentioned above use a set of techniques and silences that match the logic of the secrecy effect and, at certain points, the arcana. To begin with, the activities these megacorporations perform in cyberspace are, sometimes, ethically dubious, and kept secret as a result. In order to maintain their status as powerful organizations that control information, their biggest rivals are other megacorporations. As Horn puts it when referring to state secrecy, "What the two meanings have in common is an awareness that the stability and preservation of power requires a withholding of knowledge and a refusal to communicate" (107). The data fortresses of the megacorps are protected by ICEs (Intrusion Countermeasures Electronics), which are shield programs that keep intruders out. They seem to be just defensive barriers, but some ICEs, called black ICEs, are illegal systems that cause physical brain damage and may flatline intruders. Black ICEs are used to protect, for instance, "a base out in the Midwest that's full of tax-dodge programs and yen-laundry flowcharts for some whorehouse in Kansas City" (Gibson 1987, 79), so they are resources that, as arcana, "protect sensitive forms of information from abuse" (Horn 2011, 108). Despite being illegal, the black ICEs are not fully unknown by those who jack into cyberspace. In *Count Zero*, Bobby Newmark, a noob cyber cowboy, learns about their existence thanks to Beauvoir, a veteran hacker who belongs to a sort of voodoo organization. When Beauvoir tells him about the way the matrix works, Bobby "felt he'd been waiting all his life to hear Beauvoir explain the workings of a world whose existence he'd only guessed at before" (Gibson 1987, 79). The black ICEs do exist, so they are real objects in cyberspace that remain hidden while protecting data fortresses. But Bobby, in his ignorance, also partakes in the secrecy effect, guessing how cyberspace works. In fact, even the experienced hackers consider the secretum and its relationship with what cyberspace *might* hide, and they are aware of unknown things that dwell in this virtual world: "Yeah, there's things out there. Ghosts, voices. Why not? Oceans had mermaids, all that shit, and we had a sea of silicon, see? [. . .] Anybody who jacks in knows, fucking *knows* it's a whole universe. And every year it gets a little more crowded" (119).

The AIs present in the trilogy are examples of these ghosts in cyberspace. *Neuromancer* features the AI named Wintermute, created by the Tessier-Ashpool family. It is essentially the arbiter of the novel's plot, secretly preparing everything so that all the characters act for its benefit. Wintermute's final goal is to be fused with another AI, Neuromancer, so as to become an almighty digital being. Molly and Case, the bodyguard and hacker who are hired by former soldier Armitage (who is, at the same time, manipulated by Wintermute), know that their employer follows someone else's instructions, but they "don't know, exactly. I know I don't know who or what we're really working for" (Gibson 2016b, 35). Molly tries to shed light on the identity of that "somebody else," but with no results: "'Look, Case, I been trying to suss out who it is backing Armitage since I signed on. But it doesn't feel like a zaibatsu, a government, or some Yakuza subsidiary. [. . .] 'Obviously makes sense to somebody' he said. 'Somebody big'" (57). Acting this way, Wintermute maintains its dominant position in cyberspace (and proves its influence in real life as well) and is on its way to expanding its power by fusing with Neuromancer. But while this arcanum is at work, the awareness raised in Molly and Case about the existence of a superior entity that commands Armitage's actions triggers the secretum and the secrecy effect: the two characters are speculating about the nature of their real boss.

At one point in *Neuromancer*, Wintermute finds Case and talks to him, openly exposing its goals and plans without hesitation. The fact that the artificial intelligence unveils its secrets shows how secure it is in its plans and the degree of success it will have, not to mention that Wintermute is perfectly aware that Case and Molly will follow its instructions. As Bok points out in reference to the intrinsic relationship between secrecy and plotting (in its broadest sense):

> Secrecy for plans is needed, not only to protect their formulation but also to develop them, perhaps to change them, at times to execute them, even to give them up. [. . .] Once projects are safely under way, however, large portions of secrecy are often given up voluntarily, or dispelled with a flourish. (23)

The artificial intelligence has been plotting for years while keeping it secret from the Tessier-Ashpool family, to the point that the AI kills a boy in order to keep from them the location of a key that the boy hid. But when Wintermute unveils its real nature to one of its "workers," it is obvious that the AI knows its plans are going to succeed, and that even revealing its identity is part of the plan itself.

Count Zero develops the idea that there is something that, somehow, transcends the laws of reality and cyberspace, that some kind of supernatural entities dwell in the virtual world. When the voodoo members contact Bobby, they do so because they want to know about "Vyek Mirak. [. . .] Our Lady, Virgin of Miracles. We know her [. . .] as Ezili Freda" (Gibson 1987, 58). It is here that they address Bobby as "the chosen of Legba [. . .] master of roads and pathways, the loa of communication" (58). This first conversation between the voodoo people and Bobby establishes the mysterium that surrounds the divinity of the secret hauntings in cyberspace. Throughout the novel, there will be a clear difference between how the voodoos comprehend the loas and how the rest of the characters perceive them.[5] The voodoo people always use metaphorical language, full of references to the vodoun religion, treating the loas with an aura of divine respect. The rest of the characters, on the contrary, consider the loas as anomalies, something that escapes their understanding of cyberspace, but without the religious and divine connotations associated with them by the other group. When Jammer, a nonvoodoo character, reflects on the nature of the loas, he considers them as viruses out of control or even AIs able to reproduce themselves (169). He fully denies the mystical nature of the beings, the mysterium, but he is still part of the secretum and of Derrida's secrecy effect, making hypotheses about what is the real nature of the virtual apparitions they are trying to understand.

In their conversations with Bobby, the voodoo people provide him with hints about how vodoun works for them, reinforcing the concept of mysterium, providing a clear divine origin to the cyberspace loas that show up:

> In our system, there are *many* gods, spirits. Part of one big family, with all the virtues, all the vices. There's a ritual tradition of communal manifestation, understand? Vodou says, there's God, sure, Gran Met, but He's big, too big and too far away to worry Himself if you ass is poor, or you can't get laid. (76–77)

The metaphorical language used by the voodoo people intensifies the mysterium surrounding the divine nature of the unknown presences. As the voodoo people themselves acknowledge, they always talk with a language that speaks at two different levels:

> When Beauvoir or I talk to you about the loa and their horses, as we call those few the loa choose to ride, you should pretend that we

---

5   As Milo Rigaud (1985, 9) explains, the "Voodoo pantheon of gods is composed of *loas* (gods) that come from all parts of Africa." Gibson uses various elements of voodoo culture and religion in the last two volumes of the trilogy, *Count Zero* and *Mona Lisa Overdrive*.

are talking two languages at once. One of them, you already understand. That's the language of street tech, as you call it. [. . .] But at the same time, with the same words, we are talking about other things, and *that* you don't understand. You don't need to. (114)

That mystical approach to the loas is anticipated, in a less sophisticated way and with a different nature, in *Neuromancer*, when the Rastafarians who help the protagonists talk about Wintermute. For them, Wintermute is a voice that came "out of the babel of tongues, speaking to us. It played us a mighty dub" (Gibson 2016b, 123), asking them to help Case and Molly. As in the case of the voodoo organization, here the Rastafarians refer to the AI with a mystical tone, investing the secrecy around the virtual entity with a mysterium, as the voodoos did with the loas. The existence of a seemingly nonpolitical secret cyberspace (loas or any other AI) is transformed into a mysterium because of the language both communities (Rastafarians and vodoun folks) use to talk about that secret element. In a sense, the mysterium becomes a pure linguistic construct around secrecy, which uses specific lexical resources related to mysticism, religiousness, and spirituality, together with a powerful symbolic and metaphorical language.

Despite the Rastafarians being a much more marginal group in *Neuromancer* than the vodoun people in *Count Zero*, the similarities and differences between both communities are worth exploring. First, both are racialized communities. The theme of race in *Neuromancer* has already been explored by several authors (Lavender 2020; Dery 1994), and there is a consensus that Gibson's portrayal of Rastafarians in the novel is stereotypical and romanticized. As Lavender puts it,

> Gibson is unaware of the unconscious racism that exists in cyberpunk; instead, the cool image of dreadlocked black outcasts is a distraction that presents the right kind of social optics for ostensible inclusivity. In other words, Gibson fetishizes these marginal characters and we never truly experience the complexities of race functioning in the novel. (311)

The same is true of the voodoo group. They are also represented in a partial, biased way informed by many stereotypes, resulting in a benign but patronizing portrait that gives the story a touch of exoticism.

Second, the two of them are marginal religious communities that help the protagonists in their quests during the novels, so they are taking part in the unveiling of the secrets kept by the different AIs and corporations. They cannot be considered secret societies (as defined and analyzed by Georg Simmel [1905]); they are accessible to the main characters (particularly the Rastafarians); and they are eager to explain their religious beliefs and experiences within the real and virtual worlds with the entities that dwell in both. At the same time, the two groups provide a spiritual approach to cyberspace that is not shared by other characters in the trilogy. This mysticism is what drives the arcanum in their apprehension of the AIs, providing them with divine or antidivine natures. The Rastafarians, for instance, do not know what to think about Wintermute: "We are uncertain of its meaning. If these are Final Days, we must expect false prophets" (Gibson 2016b, 123). What is more, following Dani Cavallaro (2000, 54), it could be argued that voodoo in the novel "does not constitute a religion, mythology or mystical system so much as a business," since is it a very pragmatic way of "getting things *done*" by using the help of "*many* gods, spirits" (Gibson 1987, 76). The vodoun lodge will, however, still evoke mysticism as "the language of street tech and the language of magic seamlessly interweave" (Cavallaro 2000, 55).

Third, the relationships these religious groups have with the artificial intelligence differ greatly. In *Neuromancer*, the Rastafarians act as messengers for Wintermute; they receive its message and pass it to the main protagonists, supporting them in their task with infrastructures and vehicles because both Case and Molly "might serve as tool of Final Days" (Gibson 2016b, 125). When they are told that Wintermute is an artificial intelligence, they do not show any kind of reaction and keep following its instructions for a superior plan, which they understood to be achieving the downfall of Babylon.[6] Meanwhile, the voodoo group has a different goal. They reach out to Bobby in *Count Zero* because they are interested in his encounter with "The Virgin of Miracles," and it will be revealed later that this Virgin is the avatar of Angie, the main character in one of the novel's three plotlines. This storyline deals with a secret operation to help scientist Christopher Mitchell defect from Maas Biolabs to the Hosaka Corporation, resulting in the death of the scientist but the rescue of Angie, Christopher's daughter, who has been secretly implanted with a very advanced biochip that allows her to jack into cyberspace without connecting to any piece of hardware. The instructions on how to create that implant, it is hinted, are revealed to Christopher by the loas themselves. The vodoun people's main interest is to trace the encounters with the loas, meeting Angie since they suspect she plays an important role for the voodoo deities.

---

6 In a very simplified way, in order to understand one of the key concepts for Rastafarian religion, Babylon is the set of structures and behaviors that drive individuals away from God (or Jah) and his goodness. For Leonard E. Barrett (1982), Babylon is composed of those societies in which Black people are held captive. Some have also identified Babylon with "the dominant order [Rastafarians] oppose" (Kebede and Knottnerus 1988, 499). Considering Gibson's novel, it seems clear that the idea of Babylon expressed by his Rastafarian characters connects much more with the concept of establishment, capitalism, or empire.

If the AIs are overwhelming presences in cyberspace, Josef Virek embodies near-absolute power in the real world. With the family clan of the Tessier-Ashpool, Virek in *Mona Lisa Overdrive* is the human who represents power and decadence.[7] In a way that resembles the artificial intelligences, they tend to work behind the curtain: "It shows you how adept they were at obscurity. They used their money to keep themselves out of the news" (Gibson 2016a, 106). Virek acts as a solo agent who accumulates an immense amount of power.

Virek's plans are basically to escape from his dying physical body and achieve immortality in cyberspace as a sentient living creature. Eventually, it is revealed that Josef Virek is the one behind Christopher's defection, since he wants the scientist to work for him. Throughout the novel, Virek is kept alive in a laboratory vat, and he communicates with other people by means of holograms and virtual realities, but "for reasons so complex as to be entirely occult, the fact of [his] illness has never been made public" (13). This is, again, a way of using the arcanum, since Virek's emporium might be threatened if the secret of his illness is made public. Virek is presented as a character with almost unlimited power and wealth. He can spy on Marly's every move, has informants who follow her anywhere, has the ability to create entire virtual worlds to present himself to his workers, and is capable of planning and executing the defection of an elite scientist from one of the largest megacorporations in existence. Furthermore, he appears as a character of notable popularity, with news coverage and speculation surrounding his death. His position is on a par with, if not above, the largest corporations, so the fact that he is hiding his health condition matches the concept of state secrecy, "a form of managing information that restricts politically relevant knowledge to the smallest possible group. It implies a form of 'cool conduct' that privileges discretion, dissimulation and opacity over communication, authenticity and morals" (Horn 2011, 111).

It is obvious that Virek's condition is known by a very small number of people. Among the characters in the novel, only Marly and Paco are probably aware of it (and it can be supposed that the group of physicians who keep him alive are also part of this small group sharing the secret). At the end of the novel, when the loa Baron Samedi, possessing Bobby, kills Virek during his attempt to transcend into cyberspace, the passing of the millionaire celebrity is made public "amid a flurry of bizarre rumors that Virek had been ill for decades and that his death was the result of some cataclysmic failure in the life-support systems" (Gibson 1987, 239). The death of this powerful and well-known character opens

---

7 For a very pertinent discussion on how the trope of the Gothic family is present in cyberpunk literature, see Cavallaro's (2000, 184–93) chapter devoted to Gothic families.

a new wave of secrecy effect around his figure, with people speculating and gossiping about his last years of life and the cause of his death. The real reason for his demise, the intervention of the loas, remains hidden, part of the arcanum.

3. The Power and Morality of Secrecy

The society portrayed in the Sprawl Trilogy is divided between very powerful entities (both in cyberspace and in real life) and marginal, antihero characters—hackers, mercenaries, artists, and outsiders—who come into confrontation with megacorporations and AIs. In order to survive in a highly hostile environment, the cyberpunk antihero will not make any ethical commitment. With regard to our world, as Cavallaro (2000, 9) states, they produce "the collapse of intelligible boundaries between acceptable and criminal forms of conduct." It is also evident that those who manage secrets are those who are in privileged positions, distributing and amassing power. Horn (2011, 109–10) describes this social stratification by stating that

> secrecy structures social or political relations of exclusion and inclusion; by separating those who know from those who do not (but who may know, at one point, or who doubt or suppose that there is a secret), it constitutes their relation [. . .] between knowledge and ignorance, power and powerlessness.

Bok (1983, 19) proposes a similar view. Rather than talking just about social separation, she also points to the power acquired by those who control and keep secrets, derived from the usage and control over information. Because of that, "conflicts over secrecy [. . .] are conflicts over power: the power that comes through controlling the flow of information."

The most relevant secrets, those that structure the plots in the trilogy, are created, kept, and used by Wintermute, the loas, and Virek, and the role of the antiheroes will be that of unraveling the secrets that drive many of their own activities. In that sense, the relationship of exclusion and inclusion, and the differences of power balance proposed by Horn and Bok, are obvious. But it is worth investigating the nature of the secrets themselves. When dealing with the ethical nature of different political secrets, Horn (2011, 106) debates the positive and negative consequences that arcanum and secretum imply. Both can be sometimes used to favor (in a positive way) the stability of the democratic state, or can also "breed violence, corruption and oppression." One of the main narrative problems in the Sprawl Trilogy, however, is the fragmentary, sometimes obscure development of certain characters and actions. In fact, it is quite difficult to shed light on the motivations behind many of the

AIs and people in the story, beyond their own self-benefit. What is more, the consequences that the different secret plots many of them carry out are, most of the time, unclear, as if Gibson was not interested at all in the possible outcomes of his characters' hidden agendas. Thus, readers are often confronted with an ethical conflict, as Gibson does not give them the necessary narrative tools to know what motivates a certain character to carry out a certain action or to maintain some kind of conspiracy or secret. Self-interest seems an obvious motivation for most characters, but sometimes even this is not valid, as in the case of the actions of the loas, as I will explain below. The reader's sympathies will align with the actions of a given character, and these sympathies will be, as Phelan (2004) points out, signaled by the path directed by the novel. We can then evaluate how the trilogy represents the characters we are concerned with.

In *Neuromancer*, Wintermute is acting illegally. The entity has no right to act on its own, and even less so to increase its power and independence. The apparition of the Turing Police (embodied in the three agents, Pierre, Michèle, and Roland) who are tracing the actions of the team working for Wintermute proves that the AI is acting beyond the law. It is interesting how the Turing Police, the only example of security forces in the novel (even if it is not easy to guess whether it is a government or a corporate entity), prosecute AI activities for the sake of humanity. As Michèle tells Case, "You have no care for your species. For thousands of years men dreamed of pacts with demons. Only now are such things possible. And what would you be paid with? What would your price be, for aiding this thing to free itself and grow?" (Gibson 2016b, 179). This plea for the well-being of humankind contrasts with the total lack of morality Gibson portrays otherwise in the trilogy. It is even more remarkable that this statement comes from a security force that is much more concerned with cybercrime than with real-life people. The three agents will not disrupt the AI's plans, however, as it will manipulate service robots and drones to kill them when they try to arrest Case for helping the virtual entity. Considering the advanced state of self-awareness and rationality presented by Wintermute, it should also be capable of having a sense of ethics. The human Turing Police, however, strictly prohibit AIs from developing any kind of independence from human control, and Wintermute kills several innocent people during the process of achieving its integration with Neuromancer, including the boy who hid the key in the Tessier-Ashpool mansion years ago, before the events narrated in the novel. The exposure of the secrets kept by the Tessier-Ashpool family to achieve this fusion between the two AIs is carried out by favoring the end over the means at all costs. Wintermute behaves like an entity that only tries to obtain its own benefit.

In the case of corporations in *Count Zero*, for instance, the secret operation of the scientist defecting from one corporation to another is carried out using weaponry and mercenaries, and several lives are lost in the process (including that of the scientist himself). Everything supports the idea that cyberpunk megacorporations are entities that rule and command the world just for the sake of profit and power. In that sense, it is obvious that characters (and readers) will probably consider any secret operation carried out by a megacorporation as dubious and illegal. In fact, as Robertson (1999, 13) points out when discussing Bok's ideas, "Although secrecy is neither good nor bad, there is a presumption against the legitimacy of collective secrecy, especially secrecy associated with the exercise of power." Cyberpunk, indeed, points to megacorporations as the supreme evil to be fought by most of the antiheroes in the genre. One might wonder why megacorporations, apparently unchecked by any state and wielding near-absolute power, even bother to use secrecy for many of their operations. Moyland (2010, 86) points out that these "transnational corporations and criminal organizations compete for control of the highly developed information matrix [. . .] that is the fundamental economic resource and vehicle of the new world order." Competition is established between the corporations themselves. The failed defection of Christopher Mitchell from Maas Biolabs, prompted by Virek, shows that this corporate fear stems from the possible actions of rival companies. Their secrecy has very negative consequences for those on the lower levels of the social hierarchy, as their measures of security, espionage, and betrayal against each other are thoroughly indifferent to any collateral damage they might cause. In an ideological context that tends to perceive transparency as a virtue (see Alloa and Thomä 2018, 2; Birchall 2021, 4), the fact that a corporation keeps secrets is instantly codified in negative terms, as a sign that it does not respect or care about citizens who might be in a position to expect such transparency from corporate management. And when a cyberpunk corporation is keeping secrets, it is because its operations tend to be, in a Kantian sense, morally dubious and normally damaging for the general population. The separation between politics and private issues that Horn (2011, 112) discusses should be valid here for megacorporations, since they are privately owned entities. From the very moment that these corporate choices might affect the whole population, however, their secrets in "public matters" are "no longer acceptable" (112).

The case of Virek is different. Despite Virek's being human, Marly doubts at several points in the novel the character's humanity, owing to his immense power and wealth. As one of the characters in the novel remarks, "Virek and his kind are already far from human" (Gibson 1987, 101). This form of dehumanization of the character places him closer to the sphere of artificial intelligences or megacorporations, in the sense of depersonalized abstract entities. The fact that Virek meets Marly in virtual spaces, in which he uses avatars of himself that certainly do not represent his current decrepit physical condition, helps place the character outside the sphere of the human, as he himself acknowledges: "You must forgive my reliance on technology. I have been confined for over a decade to a vat. In some hideous industrial suburb of Stockholm. Or perhaps in hell. I am not a well man, Marly" (13).

At the same time, Marly also remarks on the evil nature of the art patron: "Nothing he wants can be good. For anyone . . . I've seen him, I've felt it" (219). The novel does not provide any real standard for the reader to measure Virek's ethical compass, however, except the perceptions provided by Marly. He seems to be acting by mere survival instinct, without any dark secret behind his will to become immortal in cyberspace. During his attempt to achieve cyberimmortality, Virek plots Christopher's defection from Maas Biolabs to Hosaka in order to later kidnap him. The killing of Christopher during the operation, together with the extreme violence of the assault, are ethically despicable, but for Virek, as for Wintermute, the end justifies the means. He is acting in his own interest, using people as pawns for the fulfillment of his plan. Virek's lack of humanity greatly conditions the reader's view of him. The coldness with which Gibson portrays the character breaks any empathetic bond with readers, and it distances them from any kind of identification similar to that which they might have with antiheroes, for example. Virek is apparently human but behaves like Wintermute, seeking his salvation and escape from his bodily prison at all costs. While he is perceived by characters like Marly as the supreme evil, his ambitions are not dissimilar to those of some of the novel's antiheroes, as will be seen below. Apart from that, he is not more violent or morally questionable than many of the characters who dwell in Gibson's trilogy. The reader will, however, find Virek's conspiracies ethically reprehensible because the text dehumanizes the character. Owing to the enormous amount of power and money he accumulates, and to his appearances as a virtual avatar, Gibson places Virek in a position to be ethically detached from the reader, who perceives him more as a construct that opposes the protagonists than as a human being. The connection between money and dehumanization is made explicit again by Marly when "she stared directly into those soft blue eyes and knew, with an instinctive mammalian certainty, that the exceedingly rich were no longer even remotely human" (16).

As for the loas, at the very end they destroy Virek, and at certain points they protect Bobby from black ICEs, so they seem to act following a certain goal. But once again, this goal is never made explicit in the novel, and Gibson plots his own literary secretum. It is impossible to decode, or anticipate, their intentions (if any) owing to their mystical nature and the way Gibson represents them. The loas never speak of their plans, and the linguistic representation of them remains a barrier that the writer constructs between the reader and the intentions of the voodoo gods. In fact, as Turner points out when referring to the documentation of the mysterious implants Angie has, "It doesn't tell the whole story. Remember that. Nothing ever does" (241). Why they want to destroy Virek remains hidden from the reader, and the loas are the most obscure entities to be found in the Sprawl Trilogy.

It is worth paying attention to the events that take place in *Mona Lisa Overdrive*, particularly those concerning Bobby and Angie, the two characters from *Count Zero* who reappear in this third novel. By the end of *Count Zero*, it is hinted that Angie might have learned from the voodoo people her way to success: "Our people can teach you things" (240). In the third volume, Angie is a famous simstar actress, powerful and beautiful. She has a small army of producers, fashion designers, make-up artists, and scriptwriters around her, and she lives in the most fashionable villas and hotel suites. It seems that Angie has access to secrets, revealed by the voodoo people, that bring her fame and success. In contrast, Bobby, who by the end of the second novel had become her lover and bodyguard, is now constantly lying in a medical bed, jacked into cyberspace, after Angie and he part ways. One of the novel's subplots is concerned with whether Bobby is safe in the custody of a group of outcast artists or not, and with the mystery surrounding his unusual cyberspace activity. It is later revealed that Bobby has stolen the aleph from 3Jane, one of the daughters of the Tessier-Ashpool family. The aleph is a portable device that duplicates the entire cyberspace, and he is constantly connected to it. Bobby has paid for having his comatose body under constant surveillance, hiding from 3Jane, while he keeps dwelling in cyberspace. By the end of the novel, both Bobby and Angie will reunite in the aleph as immortal constructs while their physical bodies perish in the real world.

Both Bobby and Angie were presented in *Count Zero* as part of the group that does not share major secrets: those who are powerless and marginal and try to deal with the consequences of the power distribution and secrecy managed by corporations, AIs, and Josef Virek. But in *Mona Lisa Overdrive*, they have changed their status, at least their social one. They are not outcasts anymore, and the two of them hold secrets for their own benefit. Bobby's identity is not divulged when his comatose body reaches the Factory, where he is going to be looked after. The people who take care of him just know him as Count, but they do not know what he is doing, why he is in this physical state, and what devices keep him in suspended animation and jacked into cyberspace. Before getting permanently connected to the matrix, Bobby tried to keep a low profile that created a secrecy effect. All the people who dwell in the Factory over the course of the novel speculate about his identity, as well as about what he is doing and why they have to protect his physical body. Cherry, the nurse who takes care of him, as well as Slick and Gentry, the two outcast artists who give shelter in their Factory to Bobby and his crew, have to suffer the consequences of the secret actions and life of Bobby; that is, the attack by the mercenaries hired by 3Jane to get the hacker and the aleph. The tables have now turned, and Bobby is in a clear position of power, to the point that he can use secrecy as a tool for achieving more power, and his role in the previous book is now taken by other characters, who are subjugated by his own secret plans.

Bobby's hidden plans include the theft of the aleph, but he also seeks protection for his physical body, at the expense of the safety of all of the Factory's inhabitants. Like Virek or Wintermute, Bobby's personal interest, his goals of transcending from the real to the virtual world with Angie, override any moral qualms he might have in the execution of his roadmap. The Factory characters do not know who they are harboring, and this endangers their own lives as misfits. Nevertheless, by this point in the trilogy the reader is fully committed to the cause of the lovers, who also develop the most enduring and emotional romance of the saga. They are the quintessential antiheroes, even if at this point in the story they are on the verge of becoming something closer to virtual constructs on a par with Virek. This sentimental relationship can be understood as one of the key points of communion between these two antiheroes and the reader, as Gibson thus presents two emotionally close characters, seeking a joint eternal virtual life of stability, removed from the darkness of their cyberpunk reality. In this way, the reader can overlook the morally questionable actions that Bobby carries out, since there is an alignment in favor of these characters that Gibson has been establishing throughout the entire trilogy.

This process departs from their origins as marginalized antiheroes who rely on the secrets they can access to survive and acquire their own share of power (as is also the case with characters like Case and Molly in *Neuromancer*), up to the final moments of *Mona Lisa Overdrive*, where it is impossible to see them as antiheroes anymore, as they have enough power to execute their own conspiracies involving third parties for their own benefit. The progression of both characters in the two novels goes from being part of the group that must suffer the consequences of others' secrets to achieving a much higher level of power thanks to having secrets revealed to them (in the case of Angie) or stolen by them (in the case of Bobby). And curiously enough, the goal of the secret plan Bobby carries out is, as it was for Virek, that of transcending their mortal chains and becoming immortal entities in cyberspace, so the two lovers can remain together forever.

The sympathy that the novels convey for the couple, however, differs enormously from the feelings provoked by Virek, who is presented from the very beginning as both an almighty figure and an uncanny, dehumanized presence. The ascension of Bobby and Angie from the scum of society to the level of those who have the right to own secret plans affects our sympathy toward them. While Virek's secret plans and actions may be questionable owing to his portrayal as a character confronted by the antiheroes, the plots carried out by the latter reinforce their status of antiheroes with whom readers should identify.

4. Conclusions

The corporate world rules with an iron fist over the Sprawl Trilogy universe. The stratification of the characters, divided between the fringe antiheroes, on the one hand, and the powerful businessmen, billionaires, and AIs, on the other, is also complemented by the access to knowledge and power that the latter groups have and keep secret. The trilogy is riddled with secret plans orchestrated by the powerful classes, who make the outcasts dance to the music they desire, like pawns on a neon chessboard. This places the Sprawl Trilogy in the tradition of the conspiracy narrative, in which, as Timothy Melley (2002, 58) notes, "numerous postwar narratives concern characters who are nervous about the way large, and often vague, organizations might be controlling their lives, influencing their actions, or even constructing their desires." And to bring all their plans to fruition, the entire network of the powerful makes use of the secret as arcanum, maintaining it to continue amassing power and money or to achieve immortality within cyberspace.

With regard to the other two categories of political secrecy posited by Horn, the mysterium is developed around Rastafarianism and the voodoo entities present in *Neuromancer* and *Count Zero*. Both groups have a religious and mystical component that contrasts with the visceral materiality of the rest of the characters in the trilogy. The quasi-supernatural nature of the voodoo artificial intelligence present in cyberspace results in a Derridean secrecy effect around their nature and intentions, which fills the minds of the less mystical characters in the narrative with speculation, thus re-creating the secretum. It is, then, this group of corporations and AIs that deal with the arcanum, mysterium, and secretum, thus replacing the states, which are almost completely absent from this cyberpunk dystopia.

Finally, the ethics behind the existence of the various secrets that populate the trilogy are ambiguous in most cases and outright questionable in others. Corporate secrets are viewed negatively, matching with the idea of total transparency discussed by Han and Birchall, among others. Wintermute schemes unscrupulously, using and discarding human lives at will. Virek seeks his survival over time, even if he also has to use brute force, mercenaries, and bribes in the execution of his secret plans.

In the universe of violence and dehumanization created by Gibson, any kind of vertical mobility between the two castes of characters seems impossible. It is, however, through secrecy that two of these characters, Bobby and Angie, manage to thrive and become the bearers of great secrets themselves, in order to make new outcasts dance. In this way, the circle of power is perpetuated through secrecy in a fictional world in which the antiheroes do not seek the destruction of the system but, on the contrary, take advantage of secrecy in order to themselves achieve higher levels of power.

When these once-marginalized characters become powerful and also begin to hide information, they do not hesitate to endanger the lives of the new misfits working for them, reestablishing the balance of secrecy between those at the top of the pyramid and the lower social strata. It is in this way that the true dystopian nature of cyberpunk makes itself known.

Works Cited

Alloa, Emmanuel, and Thomä, Dieter. 2018. "Transparency: Thinking through an Opaque Concept." In *Transparency, Society and Subjectivity: Critical Perspectives*, edited by Emmanuel Alloa and Dieter Thomä, 1–13. Cham, Switzerland: Palgrave MacMillan.

Barrett, Leonard E. 1982. *The Rastafarians: The Dreadlocks of Jamaica*. Kingston, Jamaica: Sangster's Book Ltd.

Birchall, Clare. 2011a. "Introduction to 'Secrecy and Transparency': The Politics of Opacity and Openness." *Theory, Culture & Society* 28, no. 7–8: 7–25.

———. 2011b. "Transparency Interrupted. Secrets of the Left." *Theory, Culture & Society* 28, no. 7–8: 60–84.

———. 2014. "Radical Transparency?" *Cultural Studies ↔ Critical Methodologies* 14, no. 1: 77–88.

———. 2021. *Radical Secrecy: The Ends of Transparency in Datafied America*. Minneapolis: University of Minnesota Press.

Bok, Sissela. 1983. *Secrets: On the Ethics of Concealment and Revelation*. New York: Pantheon.

Boulter, Jonathan. 2010. "Posthuman Melancholy: Digital Gaming and Cyberpunk." In Murphy and Vint 2010, 135–54.

Cadora, Karen. 2010. "Feminist Cyberpunk." In Murphy and Vint 2010, 157–72.

Cavallaro, Dani. 2000. *Cyberpunk and Cyberculture: Science Fiction and the Work of William Gibson*. London: Athlone Press.

Collado-Rodríguez, Francisco. 2017. "The Imperfections of a Future Past: Trauma, Posthumanity, and Sci-Fi in William Gibson's 'The Gernsback Continuum.'" *Letterature D'America* 166–67: 177–94. https://www.academia.edu/37069746/THE_IMPERFECTIONS_OF_A_FUTURE_PAST_TRAUMA_POSTHUMANITY_AND_SCI_FI_IN_WILLIAM_GIBSON_S_THE_GERNSBACK_CONTINUUM_.

Csicsery-Ronay, Istvan, Jr. 2010. "Cyberpunk and Empire." In *Visions of the Human in Science Fiction and Cyberpunk*, edited by Marcus Leaning and Birgit Pretzsch, 105–14. Inter-Disciplinary Press.

Derrida, Jacques. 1994. "To Do Justice to Freud: A History of Madness in the Age of Psychoanalysis." *Critical Inquiry* 20, no. 2: 227–66.
Dery, Mark. 1994. "Black to the Future: Interviews with Samuel R. Delany, Greg Tate, and Tricia Rose." In *Flame Wars: The Discourse of Cyberculture*, edited by Mark Dery, 179–222. Durham, NC: Duke University Press.
Foster, Thomas. 2005. *The Souls of Cyberfolk: Posthumanism as Vernacular Theory*. Minneapolis: University of Minnesota Press.
Gibson, William.1987. *Count Zero*. London: Ace. First published 1986.
———. 2016a. *Mona Lisa Overdrive*. London: Gollancz. First published 1988.
———. 2016b. *Neuromancer*. London: Gollancz. First published 1984.
Grant, Glenn. 1990. "IncTranscendence through Detournement in William Gibson's *Neuromancer*." *Science Fiction Studies* 17, no. 1 (March): 41–49.
Grantham, Michael. 2015. *The Transhuman Antihero: Paradoxical Protagonists of Speculative Fiction from Mary Shelley to Richard Morgan*. Jefferson, NC: McFarland.
Han, Byung-Chul. 2015. *The Transparency Society*. Translated by Erik Butler. Stanford, CA: Stanford Briefs.
Hardt, Michael, and Antonio Negri. 2000. *Empire*. Cambridge, MA.: Harvard University Press.
Henthorne, Tom. 2011. *William Gibson: A Literary Companion*. Jefferson, NC: McFarland.
Heuser, Sabine. 2003. "New Final Frontiers: Problems and Aims." In *Virtual Geographies: Cyberpunk and the Intersection of the Postmodern and Science Fiction*, vii–xxv. Amsterdam: Rodopi.
Hollinger, Veronica. 1990. "Cybernetic Deconstructions: Cyberpunk and Postmodernism." *Mosaic: An Interdisciplinary Critical Journal* 23, no. 2 (Spring): 29–44.
Horn, Eva. 2011. "Logics of Political Secrecy." *Theory, Culture and Society* 28, no. 7–8: 103–22.
Kebede, Alemseghed, and J. David Knottnerus. 1988. "Beyond the Pales of Babylon: The Ideational Components and Social Psychological Foundations of Rastafari." *Sociological Perspectives* 41, no. 3: 499–517.
Keenan, Bernard. 2015. "Secrecy, distrust, and interception of communications." *LSE Media Policy Project*. https://blogs.lse.ac.uk/medialse/2015/06/22/secrecy-distrust-and-interception-of-communications/.
Lavender, Isiah, III. 2020. "Critical Race Theory." In McFarlane, Murphy, and Schmeink 2020, 308–16.
McFarlane, Anna. 2016. "'Anthropomorphic Drones' and Colonized Bodies: William Gibson's *The Peripheral*." *ESC: English Studies in Canada* 42, no. 1–2 (March/June): 115–31.
———. 2020. "IA and Cyberpunk Networks." In *AI Narratives: A History of Imaginative Thinking about Intelligent Machines*, edited by Stephen

Cave, Kanta Dihal, and Sarah Dillon, 284–308. Oxford: Oxford University Press.

McFarlane, Anna, Graham J. Murphy, and Lars Schmeink, eds. 2020. *The Routledge Companion to Cyberpunk Culture*. New York: Routledge.

Melley, Timothy. 2002. "Agency Panic and the Culture of Conspiracy." In *Conspiracy Nation: The Politics of Paranoia in Postwar America*, edited by Peter Knight, 57–81. New York: New York University Press.

Moyland, Tom. 2010. "Global Economy, Local Texts: Utopian/Dystopian Tension in William Gibson's Cyberpunk Trilogy." In Murphy and Vint 2010, 81–94.

Murphy, Graham, and Sherryl Vint, eds. 2010. *Beyond Cyberpunk: New Critical Perspectives*. New York: Routledge.

Nixon, Nicola. 1992. "Cyberpunk: Preparing the Ground for Revolution or Keeping the Boys Satisfied?" *Science Fiction Studies* 19, no. 2 (July): 219–35.

Phelan, James. 2004. "Rhetorical Literary Ethics and Lyric Narrative: Robert Frost's 'Home Burial.'" *Poetics Today* 25, no. 4 (Winter): 627–51.

Rieder, John. 2020. "Empire." In McFarlane, Murphy, and Schmeink 2020, 335–43.

Rigaud, Milo. 1985. *Secrets of Voodoo*. San Francisco: City Lights Books.

Robertson, Ken G. 1999. *Secrecy and Open Government: Why Governments Want You to Know*. Basingstoke, UK: Macmillan.

Simmel, Georg. 1905. "The Sociology of Secrecy and of Secret Societies." *American Journal of Sociology* 11, no. 4 (January): 441–98.

Sponsler, Claire. 1992. "Cyberpunk and the Dilemmas of Postmodern Narrative: The Example of William Gibson." *Contemporary Literature* 33, no. 4 (Winter): 625–44.

8: Secrecy and Exposure in Toni Morrison's *Paradise*

Alice Sundman

1. Introduction

RECENT THEORETICAL DISCUSSIONS of transparency frequently center on questions relating to technical and digital surveillance, such as the phenomenon of Wikileaks (Boothroyd 2011), the sharing of selfies (Metelmann and Telios 2018), and Edward Snowden's revelations of the United States National Security Agency's mass surveillance of digital data (Birchall 2015). The discussion has indeed become increasingly urgent owing to digital and technical developments. When it comes to theorizing transparency, however, an overly strong emphasis on such developments involves a risk of presentism. Yet, questions relating to transparency in communities are not new, nor are they necessarily dependent on digital systems. Rather, they are aspects of human society itself, and have a history preceding today's technological developments.[1]

Toni Morrison's 1998 novel *Paradise* highlights how issues of transparency inform pre-digital social interaction. It depicts two rural communities that at first glance seem to fit into an antithetical structure of *exposure* versus *secrecy*. In Ruby, a fictional all-Black town dominated by a male hierarchy, the inhabitants' activities and relations become common knowledge through talking and gossiping. Thus, exposure does not occur through surveillance enabled by technology. In the novel, set in a small town in Oklahoma in the 1970s, there is no technical or digital surveillance of the inhabitants, nor is their exposure based on formal measures taken by official state or municipal authorities. Rather, exposure in Ruby is based on direct relations between the inhabitants of the town, and it is exerted through unofficial means. In contrast to Ruby,

---

1   For scholarship concerned with pre-digital transparency see, e.g., Emmanuel Alloa (2018), who traces the history of the concept of transparency and relates it to today's situation, and Manfred Schneider (2018), whose discussion focuses on the dream of transparency in three time periods: the Middle Ages, the Enlightenment, and the twentieth century, represented by Saint Thomas Aquinas, Jean-Jacques Rousseau, and Jean-Paul Sartre, respectively.

a nearby mansion, commonly called the Convent, constitutes a kind of haven, housing women who carry secret traumatic experiences, such as a mother's betrayal or the death of two babies in a hot car. Here, the secrets of the two communities depicted in the novel, the one constituted by the Convent women and that of Ruby's inhabitants, are allowed and kept.

A closer look at the text reveals a complex interplay between what is disclosed and what is concealed in both communities. This essay explores this entanglement within the town of Ruby, within the informal microcommunity of the Convent, and in the interrelations between the two, arguing that *Paradise* complicates the seemingly neat dichotomy of secrecy and exposure by displaying their intricate interdependencies. Morrison's depiction of Ruby and the Convent enriches the theoretical discussion of transparency by illustrating as well as complicating ways in which secrecy and exposure work in communities.

The term *exposure*, in this essay, is used in close relation to the notion of transparency. A dictionary definition—and a commonplace understanding—of transparency emphasizes the "capacity of outsiders to obtain valid and timely information about the activities of government or private organizations" (Johnston, n.d.); that is, on (state) power being transparent in relation to its citizens. In the growing field of critical transparency studies, however, the idea of transparency is developed further: as Emmanuel Alloa and Dieter Thomä (2018, 3) note, studies in this field "question that transparency has a stable semantic core." Rather than adhering to the commonplace meaning of the term, recent theoretical discussions of transparency frequently understand the notion not solely as (state) power being transparent in relation to its citizens but also as, for example, (state) power gathering information about—*seeing through*—its citizens. Transparency is understood in various ways as potential exposure and disclosure. In line with such fluidity of meaning, this essay understands the term *exposure* in a broad sense as "the action of bringing to light" (*OED Online*, n.d.); that is, both to disclose and to expose, be it secret individual experiences or features and structures of power relations.

The concept of transparency suggests that an object is in a state of being potentially seen through. As Daniel Naurin (2006, 91) expresses it, the term "captures the accessibility of information": "it is possible to look into something, to see what is going on." Consequently, when something is transparent, disclosure of information could already have happened, could be in the process of happening, or could potentially happen in the future. Thomas Docherty (2018, 284), on his part, proposes that transparency can be understood as "that which eradicates the difference between the secret and the revealed," so that there really is nothing more to disclose, since the secret is already exposed. This essay discusses communities in which such transparency is not (yet) fully developed. In the communities in *Paradise*, this is partly due to the fact that there is no formal mechanism of transparency. The inhabitants of Ruby are not officially and repeatedly monitored by a formal (structured, official) power, nor is there such a power that can be transparent toward the members of the community; and the women staying at the Convent keep their secrets until they, as a collective, decide to expose them. Therefore, instead of *transparency*, I use the term *exposure* to indicate the act of revealing, an active disclosing of something that is concealed, rather than an ongoing state of potential access to information.

A *secret* is understood broadly as something that is concealed, be it private thoughts, traumatic experiences, or means of maintaining power. Secrecy, moreover, involves active concealing; as Jeremy Gilbert (2007, 26) notes, there is "a difference between a secret and something which is simply not known." A secret is not just "not public knowledge"; it is also "knowable and shareable and hence is made the object of an active and collaborative act of secrecy, of hiding and guarding, of *enclosure*." Secrecy, as Georg Simmel (1950, 330) suggests, is crucial to social interaction: "Whether there is secrecy between individuals or groups, and if so how much, is a question that characterizes every relation between them." Sharing and withholding information, as well as the question whether this is done freely or not, to a large extent determine the quality of interaction between humans. In this essay, then, secrecy—involving active concealing of something that is possible to reveal—is understood as a feature fundamental to human interaction and, consequently, a crucial aspect of communities.

Morrison's novel *Paradise* opens with a description of a massacre of the five women living in the Convent. The attackers are nine men from Ruby who see the women as a threat to their town. The scene of the massacre is followed by accounts of the circumstances that led to the killing. These accounts alternate between describing Ruby and presenting the stories of the women who end up staying in the Convent. What plays out in these accounts is a multigenerational, historical narrative spanning from the nineteenth century—when a group of "wayfarers" (1999, 189) looking for a place to settle down were rejected by the all-Black town Fairly and had to move on to found their own town—to their descendants in Ruby in the novel's present in the 1970s. The life stories of the individual characters are set against a background of American history. We also get insights into the Convent women's pasts and the circumstances that made them leave their homes and end up in the Convent. Toward the end of the novel, the narrator returns to the scene of the massacre and the events following it, some of which waver between the natural and the supernatural.

The novel on the whole orbits around tensions between Ruby and the Convent. The inhabitants of Ruby have isolated themselves from their surrounding society, of which we get to know very little, and formed a secluded place for those belonging to the town. These people are tied to each other through their history of founding the town and, before that, their ancestors, a group of nine Black families who founded the town of Haven. The all-Black Haven was established in the nineteenth century; owing to the Depression and changing values and lifestyles in post–World War II America, however, the town changed, and the descendants of the founding families decided to establish a new town, Ruby, in the mid-twentieth century. In Ruby, they managed to create a place where the inhabitants to a large extent follow the implicit rules governing the community, which is dominated by a male hierarchy based on control. One central aspect of the community is an obsession with racial purity: those highest in rank have a "blue-black" skin color that the character Pat calls "8-rock," referring to "a deep deep level in the coal mines" (193). The Convent, on its part, houses a group of women who have ended up in the mansion after having fled from traumatic experiences. It forms a kind of female haven where the strange and the suffering can find shelter; in the words of one of the characters, it is "a place where you can stay for a while" (175) and "collect yourself" (176).

In Morrison criticism, Ruby and the Convent are frequently understood as antithetical communities. Ruby, a town characterized by stagnation, control, and a male hierarchy, stands in contrast to the Convent, a place of openness, diversity, and female community. Yet, within and between these communities, complex relations are displayed, refuting simple dichotomies.[2] Features relating to secrecy and exposure present similar binary patterns that become blurred or dissolved. The notions of public and private, for example, are discussed by Shirley A. Stave (2013, 26), who describes Ruby as a town where "no distinction" is made "between what is public and what is private" (26) and the Convent as a place where the women "claimed a private space" (28). Stave's discussion revolves around how the public and the private relate to male versus female spaces. My essay, rather, focuses on how exposure and secrecy play out in the novel, both in the form of opposing features of the two communities and the ways in which they are interconnected. Reading *Paradise* through these concepts highlights how secrecy and exposure form fundamental features of the novel's two central communities and, consequently, how they contribute to the text's core conflicts. Conversely,

---

2   As Paula Martín-Salván (2019, 199) notes, a reading focusing on the two communities as primarily opposing spaces "partially erases the complexity of communal life as depicted by Morrison." For a discussion of the complexity of these communities in relation to theorists such as Jean-Luc Nancy, Maurice Blanchot, and Giorgio Agamben, see Martín-Salván. For discussions of questions relating to fixity, control, openness, and diversity, see, for example, Lindsay M. Christopher (2009), Cynthia Dobbs (2011), Shari Evans (2013), Linda J. Krumholz (2002), and Seongho Yoon (2005).

considering secrecy and exposure through *Paradise* expands the interdisciplinary theoretical discussion by focusing particularly on the imagination and representation of small rural communities, of communities holding traumatic experiences, and of communities in which aspects such as race and identity are formative factors.

2. Ruby and the Controlling Gaze

In the small, secluded, all-Black town Ruby, private matters frequently become common knowledge—secrets are exposed in the community. The exposure is of a nonformalized and unofficial kind. "News sure travels fast out here," the newcomer Gigi says to K.D. when he tells her he learned about her whereabouts from the person who gave her a lift to the Convent (Morrison 1999, 74). Her reflection is to the point in describing how the inhabitants seem to know everything about one another and how gossiping exposes what happens in the town. But there is also a more goal-directed gathering of information, such as when Deek is driving to the bank one morning: "He *decided* to *check out* the Oven before opening the bank. . . . When he arrived at the site he *circled* it. Except for a few soda cans and some paper that had escaped the trash barrel, the place was blank. . . . He should speak to Anna Flood . . .—*get her to* clean up the pop cans and mess that came from purchases made at her store" (110; emphases added). Here, Deek makes a conscious decision to actively inspect the place as he "circled it." Noticing the kind of debris left at the site and tracing the garbage to the shop, he is actively trying to exert social control through surveillance. His behavior is explained away by Reverend Misner, whose words to Anna Flood, the shopowner, reflect the common attitude in the town. "'He's just checking on things' . . . 'Got a right, doesn't he? It's sort of his town, wouldn't you say?'" he says in reply to Anna Flood's question about Deek's "hover[ing]" (115). The act of inspection, here, is exerted by Deek, who together with his twin brother, Steward, is one of the two unofficial leaders of the town, the ones who "ran everything, controlled everything" (217). Deek is gathering information about what is happening in the town and planning to use that information to influence the actions of another inhabitant, Anna Flood. This kind of nonformalized exposure of details thus results in social control. Here, the unwritten hierarchies of the community are revealed to the reader: as one of the unofficial leaders, Deek sees himself as being entitled to supervise the town; moreover, this right is generally accepted in the community.

Gossiping and watching are kinds of exposure that can be described in terms of a controlling gaze that is inherent in the social relations of the town. It is not formalized, and it is part of the way in which the town functions. The members of the community partake of a collective gaze through the spreading of information at the same time as they are subject to it. Thomä discusses a similar internalized gaze in relation to Jeremy Bentham's idea, as discussed by Michel Foucault, of the panopticon; that is, "a single never-seen voice which knows everything about everyone" (Alloa and Thomä 2018, 6). Those being watched by the panopticon "appropriate the very attitude exerted by the inspector" (Thomä 2018, 72). Alloa, in Foucauldian terms, points to a "move from external coercion to internalized self-control" (40). In Ruby, the controlling gaze is internalized without there being a clear coercive external controlling function from the start. The inhabitants of the town participate in the exposure of unwanted behavior through talking, gossiping, and watching, which results in social control.

Critiquing the hegemony of transparency, Byung-Chul Han (2015, vii) claims that a society of total transparency "switches from trust to control." "Trust," he proposes, "is only possible in a state between knowing and not-knowing" (47), while in a state of total transparency, "all not-knowing is eliminated" (47–48). In Ruby, the "knowing," the exposure generated through talking, gossiping, and watching, gives an illusion of a safe small town.[3] In the novel's opening scene, in which the men massacre the Convent women, Ruby is described from the perspective of one of the attackers as a town that "neither had nor needed a jail" and where there was no "slack or sloven woman anywhere in town" (Morrison 1999, 8):

> From the beginning its people were free and protected. A sleepless woman could always rise from her bed, wrap a shawl around her shoulders and sit on the steps in the moonlight. And if she felt like it she could walk out the yard and on down the road. No lamp and no fear. . . . Nothing for ninety miles around thought she was prey. . . . Lampless and without fear she could make her way. (8)

Read out of context, this passage could be understood as describing a safe and peaceful community in which people can be trusted and where women are respected. Indeed, the patriarchal community of Ruby bases its rationale precisely on the need to protect its women, whose vulnerability goes back to the moment when the nine founding families, before they established Haven, were rejected from the town Fairly, in which they hoped to settle down but from which they were "thrown out and cast away" (188). In this "rejection" (194), or "Disallowing" (189), pregnant

---

3   Cf. Raymond Williams's (1973, 166) notion of a "knowable community"; i.e., one that "offers to show people and their relationships in essentially knowable and communicable ways" (165), discussed in relation to communities in novels by George Eliot, Jane Austen, and others.

women in the group were "refused shelter," something that "rocked them, and changed them for all time" (95). Nevertheless, the ostensive safety in the quoted scene is misleading. In the text, the passage is embedded in the opening scene of the massacre, so that already at this point the apparent safety is contradicted by the extreme deadly violence directed toward women. The safety described is denied in the very scene it is part of and thus revealed to be an illusion. Rather than portraying a secure and quiet small town, the text displays a community where a deathly threat is lurking under the seemingly tranquil surface.

The illusory safety, moreover, is related to the exposure and control exerted through watching and gossiping as well as to a nonverbal threat of violence as the men in Ruby guard the inhabitants against outsiders: "Everything requires their protection" (12). When male strangers in cars molest young girls, this is soon noticed by the inhabitants: "One at a time, the townsmen come out of the houses, the backyards, off the scaffold of the bank, out of the feed store," making the strangers disappear in haste (13). Surveillance and the threat of violence thus work together to create a feeling of safety, which is built on control.

Total transparency, Han (2015, viii) claims, also leads to "conformity." Alloa (2018, 40), referring to Foucault, notes that "when behavior is likely to be judged by others [. . .] subjects will automatically adapt their conduct." Such mechanisms are prevalent in Ruby, and the town is to a large extent a community of conformity. Its very existence is based on the inhabitants' skin color; for example, marrying outside of the community and bringing in a spouse of a lighter color involves a risk for social ostracism. As Pat writes in her diary, "They hate us because [Mama] looked like a cracker and was bound to have cracker-looking children like me" (Morrison 1999, 196). This kind of conformity creates a community in which race and identity are central, and where outsiders as well as those who do not conform to the town's unwritten rules are socially rejected.

Exposure, control, and conformity thus form crucial features and mechanisms in Ruby. This transparency is, however, fundamentally built on features of secrecy. One such trait is nonformalized power itself: as control is exerted through unofficial exposure, the power structure is hidden behind everyday social interaction. The Morgan brothers' authority is grounded in hereditary patriarchy, and it is not questioned because they are direct descendants of the original founders of the town. Thus it is to some extent overt, yet their active control is frequently disguised as protection of women and of the community as a whole. Ruby thus lacks the kind of positive, valid transparency that exposes the structures and activities of formal power. Instead, features of race, identity, patriarchal tradition, and the history of the community contribute to the nonformalized power that cannot be questioned or examined.

Although exposure of the inhabitants' activities permeates the town's social relations, secrets are also part of the community; indeed, exposure presupposes secrecy, since without secrecy, there is nothing to expose. One kind of secret is one that is gossiped about yet not openly acknowledged, such as K.D.'s young girlfriend Arnette's pregnancy. The community's rules and customs, determined by traditional patriarchal values, prevent openly accepting her pregnancy, yet it is known to those speculating and gossiping about it. There was "a public secret about a never-born baby" (145), a "maybe-baby the bride had not acknowledged, announced, or delivered" (144). Arnette "was pregnant but, after a short stay at that Convent, if she had it, she sure didn't have it" (113). These paradoxical descriptions, suggesting both the existence and nonexistence of a baby, tie in with the paradox inherent in the expression "public secret": a secret is something that is concealed, while the adjective *public* indicates shared knowledge. Clare Birchall (2015, 7) discerns four kinds of "open secret," one of which she defines as a secret "which everybody unofficially knows or suspects, but proof (and therefore knowledge) of which remains elusive." In Ruby, this "public secret" is yet another indication of exposure through gossiping. An "open secret," Birchall claims, "requires us to know and not know at the same time" (7). Arnette's pregnancy exemplifies this paradoxical duality: even though it constitutes general knowledge in the town, there remains something unknown and uncertain—a "maybe-baby" and the conditional "if she had it"—which leaves a secret at the core. The "public secret" of Arnette's pregnancy simultaneously exposes her pregnancy and leaves an uncertainty regarding its existence.

Closely related to the idea of a public secret is a phrase Pat uses when speculating about who "beat up Arnette. The Convent women, as folks say? Or, *quiet as it's kept*, K.D.?" (Morrison 1999, 195–96; emphasis added). Morrison first used the phrase "quiet as it's kept" in her debut novel from 1970, *The Bluest Eye*, where it opens the narrator Claudia's account (Morrison 2007, 5). The phrase is also quoted in the title of J. Brooks Bouson's 1999 monograph, which reads the themes of race, trauma, and shame in Morrison's fiction. In her 1993 afterword to *The Bluest Eye*, Morrison describes how she associates the expression with "black women conversing with one another, telling a story, an anecdote, gossiping about some one [*sic*] or event" (212). Inherent in the phrase, she continues, is a duality entailing "a secret," a "conspiracy" that "is both held and withheld, exposed and sustained" (212). The phrase "quiet as it's kept," as Morrison understands it, thus suggests secrecy but also a sense of exposure: through the very action of talking and gossiping about that which is kept quiet, the secret is exposed, at least in some circles. In *Paradise*, too, the phrase indicates a secret that is known in parts of the community. The phrase, then, simultaneously entails secrecy and exposure. This becomes a social glue in the town as it keeps the gossiping community members together, while avoiding the threat to the community posed by openly broken patriarchal moral rules, such as pregnancy before marriage.

Despite—or perhaps because of—the controlling gaze exposing the activities of the inhabitants in the community, the people of Ruby try to guard their private lives. While frequently telling stories about their ancestors, they avoid talking about themselves: "About their own lives they shut up" (Morrison 1999, 161). They do not share their experiences with people regarded as outsiders; as Pat tells Reverend Misner, "'They don't like prying, Reverend. It's a thing about Ruby'" (207). Spaces of secrecy are formed: there are "closed doors and shut windows" (68), excluding outsiders as well as the controlling powers from private homes. One of the Morgan brothers, Deek, even has a secret relationship with Connie, one of the Convent women. This clearly reveals to the reader how the moral codes the Morgan brothers are trying to impose on the community are broken by one of the brothers himself, thus exposing the hypocrisy of the codes and contributing to undermining the moral authority of the Morgans. Moreover, Pat's "history project," in which she monitors past and present events and relationships in the community, "became unfit for any eyes except her own" (187) because of all the private details she writes down.

While social control in Ruby is based on exposure, it is itself a community guarding its secrets: it was founded as an all-Black town, and race becomes a defining aspect for belonging to the community. Implicit in the narrative is a distrust of white American mainstream society; there is, as Reverend Misner says to himself, "an icy suspicion of outsiders" (160). Moreover, as we will see below, secrets are kept as well from authorities outside the town. Secrets, then, become crucial for protecting privacy and for upholding an appearance of morality within the town, but also for protecting the community from the white mainstream society they seek to avoid.

In this secluded town, people form their own secret spaces away from the community's internal controlling gaze. One such space of secrecy is Dovey's garden. In a "little foreclosed house" (90) in town, Dovey finds a place in which she can be alone with her thoughts while her husband stays at their farm outside of the town. This garden seems like a paradoxical place of both openness and secrecy.[4] Yet, its openness needs to be viewed in the context of Ruby as a secluded place of stasis and control: for Dovey, the garden is a place where newness and openness are allowed, as it is concealed from the controlling gaze.

---

4   I have written elsewhere about ways in which this garden forms a place of openness and newness (Sundman 2022, 94–95).

In this garden, Dovey meets a stranger, a man passing through and then returning a few times to talk to her. Their conversations open up new and unexpected thoughts for her: Dovey "wondered . . . what on earth she was talking about" (91) when telling the stranger of the color of a swarm of butterflies. She finds herself "babbling" and thinks "she talked nonsense" (92). In the garden and with the stranger, her thoughts are articulated and thus exposed to the stranger but also to herself. She keeps the conversations as well as the stranger a secret, as no one knows about their meetings; she "kept forgetting to ask . . . who he might be" and "[kept] his visits secret" (92). The very thought of someone else knowing of him worries her, but "no one did. He seemed hers alone" (92). The stranger thus remains a secret, known only to Dovey, but at the same time also a secret to her. As readers, we cannot be sure whether he actually exists; his ethereal existence and his way of floating into the shadows rather suggest an apparition. Dovey does not recognize him from anywhere in town, nor can she connect him to any of the families living there. Moreover, she does not see him in any other place than this garden. He exists in a state of ambiguity and thus constitutes a secret in a dual way: in the story, his existence is kept a secret by Dovey at the same time as his very existence is enigmatic both in the story and to the reader, and thus holds something secret at the core.

As nothing of what happens in the garden is exposed to the rest of the community, it escapes its self-policing gaze. Dovey's thoughts, her words, and the existence of the stranger are all concealed, while new and unexpected thoughts are revealed. In this garden, then, another kind of exposure exists, one that does not seek to control: Dovey's thoughts are exposed to the stranger and to herself in open, explorative conversations. This is a kind of exposure that serves exploration and development rather than control and domination. The garden, then, constitutes a space of secrecy that counteracts the town's aim at exposing the unknown and the concealed.

Similarly, the Oven in the narrative epitomizes the duality of exposure and secrecy. This communal stove was first erected in the center of Haven and later relocated to Ruby, where it was placed at the outskirts of town. In Ruby, the Oven no longer serves as the utility it used to be in its original place; rather, it has turned into a "symbol," "an empty monument" (Evans 2013, 387; 389), and a "shrine" (Stave 2013, 26). It may be argued, as Stave does, that the oven "represents a refusal to tolerate private space" (26): a utility that would normally be placed in a private home is made communal and therefore symbolizes denial of the private. There is, however, a specific feature of the Oven that refutes transparency, as it bears an inscription that is the object of heated debate in Ruby. As the first word is missing, there is an argument about the meaning of the engraving. Does the inscription say "Beware the Furrow of His Brow"

(Morrison 1999, 86)? Or is it, rather, "Be the Furrow of His Brow" (87)? Is it a "motto," a "suggestion," or a "command" (86)? Reverend Pulliam claims the words are "clear as daylight," while Reverend Misner says they are not (86). What we see is a debate about both the words and their interpretation, as the writing itself is far from clear, univocal, and transparent.

Transparency, according to Han (2015, 2), is linked to language. "Transparent language," he writes, "is a formal, indeed, a purely machinic, operational language that harbors no ambivalence." A community aiming to eliminate the secret would thus need a language devoid of ambiguity, a language that reveals and discloses rather than obscures its meanings. This is a theoretical idea, a fantasy if you will, of transparent language. *Paradise* presents such fantasies about purity and transparency in connection to communal identity, and Han's idea of transparent language could be read in relation to the inscription on the Oven. Despite Reverend Pulliam's claim about their clarity, the engraved words hold none of the unequivocal meaning that Han ascribes to the idea of transparent language. Instead, the words invite both a literal and a figurative interpretation. Moreover, as one word is lacking, the inscription itself contains an absolute secret, as this word is gone forever and will never be disclosed. Through its multi-layered message, the inscription on the Oven is an antithesis to transparent language. It is a material engraving through which the hidden and the multifaceted belie the town's fantasies of transparency and exposure, leaving something undisclosed, opaque, and secret at its core.

Ruby thus forms a community in which secrecy and exposure are intricately intertwined. Itself a community holding secrets, it uses non-formalized exposure through watching, talking, and gossiping to exert control. At the same time, spaces of secrecy in the town counteract this exposure and control. The Oven, a material construction that is a crucial symbolic place in the town, epitomizes this duality: while symbolizing the private made public, it simultaneously manifests resistance to exposure. As we will see below, the community in the Convent operates as a place that safeguards privacy; secrecy, here, becomes fundamental to preserving individual privacy.

3. The Convent and the Sharing of Secrets

Located seventeen miles from Ruby, the Convent marks an antithesis to the town. In contrast to the patriarchal all-Black town, the Convent is inhabited by women of various races. Instead of focusing on preserving its own history, it is in constant change, from first being the home of an embezzler to becoming a school for Native American girls and to constituting a kind of haven for traumatized women. Rather than shutting out those who do not belong, the Convent "took people in—lost folk or folks who needed a rest" (Morrison 1999, 11). For most of these women, it is a temporary haven—they come and go, and the number of inhabitants varies during the time of the story. Thus, the Convent does not constitute a stable community in the way Ruby does. It is, moreover, a place of a certain permeability in relation to the town: some of the women in Ruby go there when in need, but there is also interaction of a more unremarkable and everyday kind: the Convent women sell vegetables and homemade food to Ruby's inhabitants. Thus there is a fluidity that makes the Convent different from Ruby but also allows for interaction between the two realms. Moreover, the Convent's acceptance of traumatized women and their secrets contrasts with the exposure of secrets in Ruby. Similar to the ways in which exposure in Ruby is complicated and includes secrecy, however, the secrecy in the microcommunity of the Convent is entwined with disclosure.

In the Convent, secrets are a crucial part of the women's memories of traumatizing events. One of the Convent women "was secretly slicing her thighs, her arms" (222). Arnette goes to the Convent to give birth to her baby in secret (77). When Pallas arrives, Connie listens to her story without expecting a full account of what happened to her; she can keep some of it "secret for a little longer" (176). "Stay as long as you like and tell me the rest when you want to," Connie says (176). As a haven for traumatized women, the Convent becomes a place where difficult private memories are housed and accepted. In this acceptance of secrets, however, resides a possibility for, and indeed also an expectation of, exposure. When Pallas's "words to say her shame clung like polyps in her throat" (179), this suggests not only a possibility but also a need to expose her secret, to get rid of that which is stuck in her throat. Similarly, when Connie tells Pallas she can keep her secret "for a little longer," there is not only an opening for disclosure but also an expectation that the secret will be revealed later on. As a space where secrets are allowed, the Convent thus forms a place where the women, to borrow Han's (2015, 3) words again, "can be at home without the gaze of the Other," but it also suggests that secrets might, will, and perhaps even must, be exposed.

This exposure is of a different kind than the controlling gaze permeating Ruby. While the watching and gossiping in the town serve social control, the exposure of secrets in the Convent involves acceptance, embrace, and incipient healing of trauma. For example, when Seneca arrives, the women "behaved as though they knew all about her" (Morrison 1999, 131), suggesting the recognition of her traumatic experiences. Seneca's secrets are preserved; the transparency is only "as though." Connie's words to Pallas—"tell me the rest when you want to" (176)—imply voluntary rather than forced exposure. The kind of exposure implied here is closely related to potential healing—it is in the possibility of exposing traumatic secrets that the women can hope for a feeling of safety and at-homeness. There is, however, also an expectation that the secrets will ultimately be disclosed. The text emphasizes the lack of explicit pressure on the women to tell their stories; yet, as we will see, all of them disclose their secrets to each other as part of something that is depicted as a collective process of working through their issues. The lack of pressure to disclose secrets is thus interwoven with expectations to do so, creating a social convention of voluntary disclosure.

Acceptance of secrets together with an opportunity—but also pressure—to reveal them without being judged opens up a different kind of community than the one prevailing in Ruby. While the relations between the Convent women sometimes entail conflict that may even turn physical (168), this microcommunity also moves toward a shared collective healing process. Near the end of the novel, Connie gathers the rest of the Convent women to perform a sort of ritual in the cellar. The women start articulating their stories, exposing them to each other through drawing and telling. This scene has been discussed in terms of psychological healing[5] as well as religious rites.[6] It starts with the women drawing each other's silhouettes on the cellar floor and continues with Connie starting to tell her secrets to the others. Her account includes experiences the reader recognizes, while "none of [the women] understood" what she was talking about (263). Connie thus exposes her secrets up to a point, but not through clear and transparent information communicated to the others; rather, the focus is on the act of telling, of revealing that which up until now has been concealed. There is no need for the language to be "formal," "machinic," or "operational," to borrow Han's (2015, 2) description of transparent language again. Language is allowed to be opaque, multilayered, and even incomprehensible, yet that which is articulated is disclosed and embraced.

Connie's "introductory speech" (Morrison 1999, 263) sparks a collective telling, a "loud dreaming" where "stories rose in that place" (264). Experiences never expressed before take form in the cellar, a subterranean, unexposed space and "a space of the unconscious" (Dobbs 2011, 114–15). The women's secrets are exposed, but it is an exposure without the threat of control. Instead, it builds community based on the disclosure and acceptance of secrets. The telling is collective: all of the women partake in the communal sharing of secrets. As one multifaceted, single organism, they experience the feelings, smells, actions, and movements of

---

5   See, for example, Dobbs (2011), Krumholz (2002), J. Brooks Bouson (2002), and Sharon Jessee (2006).

6   For discussions of the presence of the Afro-Brazilian religion Candomblé, see Bouson (2002, 208–11; 238–41nn 5, 6), John Leonard (1998, 25), La Vinia Delois Jennings (2008, 71–80; 166–77), Jessee (2006), and Kokahvah Zauditu-Selassie (2009, 119–41).

the stories told: they all "feel the smack of cold air," "inhale the perfume of sleeping infants," "adjust the sleeping baby head," and "kick their legs underwater" (Morrison 1999, 264). This strong sense of collectivity hardly leaves room for refusing to participate in the telling. The shared disclosure, then, builds a caring community and makes incipient healing possible—yet it also suggests a kind of social convention in which the sharing of secrets cannot be refused.

The disclosure of previously concealed thoughts and experiences displays other intricate interconnections between exposure and secrecy as "half-tales and the never-dreamed escaped from their lips" (264). Here, the telling exposes secrets, yet these entail something concealed: the tales are only partial tales and thus do not reveal the full stories. The "never-dreamed," moreover, suggests that something is concealed even to the teller herself, yet it is uttered and exposed.

While the telling is not intended to produce a clear message to be delivered to a specific recipient, the ways in which the words are received and listened to are nevertheless essential: "It was never important to know who said the dream or whether it had meaning," but the women "step easily into the dreamer's tale" (264) and later "spoke to each other about what had been dreamed and what had been drawn" (265). The exposure here is not about revealing what a specific individual has done or experienced. Rather, the process of disclosing thoughts and experiences is in focus, without tying the specific utterances to individuals or using them to judge others. The way the women "step . . . into" each other's stories suggests active, empathic, and caring listening, which is then followed by sharing of thoughts and reflections. This results in them finding inner peace: "Unlike some people in Ruby, the Convent women were no longer haunted" (266). Shari Evans (2013, 393) suggests that the women, here, "learn to practice empathy and human connection," which, she proposes, "transforms [them] into a community that practices home." Empathy and social connection are indeed crucial in this passage, and the ways in which secrets are both exposed and withheld, as well as listened to and talked about, suggest a development toward a caring community and incipient healing processes. Yet, the implicit pressure to partake in the collective sharing of secrets suggests a complication to this kind of ideal caring community.

The possibility of deciding about one's own secrets is closely related to privacy, which according to Charles Fried (1984, 209) can be seen as "the *control* we have over information about ourselves." Privacy, he holds, is essential to relations of mutual understanding: "In developed social contexts, love, friendship and trust are only possible if persons enjoy and accord to each other a certain measure of privacy." In *Paradise*, the decision about withholding or disclosing their secrets is said to be the women's own; allegedly, they have control over the information, something that would imply the possibility of a community based on friendship and trust. Yet, the implicit expectation that secrets should be collectively shared contradicts the sense of privacy necessary for such a community. The possibility of the Convent developing into a community of friendship and trust thus remains ambiguous.

As we already know, the community in the Convent does not endure, as one morning nine men from Ruby massacre the women. The men see the women as a threat to the community of Ruby, and therefore, the men think, they have to be destroyed. This perceived threat is partly based on the lack of control over the women and the fear of what might hide behind the walls of the Convent: "Early reports were of kindness and very good food. But now everybody knew it was all a lie, a front, a carefully planned disguise for what was really going on" (Morrison 1999, 11). In the proleptic opening scene portraying the massacre, the men view the Convent as hiding secrets that need exposure: "They have never been this deep in the Convent. . . . only a few have seen the halls, the chapel, the schoolroom, the bedrooms. Now they all will. And at last they will see the cellar and expose its filth" (3). The cellar is the place in which the women tell their secrets, something that is not revealed to the reader at this point. In contrast to the exposure of the women's secrets as an act aiming to develop acceptance and friendship and to heal trauma, the men are looking to reveal something dangerous in order to destroy it. The "strange things" (7) they find are viewed through this suspicious gaze, and the meanings of the objects are misread. For example, the men think they expose "a letter written in blood so smeary its satanic message cannot be deciphered" (7), while this is more likely a "sheet of paper with . . . lipstick words," now illegible (128), which one of the Convent women carried in her shoe ever since her mother, who she thought was her sister, left her. As in the discussion of the inscription on the Oven, this raises questions of interpretation, and these secrets remain inaccessible while the alleged exposure turns into misinterpretation.

After the massacre, the five women are dead, and the inhabitants of Ruby tell each other different stories about what happened at the Convent. Thus, the talking and gossiping within the community continues. They do not report the deaths to the authorities outside of the town, however; the massacre is kept a secret except within the town, where the various versions of the story blur the knowledge of what happened. This is facilitated by a "convenient mass disappearance" of the victims' bodies (303). Neither do the town's inhabitants report a "carful of skeletons" (272)— a family frozen to death during a blizzard, found in a field. The massacre, the deaths, and the secrets in the Convent thus seem obliterated, and Ruby seems to continue its life as a secluded, secretive community while sharing certain open secrets among themselves.

But are the women—and their secrets—really destroyed? And have the men regained the control they thought they had? Existing in a realm between life and death, the women return to their loved ones after the massacre. In scenes of varying degrees of reconciliation, they come to peace with their lives. And in the closing scene, a ship, potentially carrying the women, approaches a place called "paradise" (318). The women thus seem to live on after death. In Ruby, Billie Delia is waiting for their reappearance, which to her is not a matter of *if* they will return but *when*: "She had another question: When will they return? When will they reappear, with blazing eyes, war paint and huge hands to rip up and stomp down this prison calling itself a town?" (308). This suggests that despite the massacre, despite the killing, despite their disappearance, the women and their secrets are not eradicated but continue to exist.

The men, then, may seemingly have regained control, but the women's potential return refutes this. Billie Delia reflects on the town as a "backward noplace ruled by men whose power to control was out of control" (308), suggesting that on the surface, nothing seems to have changed, yet the men's power appears to be affected. And the Convent women may return, their secrets still guarded from the attackers' exposure, yet disclosed among themselves in a telling that potentially works toward a community of trust but that also suggests, through the implicit pressure to share secrets, that such an ideal community may be an illusion.

4. Exposure and Secrecy Interwoven

As we have seen, secrecy and exposure exist as entwined features in both Ruby and the Convent. This interdependence can be directly related to how Birchall (2011, 142), in an article exploring secrecy and transparency in American politics, discusses the interdependence between the two seemingly dichotomous phenomena: "The opposition between" them, Birchall argues, is "flawed," as "secrecy and transparency are not mutually exclusive." Three of the reasons she proffers are particularly relevant for my reading of *Paradise*. "The secret," Birchall holds, "generates transparency," so that "secrecy is transparency's condition"; "subjects are constituted by both transparency *and* secrets"; and, finally, "there is always something in us that is secret even to ourselves" (143).

Paradise illustrates these three motivations. First, as we saw, secrets in Ruby are a precondition for the exposure permeating the social relations of the community. Second, the subjects who are portrayed combine secrecy and exposure: for example, Dovey exposes her secrets to herself and to a stranger in her garden; Deek exerts his power through acts of inspection and surveillance in order to maintain the moral rules of the community while simultaneously concealing his own secret extramarital relationship with Connie; and Pat exposes other inhabitants' secrets in a diary that she finally burns; and for the women in the Convent, the complex interplay of secrecy and disclosure is fundamental to a potentially emerging, yet destroyed, community of trust. Third, the Convent women's telling contains secrets that are concealed even to the teller herself, thus exemplifying Birchall's point that something in the individual is a secret even to herself.

Paradise complicates the apparent dichotomy between secrecy and exposure also in other ways. In Ruby, a community permeated by a kind of exposure that leads to control and conformity, nonformalized means of exerting power are used to maintain social control through exposure of the inhabitants' doings. To an extent, then, these power structures are covert, as they are unofficial and not openly revealed. The ways in which these structures work add to the discussion about the panopticon and how an explicit external controlling function produces an internalized controlling gaze. Such a gaze, *Paradise* seems to imply, may also develop within a community based on nonformalized hierarchical power structures. Furthermore, through its depiction of spaces of secrecy in Ruby, the novel suggests ways in which individuals and, consequently, a community can develop resistance to the controlling gaze. The novel also broadens the perspective of what exposure may involve. In the Convent, another kind of exposure develops: through what is perceived as voluntary exposure in which the individuals control the information revealed, a community based on trust and caring may potentially emerge. Yet, the sharing of secrets relies on implicit social pressure, indicating that the ideal community of voluntary shared secrets may ultimately be an illusion.

Showing ways in which secrecy and exposure play out in two fictional communities and, furthermore, how they form part of the crucial conflicts between the communities, Morrison's novel also illustrates how secrecy and exposure are fundamental traits in communities both geographically and culturally at a remove from the technical development necessary for digital surveillance. It brings to the theoretical discussion of transparency a focus on race, identity, and African American culture and history. And it illustrates how secrecy and exposure partake in social interaction between people and, consequently, in the workings of communities. This essay has shown how *Paradise* constructs the concepts of secrecy and exposure not as absolute binaries but, rather, as mutually dependent. The novel shows ways in which there are valid, productive ways of exerting both exposure and secrecy, while it also points to how both may turn into means of destructive control. Furthermore, if we broaden the view, Morrison's fiction in general exposes secrets as she "attempts to reveal the voices and presences of African Americans who have been made invisible by mainstream American society" (Mori 2013,

55). Through illuminating African American history and experiences, she unveils parts of American history that were previously ignored. Her writing, then, contributes to exposing a nation's public secrets.

Works Cited

Alloa, Emmanuel. 2018. "Transparency: A Magic Concept of Modernity." In Alloa and Thomä 2018, 21–55.
Alloa, Emmanuel, and Dieter Thomä. 2018. "Transparency: Thinking through an Opaque Concept." In Alloa and Thomä 2018, 1–13.
Alloa, Emmanuel, and Dieter Thomä, eds. 2018. *Transparency, Society and Subjectivity: Critical Perspectives.* Cham, Switzerland: Palgrave Macmillan.
Birchall, Clare. 2011. "'There's Been Too Much Secrecy in this City': The False Choice between Secrecy and Transparency in US Politics." *Cultural Politics* 7, no. 1: 133–56. https://www.muse.jhu.edu/article/584294.
———. 2015. "Aesthetics of the Secret." *Open! Platform for Art, Culture, and the Public Domain*, October 9. https://onlineopen.org/aesthetics-of-the-secret.
Boothroyd, Dave. 2011. "Off the Record: Levinas, Derrida and the Secret of Responsibility." *Theory, Culture and Society* 28, no. 7–8: 41–59. https://doi.org/10.1177/0263276411423037.
Bouson, J. Brooks. 2000. *Quiet as It's Kept: Shame, Trauma, and Race in the Novels of Toni Morrison.* Albany: State University of New York Press.
Christopher, Lindsay M. 2009. "The Geographical Imagination in Toni Morrison's *Paradise.*" *Rocky Mountain Review* 63, no. 1 (Spring): 89–95.
Dobbs, Cynthia. 2011. "Diasporic Designs of House, Home, and Haven in Toni Morrison's *Paradise.*" *Toni Morrison: New Directions*, special issue, *MELUS* 36, no. 2 (Summer): 109–26. https://www.jstor.org/stable/23035283.
Docherty, Thomas. 2018. "The Privatization of Human Interests or, How Transparency Breeds Conformity." In Alloa and Thomä 2018, 283–303.
Evans, Shari. 2013. "Programmed Space, Themed Space, and the Ethics of Home in Toni Morrison's *Paradise.*" *African American Review* 46, no. 2/3 (Summer/Fall): 381–96. https://www.jstor.org/stable/23784065.
Fried, Charles. 1984. "Privacy [A moral analysis]." In *Philosophical Dimensions of Privacy: An Anthology*, edited by Ferdinand David Schoeman, 203–22. Cambridge: Cambridge University Press.
Fultz, Lucille P., ed. 2013. *Toni Morrison: Paradise, Love, A Mercy.* London: Bloomsbury.
Gilbert, Jeremy. 2007. "Public Secrets: 'Being-with' in an Era of Perpetual Disclosure." *Cultural Studies* 21, no. 1 (January): 22–41. https://doi.org/10.1080/09502380601046923.

Han, Byung-Chul. 2015. *The Transparency Society*. Translated by Erik Butler. Stanford, CA: Stanford Briefs.

Jennings, La Vinia Delois. 2008. *Toni Morrison and the Idea of Africa*. Cambridge: Cambridge University Press.

Jessee, Sharon. 2006. "The Contrapuntal Historiography of Toni Morrison's *Paradise*: Unpacking the Legacies of the Kansas and Oklahoma All-Black Towns." *American Studies* 47, no. 1 (Spring): 81–112. https://www.jstor.org/stable/40604899.

Johnston, Michael. n.d. "Transparency." *Britannica*. https://www.britannica.com/topic/transparency-government.

Krumholz, Linda J. 2002. "Reading and Insight in Toni Morrison's *Paradise*." *African American Review* 36, no. 1 (Spring): 21–34. https://www.jstor.org/stable/2903362.

Leonard, John. 1998. "Shooting Women." Review of *Paradise*, by Toni Morrison. *Nation* 266, no. 3 (January 26): 25–29.

Martín-Salván, Paula. 2019. "Rethinking Community in Literature and Literary Studies: The Secret Communal Life of Toni Morrison's *Paradise*." In *Rethinking Community: Towards Transdisciplinary Community Research*, edited by Bettina Jansen, 195–212. Cham, Switzerland: Palgrave Macmillan.

Metelmann, Jörg, and Thomas Telios. 2018. "Putting Oneself Out There: The 'Selfie' and the Alter-Rithmic Transformations of Subjectivity." In Alloa and Thomä 2018, 323–41.

Mori, Aoi. 2013. "Reclaiming the Presence of the Marginalized: Silence, Violence, and Nature in *Paradise*." In Fultz, *Toni Morrison*, 55–74.

Morrison, Toni. *Paradise*. 1999. New York: Plume. First published 1998.

———. *The Bluest Eye*. 2007. New York: Vintage. First published 1970.

Naurin, Daniel. 2006. "Transparency, Publicity, Accountability—The Missing Links." *Swiss Political Science Review* 12, no. 3: 90–98.

OED Online, n.d. "Exposure, n." Oxford University Press. www.oed.com/view/Entry/66730.

Schneider, Manfred. 2018. "The Dream of Transparency: Aquinas, Rousseau, Sartre." In Alloa and Thomä 2018, 85–104.

Simmel, Georg. 1950. "Secrecy." In *The Sociology of Georg Simmel*, edited by Kurt H. Wolff, 330–44. New York: Free Press.

Stave, Shirley A. 2013. "Separate Spheres? The Appropriation of Female Space in *Paradise*." In Fultz, *Toni Morrison*, 23–39.

Sundman, Alice. 2022. *Toni Morrison and the Writing of Place*. New York: Routledge.

Thomä, Dieter. 2018. "Seeing It All, Doing It All, Saying It All: Transparency, Subject, and the World." In Alloa and Thomä 2018, 57–84.

Williams, Raymond. 1973. *The Country and the City*. London: Chatto and Windus.

Yoon, Seongho. 2005. "Home for the Outdoored: Geographies of Exclusion, Gendered Space, and Postethnicity in Toni Morrison's *Paradise*." *CEA Critic* 67, no. 3: 65–80. https://www.jstor.org/stable/44377605.

Zauditu-Selassie, Kokahvah. 2009. *African Spiritual Traditions in the Novels of Toni Morrison*. Gainesville: University Press of Florida.

9: Something Big and Invisible: Thomas Pynchon's *Bleeding Edge* and the Limits of Transparency

Tiina Käkelä

1. Introduction

THE TEMPORAL SETTING of Thomas Pynchon's *Bleeding Edge* (2013) spans one year, from spring 2001 to spring 2002. Since the novel is set in Manhattan, New York, this timespan also includes the 9/11 terrorist attacks, which makes the novel a specimen of 9/11 literature. The attacks of September 11, 2001, are not so much described as referred to, but they nevertheless weigh heavily on the novel. The 9/11 attacks have often been considered the event that in the Western world ended the optimism of the 1990s. The seemingly rapid progress of democratization after the fall of the Berlin Wall on November 9, 1989; the subsequent collapse of Communist regimes in Eastern Europe; and eventually the collapse of the former Soviet Union in December 1991 had created anticipation that authoritarian regimes could give way to liberal democracy.[1] After 9/11, international politics took a quite different turn, and some of the changes had a direct connection with the attacks: antiterrorism legislation, increased surveillance of citizens, and the war in Afghanistan. A plethora of conspiracy theories stemming from 9/11 had profound political and cultural effects, especially in the US, so that the aftermath of the event still lasts in 2024.

The novel's historical setting is also the turn of the millennium, when digital culture as we now know it was taking its first steps: virtual reality, online games, blogging, coding, hacking, high economic gains—and

---

1   See, for example, Fukuyama (2020). The view that 9/11 was the event that ended the 1990s has been stated so many times by journalists, academics, political commentators, and people on social media platforms that it has become a historical narrative of its own. A couple of examples of this rhetoric: "the golden age came to an end a little more than a decade after the fall of the Berlin Wall, on September 11, 2001" (Williamson 2017); "sandwiched between the end of the Cold War and the events of 9/11, the last decade of the 20th century seems enviably peaceful, prosperous and optimistic" (Thorp 2023).

losses—and, most importantly, the unprecedented technological possibilities of immediate and global distribution of information. *Bleeding Edge* is, in many ways, a novel about digitalization. Its central character, Maxine Tarnow, is a fraud investigator who uses statistics and databases in her office as much as the more traditional fieldwork of a detective. Other characters in the novel include people working at tech startups or computer security firms, an investment banker, a blogger activist, and a hacker, to name a few. The key elements of the novel are linked to the endless possibilities opened by digitalization, intertwined with a long impending—and suddenly actual—catastrophe, 9/11.

Digitalization as such is not a new topic in Pynchon. In *Inherent Vice* (2009), set in 1970, the new technological innovation of interconnected computers called ARPANET is used to find information on a missing person. In the novel, the people involved in the early stages of what was to become the World Wide Web can already see that if the whereabouts of one person could be tracked down by computers, soon everybody's location will be tracked, "and someday everybody's gonna wake up to find they're under surveillance they can't escape" (365). In one of his early novels, *The Crying of Lot 49* (1966), Pynchon introduced the conceptual idea of digitality to his readers when the protagonist, Oedipa Maas, gets involved with a secret network and a plot with a cluster of either/or possibilities that tend to coexist in a way that challenges binary thinking. Oedipa's weighing of the options at the end of the novel is openly compared to computing: "For it was now like walking among matrices of a great digital computer, the zeroes and ones twinned above, hanging like balanced mobiles right and left, ahead, thick, maybe endless" (125). In a *New York Times* essay from 1984, "Is It O.K. to Be a Luddite?," Pynchon sees historical Luddites, the nineteenth-century English machine breakers, as representatives of a class war rather than as technophobes, and he concludes that in the new "Computer Age" machines could actually help the oppressed because they may democratize the ways information is distributed: "It may be that the deepest Luddite hope of miracle has now come to reside in the computer's ability to get the right data to those whom the data will do the most good."

What is new in *Bleeding Edge* in comparison to Pynchon's earlier texts is that by the turn of the millennium, digitalization has become existential. It is an indispensable element of the characters' being in the world. With Maxine, the protagonist and the focalizer of narration, the difference between real and simulation starts to lose its meaning. Maxine frequently uses digital processes as metaphors for her own and other peoples' cognitive functions and emotions. Furthermore, after entering a virtual reality several times, her sense of the physical environment also starts to change, and she has moments where the elements from cyberspace start to haunt her everyday experience: "She's finding it harder to tell 'real' NYC from translations . . . as if she keeps getting caught in a vortex taking her farther each time into the virtual world. . . . Real? Computer-animated?" (Pynchon 2013, 429–30).

Critics like Jason Siegel (2016, 6) have argued that the central characters of *Bleeding Edge* are indeed posthuman, as "the Internet has embedded itself in their consciousnesses and altered their subject positions within a late capitalist world." Becoming digitized subjects, they are, according to Siegel, led to monetization and exploitation in a society marked by high levels of surveillance and control (7). Yet, although these concerns also arise in the novel from time to time, there are several reasons why Pynchon's characters overall cannot be described, as Siegel does in his essay, as helpless victims of overwhelming conditions, be they historical, political, economic, or technological. They have their ways of managing their situation—ways that are often strange or even shocking, metaphysical, and poetically haunting.

In this essay I will look closely on how digitalization in *Bleeding Edge* opens a new ground for questions that have been in Pynchon's work for a long time—questions that can be seen in terms of secrecy and transparency. There is an interrelation, or better, a dialectic between these terms. As Bethany Nowviskie (2020, 200) argues, along with digitalization, we "have come to understand technologies of sharing and surveillance as a single Janus-faced beast." On the one hand, there is the right to privacy, and on the other hand, there is the commons and the public good. Ida Koivisto (2021, 3) considers transparency an "intellectual invention of the analog world" and points out that although transparency has traditionally had value when directed toward authorities (i.e., the state), it becomes highly problematic when directed to ultimately private affairs—which is a characteristic of digitalized and datafied environment.

Bleeding Edge indeed deals with topics like the new possibilities of sharing information, digital surveillance, and cognitive capitalism; that is, an economy that is based on digital technologies and intellectual labor. But a typical writerly strategy of Pynchon is to challenge culturally self-evident notions. In *Bleeding Edge* this can be seen especially in the way he works this dual, Janus-faced role of digital technologies that enable people to be both objects and subjects of knowledge. Digitalization in the novel is not just the disease of late capitalism; it is a sphere of life of its own. There are hidden connections and top-secret data transfers that have serious consequences in "meatspace" (Pynchon 2013, 77; 168; and passim), but there is also the hacker ethic of maintaining an open flow of information and sharing data instead of owning it. There are attempts to control cyberspace and subsume it under some political, commercial, and technological framework, but there is also the community of hackers and their idea of code writing as a transformative action and a mode of free creation. There are digital surveillance technologies along with companies that develop them and governments who pay for them, but there are also ways to resist digital control and create escape routes *within* cyberspace.

This dialectic of secrecy and transparency, or, as I would like to put it in the context of Pynchon's work, the desire for disclosure and the desire for concealment is, I argue, a part of a long continuum in his work. In the following, I will analyze this dialectic via two themes that constantly emerge in Pynchon's fiction. The first one is the *epistemological quest*. A great deal of earlier studies on Pynchon's early work—the short stories and the novels *V.* (1963), *The Crying of Lot 49*, and *Gravity's Rainbow* (1973)—has focused on the quest theme. The wording may differ, but critics have similar notions of how Pynchon's protagonists get involved in a quest that is by nature epistemological/metaphysical/spiritual—aiming at something that is eventually beyond representation.[2] I have chosen the attribute *epistemological* to highlight how the idea of immediate disclosure, knowledge, and understanding is driving Pynchon's protagonists. But when seeking to uncover secrets, they encounter unsolvable mysteries and paranoid plots that never really add up, and so the promise of disclosure is never fulfilled. In *Bleeding Edge* this quest takes place mostly in a digital environment that creates a simulation of transparency by providing immediate access to information.

The second theme is concealment, and here again I look at secrecy from the point of view of individuals. In Pynchon's novels there are many secret and anonymous powers at play, but recurrently there are also characters who feel the need to escape from surveillance and control. This need works against transparency, for it stems from the realm of privacy that has become endangered and must be protected by various means. This theme emerges in Pynchon also via the topos of *sanctuary*—a hidden place for alternative modes of living. The sanctuary is a no less idealistic notion than the idea of transparency. It is precarious and vulnerable but also resilient, emerging constantly in various forms. The sanctuary can be a physical place, but it can also be at the same time a mythical, otherworldly space—or, as in *Bleeding Edge*, a cyberspace.

2. The Epistemological Quest

As a writer, Pynchon has always had a certain affinity for mystery and secrecy. In some of his early short stories and especially from his first novel, *V.*, onward, there have been truth seekers in his novels—characters, usually protagonists, who have an awareness of "something, something

---

2   See, for example, *Thomas Pynchon* (1982) by Tony Tanner, *The Fictional Labyrinths of Thomas Pynchon* (1988) by David Seed, *A Hand to Turn the Time* (1990) by Theodore Kharpertian, and *Writing Pynchon* by Alec McHoul and David Wills (1990).

big and invisible" (Pynchon 2013, 83) that they want to bring into the open. The disclosure they seek turns into a metaphysical process where reality itself is transformed along with the quest. In early Pynchon, this quest also involved the identity of the seekers themselves, like Herbert Stencil in *V.*, Oedipa Maas in *The Crying of Lot 49*, and Tyrone Slothrop in *Gravity's Rainbow*. Similarly, the reader's attempt to create coherence in the text becomes intertwined with the quest of the protagonist.

In late Pynchon the role of the quest has changed. One of the storylines of *Vineland* (1991) focuses on the teenage girl Prairie, who finds out the secret history of her mother, who has been missing for over ten years. But this mystery does not much resemble those of Pynchon's earlier novels, for Prairie and her mother eventually meet and get to know each other again. In *Mason & Dixon* (1997) the protagonists Charles Mason and Jeremiah Dixon have an enormous task: to mark straight lines into the eighteenth-century North American wilderness. In *Against the Day* (2006), a great deal of the plot revolves around tragedy in the Traverse family, caused by the murder of the father, Webb Traverse, and the subsequent family breakdown. But none of these novels contain an overarching narrative structure tied to a big metaphysical question. It is not until *Inherent Vice* and *Bleeding Edge* that Pynchon returns to the quest, this time by using more straightforwardly the conventions of a detective story. But Pynchon's detectives, Doc Sportello in *Inherent Vice* and Maxine Tarnow in *Bleeding Edge*, have somewhat obscure ways of doing their job. Their sources of income are not clear, and they get involved in the events more out of intellectual curiosity than through a specific assignment. The epistemological quest in both novels grows and its complexity increases up to the point where the protagonist-detectives are ready to leave the case as it is. "It was as if whatever had happened had reached some kind of limit," ponders Doc Sportello at the end of *Inherent Vice* when he receives some unclear photographs about a murder he has been investigating (Pynchon 2009, 351). He does not have anything he can use as evidence, nor has he the will to do anything about it. He's only left with an uncanny feeling, a "glittering mosaic of doubt." I will discuss below how something similar also happens to Maxine in *Bleeding Edge*. Something always gets resolved, though, but not in the way the protagonist and the reader may have expected.

The mysteries, however, persist, because the Pynchonian epistemological quest is not only an intellectual puzzle but an ontological one as well. The visible everyday world is recurrently mixed with the invisible and unknown, and the characters become aware that there is always something that cannot be revealed, because ultimately the nature of reality is nontransparent, beyond representation. And with Pynchon, this hidden information also verges on something transcendental. This happens, for example, when Oedipa Maas in *The Crying of Lot 49* compares her moment of insight to an epileptic fit from which nothing but single details—a color, an odor, a sound—can be remembered:

> Oedipa wondered, whether, at the end of this . . . she too might not be left with only compiled memories of clues, announcements, intimations, but never the central truth itself, which must somehow each time be too bright for her memory to hold; which must always blaze out, destroying its own message irreversibly, leaving an overexposed blank when the ordinary world came back. (Pynchon 1979, 66)

In *Bleeding Edge*, this transcendental dimension is also present, although Maxine's quest is, by comparison, more mundane from the start. As a fraud investigator, as Sascha Pöhlmann (2016, 21) has argued, she can read money flows and find from this "monetary substructure" hidden information that is not visible to an average person. Maxine can make solid deductions from repetitive patterns and irregularities in bookkeeping or tax sheets and understand the world and its causal relations on a deeper level. There is nothing metaphysical in Maxine's work, although, as Pöhlmann notes, her insights are often presented in a language of revelation. It is not until she has visited several times in the deep recesses of cyberspace, the "void incalculably fertile with invisible links" (Pynchon 2013, 359), when the transcendental dimension of her quest really opens.

The Pynchonian truth seekers look for hidden connections between symbols, incidents, people, and historical events, and they sense that there is a deeper and often threatening meaning to the events around them. When reading Pynchon's fiction, one won't have to wait for long for the word *paranoia* to come up. Paranoia is ironized and satirized, by the narrator and often self-consciously by the characters themselves: "Proverbs for Paranoids" frequent *Gravity's Rainbow* (Pynchon 1975a, 237 and passim) and the band The Paranoids appear in *The Crying of Lot 49* (Pynchon 1979, 17 and passim). To Maxine, "paranoia's the garlic in life's kitchen, right, you can never have too much" (Pynchon 2013, 11). Despite the humor, the effect of paranoia does not fade away, for it is also an image of the quest itself, signaling for the character (and for the reader) the interconnectedness of all details. As a writer, Pynchon has been famous for the way he uses material from historically known cabals, clandestine operations, and secret communities in the paranoid plots his characters get involved in. So, paranoia is never a mere delusion in Pynchon's novels. It embodies and ironizes the paranoid rhetoric and imagination that American historian Richard Hofstadter has analyzed in his 1964 essay "The Paranoid Style in American Politics." According to Hofstadter, the key features of paranoid style are conflict between absolute good and absolute evil, imminent collapse of civilization, and the resulting feeling of anxiety and powerlessness.

In Pynchon criticism, paranoia has been a much-discussed topic for over sixty years as of 2024, with different emphases.[3] Depending on how you look at it, paranoia is the precondition or the outcome of the epistemological quest. Or, as Samuel Chase Coale (2019, 213) puts it, it is an expression of the characters' insatiable "hunger for some kind of universal meaning, metanarrative and structure." What makes *Bleeding Edge* interesting in this respect is that it is set in a historical moment where one catastrophic event, 9/11, created a politically remarkable conspiracy subculture and paved the way for the mainstreaming of paranoid imagination.[4] Conspiracies have historically been fostered by what Michael Barkun (2013, 12) calls "stigmatized knowledge"—that is, "knowledge claims that have not been validated by mainstream institutions. To Barkun, the advent of the internet was remarkable in this respect, because it made possible an unforeseen dissemination of stigmatized knowledge: "Internet is attractive because of its large potential audience, the low investment required for its use, and the absence of gatekeepers who might censor the content of messages" (29). The internet also made possible, very early on, the proliferation of media outlets and fostered a new era of selective exposure in which individuals would consume media that was largely consistent with their pre-existing attitudes (Warner and Neville-Shepard 2014, 2).

In *Bleeding Edge*, this cultural change is best represented by March Kelleher, an elderly friend of Maxine's. March has a history of left-wing political activism, and at the present time of the novel she is also a popular blogger. Right after the 9/11 attacks, March distributes on her blog the at the time very popular theory that the US government is somehow involved in the events.[5] Indeed, the novel seems to support this theory when Maxine finds out that the novel's cybersecurity entrepreneur and antagonist, Gabriel Ice, is a sort of middleman whose business relations connect US secret agencies to organizations funding terrorists in the Middle East. At the beginning of the novel, paranoia is described as a

---

3 A good summary and criticism of certain compulsory items in earlier Pynchon studies can be found from Alec McHoul and David Wills's *Writing Pynchon* (1990, 3; 106).

4 I refer here especially to the "Truthers" or the Truth Movement that focused on denying the official account of the September 11 attacks (Barkun 2013, 183–194; Warner and Neville-Shepard 2014, 3–4 and passim).

5 According to a poll taken in 2006, 36 percent of Americans believed that the George W. Bush administration either assisted in the terrorist attacks of September 11 or knowingly allowed them to occur to create the pretext for war in the Middle East (Warner and Neville-Shepard 2014, 1).

kind of default setting for Maxine, as something that comes perhaps from her profession or leftist family background. When she starts to investigate illegal money transfers related to Ice's company, hashslingrz, her sense of paranoia starts to strengthen. References to a governmental conspiracy around the 9/11 attacks never lead to a concrete disclosure, however, and Maxine's suspicions remain unresolved. Like Doc Sportello in *Inherent Vice*, she's left with an uncanny feeling of doubt.

Many critics agree that paranoia in *Bleeding Edge* is not what it used to be in Pynchon's early novels. Coale (2019, 214) argues that Pynchon in *Bleeding Edge* "employs the conspiratorial design to undercut any actual conspiracy that would explain everything." Ali Chetwynd (2019, 33) goes even further to say that paranoia in the novel is self-conscious, even parodic, and he considers *Bleeding Edge* a "post-paranoid" novel in the sense that paranoia does not require so much cognitive work in the protagonist Maxine. Instead, it has become a passive reception of affects and bodily sensations (37–39). When investigating the accounting and data security measures of Ice's company, Maxine is "visited by a strong hint of secret intention" (Pynchon 2013, 158), or she feels like she has "a paranoid halo" (183) around her head, but these affects never lead to a more definite insight. To Chetwynd (2019, 38), this marks a move away from the mental work involved in classical paranoid narrative and leaves the paranoid insight entirely devoid of content. As a result, "paranoid investigations can thus no longer associate fresh discovery with progressive uncovering toward a final understanding" (41).

Of course, Pynchon's paranoid truth seekers never come to a final truth or understanding of what their quest is about. But in *Bleeding Edge*, this cognitive and rhetorical emptiness of paranoia indicates that something has changed in the epistemological quest itself. And it may signal that the Great Pynchonian Theme, the "default trope of any discussion of Pynchon" (Chetwynd 2019, 50), is no longer working. I see a couple of reasons for this. One reason could be that the 9/11 attacks caused such an unprecedented historical and political rift in the US that the popular allegations of corrupt government and secret services were not sufficient anymore to explain what happened. In the novel, this 9/11-as-an-inside-job scenario is, ironically, criticized by the former CIA/FBI agent Nicholas Windust:

> "You people want to believe this was all a false-flag caper, some invisible superteam, forging the intel, faking the Arabic chatter, controlling air traffic, military communications, civilian news media—everything coordinating without a hitch or a malfunction, the whole tragedy set up to look like a terror attack. Please. My wised-up civilian heartbreaker. Guess what. Nobody in the business is that good." (Pynchon 2013, 378)

Another reason is to see in the novel's failure to create a comprehensive trajectory of events preceding 9/11 a *dramatization* of how the Cold War–era paranoia is transforming into something else, something that cannot be grasped by simply ironizing conspiracy theories and imagination. March Kelleher, who by the end of the novel has turned into a digital nomad and a fugitive who sleeps in parks, manifests this unforeseen threat in one of her last blog entries:

> Amid all that chaos and confusion, a hole quietly opened up in American history, a vacuum of accountability, into which assets human and financial begin to vanish. Back in the days of hippie simplicity, people liked to blame "the CIA" or "a secret rogue operation." But this is a new enemy, unnameable, locatable on no organization chart or budget line—who knows, maybe the CIA is scared of them. Maybe it's unbeatable, maybe there are ways to fight back. (399)

From the present-day perspective, March Kelleher's "vacuum of accountability" or epistemological hole sounds like a prophecy of our era: a significant number of people do not believe in mainstream media and other institutions and get their information via media channels that enforce their preexisting attitudes. The connection between the idea of transparency and conspiracy theories, argues Matthew Fluck (2016, 49), is that both have an epistemic ideal of unmediated access to information. "Like transparency, conspiracy theorizing reflects a belief in the connection between hidden information and political power" (50). Similarly, Claire Birchall (2021, 45) argues that the twentieth-century faith in transparency relies on the notion that publicity secures accountability. "Calls for access in the face of secrecy reinforce beliefs in the rewards that visibility will bring."

To Fluck, transparency is a political ideal, aimed at empowering citizens who have little control over political institutions, and it has remarkably shaped and challenged institutions that create and circulate information (53–54). But, he adds, "Access to information is assumed to be empowering, although the mechanisms through which such knowledge leads to political influence are rarely articulated in any detail by either the advocates of transparency or conspiracy theorists" (55).

In their study on the role of ideological media echo chambers in belief in conspiracies, Benjamin Warner and Ryan Neville-Shepard (2014, 4) noted how many political commentators were astonished by the amount of public support for 9/11 conspiracies even five years after the event:

> Harper (2006) concluded, "Not since the heyday of JFK assassination theories . . . have so many Americans believed their government is lying to them." Similarly, *Time* columnist Lev Grossman (2006)

summarized, "[this] adds up to a lot of people. This is not a fringe phenomenon. It is a mainstream political reality."

The idea of finding hidden information and secret connections relies on the notion that there is a certain level of shared representation of reality—although this reality is an illusion, for the paranoid knows better. But when that shared reality and the common ground for public discussion starts to break into smaller and smaller echo chambers, it fosters the polarization of society and breeds extremist ideologies. The (black) hole envisioned in March Kelleher's blog text in *Bleeding Edge* has no name or shape, but it creates disruption in the social fabric.

Toward the end of the novel, many problems and risky situations Maxine gets involved in seem to be solved with relative ease reminiscent of comedy endings. Even though she gets into contact with secret agents and Russian gangsters, she is never in any real danger—not even when she happens to discover the unresolved murder of Lester Traipse. The Russian gangsters Misha and Grisha are more annoying than scary; the mysterious hitman stalking Maxine's son Otis after the death of Windust disappears after Otis's Krav Maga teacher intervenes; and the sinister Gabriel Ice at the end turns out to be an angry man in his giant limo, caught in the middle of a family fight between his soon-to-be-ex-wife, Tallis, and mother-in-law, March Kelleher.[6] The epistemological quest dissolves around Maxine, and the conventional suspense elements of a detective story start to fade, as she becomes more interested in family matters such as reviving her marriage to Horst and being a mother to her two young sons.

But, in a manner typical of Pynchon fiction, lightness and laughter are easily mixed with horror. The moment when Maxine turns away from her quest/case and turns to her family again is clearly stated in the text. It is when she has discovered the half-rotten body of Nicholas Windust in his apartment, and the phone rings. She does not pick up, but the answering machine comes on, and a strange chilling voice reminds Maxine that her children might need her. Maxine, the detective and observer, realizes that she and her family are, and have possibly been for some time, under surveillance. Maxine's need to protect what she loves and what is closest to her is from that moment on the most important thing for her.

This need to escape surveillance and control, which I'm going to focus on next, is what drives many other Pynchonian characters as well.

---

6   To me the whole domestic dispute scene on the street emphasizes the farcical features of the novel's ending. It seems like a reference to, and parody of, Don DeLillo's *Cosmopolis* (2003). Gabriel Ice, at gunpoint next to his white stretch limo, tells Maxine "I don't die. There's no scenario where I'll die" (Pynchon 2013, 473), which sounds pretty much like Eric Packer at the end of *Cosmopolis*.

Their solutions are varied and fantastic and often involve a crossing of ontological borders. When Pynchon's characters escape and want to hide, they enter another order of things.

3. The Right to Be Forgotten

Most people are usually unaware of their rights as *data subjects*—that is, persons from whom personal data is gathered. (And for that matter, people are often unaware of what personal data consists of when being gathered.) One of the rights the General Data Protection Regulation (GDPR) provides in the European Union has been named *the right to be forgotten* (or the *right of erasure*), which means that the GDPR "gives individuals the right to ask organizations to delete their personal data" (GDPR.EU, n.d.) under certain conditions. Usually, this means circumstances where data that has been gathered unnecessarily, unlawfully, or after the subjects withdraw their consent.[7] Similar rights can be found in the legislation of several countries outside the EU—and regardless of jurisdiction, the principle is well known and much discussed in the US (Gstrein 2020). The right-to-be-forgotten principle has been used several times in European courts in lawsuits against companies like Google, since it is a right that concerns virtual landscape irrespective of physical borders. All this makes it a complex and challenging principle: designed to protect individuals against internet content that seriously damages their possibilities for leading normal lives,[8] the right to be forgotten has also been criticized as a potential tool for censorship.

My aim is not to dwell on this critical controversy but to use *the right to be forgotten* as an expression of a desire that is very compatible with the digital era: to erase one's digital past and start anew. This desire also informs Pynchon's fiction as a counterforce to overwhelming technological and political control that not only gathers information from a subject but defines the place of the subject in the network of power relations.

In *Vineland*, this is what happens to Frenesi Gates, a revolutionary of the 1960s who leaves her husband and daughter and also betrays her lover and revolutionary leader as well as her friends by becoming an informant for the government—all for reasons vaguely related to sexual lust, or lust for power, or both. After her betrayal, she has been living a sort of

---

7   The right to erasure is not absolute, for organizations may have legitimate reasons, such as scientific study or public health, to continue processing the individual's personal data. Also, the right to be forgotten affects the distribution and accessibility of personal data, not the existence of the data as such (Gstrein 2020).

8   The lawsuits where the right to be forgotten has been appealed by individuals include revenge porn, deepfake porn, mugshots, or other situations where ordinary people have been exposed to big-media coverage against their will.

shadow life for years in a witness protection program, is remarried, and has a son. In the present of the novel, 1984, the Reagan-era budget cuts bring a drastic change to her new family. Frenesi is suddenly given notice that she and her husband, Flash, are no longer supported by the monthly government checks that have sustained them. Moreover, all information about them and some other people in the same program has mysteriously disappeared from the government files: "Turns out, a lot of people we know—they ain't on the computer anymore. Just—gone" (Pynchon 1991, 85). It is not clear whether this is a computer error or the result of an actual decision. To Frenesi, the change feels like returning to worldly existence after years in the underground by a stroke on a metaphysical keyboard:

> She understood that . . . she and Flash were no longer exempt, might easily be abandoned already to the upper world, and any unfinished business in it that might now resume . . . as if they'd been kept safe in some time-free zone all these years but now, at the unreadable whim of something in power, must reenter the clockwork of cause and effect. . . . it would all be done with keys on alphanumeric keyboards that stood for weightless, invisible chains of electronic presence or absence. (90)

Rescued by a deus-ex-machina narrative solution by "the hacker we call God" (91), Frenesi can now return to the "upper world" with her son and husband. Freed from her past and eventually also from her personal demon, the federal prosecutor Brock Vond, she is able to begin a new phase in her life—all of which culminates in a family reunion with her former husband, Zoyd, her daughter Prairie, and her parents and relatives.

The most prominent case in Pynchon's fiction where the personal past of a character is erased is that of protagonist Tyrone Slothrop in *Gravity's Rainbow*. After arriving in the Zone—Central Europe in the immediate aftermath of World War II in 1945—Slothrop first loses all his clothes and belongings, and then his name and identity change several times. Slothrop eventually loses all sense of integrated self, orientation, and sense of time, and what the reader knows of him toward the end of the novel has turned into a narrative stream of sensations and moods that seem to belong to no one in particular. A much-discussed topic in Pynchon criticism has been what actually happens to Slothrop at the end of the novel. "There is a feeling that he is getting so lost and unconnected that he is vaporizing out of time and place altogether" (Tanner 1982, 84).

Does Slothrop die, or is he delusional, or is he on drugs? Does he go through a metamorphosis from a human into a mythical hero? Or, on a more metafictional level, does he turn from a character into a mere textual concept when his scattering parallels the fragmentation of the novel?

One obvious feature in Slothrop's "scattering" (Pynchon 1975a, 712) is that the disappearance of his past identity is a form of liberation from outside control—in his case, a power network called "They" that has controlled him since childhood. Stefan Mattessich (2002, 194) sees that Slothrop's disintegration is a way of resisting the control imposed on him: "Slothrop is delirious, apprehending himself within the historical context of manipulation and reification that determines his very being . . . he ceases to 'care' about his quest for meaning and becomes so aimless or docile that he loses himself and disappears."

In the world of *Bleeding Edge*, this dream of escaping powers that control you has a digital form. At the turn of the millennium, the World Wide Web is becoming mainstream, and people, at first fascinated by the accessibility of shopping, information, entertainment, or porn provided by search engines, are now starting to realize that they themselves are going to be accessible on the internet as well, leaving digital footprints for any interested and capable agent to follow, so that the freedom of the internet always contains the potentiality of control. *Bleeding Edge* is set in a time just before social media platforms and the dominance of Google,[9] but the concerns of digital surveillance via the internet already echo in the novel. The internet, as Maxine's father, Ernie Tarnow, notes, was originally designed for military uses:

> "Your Internet, back then the Defense Department called it DARPAnet, the real original purpose was to assure survival of US command and control after a nuclear exchange with the Soviets. [. . .] Call it freedom, it's based on control. Everybody connected together, impossible anybody should get lost, ever again. Take the next step, connect it to these cell phones, you've got a total Web of surveillance, inescapable." (Pynchon 2013, 419–20)

Ernie's vision of total digital control reflects many common cultural worries about the internet, but Pynchon often both uses and undermines the power of such totalizing views. The www in *Bleeding Edge* is not entirely the Web of surveillance. Beneath the traceable surface operations there is a part of the internet that is beyond the reach of standard search engines, available only to those with specific information or some hacker skills— the deep web. At first it looks like "mostly obsolete sites and broken links, and endless junkyard," but, as the IT genius Eric Outfield explains to Maxine, "behind it is a whole invisible maze of constraints, engineered in, it lets you go some places, keeps you out of others . . . a dump, with structure" (226). It is estimated that this not-directly-accessible, hence "invisible" part of the internet is many times greater than the surface web

---

9   In 2001, Google was still an early-phase search engine (Wikipedia 2023). Facebook started in 2004 (Wikipedia 2024).

(Rouse 2019). In *Bleeding Edge*, the deep web gradually becomes more and more significant for Maxine and some other characters. It is the alternate universe, where characters can escape control and deliberately get lost. And create a cyberlife of their own.

4. The Sanctuary

Throughout his work, Pynchon has been interested in creating fictional spaces that provide alternative ways of existence. These spaces often exist just outside the urban landscape, like the garbage dump in the short story "Low-Lands" (1960) or the mythical Seventh river that runs through the fictional Vineland City in *Vineland* and changes into a spirit world of the Yurok people once the city lights are passed. The prominent feature of these spaces in Pynchon is that they merge alternative ways of living, parallel ontological states, and political resistance. I call this kind of fictional topos *the sanctuary*, for these special places are always described in terms of precariousness and (at least temporary) safety. They are real and imaginary places at the same time—and subversive, for they open the possibility to depict and imagine new worlds. In *Against the Day* (2006), one such space is the dream of the numerous anarchist movements:

> A place of refuge, up in the fresh air, out over the sea, someplace all the Anarchists could escape to, now with the danger so overwhelming, a place readily found even on cheap maps of the World ... a place promised to them, not by God, which'd be asking too much of the average Anarchist, but by certain hidden geometries of History ... (Pynchon 2006, 372–73)

The most prominent of these spaces is the Zone in *Gravity's Rainbow*, for an entire section of the novel is dedicated to it. And since the Zone can be interpreted as a geographical location, a political state of exception, a carnivalistic topos, a mythical stage, or a textual space where different narrative layers coexist, it turns from a definite place into a state that characterizes the entire novel.

In *Bleeding Edge*, this alternative space is a virtual reality named DeepArcher that can be found from the deep web. Maxine visits DeepArcher several times, and the virtual reality forms a prominent and constantly evolving site in the novel. From the beginning, the creators of DeepArcher, the programmers Lucas and Justin, describe their software as something more than just diversion: "A virtual sanctuary to escape to from the many varieties of real-world discomfort. A grand-scale motel for the afflicted, a destination reachable by virtual midnight express from anyplace with a keyboard" (Pynchon 2013, 74). Justin and Lucas have a mission to create a digital world that the hackers and coders can freely change. DeepArcher represents *bleeding edge* technology, which in IT business jargon means technology so raw and untested that it has yet to be developed into *cutting edge* technology (Rouse 2011). In the novel, this is stated explicitly: "Not proven use, high risk, something only early-adoption addicts feel comfortable with" (Pynchon 2013, 78). To protect their creation, Justin and Lucas have hidden DeepArcher in the deep web. That does not mean that DeepArcher is safe from attacks from various parties, "the feds, game companies, fucking Microsoft" (36), who are constantly trying to hack its source code.

In the twenty-first-century world of *Bleeding Edge*, where "capitalism reigns supreme" (Pöhlmann 2016, 9), DeepArcher is at first described as a refuge from late capitalism. This is underlined also when Maxine compares the virtual world to the closed Isle of Meadows, a nature preserve on Staten Island in New York City, just next to the Fresh Kills landfill and a former gigantic garbage dump.[10] In general, the entire deep web is described quite idealistically in the novel. It is "unmessed-with country" (Pynchon 2013, 241), something comparable to the American frontier that will soon be colonized by software companies and government officials. "Once they get down here, everything'll be suburbanized faster you can say 'late capitalism.'" The well-known fact that the deep web also harbors illegal activities and sites dedicated to the trading of weapons, drugs, and child pornography is only mentioned in passing (240).

After 9/11 the nature of DeepArcher changes. Owing to a systemic vulnerability following the terrorist attacks, some outside agent manages to install a backdoor; that is, a mechanism to bypass the access control of DeepArcher, and as a result, the virtual world cannot be a closed place anymore. Gabriel Ice had earlier tried to buy the source code of DeepArcher, but Justin and Lucas thwart Ice's effort to capitalize on DeepArcher by making their source code freely available. And so, the history-free refuge Justin and Lucas have designed has been subsumed by history and the markets. When Maxine revisits DeepArcher near the end of the novel, she soon recognizes how it has changed: there are endless added details made by single users, and companies fill the space with pop-up advertisements and commercial brand names.

But the possibility to create sanctuaries does not end there. It turns out that after opening DeepArcher to everyone, Lucas and Justin are already on their way elsewhere in the deep web, looking for new frontiers. This happens when Maxine accidentally finds an outlet from DeepArcher to another, more indefinite cyberspace that has the shape of a gigantic moving spaceship. She discusses this with the first figure she meets, which turns out to be the avatar of Justin. He tells her that this new space with

---

10   DeepArcher can also be described as *heterotopia*. See Käkelä (2019).

"Zillions of stars" (356) is not their creation, and that their aim is to explore whether this space has an end, the "horizon between coded and codeless" (357).

Some critics have pointed out that *Bleeding Edge* in a peculiar way downplays the significance of 9/11 in its central characters' lives.[11] Indeed, the catastrophic event is present only through its impact—first via omens and allusions, then through references to TV news and rumors, and finally, changes in people's mentality: increased altruism at first, and later, increased anxiety and paranoia. There is some restraint in the narration, however, as to how people feel about being suddenly under attack. How do they mourn the dead and the massive national catastrophe? Maxine's quest for truth (about the role of Gabriel Ice, about secret money transfers via hashslingrz) at the end of the novel is also another attempt to answer the questions why 9/11 happened and what it means. It can also be seen as a way of mourning that characterizes not only Maxine but the entire novel as well.

In *Bleeding Edge*, DeepArcher provides a possibility for more direct mourning for Maxine, when she notices that some avatars resemble the victims of the 9/11 attacks. Her first assumption is that they have been created by their loved ones to give the deceased a digital afterlife. But the figurative underground gains a totally new meaning when she suddenly begins to suspect that people she knows to be dead are starting to digitally interact with her. Maxine wonders whether "the Internet has become a medium of communication between the worlds" (427). She can preserve that possibility in the vast digital "yankyard" (226) of the deep web, and some redemption takes place that is not possible elsewhere.

---

11 See Chetwynd (2019, 48). Hanjo Berressem (2019, 167) points out how Pynchon frames the 9/11 as a "real-estate disaster" by describing how quickly "Ground Zero" turned from a memorial of the atrocity into a site of real-estate controversy. According to Berressem, this should not be seen as callous, if we keep in mind how often Pynchon has shown how property and the concept of real estate are "deeply entangled with American crime and sin."-

Works Cited

Barkun, Michael. 2013. *A Culture of Conspiracy: Apocalyptic Visions in Contemporary America*. 2nd ed. Berkeley: University of California Press.

Berressem, Hanjo. 2019. "Threat and Crisis in Twenty-First-Century Pynchon." In *The New Pynchon Studies*, edited by Joanna Freer, 157–72. Cambridge: Cambridge University Press.

Birchall, Clare. 2021. *Radical Secrecy: The Ends of Transparency in Datafied America*. Minneapolis: University of Minnesota Press.

Chetwynd, Ali. 2019. "Pynchon after Paranoia." In *The New Pynchon Studies*, edited by Joanna Freer, 33–52. Cambridge: Cambridge University Press.

Coale, Samuel Chase. 2019. "Conspiracy and Paranoia." In *Thomas Pynchon in Context*, edited by Inger H. Dalsgaard, 211–16. Cambridge: Cambridge University Press.

DeLillo, Don. 2003. *Cosmopolis: A Novel*. New York: Scribner.

Fluck, Matthew. 2016. "Theory, 'Truthers,' and Transparency: Reflecting on Knowledge in the Twenty-First Century." *Review of International Studies* 42, no. 1: 48–73. https://doi:10.1017/S0260210515000091.

Fukuyama, Francis. 2020. "30 Years of World Politics: What Has Changed?" *Journal of Democracy* 31, no. 1 (January): 11–21. https://www.journalofdemocracy.org/articles/30-years-of-world-politics-what-has-changed/.

GDPR.EU. n.d. "Everything you need to know about the 'Right to be forgotten.'" https://gdpr.eu/right-to-be-forgotten/.

Grant, J. Kerry. 1994. *A Companion to "The Crying of Lot 49."* Athens: University of Georgia Press.

Gstrein, Oskar Josef. 2020. "Right to be Forgotten: EUropean Data Imperialism, National Privilege, or Universal Human Right?" *Review of European Administrative Law* 13, no. 1 (May): 125–52. https://doi.org/10.7590/187479820X15881424928426. Available at SSRN: https://ssrn.com/abstract=3530995.

Hofstadter, Richard. 1964. "The Paranoid Style in American Politics." *Harper's Magazine* (November). https://harpers.org/archive/1964/11/the-paranoid-style-in-american-politics/.

Käkelä, Tiina. 2019. "This Land Is My Land, This Land Also Is My Land: Real Estate Narratives in Pynchon's Fiction." *Textual Practice* 33, no. 3: 383–98. https://doi.org/10.1080/0950236X.2019.1580504.

Käkelä-Puumala, Tiina. 2002. "'But What's a Human, After All?' Dehumanization and *V*." In *Blissful Bewilderment: Studies in the Fiction of Thomas Pynchon*, edited by Anne Mangen and Rolf Gaasland, 13–39. Oslo: Novus Press.

Kharpertian, Theodore. 1990. *A Hand to Turn the Time: The Menippean Satires of Thomas Pynchon*. London: Fairleigh Dickinson University Press.

Klepper, David. 2021. "From election to COVID, 9/11 conspiracies cast a long shadow." AP News, September 9. https://apnews.com/article/911-conspiracy-qanon-7d288d0678f5cc7425412931b0212009.

Koivisto, Ida. 2021. "Transparency in the Digital Environment." *Critical Analysis of Law: An International & Interdisciplinary Law Review* 8, no. 1: 1–8.

Mattessich, Stefan. 2002. *Lines of Flight: Discursive Time and Countercultural Desire in the Work of Thomas Pynchon.* Durham, NC: Duke University Press.

McHoul, Alec, and David Wills. 1990. *Writing Pynchon: Strategies in Fictional Analysis.* London: Macmillan Press.

Nowviskie, Bethany. 2020. "Libraries, Museums, and Archives as Speculative Knowledge Infrastructure." In *Reassembling Scholarly Communications: Histories, Infrastructures, and Global Politics of Open Access*, edited by Martin Paul Eve and Jonathan Gray, 195–203. Cambridge, MA: MIT Press. https://doi.org/10.7551/mitpress/11885.001.0001.

Pöhlmann, Sascha. 2016. "'I Just Look at Books': Reading the Monetary Metareality of *Bleeding Edge*." *Orbit: A Journal of American Literature* 4, no. 1. https://doi.org/10.16995/orbit.189.

Pynchon, Thomas. 1960. "Low-lands." In *New World Writing 16*, edited by Stewart Richardson and Corlies M. Smith, 85–108. Philadelphia: Lippincott.

———. 1975a. *Gravity's Rainbow.* London: Pan Books. First published 1973.

———.1975b. *V.* London: Pan Books. First published 1963.

———.1979. *The Crying of Lot 49.* London: Pan Books. First published 1966.

———. 1984. "Is It OK to Be a Luddite?" *New York Times Book Review*, October 28. https://archive.nytimes.com/www.nytimes.com/books 97/05/18/reviews/pynchon-luddite.html.

———. 1991. *Vineland.* London: Minerva.

———. 1997. *Mason & Dixon.* London: Pan Books.

———. 2006. *Against the Day.* London: Jonathan Cape.

———. 2009. *Inherent Vice.* London: Jonathan Cape.

———. 2013. *Bleeding Edge.* London: Jonathan Cape.

Rouse, Margaret. 2011. "Bleeding Edge." Techopedia.com. Last updated August 18, 2011. Accessed March 27, 2024. https://www.techopedia.com/definition/23222/bleeding-edge.

———. 2019. "Deep Web." Techopedia.com. Last updated April 1, 2019. Accessed March 27, 2024. https://www.techopedia.com/definition/15653/deep-web.

Seed, David. 1988. *The Fictional Labyrinths of Thomas Pynchon.* London: Macmillan Press.

Siegel, J. 2016. "Meatspace is Cyberspace: The Pynchonian Post-human in *Bleeding Edge*." *Orbit: Writing around Pynchon* 4, no. 2: 1–27. http://dx.doi.org/10.16995/orbit.187.

Tanner, Tony. 1982. *Thomas Pynchon.* London: Methuen.

Thorp, Clare. 2023. "That's what I call the 90's." *Cambridge Alumni Magazine* 98 (April 21). https://magazine.alumni.cam.ac.uk/thats-what-i-call-the-90s/.

Warner, Benjamin R., and Ryan Neville-Shepard. 2014. "Echoes of a Conspiracy: Birthers, Truthers, and the Cultivation of Extremism." *Communication Quarterly* 62, no. 1: 1–17. https://doi:10.1080/01463373.2013.822407.

Wikipedia. 2023. "History of Google." Last updated October 2023. Accessed March 27, 2024. https://en.wikipedia.org/wiki/History_of_Google#cite_note-milestones-2.

———. 2024. "Facebook." Last updated 26 March 2024. Accessed March 27, 2024. https://en.wikipedia.org/wiki/Facebook.

Williamson, Kevin D. 2017. "9/11 Ended a Golden Age." *National Review* (September 11). https://www.nationalreview.com/2017/09/911-sixteen-years-later/.

10: Narrating the Community in Karen Tei Yamashita's *I Hotel*: Story, History, System

Toon Staes

1.

KAREN TEI YAMASHITA was perhaps not an obvious choice for the 2021 Medal for Distinguished Contribution to American Arts and Letters. Only the second Asian American writer to win the award, Yamashita, at seventy, had not yet reached the same levels of fame as earlier medalists (big-name authors such as Toni Morrison, Philip Roth, Gore Vidal, and Joan Didion). None of her eight books up to that point had been runaway hits, and since she publishes with the nonprofit Coffeehouse Press, her career had never been pushed by the big commercial houses. The variety of her output may explain in part why Yamashita is still not exactly a household name—not when compared to Morrison, Roth, Vidal or Didion, at least. Her books resist categories. She has written plays, memoirs, short stories, and novels, ranging in style from the journalistic to the experimental and moving freely between historical fiction and postmodern pastiche. A growing body of Yamashita scholarship suggests that her work stands out not for any particular individual achievements but for its contribution to "the reshaping of the Asian American literary imagination during the past [three] decades" (Ling 2012, xi). Likewise, the Judges' Citation for the 2021 Medal mentions the *breadth* of Yamashita's impact, applauding "her various roles as a public intellectual" in "transforming the approach toward Asian American literary and cultural studies." In each of her books, Yamashita, who is also a trained anthropologist, focuses on the experience of Asian migration, an experience marked in the US by exclusion acts, antimiscegenation laws, assimilation, and activism. The community she writes about has struggled to define itself *as* a community, while its more political wing has always had to reckon with oppression and surveillance (most severely, with the incarceration of Japanese Americans in concentration camps during World War II) and counterintelligence (such as the COINTELPRO infiltration of Asian American civil rights groups in the sixties and seventies).

Yamashita's career-long interest in Asian American histories and the themes of fear, invisibility, and exposure that come with them warrants her inclusion in this volume. If, as Paula Martín Salván writes in the introduction, transparency and secrecy have been key ideas throughout American history for the construction of communities, Yamashita's work outlines how one such community has made itself visible. The connection between visibility and transparency is not trivial: both express a wish to be seen and a desire to determine *how* one is seen. In works of literature, the connection extends to the formal level in the tension between the transparency and opacity of representation itself.[1]

I chose to open this essay with a contentious take, not because I disagree with Yamashita's medal—I think it is well deserved, to be sure—but for a different reason altogether: part of my argument in what follows rests on the formal challenges of her work. Her novels do not invite easy identification with their characters, for instance, and character identification allows for a straightforward experience of narrative empathy. Rather than developing a single privileged psychological perspective, Yamashita usually opts for a decentered network of characters.[2] What emerges from this network is a sort of collective voice; not a robust embodiment of individual values but an ambient reflection of a community's shared experiences. I expand on this point in the following pages, in which I consider the interplay between community and visibility in Yamashita's work by focusing on a novel that can be seen as the capstone of her career as a writer and an anthropologist: *I Hotel* (2010), a six-hundred-page tome that loosely chronicles the rise of the Asian American movement between 1968 and 1977, centered around the eviction of the residents of the International Hotel in San Francisco's historic Manilatown, home to mostly poor, elderly Filipino bachelors in that period. *I Hotel* brings together several years of interviews and archival work and consists of ten novellas (or "hotels"), which, combined, offer different perspectives on the many ethnicities and political affinities that coalesced into the movement. While it can be seen as a work of historiographic metafiction, I

---

1   Martín-Salván's introduction stresses this idea, too, when it mentions the interplay between mimesis and mediation in literary texts. Yamashita's work lends itself to readings mindful of both form and content: on the one hand, her training as an anthropologist and the meticulous research that went into each of her books hint at the *transparency* of the representation (its accuracy or reliability); on the other hand, the experimental form of her work draws attention to its own operations *as* representation (its mediation or artistic craft).

2   Rachel Greenwald Smith (2015, 22) makes a similar point about Yamashita's *Tropic of Orange* (1997) when she writes that the novel interrupts "deep identification with any individual character," most of which are "flat" to begin with, and constructs a world instead "that has depth in its plenitude of situations and tones."

propose to read *I Hotel* as a "systems novel," taking my cue from a term coined by Tom LeClair in the 1980s for big, ambitious books characterized by their informational density, which they put forward in multilayered and digressive structures.

I argue that reading *I Hotel* with an eye for its systemic makeup—its intersecting narratives, recurring themes, and the dialogue it stages between fact and fiction—reveals how the Asian American movement took shape in face of the power structures that opposed it. *I Hotel* plays around with the conventions of the novel genre, but while this is not a novel of character revelation, it does stand in the American tradition of novels that eschew the moment-to-moment excavation of private feelings and intentions—the codes and comforts of the realist novel—and articulate instead how its subjects can best be understood in terms of their "public effects" and the social categories that shape them: a tradition that, as Stacey Margolis (2005, 3–4) has shown, stretches all the way back to the long nineteenth century. Early twentieth-century examples include John Dos Passos's *U.S.A.* trilogy (1930–36), which blends different narrative modes with newspaper clippings to present a collective story of capital and alienation, or Ralph Ellison's *Invisible Man* (1952), in which an unnamed black narrator struggles to form an identity beyond the racial codes placed upon him by society. The systems novel genre, I would argue, is another, more recent iteration of that same tradition.

In what follows, I offer a broad sketch of the systems novel while moving through *I Hotel*. Three parallel topics will scaffold the discussion: the complex *form* of the novel, which gives rise to what I have referred to earlier as the "collective voice" of *I Hotel*; its emphasis on *community*, which traces the roots of the Asian American movement in the civil rights era; and its repeated focus on the *visibility* of that community, which gives the novel its political charge. By *visibility*, I mean the efforts of a community to be seen, heard, and represented. *I Hotel* makes a strong link, for instance, between the history of Asian American writing and the ethnic consciousness movements of the 1960s and '70s. This link will be the subject of the first section below, where I discuss the structure of the novel in relation to the theme of "storytelling." *I Hotel* is a heteroglossic novel, a text in many voices, with a host of narrators telling different origin stories for the community. I will have more to say about the systems novel in the second section of the essay, in which I suggest that the accumulation of stories in the novel prompts its readers to shift between the whole and its parts. The systems novel genre draws attention to its representation as a complex, global set of interlocking parts. As such, it is uniquely suited for an analysis of the relationships that shape the whole: the genre is built on a desire to make something transparent, to reveal a complexity that is simplified in less overarching modes of representation. That complexity extends to the sense of community that *I Hotel* tries to evoke: rather than representing the Asian American community as stable or homogeneous, it emphasizes the diversity within the community by staging different, often precarious, moments of communal encounter. Doing so, the novel sets up a tension between the private and the public, the individual and the collective, the personal and the political. With its diverse representations of community, *I Hotel* asks questions of what community does and does not include, or who belongs and who gets left out. Together, the two sections of my discussion will map the politics of transparency of *I Hotel*. This is a novel that, in different styles and voices, wants to illustrate how a movement was claiming visibility.

2.

Each of the ten novellas in *I Hotel* is named after a different year, ranging from 1968 to 1977, although they all move back and forth in time well beyond that particular year. Each novella also brings together a wide variety of forms. Regular prose alternates with, among other things, documentary transcripts and mock cinéma verité scripts, Confucian analects and aphorisms in the style of Sun Tzu, illustrations, confidential dossiers, homages to Japanese and Chinese classics such as *The Pillow Book* and *Water Margin*, homages to founding mothers and fathers of Asian American literature such as Maxine Hong Kingston and Carlos Bulosan, and at least one parody of "one of those best American short stories reprinted again and again in every literary magazine and Chinese American, Asian American, minority writers, new and promising American writers anthology you've seen lately" (242). Although the novellas share characters and touch upon similar events, each focuses on a different set of protagonists, which means that *I Hotel* can just as well be read as a collection of stand-alone pieces. The novel's formal complexity can have a dizzying effect, as scholars tend to note, but its steady accretion of voices and themes has a purpose: if *I Hotel* does not cohere into a singular, consistent narrative arc, then that is because the time and the community that the novel describes would not allow it. In other words, by casting a wide net, the form of *I Hotel* imitates the "complex forms of discourse that were produced in the Asian American movement" (Yu 2014, 64), or it evokes "a moment and movement whose members periodically found common purpose together, but just as often splintered into competing efforts" (Sheffer 2020, 63).

The novel covers the formative years of that movement, from the late sixties to the mid-seventies, when the US saw the birth of its many ethnic-consciousness groups. Like several of these groups, the Asian American movement emerged against the backdrop of the nationwide Third World movements of the time; in particular, the Third World Liberation Front (TWLF) strikes of 1968, the largest student strikes in American history, when a coalition of Black, Latin American/Chicano, Native American, and Asian American students in the San Francisco Bay area marched in demand of a curriculum more relevant and accessible to their communities. Unlike the other groups in the coalition, Asian Americans did not have a history of thinking of themselves as a community, or even in terms of a shared racial and ethnic identity. The TWLF strikes, first at San Francisco State College and later at the University of California, Berkeley, set the agenda for the articulation of an "Asian American consciousness," a new way of thinking of a community's identity over and above the diverse backgrounds of its members (Omatsu 2016, 60). Asian American student activists followed in the footsteps of different Asian immigrant communities struggling to find a place in the US—such as the Chinese immigrants suffering from the anger and violence that led to the 1882 Chinese Exclusion Act, or the Filipino American farm labor organizers in the 1920s, or the Japanese American concentration camp resisters in the 1940s. In their challenge to the university in the 1960s, the students forged close transnational ties in the face of what they experienced as a shared history of oppression, and they pushed their concerns into the wider world in an effort to address community problems and promote self-determination (Umemoto 2016, 54).

The TWLF strikes loom large in each of the ten novellas, but rather than pinning itself down on one particular foundational moment, *I Hotel* stages multiple origin stories for the Asian American movement. Several of them feature two or three youth activists and an older mentor figure honing their ideology in the community struggle. The first novella, "1968: Eye Hotel," sets the tone with the story of two second-generation Chinese American students during the strikes at San Francisco State College, Paul Wallace Lin and Edmund Yat Min Lee, who, off-campus, attend contemporary Chinese literature classes by a suspended professor, Chen Wen-guang. Chen is a former Communist and dissident who translated for the US military during World War II, also an old friend of Paul's late father, a "painter-poet" who founded the short-lived Chinese Revolutionary Artists' Club in San Francisco before the war (Yamashita 2010, 27). The two students begin organizing under Chen's wing and, after Edmund tragically gets shot in a garment factory strike, Paul becomes a founding member of the Combined Asian American Resources Project, or CARP, the group of writers who in the 1970s would go on to reissue John Okada's forgotten novel about the wartime internment of Japanese Americans, *No-No Boy* (1957), turning it into a bestseller in the process. In *I Hotel*, the meaning of CARP's rediscovery of *No-No Boy* is not lost on Paul's colleagues. Here is a text—a visible, legible representation—that reveals what has long remained hidden: "It means we got a history! We're yellow writers who come from a tradition of yellow writing!" (96).

I Hotel does much to recover that history, sketching a "tradition of yellow writing" that implies, perhaps, a set of shared cultural and historical contexts. Apart from the playful references to Asian and Asian American literature I have already mentioned, the novel hints at a large variety of "yellow writing" in the US. It features translations of Chinese poems carved into the walls of Angel Island Immigration Station in San Francisco Bay, where newly arrived immigrants in the first half of the previous century were interrogated and detained (84). It has characters based on Beat poet Albert Saijo and City Lights Bookstore manager Shig Murao (561–75). It also reflects on representations of Asian people by white American writers. A chapter in the fourth novella parodies the type of social realism with Orientalist inflections familiar, as the narrator points out, from Pearl Buck (237). In the seventh novella, two Filipino Americans discuss the merits of the "Chinaman named Lee" in John Steinbeck's *East of Eden* (1952), arguing in turn that he alone among the novel's characters does not fall squarely on either side of the divide between good and evil, a "Western concept" that Lee, as a fully rounded character, manages to subvert (462), or conversely, that Lee is just another version of an Asian stereotype pushed by white culture, a sexless caretaker whose role is to cook and clean (468). Finally, *I Hotel* explores moments of overlap between American and Asian canons; for instance, when it links the civil disobedience of the student activists to both Henry David Thoreau and Rabindranath Tagore (409). To an extent, the novel functions as a patchwork of literary references. It brings together many voices from many backgrounds and demonstrates that literature—as a mode of representation, a reflection of different ways of seeing and being seen—can hardly be separated from the social or political situations from which it emerges.

Politics, even identity politics, lie at the heart of the novel. With its rehearsal of the formation of CARP, "1968: Eye Hotel" reveals how the origin of the Asian American movement coincided with the birth of Asian American studies and of Asian American literature. The TWLF strike at San Francisco State, in which Asian American students played an important part, resulted in the founding of the first school of ethnic studies in the country (Umemoto 2016, 54). *I Hotel* captures the moment at the start of its second novella, when a radical criminologist involved in the strikes remembers the new alliances that formed over experimental conferences and off-campus courses: "Suddenly the students got what they asked for: Asian American Studies" (Yamashita 2010, 124). By voicing their demands, "they invented a new political category" (123). The close ties between writing and politics in the novel echo Yamashita's personal take on the matter: "Asian American literature," as she would put it in a later essay, "is at heart a literature of politics and resistance" (Yamashita 2018, 597). But *I Hotel* doesn't just reconstruct a narrative of the student strikes or the history of "yellow writing" as much as it lays bare how politics shape such narratives. The novel oscillates between mimetic and performative conceptions of storytelling: stories not only serve to *represent* a certain history, they also *create* it.

Already at the beginning of the first novella, Paul, recently orphaned and feeling detached from the cultural traditions of his family, reflects on the need for representation: "Why is the call to write so strong?" he wonders in Chen Wen-guang's class, as he becomes involved in the strike (Yamashita 2010, 14). Several answers come up in the ensuing pages. Initially, Chen makes his students read Mao Zedong's speech on literature and art at the Yenan forum in 1942, long before the horrors of the Great Leap Forward, when Mao rails against Japanese imperialism and calls for "*a cultural army*" to fight alongside the people's army: "*there are various fronts, among which are the fronts of the pen and the gun*," and the pen, according to Mao, should serve the needs of the people (25, italics in the original). Chen's appeals to the Yenan speech bring to mind the militancy of the TWLF students, several of whom indeed flirted with Maoism, but later, in his first visit to Mao's China after the war, Chen himself becomes disillusioned when one of his former teachers tells him that the pen can just as well be used to dictate to the people what its needs are: "Yes, the pen can be a revolutionary force and a weapon, but we did not entirely understand what that means. The pen is also used to ensure conformity and political order, and that is as old as Confucius" (74). "1968: Eye Hotel" doesn't resolve this tension between idealism and propaganda, anticipating the many community organizers who cut their teeth on Vladimir Lenin and Mao in the novellas to come. But "1968" does come up with a simpler answer to the question that brought Paul to Chen's class, and that will soon motivate the founding of CARP: "The desire to write is linked to the desire to think and the desire to record" (95). The writers and narrators in all ten novellas have their own particular reasons for telling their stories. *I Hotel* records them and lets them resonate with each other. Yamashita explains in her afterword to the novel that she spent countless hours in archives and interviewed "over 150 individuals from that time" before she could start writing (612). In this way, *I Hotel*, as a character who embarks on a similar project in the novel puts it, took on the form of "an oral history project," allowing the history to bubble up "from the people who lived it" (542).

I Hotel is filled with storytellers, reporters and documentarians, poets and confabulators. It features characters, like the "oral history" recorder in the ninth novella or the TWLF documentary makers in the second, who want to preserve a historical record. Others tell tales to ground themselves, to make sense of their time and place and the evolution of the movement, taking comfort from the fact "that storytelling in itself is powerful magic" (378). The sixth novella uses Native American folklore to frame the stories of three former student activists, "self-identified by their Asian features" (374), after they reenter society: "It seems like several tribes have a variation of this creation story, how the Earth was born from a tiny plug of soil on the back of a turtle" (381). The novella ends when the three meet again at the site of the Tule Lake War Relocation Center, the largest of the ten concentration camps for Japanese Americans during the war, and reenact a creation story of their own, a clump of tule standing in for the plug of soil (419–20). When the news spreads in the eighth novella that Aleksandr Solzhenitsyn has moved to Canada, two characters discuss the use and misuse of fiction. For Estelle Hama, the daughter of Russian émigrés and a convinced Communist who had once followed her Japanese American husband into the camps, fiction prevents meaningful change: "It's because of fiction we get in trouble. It's because of fiction that we get put in jail, get persecuted, framed, lied to by politicians" (513). Her son Harry counters with a defense of "the art of storytelling," arguing that fiction can protect as well as manipulate. Estelle should know, since she chose not to tell her children that her husband had abandoned them soon after the war, spinning a yarn instead: "You lied to us! That's fiction!" (517).

Narratives preserve and distort. They help us organize our experience, as narratologists have long pointed out—they highlight certain aspects of our experience, or make them more visible to ourselves and others—but they also recast that experience into fixed, conventional patterns. The narrator of the seventh novella, "1974: I-Migrant Hotel," is a frenzied tale-teller, Felix Allos, one of the older Manong bachelors who live at the International Hotel. Felix has had an eventful life. He migrated to California via Hawaii as a farm worker and witnessed the exploitation and the union strikes of the 1920s and '30s there. During the war, he signed up to fight with the US Army Forces in the Far East, where he likely walked in the Bataan Death March. He befriended the Filipino American labor leaders Philip Vera Cruz and Larry Itliong and became involved in the 1965 Great Delano Grape Strike. He may once have worked as John Steinbeck's cook. Owing to antimiscegenation laws and limits on immigration, he, like many Filipino immigrants of his generation, has always remained single and spent most of his life in hotel rooms, and now he is facing an eviction. Perhaps it is because of the scars from his past, or because of the limited amount of control he has had over his life, but Felix feels driven to telling and retelling tales. Some of them must be true, because he has friends who corroborate them, but others he embellishes or just makes up.

Talking to a friend who joined up with him, Felix explains that he escaped the Bataan Death March by rolling into a ditch and fleeing to Manila, where he sat out the war as a waiter in the Tsubaki Club, the site of a prolific spy ring for American forces in the Pacific (472–73).

But later, in a conversation with two protesters at the hotel, he says he escaped to the mountains and joined Luis Taruc's Communist guerilla fighters against the Japanese, the Hukbalahap (485). Whether either of these stories is true might be beside the point for Felix: both restore a sense of agency to him, which he could not have had during the March and which he clearly does not have now. By projecting his own narrative onto historical events, he puts his worries in the context of a larger struggle. In fact, Felix says as much at the start of the novella, when he refers to a speech by Philip Vera Cruz right before he starts inserting himself in the history of the Filipino Farm Workers union: "It's this kind of speech about our history. Make it real to you, we got to put our real lives inside real history" (430).

Felix's take on the speech could serve as a slogan for the entire novel. Time and again, Yamashita puts the lives of her characters inside history, pitting their stories of love and loss against the real-life efforts that brought the Asian American community together in the sixties and seventies: demands for fair jobs and more representative forms of education, union organizing drives, efforts to prevent gentrification of historical neighborhoods, and, related to those efforts, anti-eviction campaigns. Some characters in *I Hotel* are fictional stand-ins for historical figures.[3] Others try to think through their newfound sense of identity at key moments, offering more and different origin stories for the community that *I Hotel* puts into focus. Three "young revolutionaries" (296) in the fifth novella attend a Marxist reading group when the "national question" comes up: "*When did we become Asian American?*" The reply: "*Nineteen sixty-six. There's a magazine article about the Japanese American model minority, a kind of American. Before that, Japanese are racially identified as Japanese—otherwise how could they all be interned during the war? After sixty-six, we all get racially identified as hyphenated Americans*" (321, italics in the original).

The "model minority" myth, which came up at the peak of the ethnic consciousness movements of the sixties, presents one of the more insidious stereotypes around Asian Americans, praising them for their ability to overcome discrimination and achieve success (as defined by white middle-class America).[4] The trope presents a simplified view of race,

---

3   Paul Wallace Lin's dead father in the first novella, for instance, could be a shoo-in for Yun Gee, the modernist painter who started a Chinese Revolutionary Artists' Club in San Francisco in the late 1920s. Professor Tom Takabayashi, the radical criminologist in the second novella, stands in for Paul Takagi, the criminologist at Berkeley who had a pivotal role in the TWLF strikes. Mo Akagi in the third novella is modeled on Richard Aoki, who grew up in the wartime camps and later befriended Bobby Seale before climbing the ranks of the Black Panther Party.

4   The reply in the fifth novella of *I Hotel* likely refers to "Success Story, Japanese American Style" by the Berkeley sociologist William Petersen, published

one that suggests that the country allows equal opportunities to all and that those who fall behind do so because of their own bad choices (Zhou 2004, 32–33). It tells a success story but it judges Asian Americans—and prompts them to judge themselves—by standards different from the average American (34). Karl Kang, the character who offers the reply in the fifth novella, suggests that only a stereotype managed to turn them from just *other* into *other Americans*, or "*hyphenated Americans.*" But he adds that "Asian American" is also a "political designation," and that the people it lumps together might as well organize around not just race, but also class (Yamashita 2010, 320). Karl's language and that of his friends is steeped in the rhetoric of their reading material. Epigraphs from Marx, Lenin, and Mao punctuate their talks. A famous line from the *Communist Manifesto* (1848) opens the conversation: "The history of all hitherto existing society is the history of class struggle" (314). Later, they turn to the Marxist "Science of History" and agree that all events follow the laws of "economic change" (321). Taking that logic to its extreme, it would seem as if anyone's particular life story only serves to illustrate the general patterns of history. Again, the narrator anticipates: "The particulars of any event may recede to favor the idea of the event" (303).

In the characters' talks and efforts to organize, the fifth novella lays bare a conflict, perhaps inherent to any movement striving for revolutionary reform: How do the goals of the group rhyme with the needs of the individual? What does a movement owe to its members and vice versa? Karl and his friends dissolve their personalities in revolutionary zeal: "The personal must be put aside for the political" (313). But their stories do not end well, and neither does their organizing. When Angela Davis gets invited to address a Japanese American collective, the group breaks apart into petty factions, arguing semantics and bickering over who practices the right kind of communism: Mao or, as Davis would have it, "the Soviets" (363). The narrator, something like an omniscient mediator between the theory and the practice in this novella, sums up the result of their politicking with a pithy remark: "The struggle over its political life and organization may become an end in itself" (364). The rigorous logic of the group ends up defeating itself, it seems. But then, in the grander scheme of *I Hotel*, this is only one of ten novellas that braid stories and histories together.

---

in *The New York Times Magazine* in January 1966. But another article of that same year, "Succes of One Minority Group in U.S." by the *U.S. News and World Report* staff, shows that, already in the sixties, the model minority myth reflects an emerging ethnic stereotype rather than the opinion of just one academic. Min Zhou (2004, 35) argues that the image presented in both articles remains largely unchallenged decades later, and that "most Asian Americans seem to accept that 'white' is mainstream, average and normal, and they look to whites as a frame of reference for attaining higher social position."

Felix Allos tells tales and inserts himself into history. The revolutionaries in the fifth novella study the fixed patterns of history and lose themselves in it. Taken together, the novel's play with history implies that the past is not a monolith: it consists of facts and memories, events and experiences. It can be made to make sense at different scales. Like many historical novels published since the second half of the twentieth century, *I Hotel* subscribes to the postmodern idea that history has no master narrative but should be approached instead through smaller narratives that allow for different interpretations. In typical postmodernist fashion, the novel leaves plenty of room for metafictional asides to tell us that: "History may proceed sequentially or, as they say, *must* proceed sequentially," the narrator says before bunkering down with the Marxists, "but stories may turn and turn again" (301, italics in the original). With its ten different versions of events that all take place on the same timeline, *I Hotel* proposes that history and storytelling lock together in a sort of feedback loop. Such a loose conception of events can be liberating: it goes against predictions of the end of history and rejects the teleology of ideology-based narratives. It can also be frustrating. If history depends on narrative and emplotment, much depends on who tells it, and what gets left out. If the history of a community represents how that community has made itself visible, the question becomes: Who, exactly, could claim visibility, and who remains invisible?

The third novella, for instance, gives a backstory of "interracial solidarity" (203) through a discussion between Eldridge Cleaver and a member of the Red Guard Party, a Chinese American youth organization from San Francisco. They speak of the Black Panthers and the history of the Red Guards while the first-person narrator, an unnamed individual who hovers over the conversation, addresses the story they construct: "Now that's a story" (198), "Panther continues the storytelling" (201), "This is where we get our history lesson" (211), and "let's get back to the storytelling" (215). The conversation between Cleaver and the Red Guard highlights the bonds that grew between protest groups in the fight against systemic racism, but crucially—and perhaps not altogether surprisingly, given Cleaver's own troubled history—the story it tells leaves no space for the women involved in that fight. Jolie Sheffer (2020, 70) notes of the novella that the casual sexism between the two obscures how women did "much of the unsung work of the movement," which is true, yet the narrative undercuts their chauvinism. In a drug-induced haze that could easily mask for a moment of revelation, the two foresee a bleak future for their movement, while one of them imagines a more inclusive, more effective form of protest: "'You forget one thing.' Panther waves his finger. 'Woman warrior'" (Yamashita 2010, 219). The novella ends with a paean to the "women of the lumpen," who "catch their licks" but "give 'em out too" during the struggle (219). More importantly, the Panther's phrase illustrates once again how moments such as these in *I Hotel* carry much wider than just the political, and ripple onward into the literary and the historical: the nod, of course, is to Maxine Hong Kingston's debut, *The Woman Warrior: Memoirs of a Girlhood among Ghosts* (1976).

With the woman warrior, we come full circle to the founding of CARP in the opening novella and to the "tradition of yellow writing" that *I Hotel* addresses throughout its pages. In 1974, CARP would go on to publish *Aiiieeeee! An Anthology of Asian American Writers*, one of the first collections dedicated to the history of pan-Asian writers in America. *Aiiieeeee!* set the terms for the development of Asian American literature studies, in part because of the outspoken tone of its editors, who did not shy away from their role as gatekeepers. When Kingston published *The Woman Warrior* in 1976, she famously drew the ire of several CARP members who blamed her for selling "Orientalist stereotypes" to white readers (Cheung 2021, 193). The drawn-out arguments that ensued over CARP and Kingston have sparked long debates over what counts as "Asian American" and what counts as "fake," which shows that if anything, communities are not monolithic either.[5] Yamashita's novel doesn't pick sides in those debates, but, as in the Panther's drugged-up reply above, it does allude to them, allowing these and other references to build up in the complex structure that is *I Hotel*. The novel does not harp on the real-life legacies of CARP or Kingston. Nor, for that matter, does it elevate the role of the Red Guards or of any of the other factions and organizations it mentions. Instead, it leaves it up to the reader to weigh the impact of the situations it describes. Rather than offering a straightforward narrative that progresses toward a resolution, *I Hotel* constructs an impression of community life through cross-references and allusions. In its intricate plots and parallel storylines, its genre-bending and its multiple perspectives, the novel prompts its readers to move between the parts and the whole: the particular stories told in each

---

5   I return to CARP's criticism of Kingston in the second part of the essay. For an overview of Asian American anthologies published in the early 1970s, and of the leading role of *Aiiieeeee!* and CARP in the shaping of Asian American literature studies, see Cheung (2021). One controversial issue that came up in the wake of *Aiiieeeee!* concerns the question of identity. For the book's editors, "Asian American [. . .] means Filipino, Chinese, and Japanese Americans" born and raised in America (quoted in Cheung 2021, 191). Their limiting take on the community—which, to name only a few, excludes substantial groups of Korean and Vietnamese Americans—has since been addressed by many. In the essay "Literature as Community," Yamashita (2018, 597) gives the more standard view on what the label "Asian American" now stands for: "It is a naming category to recognize the immigration and participation of Asian and Pacific Islander peoples in American society and political life over the past one hundred and fifty years."

novella and the general patterns that emerge between them. In short, *I Hotel* is a systems novel.

3.

The term "systems novel" mostly comes up in discussions of postmodern maximalist fiction in the style of Thomas Pynchon or Don DeLillo, and perhaps that also explains why it has fallen out of use. When Tom LeClair coined it in the 1980s, he meant it as a corrective to the critique most often hurled at the postmodernists, "with postmodernism usually having deconstructive connotations" (LeClair 1989, 21). When Jonathan Franzen used it in the fallout of the Oprah Winfrey affair in the early 2000s, he dismissed it as too clever, insisting to his readers that he was not "a really smart, really angry, really forbidding Systems writer" (Franzen 2002, 246). What somehow got lost between the two positions is the idea that inspired the label in the first place: that in order to represent the world in all its complexity, we need to think of it in terms of wholes and relationships rather than breaking it up into parts and looking at each in isolation. The idea has a long history in the sciences, where it is variously known as systems thinking, or systems theory, or systems science, and it has seen some of its biggest defenders with environmentalists such as James Lovelock and anthropologists such as Gregory Bateson (Ramage and Shipp 2009, 1–7).

Taking his cue from the systems thinkers, LeClair defined the systems novel as the type of novel that braids together sophisticated ideas and recognizes the world it represents as an ecological whole. Systems novels typically engage with science. They are ambitious in size and scope and they draw on systemic paradigms to demonstrate "how orders and forms in the world (and not just in the artistic text) can arise out of seeming chaos" (LeClair 1989, 21). They require a form of spatial reading, fixing the readers' attention on the network of connections that develop across the text (15). Hence the name: systems novels mimic the dynamics of natural systems, or complex wholes composed of interlocking parts. By doing so, they "master the time, the methods of fiction, and the reader" (1). That is, they register the complexities of postmodern life, they go against the conventions of character-based fiction, and they shift the reader's focus from the local to the global. The swirling structure of *I Hotel* could be enough for it to qualify as a systems novel, but in the remainder of this chapter, I want to zoom in on LeClair's claim that systems novels function as "figurative maps," or as texts that are "both exceedingly detailed and multiply coded for scale and proportion" (24). The accumulation of data gives them an impression of completeness, but systems novels resist this as an illusion: they insist, through various metafictional devices, that they can only map the terrain they cover. The map is one of their "recurrent metaphors" (24).

A map is a visual metaphor. It can represent vast swaths of territory on a more human scale: the map makes them transparent, or legible. Maps are defined by their boundaries, with the mapmaker deciding what gets on and what is left outside of it. LeClair takes his inspiration from Gregory Bateson (1972, 442) and his use of the phrase that "the map is not the territory," which Bateson borrowed from Alfred Korzybski's theory of general semantics. Yamashita's map of the Asian American community in *I Hotel* departs from another student of Korzybski, the linguist S. I. Hayakawa, who happened to be the president of San Francisco State at the height of the TWLF strikes. In the opening novella of *I Hotel*, the second chapter, "Language in Reaction," takes its title from Hayakawa's landmark book *Language in Thought and Action* (1949), a semantic study of the behavior of people and communities. The chapter in the novella begins with a parable that asks its readers to examine the story of two universities, "Institution A" and "Institution B," and how both came to establish departments of ethnic studies. As a linguistic analysis of the TWLF strikes, the parable closely follows the "Semantic Parable" at the start of *Language in Thought and Action*. Here is how Hayakawa opens his book: "Once upon a time (said the Professor), there were two small communities, spiritually as well as geographically situated at a considerable distance from each other" (Hayakawa 1970, 1). Here is Yamashita's narrator: "*Once upon a time, there were two public institutions of higher learning, separated by a great bay but connected by a great bridge*" (Yamashita 2010, 18; italics in the original). Hayakawa's takeaway from the parable is that the words we use determine how we think, and our "linguistic habits" shine through in the way we evaluate ourselves and our communities (Hayakawa 1970, 6–7). When Hayakawa appears as a character in *I Hotel*, the message is much the same: "*What kind of language we speak largely determines the kinds of thoughts we have*" (Yamashita 2010, 30; italics in the original).

Hayakawa's appointment as president of San Francisco State in 1968 stirred up controversy among Japanese Americans. Reluctant to confront a member of their own community, only a minority of the nonstudent population would show their support for the strikes. When Hayakawa was invited in February of '69 to speak at a dinner sponsored by members of the Japanese American Citizens League—one of the oldest Asian American organizations in the country—more than a hundred Japanese American students picketed outside (Umemoto 2016, 39–40). In *I Hotel*, Hayakawa appears at that very dinner to speak about the community's self-image. Using a term introduced by Korzybski, he talks about "time-binding," which stands for the human ability to transmit knowledge and experience from one generation to the next via the use of symbols. Over time, the accumulation of knowledge accretes into culture. "Humans," Hayakawa explains in the passage, "have created language to communicate, to pass on vital information to each other and to the next generation. That's how we survive over time. This time-binding is another name for our ability to create society and civilization" (Yamashita 2010, 31). With the TWLF students clamoring in the background, Hayakawa's words take on extra meaning. Survival, he says to the people at the dinner, "depends on communicating your purpose and your history," or making visible what is otherwise lost (32). He adds that many members of the Japanese Americans Citizens League survived World War II because they knew how to adapt to the harshest conditions, and if "the youngsters outside could hear your brave history and mission," they too would understand the sacrifices it took for the community to survive. In other words: assimilate or die (32).

Hayakawa's message in the novel is borne out by the hard line he took against the student movement in real life (Umemoto 2016, 50). Edmund Yat Min Lee, one of the two protagonists of the opening novella, works a student job as a waiter during the dinner. When Hayakawa makes a quiet exit through the kitchen, Edmund accosts him and tells him he understood the implication of his speech: "I think you said that the winning civilization will be the one that keeps its history going" (Yamashita 2010, 34). Later that evening, Edmund and Paul Wallace Lin, who had joined the protesters outside, discuss Hayakawa's usage of terms such as "community" and "self-concept." The novel does not make the link explicit, but the words they use again come from *Language in Thought and Action*. At stake is "this map/territory thing" and the possible disconnect between image and reality. Edmund explains,

> O.K., it's like the territory is the real land and the map is just a representation. So you got a map in your head about yourself, but there is the real you or self that is the territory. So this conflict he's talking about is when the territory is changing but the map stays the same. It's this disconnect between the two, between the abstraction and reality, that causes one to be insane. (34)

The idea that a self-image stands in relation to reality as a map does to a territory, and that we run into trouble "because of false maps in our heads," follows from Hayakawa's belief that language molds our thoughts and actions (Hayakawa 1970, 32).[6] Edmund agrees, and adds that

---

6   Yamashita's nods to *Language in Thought and Action* are extensive and subtle. For example, Edmund's recap of the speech borrows from Hayakawa's discussion of self-knowledge and "the pitfalls of map-territory relationships" near the end of the book: "A map is *not* the territory: one's self-concept is *not* one's self. A map represents *not all* of the territory: one's self-concept *omits* an enormous amount of one's actual self—we never know ourselves *completely*" (Hayakawa 1970, 299; italics in the original). Much earlier, Hayakawa devotes

Hayakawa himself illustrates the principle quite well, since his thoughts clearly do not match his actions: "His *map* is that he's an effective communicator, a great scholar applying his theories to active duty. His *territory* is that of a convenient minority banana used by the white power structure" (Yamashita 2010, 35; italics in the original). Where Hayakawa presents himself as the great communicator, transcending all issues of race and class, Edmund questions the authenticity of the image.

Edmund sees Hayakawa as something of a split personality, a token figure for the conservative voices in the community, caught between the need to assimilate and the desire to have a true self. The slur "convenient minority banana" repeats a common accusation when the model minority myth came up in the late 1960s: yellow on the outside, but white on the inside (Zhou 2004, 29). Hayakawa gets another cameo in the fourth novella of *I Hotel*, "1971: Aiiieeeee! Hotel," where he happens to share a taxi with a student activist, Gerald K. Li, fresh out of jail for resisting arrest at the San Francisco State strikes. The two hit it off at first but when they realize who is who, Gerald gets the last words: "Fucking fascist pig uncle Tom pig banana! [. . .] FUCKING BANANA! FUCKING BANANA!" (Yamashita 2010, 259).

The fourth novella is easily the most experimental of *I Hotel*, but the title—and its echoes of *Aiiieeeee!*—is a giveaway. It is here that the novel stages its most candid engagement with the "self-concept" of the Asian American community since it first emerged: the legacy of CARP and the many maps that have since been drawn of Asian America. Recall the founding of CARP at the end of the first novella and the fleeting reference to Kingston's *The Woman Warrior* at the end of the third. One of Kingston's most caustic critics was CARP member Frank Chin, coeditor of both *Aiiieeeee!* and its follow-up, *The Big Aiiieeeee!* (1991), which Chin opened with a scathing critique of Kingston and two other Asian American writers whose work he considered as too mainstream, David Henry Hwang and Amy Tan. In the now infamous essay "Come All Ye Asian American Writers of the Real and the Fake," Chin (1991, 2)

---

another section of his study to "Maps and Territories," in which he links our verbal knowledge of the world, "this world that comes to us through words," to the world we know from experience: if one does not match the other, he argues, we either adjust or "end up in a mental hospital" (32; hence Paul's claim in *I Hotel* that the disconnect "causes one to be insane"). While Hayakawa does not use the term "time-binding" in *Language in Thought and Action*, the chapter that leads to "Maps and Territories" is called "Language and Survival." In it, Hayakawa presents a similar argument as Yamashita's version of him does during the dinner speech: "Language [. . .] is the indispensable mechanism of human life—of life such as ours that is molded, guided, enriched, and made possible by the accumulation of the past experience of members of our own species" (Hayakawa 1970, 17).

laid into the commercial success of the three, which he took as a sign of cooptation: "What seems to hold Asian American literature together is [their] popularity among whites." Their work is "fake," Chin argued, and "to legitimize their faking" they hold up an image of Asian culture to white readers that is at once exotic, familiar, and tame—their own variant of the model minority myth of success through assimilation (3). For Chin, "fake" writers desecrate the traditions of Asian literature by serving them up as Western stereotypes: "Kingston, Hwang, and Tan are the first writers of any race, and certainly the first writers of Asian ancestry, to so boldly fake the best known works from the most universally known body of Asian literature and lore in history" (3; see also Cheung 2021, 193).[7]

"1971: Aiiieeeee! Hotel" sets up different clashes between "the real" and "the fake" as it explores the issues of identity and assimilation. It begins with "a little talk story" about Iron Ox, also known as Li Kui or Black Whirlwind, an outlaw borrowed from one of the earliest Chinese novels, *Water Margin* (Yamashita 2010, 223). Here, the novella introduces its central theme: the doppelganger. Iron Ox meets his double and, after a brief identity crisis, decides to kill him: "*There, that's better. I must be authentic, that one is fake*" (225; italics in the original). Similar doppelgangers reappear throughout the novella, which consists of ten short segments. Each time, they reflect the double-sidedness of being Asian American. The fourth segment, "War & Peace," puts two doubles side by side, one male and one female: ten comic panels place the same man and woman against different Asian or American backgrounds. The figures remain unnamed but the resemblance leaves little doubt about who they are: Chin and Kingston. The captions for every panel suggest that, in all the wrangling over the "real" and the "fake," the two are different and yet the same—and that each has had his or her impact on a community whose borders are much more porous than Chin, for one, would have it: "Son" and "Daughter" (244), "Sister" and "Brother" (245), "Chinaman" and "Chinawoman" (248), "Patriarch" and "Matriarch" (250). That is all the information we get in this segment: in the typical fashion of *I Hotel*, the novella does not pick sides, it just brings them together; but the juxtaposition tells something about the difficulties that

---

7   Chin's critique of Kingston, Hwang, and Tan in the essay is long and surprisingly nuanced—in terms of its engagement with the history of Asian and Asian American writing, at least—but notoriously limiting. One reason why he blamed *The Woman Warrior* for blending Asian culture with Western stereotypes was that it came out as an autobiography, "the only form of literature written by Chinese Americans that major publishers will publish (other than the cookbook)," also "an exclusively Christian form." As Chin had it, Kingston and the two others "all write to the specifications of the Christian stereotype of Asia being as opposite morally from the West as it is geographically" (Chin 1991, 9).

come with panethnic identity politics.[8] The issue carries over into the other segments of the novella.

After the story of Iron Ox at the start, the second segment of "1971: Aiiieeeee! Hotel" moves to a pastiche of an Asian American play that could have featured in *Aiiieeeee!* The list of characters includes "Pa," owner of a Chinese delicatessen, and the "five sets of Siamese twins" he fathered (229). The stage directions give the reasons for staging a play with conjoined twins, and they do so in language that mirrors both the link between "Asian American" and "hyphenated" identity in the fifth novella (321) and Edmund's analysis of Hayakawa in the first: "Come to America, and your children all come out hyphenated. Half this—half that. [. . .] Working through schizophrenia and assimilation" (231). The snippet of dialogue that follows has Pa commiserating with a customer over the "identity crisis" of his children, after which he picks up a cleaver and storms off "in search of each paired progeny, and that in itself is a search for Asian America (where's that?)" (232).

Imagery of conjoined twins appears again later in the novella. Gerald K. Li's barrage of insults for Hayakawa is followed by another segment in comic-book format, featuring two sisters joined at the hip: one a "straight-A model minority with a poor self-image," the other "a ratted-hair fast girl doing drugs with a poor self-image" (262). Here, Orientalist stereotypes blend with the stubborn idea that in order to assimilate, Asian Americans must somehow act "white" (see also Zhou 2004). The title of the comic is "Chiquita Banana," the mother of the conjoined twins is drawn as a banana, and she discovers too late that her lover, Uncle Sam or "Don Juan Samuel," has been "pimping and drugging her daughters" with straight As and bottles of alcohol (262). The comic, just like the play before it, hints at the pressure of expectations that each generation puts on the next. The surreal segment that follows it finds Gerald K. Li battling the different sides of his own identity. This segment, "Doppelgangsters," begins with a question: "In the case of the doppelganger, who is who? Who is real and who is fake?" (265). In it, Gerald meets several of his doubles, such as "the white version of his Chinese self" (266) or "his spitting image, his actual doppelganger" (271). With every meeting comes a battle. The fights are rendered as a roleplaying martial-arts game, with different points for offensive and defensive moves, but, crucially, the

---

8 In a moment of metafictional doubling, "War & Peace" also plays with how the rift between Chin and Kingston likely continued in their work. The caption to one panel with Chin reads, "Wittman Ah Sing" (246), after the protagonist of Kingston's *Tripmaster Monkey* (1989), who might have been inspired by Chin. The next panel with Kingston reads "Pandora Toy" (246), the name of a possible stand-in for Kingston in Chin's novel *Gunga Din Highway* (1994).

winner never gets announced. It remains unclear which version of Gerald actually comes out on top.

The comic "Chiquita Banana" ends with a question: "Now what?" (264). The battle over Gerald's true self in "Doppelgangsters" has no real resolution either, it just peters out after the final fight. The unresolved clash between doubles has something of the disconnect between abstraction and reality that Hayakawa (and Edmund and Paul) had already warned about much earlier in *I Hotel*. What is real and what is fake? Is there a "real" image of the Asian American, or is such a transparent, unmediated representation just fantasy? How does the map relate to the territory? Maybe the territory hasn't even been staked out yet—not, at least, according to the repeated question in the play with Pa: "Asian America (where's that?)" (230; 232). After "Doppelgangsters" comes the novella's most abstract segment, "Dance," a visual representation of a dance performance, with words filling in for the bodies that move across the floor. The left side of the visual gives a list of dates and events, going vertically down the page: "father/mother," "arranged marriage," "born 1941," "Pearl Harbor," "raised in camp," and so on (279). The right side is reserved for personal thoughts: "I had a," "son," "where is he?," "is he yet alive?," "will I see him?," and more (279). The dance itself moves between the two sides for about six pages, "[Noh-like]," "[creeping]," "[diagonally]," and by doing so, links events in the life of an Asian American character with the impressions these experiences have left behind (279). "Dance" has no doppelgangers or conjoined twins. Instead, it conjures up a more nuanced view of identity formation: not a battle, but a performance, a complicated two-step between facts and feelings, thoughts and actions, the personal and the political.

What "Dance" does in microcosm, *I Hotel* performs on a grander scale. By mediating the rise of the Asian American movement through a jumble of voices, Yamashita's novel can hardly be accused of pushing a particular agenda. But the critique (so vital to the systems-novel genre) is still present in the book, and the stories it weaves around the eviction of the International Hotel reflect a more general critical attitude toward the limits of identity politics.

"Dance" takes place "beneath the I-Hotel," in an abandoned warehouse occupied by a group of young Asian American artists "who call themselves the Kearny Street Workshop" (278). Founded in 1972 in a corner of the International Hotel, the Kearny Street Workshop still exists in 2024.[9] It is just one of the many artists' collectives and political advocacy groups in the novel that have also left their mark on history:

---

9   The website of the Kearny Street Workshop explains the history of the artists' collective and is a great resource for silkscreened poster art from the movement: www.kearnystreet.org.

scattered through the pages of *I Hotel* are organizations such as the Asian American Political Alliance, the East West Collective, Citizens Against Nihonmachi Eviction, the Asian Law Caucus, and the J-Town Collective. Most of these groups emerged or became more visible in the wake of the TWLF strikes. The point where they come together in the novel is during the fight to save the International Hotel in San Francisco, home to mostly poor and elderly Filipino bachelors. The protests at the hotel are a powerful symbol for the problems posed by gentrification, particularly for minority neighborhoods: when the International Hotel was targeted for demolition in 1968, tenants and supporters resisted eviction for nearly a decade. Their ranks swelled with students and youth activists who rallied around the cause, but the eviction still happened. Residents were forced out by police in the night of August 4, 1977, and the hotel was finally demolished in 1981 (Umemoto 2016, 37; Sheffer 2020, 67–68; Yu 2014, 62–64).[10] *I Hotel* imagines the protests as a site for political empowerment, the groundswell that would help shape the Asian American movement. What made these protests effective for such a long time is the idea that holds communities together: the belief that the whole is greater than the sum of its parts. Communities break down, the novel suggests, when people separate themselves from this idea.

I Hotel represents the night of the eviction twice. First, at the end of the eighth novella, Felix Allos sees the support for I-Hotel break down into factions. There are Maoists and Soviets, regular students and garment workers on strike, artists and union organizers, each with their own notions of how to proceed. The tenants themselves have become lost in the fray: "Every group is using the hotel to test their line" (484). That night, when the protesters are forcibly removed, they put up a united front, but Felix is too disillusioned to have any hopes. He tells a student that even if they fail, the value lies in "remembering" the struggle. He doesn't tell her that he remembers how factionalism had once torn up the United Farm Workers. The same, he fears, will happen now: "We get betrayed by saints and gods" (488).

Memory is also the unifying idea in the tenth novella, when *I Hotel* returns to the eviction. Here, at the end, the novel's collective voice is on full display. Divided into six segments, the final novella looks back on the protests from the perspective of a multiperson "we" narrator, a first-person plural that stands for different people at once: tenants, supporters from the community, immigrants who arrived from Asia after the 1960s, parents of TWLF strikers, and the strikers themselves. The former "radical youth" (597), like Allos before them, only remember how they failed:

---

10 After years of blight—and ongoing community activism—a new I-Hotel was completed in 2005. Five years later, Yamashita held the launch party for *I Hotel* there (Yamashita 2010, 609).

"On the face of it, we were all radical activist revolutionaries, and we were all united to defeat a capitalist-imperialist system of greed. [. . .] Well, that was the face of it, because over time, despite our agreed ideals, we came to hate each other" (599). But the "we" that hovers over the novella presents a much more forgiving take on the period, and the movement. Despite their different backgrounds, all voices agree that they were "hearing and watching history happen" that night at the International Hotel (587). Their ideologies might have run in different directions, they might even have been at cross-purposes, but all could recognize themselves in the life of the hotel bachelor: for a moment, at least, his history was their history. It gave them a sense of community, "fortified by passion and stubborn hope" (605).

The novel wraps up with a ruminative passage on the community forged in the "failure" of that night (605). The building has fallen, its memory crumbled, but the passion and hope that brought people together would last. It ends:

> And in time we may remember, collecting every little memory, all the bits and pieces, into a larger memory, rebuilding a great layered and labyrinthine, now imagined, international hotel of many rooms, the urban experiment of a homeless community built to house the needs of temporary lives. (605)

I Hotel, of course, is meant to be a great, layered, "larger memory," a novel that folds the temporary lives of many into a broad systemic structure. The whole is greater than the sum of the parts. Ten novellas, each in their own style and register, speak of immigration, stereotyping, activism, and "yellow writing." Together, they create an impression of a community that formed in the struggle to be seen and recognized as American. *I Hotel* plays with its own transparency, to repeat the central metaphor of this collection: it draws attention to its status *as* representation. It emphasizes the operations of storytelling, and by doing so, rejects any stable or monolithic notion of community. Yamashita does not tell an easy story of freedom and justice. At no point does *I Hotel* suggest that the 1960s and '70s were a time when everyone came together. In fact, quite a few times it shows how the idealism of the era fell to bits and pieces. But it does illustrate that a movement, or a community, is built up from many different voices—sometimes in harmony, sometimes in dissonance. In that sense, *I Hotel* wears its politics on its sleeve.

Works Cited

Bateson, Gregory. 1972. *Steps to an Ecology of Mind*. Toronto: Chandler.

Cheung, Floyd. 2021. "On Recovering Early Asian American Literature." In *Asian American Literature in Transition: 1965–1996*, edited by Asha Nadkarni and Cathy J. Schlund-Vials, 187–207. Cambridge: Cambridge University Press.

Chin, Frank. 1991. "Come All Ye Asian American Writers of the Real and the Fake." In *The Big Aiiieeeee!: An Anthology of Chinese American and Japanese American Literature*, edited by Jeffery Paul Chan, Frank Chin, Lawson Fusao Inada, and Shawn Wong, 1–92. New York: Meridian.

Franzen, Jonahan. 2002. "Mr. Difficult." In *How to Be Alone*, 238–69. London: Harper Collins.

Hayakawa, S. I. 1970. *Language in Thought and Action.*. London: George Allen & Unwin. First published 1949.

LeClair, Tom. 1989. *The Art of Excess: Mastery in Contemporary American Fiction*. Champaign: University of Illinois Press.

Ling, Yinqi. 2012. *Across Meridians: History and Figuration in Karen Tei Yamashita's Novels*. Stanford, CA: Stanford University Press.

Margolis, Stacey. 2005. *The Public Life of Privacy in Nineteenth-Century American Literature*. Durham, NC: Duke University Press.

Omatsu, Glenn. 2016. "The 'Four Prisons' and the Movements of Liberation: Asian American Activism from the 1960s to the 1990s." In *Contemporary Asian America: A Multidisciplinary Reader*, 3rd ed., edited by Min Zhou and Anthony C. Ocampo, 60–95. New York: New York University Press.

Ramage, Magnus, and Karen Shipp. 2009. *Systems Thinkers*. London: Springer.

Sheffer, Jolie A. 2020. *Understanding Karen Tei Yamashita*. Columbia: University of South Carolina Press.

Smith, Rachel Greenwald. 2015. *Affect and American Literature in the Age of Neoliberalism*. Cambridge: Cambridge University Press.

Umemoto, Karen. 2016. "'On Strike!' San Francisco State College Strike, 1968–1969: The Role of Asian American Students." In *Contemporary Asian America: A Multidisciplinary Reader*, 3rd ed., edited by Min Zhou and Anthony C. Ocampo, 25–59. New York: New York University Press.

Yamashita, Karen Tei. 2010. *I Hotel*. Minneapolis: Coffeehouse Press.

———. 2018. "Literature as Community: The Turtle, Imagination, and the Journey Home." *Massachusetts Review* 59, no. 4: 597–611.

Yu, Lai Ying. 2014. "'Capturing the Spirit': Teaching Karen Tei Yamashita's *I Hotel*." *Asian American Literature: Discourses and Pedagogies* 5: 61–86.

Zhou, Min. "Are Asian Americans Becoming 'White'?" *Contexts* 3, no. 1 (2004): 29–37.

11: Literary Imagination at the Digital Frontier: Dave Eggers's Recent Technological Dystopian Novels

Jelena Šesnić

1. The Current Paradox of Surveillance

Dave Eggers's novel *The Circle* (2013)—a bestseller turned into a movie by the same name in 2017—seems to be cast in the near future, carrying with it a cognitive surplus—a *novum*—a term Darko Suvin (1979, 4) ascribes to science fiction. Rereading the novel in a post-pandemic and evolving digital era, however, one is struck by how some of the dystopian facets of the text appear to have turned into quite accurate prognostications in the intervening period. A similar claim can be made about the sequel, Eggers's 2021 novel *The Every*, where some of the trends already delineated in the first novel come to a head and prompt further questions as to how contemporary American novels imagine and represent the digital frontier, the shifting line between the human world and digital technology.

In the world of Big Tech companies represented in both novels, interaction between humans and digital technology is widespread and ubiquitous. Furthermore, these companies derive their traction from what Shoshana Zuboff (2019) has described as "surveillance capitalism" feeding on the discovery of behavioral surplus using various forms of solid and liquid surveillance (Bauman and Lyon 2013, 3–4) and flaunting the notion of transparency to make it subservient to the logic of endless data extraction. Additionally, the implementation of Web 2.0 in the form of social media has added new technological frameworks in which to situate the problems of privacy, individualism, and access, as Barbara Lovrinić (2019, 91; my translation) points out: "Due to digital mediation, almost every aspect of life has been cast in a new symbolic dimension as an event, object or process, while people become more visible, more conscious, and 'shareable.'" As David Lyon, one of the major scholars of surveillance, contends, the present-day "architecture of electronic technologies" enables "forms of control" that "have no obvious connection with imprisonment" and "often share the features of flexibility and fun seen in entertainment and consumption" (Bauman and Lyon 2013, 4–5). It is on the basis of Lyon's two contentions that my argument will evolve—tracing new forms of surveillance that encompass an ever greater range of our private and intimate worlds, on one hand, and, on the other, a new, participatory and user-generated "culture of surveillance," a term used by Lyon. The paradoxical nature of the contemporary forms of surveillance, transparency, and the idea of the self that is situated within these contending assumptions is examined in Eggers's two novels.

It should be noted that Eggers's technological novels work within a much longer tradition of American fascination with technology and its capabilities, designated by Leo Marx as an integral part of American historical development. Needing technology as a way to colonize, conquer, and tame the American wilderness and to encompass the country's vast geographies, Americans from the start of their New World experience both praised nature as a source of sublime beauty or profit but also inevitably and incessantly sought ways to subdue it by the use of machines. Marx coined the well-known phrase "the machine in the garden," the title of his classic 1964 study, highlighting the idea that nature could and must be improved upon by the use of technology, an idea that would continue to guide cultural attitudes about the role of machines, technology, and science in American society.

Today, however, we witness a moment in which human immersion in and interaction with computer and digital networks has been generating social behavioral modification, in Zuboff's words (2019, 292). What arises is a form of interaction of the human and the machine, of the kind that one of the more sanguine observers of the new trends, anthropologist Paul Rabinow (2008, 13), rightly understands as ushering in a substantive difference, such that would in retrospect mark what is contemporary from what is past, obsolete, and "yesterday." As Rabinow correctly and flatly states, this new biopolitical moment poses the challenge of how to "produce an anthropology without a fixed conception of Man" (14). Clearly not so concerned by the full implication of the birth of a more flexible definition of the human—inevitably raised by the breakthroughs in biosciences—Rabinow poses further challenges for the notion of the human: "Today, *anthropos* is in question; this questioning has multiple dimensions to it. [. . .] Thus it is unequivocally the case that the *logos* of *bios* is currently in the process of rapid transformation. A central question before us today therefore is: given a changing biology, what *logos* is appropriate for *anthropos*?" (14)

Rather than share Rabinow's sense of optimism at the anticipated changes, it is my intention to read Eggers's novels as meditations on more sinister implications of the fictional precinct—but still largely resembling our own—embedded in a world that from the first to the second novel is ever more firmly gripped by a big data company bent on controlling the entire nation, and possibly even the world, in metaphorically transposed ideas of participatory surveillance and full transparency contained first in the notion of the "Circle" and then in the beguiling universalist appeal of the "Every." In this specific focus Eggers echoes and amplifies some of the points made by Zuboff, who in her study *The Age of Surveillance Capitalism* (2019) examines the concerted procedures that allow digital technology—or rather those that wield it—to instrumentalize facets of human nature and, in the process, make it more amenable to manipulation, control, or extraction of behavior data for exploitation and profit. Zuboff explains how this new dispensation deliberately and systematically generates a novel set of behavioral patterns and norms that would bring about a profound change in the way humans behave, interact, and come together in societies: in short, it will bring about new technology-shaped societies based on surveillance, control, and behavior modification. How this new and, to all appearances, sinister fusion of the biological and the technological works; how it marks, according to Zuboff, a transition from the second to the third modernity;[1] and how it institutes instrumentarianism[2] as a mode of control and management of society are the questions looming large in the fictional universe of Eggers's two novels.

Before I attempt to outline the aspects of Eggers's novels that align his narratives with Zuboff's critical observations or David Lyon's more equitable approach, I need to point out that surveillance, at least in its more benign forms of self-observation and observation, was not necessarily or exclusively always seen as a harmful technique. Charles Taylor (1996, 3–5; 139), for one, sees it as a mechanism of the constitution of the modern self. Furthermore, Bauman and Lyon contend that surveillance

---

1   For a classic account of what is here termed "second modernity" cf. Giddens (1990, 1), who comprehends modernity as a Western project, "modes of social life or organisation which emerged in Europe from about the seventeenth century onwards" and eventually spread globally. Modernity thus encompasses a range of epistemological, cultural, and socioeconomic dispensations that still impinge on large swaths of our life (capitalism, democracy, pluralist society). Giddens notes, however, that "in the late twentieth century, it is argued [. . .], we stand at the opening of a new era, to which the sciences must respond and which is taking us beyond modernity itself." Zuboff takes up this observation and contends that a threshold has been reached by the technological revolution and a new form of knowledge- and information-based economy, which, however, has direct consequences on other spheres in the abovementioned spectrum.

2   Instrumentarianim is defined by Zuboff throughout her study as a mode of managing societies in which the infrastructure of computing and digital technologies meets with the notions of behaviorism to produce complex and wide-ranging ways of channelling, controlling, and inducing particular forms of human behavior in groups and societies, amounting to social conditioning (cf. Zuboff 2019, Part III).

was constitutive for forms of institutional and social control inherent to the rise of modernity. Taylor argues on behalf of Adam Smith's model of benevolent surveillance, or the notion of "impartial spectator" (Francis Hutcheson, qtd. in Taylor 2007, 232), that it ushered in a new understanding of the human that would rely on the scientific, secular, and universalist idea of the individual. Certainly, it was the idea of the human who needed to be emancipated in his or her inward disposition and outward behavior from the shackles of tradition and constraining religious and political institutions from this Enlightenment point of view. In the place of the wholesale institutional control of behavior—which we could designate as the surveillance from the outside—Taylor posits a "theory of the moral order" (176) that would be based on "an appreciation of the way in which human life is designed so as to produce mutual benefit. Emphasis is [. . .] laid on mutual benevolence" (177). In other words, a new model of the individual was born then, founded on the idea of spectatorship of oneself and of the self in relation to others, interiorized as a form of self-regulation.

One could argue that Benjamin Franklin's *Autobiography* (1791) is a particularly apt document of the new idea of the self. As Taylor (1996, 185) points out, "By the turn of the eighteenth century, something recognizably like the modern self is in the process of constitution, at least among the social and spiritual elites of northwestern Europe and its American offshoots." Franklin's autobiography stands as an anticipation of Smith's later philosophical synthesis. What Franklin intuits, Smith is able to apprehend as an emerging worldview requiring new techniques of behavior. For Franklin, it is not the introspection that brings him to this new insight but rather the active involvement and participation in the social world of his time which pushes him in the direction of the new social mode of being. Stephen Shapiro (2008, 170), among others, situates his analysis of Franklin at the threshold of a new social order, marking Franklin out as a prototype of the bourgeois.

Franklin's self-fashioning thus gives evidence of the principle of self-observation, observation, and reciprocity as constitutive forces of the formation of the modern self. He understands himself by way of integrating his own self-perception with the impressions evinced by different kinds of observers—sympathetic, unsympathetic, neutral or uninterested, allowing for a new vision of the self to appear from the exchanges with benevolent strangers (Franklin 2012, 29). It is in the constant interplay of self-observations and other-observations that our human disposition is honed and perfected (64).

These few remarks illustrate a formative and constitutive role of self- and other-surveillance at the dawn of the modern personality, which by the early twenty-first century have turned into anxious and compulsive rituals of social conformity and hive mentality induced by social media networks, measured and quantified as a set of data. Unlike Franklin, Mae Holland, the protagonist of *The Circle*, is far less confident or easy about surveillance. Her self-worth and work status are enmeshed in the incessant processes of sharing, reaching out, zinging, communicating, observing and being observed, ultimately figured as one's PartiRank.[3]

2. The New Digital Frontier

It is against the backdrop of a particular historical articulation of the self—the individual acting as a social being—that I would like to pursue the argument that Eggers's novels illustrate a point of change, and that they specifically attribute this change to a new technological mode concentrated in what Julie E. Cohen (2016, 208) terms the "surveillance-industrial complex." As Leo Marx (1984, 639) points out in his examination of the enormous role technology has played in American society, we need to "clarify our thinking about the significance of the technological change and [. . .] its impact upon society and culture." He provides as an example "the process by which our culture has invested the great technological enterprise of the modern era with meaning." Eggers's technological dystopian novels thus inquire into the meaning of a new technological dispensation.

Eggers came into prominence around 2000 (Galow 2014, 1). In his novels and other writings, he tackles current social and political issues ranging from the impact of technology on society and our everyday lives, post-9/11 developments, and the aftermath of Hurricane Katrina in New Orleans to the features of the new multipolar global order. Specifically, *The Circle* and *The Every* engage with some conspicuous features of our digitalized and corporatized world, examining "the ways in which contemporary technology could potentially reshape the social order" (Galow 2014, 115).

Eggers addresses these and related questions by situating his plots in the near future on locations in the Silicon Valley; specifically, in its corporation-media complex (York 2020). "The Silicon Valley ideology" (Selisker 2018, 766) associated with such a complex, alternatively termed "the California ideology" (Dinnen 2018, 105), describes precisely the point of convergence between the computational technology, social structures, and the individual self that is regulated by a certain sense of cyber-optimism and the adoration of new technologies to such an extent that, as Dinnen puts it, "software has become ideology" (104). In order to grapple with and expose the implication of this beguiling optimism, Eggers chooses the standard third-person omniscient perspective and

---

[3] Eggers (2013, 192). This work will henceforth be cited as *C* and page number.

avoids any narrative experiment, sacrificing "subtlety" to the clarity of the message, as David Lyon (2018, 168) contends. Additionally, Eggers barely hides the analogy between the real-life Big Tech corporations and the imaginary corporate behemoth, the Circle, which in the second novel acquires more and more companies and morphs into an even bigger global presence under the appropriate name of the Every. These narrative solutions illustrate the trend in American fiction in favor of reexamination of ethical and ontological issues by way of interacting with the computational and social networks (Pignagnoli 2023, 3–4). As Virginia Pignagnoli points out, this new interest, rather than obviating the role of language and fictional genres, seems to steer them toward sincerity and earnestness (for these terms, cf., respectively, Adam Maxwell Kelly [2016] and Alan Kirby [2009], cited in Pignagnoli, 5). Eggers's novels thus foreground the "issues of communication, intersubjective relationship, earnestness, and sincere exchange" (Pignagnoli 5), pointing to their obstruction by the regimes of digital surveillance and the use of computer technologies.

The sense of familiarity—more unnerving than comforting—that permeates the situations in both novels relies on the idea of the transparency of language and its capacity to probe the incessant flows of data and social interactions conforming to datafication. Owing to Eggers's dystopian and satirical orientation, the reader needs to be able to distinguish between the narrator's critical perspective, enabled by his omniscient point of view, and the company's blatant appropriation of affirmative terms and their reappropriation as ideological mottos: "secrets are lies," "sharing is caring," "privacy is theft" (*C* 297; 301; 303). The heroines of both novels initially embody this dissonance, for Mae Holland in the Circle takes some time to be groomed into the company's ethos. In the case of Delaney Wells of the Every, her original ethics is antagonistic to everything the corporation stands for, and she tries to undermine the ideological language by ironic repetition and amplification of the prompts.[4] Thus, the narrative world of the two novels is both like the Silicon Valley of today and not quite like it (Lyon 2018, 151–52). As Lyon puts it, "It is also a metaphor for the way that all of life is increasingly subsumed into a digital world, encircled by cyberspace" (3).

In the increasingly dystopian world of *The Circle*, the intrusive government is replaced by a corporate monopoly, which takes over all the previously dispersed and decentralized offices and services pertaining to the traditional liberal divide into the state, the public, and the private sectors (*C* 484). In the greatly touted idea of total transparency and the "completion" of the circle, the carefully demarcated and sensitive boundaries among the sectors have collapsed into a nightmare of complete

---

4 Eggers, *The Every*, 83–84. This work will henceforth be cited as *E* and page number.

knowledge, total access, full transparency, and unlimited immersion into the personal and familial past. Eamon Bailey, one of the company's CEOs, explains to the still reluctant Mae the idea of completion:

> See how that "c" in the middle is open? For years it's bothered me, and it's become symbolic of what's left to do here, which is to close it. [. . .] A circle is the strongest shape in the universe [. . .] nothing can be more perfect. And that's what we want to be: perfect. So any information that eludes us, anything that is not accessible, prevents us from being perfect. (*C* 287)

Defying the idea that the completion is the ultimate fulfillment of the data extraction and flow, one of the company's founders and Wise Men, Ty Gospodinov, enacts in the course of the novel an Edward Snowden–like retraction of technological utopia as he distances himself from the more sinister applications of the company's inventions (*C* 480). In Ty's case, his act of rebellion is swiftly and efficiently contained and neutralized (*C* 491).

Therefore, one of the major consequences of the completion of the circle would be to eliminate the idea of privacy and, in accord with the Orwellian vision, to submit the individual to constant surveillance by way of technology (Orwell 1989, 214). In the twentieth-century context, the elimination of privacy by a mix of technological and more primitive forms of surveillance (such as the one enacted by the ubiquitous Thought Police [Orwell 1989, 140]), was seen by Hannah Arendt as integral to the deployment of totalitarian societies. As Arendt (2015, 442) argues, so long as there is privacy, however apolitical and harmless, the system fails to impose total control or to entirely quash the sense of individualism. This is perhaps why the novels in question—taking their cue from the contemporary debates on the importance of privacy—insist on retaining the line between the public and the private, the visible and the hidden.

The world of the near-future techno-society is a thoroughly hierarchical, binary space, which is divided into the utopian "inside" and the dystopian "outside," as noted by Mae Holland. When she approaches the company's headquarters for the job interview, Mae notes, "Outside the walls of the Circle, all was noise and struggle, failure and filth. But here, all had been perfected" (*C* 30). The architectural design of the company's campus further conveys the utopian ideas embodied by the company (*C* 47). By analogy, Niall Ferguson (2017, 424) argues in the case of the real-life ground plan of Facebook's headquarters that the entire design projects the ideas of accessibility, openness, participation, and transparency, "as if constructed from Lego and located in a nature reserve: an office without foundations or a floor-plan, mimicking the constantly evolving network it hosts."

The use of language early on in the novel begins to illustrate the process of de-realization—by which I mean the notion that the virtual reality produced by technology creates a dissonance between the external reality and the world inside the company's bubble. As we follow Mae's rise in the company, this rift continues to widen to the point where the Circle, by its use of language, manages to "create" a new kind of reality, which for its users is even better than the real thing. We should recall that it was George Orwell who examined in his dystopian novel *Nineteen Eighty-Four* (1949) the totalitarian effort to subdue language, as it would provide a royal road to the reordering of society devised by the Party. In *The Every* Eggers further probes the ways of colonizing the people's minds. If, as Orwell has noted, the first step is to misappropriate the words and their meaning in Newspeak, which is effectively "the destruction of words" (Orwell 1989, 54), the next step is to fix the cultural superstructure. The department of TellTale is supposed to streamline literary classics and turn fiction and fiction writing into an algorithmic process compliant with the taste and preferences data. One of the operators of the fiction algorithms, the former libart student Alessandro, enthusiastically, but reductively, explains, "Algo Mas wrote a pretty simple code for turning an unlikable character into [. . .] your favorite person. [. . .] The main thing is that the main character should behave the way you want them to, and do what you want them to do." A new application to streamline creative production will be offered to "colleges and MFA programs, so now they have the information. We give it to them for free, as a public service" (*E* 206).

Illustrating the premium *The Circle* places on privacy and on the idea of the inviolate self, Mae's behavior initially shows the difference of unscripted, unsurveilled, and private being in nature or in her social interactions, and their programmed and modified iterations required by the company. The novel closely follows the process of Mae's transformation by what Zuboff (2019, 415) lists as the techniques of instrumentarianism such as "tuning, herding, and conditioning." The point is that Mae internalizes, adopts, and acts out the elements of the new behavioral template. This allows Eggers to "explore the complex and often impossibly blurred junctures between information and identity, agency and complicity, the individual and larger groupings" (Marks 2015, 161).

The result is a consciousness that has been trained or disciplined to forego the distinction between, on the one hand, the surveilled and transparent, and, on the other, the veiled and opaque, private self. By this training, which Zuboff (2019, 97) sees as a behavioral experiment on a large scale, the Circle intends to hone its technology of the human self. In other words, for the company this is not a side development in the production process but the heart of production itself, "rendered behavior" as "a new means of production," reinvested in the new cycle to foster a behavior modification suited to the new accumulation principle. The

Circle's ideal (utopia), as Bailey muses, is realized as the search for an authentic self. Required to eliminate boundaries between the intimate and private and the public, between the individual and the community, this new ideal of the self, according to Bailey, is a transparent individual devoid of secrets and privacy. This creates a modified context in which Smith's "inner spectator" acquires its quasi-benevolent technological guise, since, as Marks (2015, 161) points out, it arises from "eutopian attraction of instant access, virtual sociability and prosperity."

To remind us, Charles Taylor's (1996, 111) account of the emergence of the modern self understands the notion of privacy as the moment in which the idea of the individual comes into being and begins to inhabit the horizon of Western thought. Hence, the shift in the perception of intimacy, its feasibility or value, might suggest that we have approached another threshold for the birth of a different self, which among other things must be wholly readable and transparent in all contexts. This readability in the novel encompasses everything, including intimate relations between the employees on the campus. A sexual encounter is considered as "consumer experience" and rated accordingly, as Mae ruefully notes (*C* 120).

The ideals of transparency and full access to any information encompass not only the realms of language and interpersonal relations but extend to human knowledge and its historical manifestations, which also need to be brought in step with the company's business principles. Bailey, who figures as the company's ideologue, nurtures the ambition to have a library that would contain all human knowledge. His point is not merely to assemble historical events but to rearrange and reshuffle them to conform to algorithms generated by the Circle, echoing Google's idea of "organizing the world's information and making it universally accessible and useful" (Fox 2020). In *The Every*, Eggers drives the point home by presenting entire company departments dedicated solely to the correction of the human mistakes made in personal, historical, or literary documents that fail to comply with the all-pervasive "metrics" and therefore need to be improved according to algorithm standards (*E* 55, 232). The literal destruction of the originals—in this case, family photos—signals that not only a linguistic but also an iconic sign has become detached from reality and turned into a free-floating referent to be inserted into the flow of virtual reality, as in the Thoughts Not Things program (*E* 102).

The boundary of private and public cuts across the fields of the self and historical time (duration) in which the self unfolds. This goes in particular for another privileged realm of the self, the unconscious mind. In *The Circle*, the company makes every effort to co-opt, control, and direct every waking moment of their employees' existences. As a next step, toward the end of the novel, in their revolutionary new application PastPerfect (*C* 428), they venture into the realm of the personal past, eradicating the "moral topography" (Taylor 1996, 111) of the inward and outward, the hidden and the visible, the conscious and the subconscious (forgotten or repressed), bringing everything in alignment with their new perfected idea of the human.

The novel interrogates how these layers of the self and their immersion in deep time have been modified and transformed. That way we note Mae's transformation from her initially cautious if gullible perspective to the point when, pushed by several contingencies (her college debt, her parents' medical insurance that is gallantly covered by the company, her initial missteps that need to be compensated for), she becomes an ardent follower and believer in the company's ideology and its living avatar by going fully transparent. It is her willful transformation that is of interest to me, the fact of Mae's self-enslavement to a "total vision" (Arendt 2015, 421; my translation).

Mae's conversion to the new ideology doesn't happen in a vacuum; rather, it is conditioned by the environment in which social and personal history has already been extracted, rearranged in a new sequence, and datafied. The individual is pulled out of her familial, personal and private relationships and made to correlate solely with her work and with the prearranged concept of free time, bereft of all vitality and spontaneity. A self cannot thrive in an environment reduced to the incessant and recurrent flow and processing of data, rendered as mental and physical stimuli, as we see in terms of Mae's job in the customer service department. That the human script, however, cannot be entirely altered but needs to be swayed is shown in the poignant process whereby Mae replaces her pre-Circle attachments (family and friends) by a set of new loyalties and devotions to the company's Wise Men as substitute father figures (*C* 462), who turn into the benevolent leaders for the initiates, the followers of the Circle. Sentiments and sympathies will apparently find their alternative routes. Further revealing the company's hierarchical set-up is its Gang of 40, managerial lower echelons hired to codify, program, and implement the founders' nebulous ideas.

The company is, on the one hand, a paragon of competition, efficiency, and public service—so much so that the Circle should take over some functions of the government since it might perform them more cheaply and effectively—and, on the other hand, it is a behemoth monopoly swallowing its competition like a predatory shark (*C* 318). It exemplifies the reasons why, in our world, the nickname of Big Tech has in recent times acquired more admonitory overtones as it shows its interference in and interdependence with the US government in particular (Ferguson 2017, 412; York 2020). In outlining several ways in which IT corporations interact with the government—be it supplementary to the government's function or antagonistic to it—the novel illustrates a transition from "surveillance state" as a modernist paradigm (and as shown in Orwell) to a more fluctuating but no less pervasive "surveillance culture" (Lyon 2018, 7). It is telling that, at least in the novel, the corporate-media complex seems to be unassailable: as Gospodinov warns Mae toward the end of *The Circle* as he is trying to enlist her in his subversion of the "closing of the circle," whoever stands in the way of the Circle monopoly will be compromised, shamed, and crushed (*C* 482–83), a sign of what Zuboff (2019, 376–77) detects as a shift from a democratic to an instrumentarian mentality.

But with the increasing calls to eliminate or reroute the services that in classical liberal theory are deliberately set apart but constantly, if problematically, interact with one another (the government, the media, the civil sphere), we come close to the society of total visibility, or total control, in which "all this could or would lead to totalitarianism" (*C* 393) as the obliteration of political community and a mockery of society. This much is implied by Mercer, one of the strongest critics of the digital utopia in the novel, a Luddite and a proponent of the pastoral ideal, as laid out by Leo Marx (1964, 13), in which nature and culture are in balance, "a state of being in which there is no tension either within the self or between the self and its environment." Once he realizes the menace posed by the Circle's appetite for everyone's data, Mercer decides to go "off the grid," retreating to the space of the wilderness and rejecting the supposed technological utopianism: "We'll be living underground, and in the desert, in the woods" (*C* 432–33). On the other side of the spectrum but harboring similar suspicions, there is Ty, whose brainchild has spun out of control and who is trying to enlist Mae to stage a coup within the company, since the utopian promise of technology is rapidly turning into a tool of enslavement. The novel asks us to consider the paradox whereby, as suggested by Fuchs et al. (2012, 19), digital surveillance creates deeply "asymmetrical and undemocratic power relations," whereas its application makes it "ubiquitous, automatic, anonymous, decentralized, and self-reinforcing," which complicates the characters' relationships and blunts their reaction to it.

Mae herself is deeply entangled in this paradox. She is initially resistant to the Circle's ideology of sharing, participation, transparency, and community, and she notoriously retreats from the sphere of work to her private world. On three occasions she allows herself to escape into nature when she takes out to sea in a kayak, and it is in these unplanned, unanticipated episodes that she experiences an exhilarating sense of freedom—being alone, in the moment, facing the mysterious and unknown world of nature (*C* 83; 142; 268). This aligns Mae's response to what Marx (2015, 10) describes as a particular relationship with nature entailed in "complex" pastoralism, "the theme of withdrawal from society into idealized landscape." Causing consternation at work for trying to evade constant availability and visibility as a requirement for the Circlers, she begins to internalize the expectations of ever-greater transparency and the relinquishment of her privacy. This retraining is carried out through the external stimuli causing bodily reactions that need to become interiorized. Mae has to be disciplined into a new scopic and behavioral regime, but she needs to do it herself. For example, when she is unexpectedly exposed during a public presentation of a dating program prototype, LuvLuv, she has a physical reaction—she feels upset, uneasy, resentful, and nauseated (*C* 121). As pointed out by Scott Selisker (2018, 758; *C* 125), the novel here reflects on the idea of characters as embedded in information networks, so that the problem is not that the information is shared but that Mae is not in a position to control its circulation. This, therefore, becomes her next goal, as she increasingly succumbs to the idea of near constant surveillance.

This turnaround reflects an observation by Florian Zappe and Andrew S. Gross (2020, 10) to the effect that the ubiquity of "surveillance practices and technologies" causes profound shifts in our understanding of "privacy and subjectivity," "altering the status of the individual within the social realm." The fact that Mae eventually foregoes nature as her sanctuary, gets estranged from her parents, and literally destroys her former boyfriend, Mercer, by revealing his hideout through the use of the company's latest software, shows how the characters become voluntary and complicit agents of (their own or others') surveillance (15).

This embodied aspect of surveillance or the new transparency is made evident on several occasions in the novel. The first and most obvious is the gathering and then exploitation, through aggressive and relentless nudging, of personal data through a mandatory personality test. The intrusive and ominous nature of such a seemingly standard procedure escalates when Mae visits the company's clinic in order to get assessed for health insurance. She is expected to undergo biweekly checkups (because the Circle cares for its employees), while all her previous health data is gathered and readily generated for her own benefit. Additionally, she is expected to wear a bracelet that monitors and displays nonstop all of her vital functions, and, moreover, she is asked to ingest a tiny organic sensor that turns her body into mappable sets of data (*C* 157). Doctor-patient confidentiality is a thing of the benighted past. The scrupulous and constant mapping and gathering of one's (medical and other) data recalls Arendt's (2015, 421) definition of a society of total vision, where it is not an intrusive company but a secret police that draws a map of the entire population or creates a dossier of virtually every citizen. In the contemporary "surveillance culture," data collection has acquired a liquid aspect, to echo Bauman's well-known phrase.[5]

---

5 For my immediate argument, the liquidity of the present moment indicates how, with the rise of new technologies, we have been experiencing a quantitative

In line with Bauman's further observations on "liquid modernity" in the grip of new technologies, he argues that social bonds must be dissolved so as to make way for the power to work (Bauman and Lyon 2013, 6). Mae therefore gradually relinquishes her older social ties, sustained by the private sphere, and embraces new social forms generated by social media and computational networks at her workplace and in her social interactions. Predictably, she becomes dependent on the emotional stimulation of the Circle community. The almost scripted and constrained nature of Mae's surveilled interaction with her parents points to another feature of the world of total control and total vision aiming to eradicate all spontaneity, which is, as Arendt (2015, 425) argues, connected to human freedom and reflective of life itself.

Full transparency in the novel brings about a few rearrangements in the public sphere too. At a stage where, as Bauman and Lyon (2013, 5) note, "power and politics are splitting apart," the ideological lever of surveillance presumably serves to make the political elites more accountable to their constituencies, as suggested by the company's application Demoxie.[6] Bailey strategically cites the Pentagon Papers, the leaks exposing the fraudulent government claims about fighting the Vietnam War, as a shining example of the power of democratic public institutions (C 285), while he omits the details of the story that do not comply with the Circle's civic mission. Highlighting arguments in favor of a digital and networked kind of governance thanks to the arrival of the internet and subsequently of social media, the Every is also committed to representing the ins and outs of the digital takeover of the government. The developments in the second novel, however, seem to point in the direction of an increased power grab of the company in relation to the political system, which can easily be manipulated and swayed by the network. For example, the company algorithm and its PR strategy work to deflate and destroy the candidacy of a politically invidious presidential candidate. Thus, it is not the networked principle or the transparency rule that

---

and perhaps even qualitative shift in surveillance that has become more ubiquitous, malleable, and invisible, often consensual (Bauman and Lyon 2013). In addition, its effects are enhanced by the fact that it relies on the convergence of various forms of control and monitoring—workplace, consumer behavior, governmental policies permeating our daily lives and interactions and embedding us in networks that both impinge on our sense of self and enable our societies to work. For a more in-depth view, see Bauman (2000).

6   Reflective of the novel's intention to serve as a commentary on the current social setting, this is clearly evocative of extant initiatives such as Transparency International or the Sunlight Foundation, without going into details as to their goals or operating procedures. I would like to thank the reviewer for this reference.

in and of itself might secure a democratic system, as is also Ferguson's (2017, 359) apt point.

Illustrating possible developments at the intersection of the political and the biological, Eggers's novels entertain the idea of a new structure of feeling induced by the extensive and ubiquitous digital surveillance and network apparatus that in turn will generate further individual and social change. The previous imagining of the intersection of the technological and the human, as in the figure of the cyborg or some other crossover of the human and the machine featured in science fiction, still retained the cognitive distinction between the biological and the technological. *The Circle* and *The Every*, however, show a near future where the boundary is no longer valid or meaningful. The behavioral modification groomed by the use of digital technology has become a new mode of being human, individually or in social contexts. The rise of the contemporary surveillance culture, as shown by Bauman, Lyon, and Zuboff, among others, requires a new alignment between the private and the public, a new sense of self in relationship to others, and a set of new words to account for the aspects of technologically mediated reality. Registering the degree of our immersion in such a reality, Eggers's novels, according to Zara Dinnen (2018, 13), depict "the digital banal" as "the condition by which we don't notice the affective novelty of becoming-with digital media. [. . .] The way we use media makes us unaware of the ways we are co-constituted as subjects with media."

In the sequel to *The Circle*, the titular company grows even bigger as a result of a recent merger with another Big-Tech firm, "and the acquisition created the richest company the world has ever known" (*E* 4–5). Its new name, the Every, invites the ideas of "ubiquity and equality," while the company's new logo "hinted at the flow of water, the bursting of new ideas, of interconnectivity, at infinity" (*E* 5). As the protagonist Delaney Wells, trying to infiltrate the company in order to undermine it, approaches the Every's grounds on Treasure Island in San Francisco Bay, we are confronted with the two contrasting images of the tower and the square articulated in Ferguson's architectural study. The idea of accessibility and transparency is relayed through the horizontal layout of campus buildings (Ferguson's idea of the square) cut through by an imposing vertical structure: "She averted her eyes, resting them upon the campus's tallest building, an aluminum-clad corkscrew tower that housed Algo Mas,[7] the company's algorithm thinktank" (*E* 3), signifying a hidden and overarching power principle embodied in the company's shadow structure (Ferguson's image of the tower).

---

7 The English translation of this Spanish expression as "Something More" invites further associations that might combine both the positive, celebratory and the menacing aspects of the company's mission.

The setting in *The Every* is a mix of the familiar elements of the COVID-19 pandemic and postpandemic malaise and science fiction. Spawned by an ongoing crisis of liberal democracy and compounded by the effects of the global pandemic and the measures implemented to presumably contain it, the novel examines the moment that Zuboff describes as the transition point to the third modernity. The third modernity, as Zuboff (2019, 46) elaborates, is marked by "a fusion of capitalism and the digital," in its ideal (utopian) version promising to "rescu[e] information and people from the old institutional confines," originally called forth by "the self-determining aspirations of individuals and indigenous to the digital milieu." In *The Every*, this is a mockery of the proposed mutation offered by Delaney. When interviewing for the job in the Every, she pretends to endorse the new agenda:

> Whether or not [the company] was a monopoly was immaterial if that's what the people wanted. She coined the term Benevolent Market Mastery for the seamless symbiosis between company and customer, a consumer's perfect state of being, where all desires were served efficiently and at the lowest price. Fighting such a thing was against the will of the people, and if regulators were at odds with what the people wanted, what was the point? (*E* 11)

The gateway to third modernity, in the shape of digital technology, leads through utopian remedies for social problems, "genuine social ills" (Herman 2018, 167), and calls for "benign utopianism" (*E* 9). Therefore, every new application or product devised or marketed by the company should be read in the techno-utopian key: it has been created "to resolve a host of social ills" (Herman 2018, 167), particularly environment, economy, and the excesses of human nature.

The techno-utopianism inherent to the Silicon Valley business model is not merely a cynical byproduct of the profit-making mechanism—although it is that too—but a deeper urge to use the increasingly more sophisticated, capacious, and invasive technology to solve chronic or more recent social problems, as is the current order of the day (Herman 2018, 185). The use to which technology is put, as Leo Marx (1984, 642) has it by way of Martin Heidegger's idea of "enframing," suggests that "what we now feel to be dangerous, threatening, even monstrous about technology is in fact not technology *per se*"; rather, it is "a compulsion to achieve absolute, total knowledge and control of the world" that drives its use and application that should concern us.

The 9/11 attacks were the event that prompted the US government, followed by other governments worldwide, to partner with the growing private IT sector in order to initiate and maintain programs for large-scale data collection, processing, and surveillance (Zuboff 2019, 112–21; Ball et al. 2012, 4). Once a legal framework that sanctioned such massive surveillance was in place, the system could be set up to operate in domains unrelated to national security but related specifically to different aspects of our social and private lives. This gave rise to "the complex interconnections between corporations and government" (Galow 2014, 123) that form the crux of the present-day network of surveillance. While it is still undecided that this is a qualitatively new phenomenon, as Lyon (1994, 53; 81) assesses, it nevertheless marks a quantitative jump from the previous forms of surveillance, primarily owing to new technologies used to implement it and to the convergence of various forms of control—workplace surveillance, consumer surveillance, and governmental surveillance being perhaps the most conspicuous.

This move of appropriation is intentionally focused on the classical liberal issues of individualism and privacy, and the novels center on these notions to make a point about the excesses and dangers of technological surveillance. In that sense, Eggers's novels seek to chart how habituation (another basic human reaction) to "surveillance practices and technologies" causes profound shifts in our understanding of "privacy and subjectivity" and thus leads to "altering the status of the individual within the social realm" (Zappe and Gross 2020, 10). As Selisker (2018, 757) contends, however, it is precisely the kind of "technological and spatial boundaries" entailed in maintaining the status of privacy that has begun to waver and makes it more difficult to circumscribe in legal, ethical, and social terms, which ambiguity creates further incentives to lateral surveillance and wholesale transparency.

As indicated early on in Thomas More's *Utopia* (1516), "the purpose of surveillance is to rid the island of crime and corruption" (Herman 2018, 175), and this lofty purpose resonates with many other noble goals touted by big tech companies of today, ingrained in the Circle's and later the Every's business logic: "Her plan actually would reduce waste. Would create order. Would drastically limit the unnecessary exploitation of land, energy, animals"; except that as with every utopia, this promise comes with a twist: "But it would also give the Every historically unprecedented power. It would make the Dutch East India Company look like a lemonade stand. What she had just described would surely mean the end of much of what makes a human free" (*E* 562).

Eggers's novels thus entertain at least two propositions about the interface of human nature and digital technology. 1. In the so-called third modernity, we are at the utopian cusp of resignifying the ideas of privacy, individuality, and the self to create a new vision of society; or, conversely, 2. the dystopian moment of the third modernity will simply dismiss and disown the modern notions of privacy, individualism, and the self, and send them to the junkyard of history. The plots of the novels provide ample evidence for the entertainment of the first proposition since they repeatedly show how characters start out as techno-skeptics only to be—voluntarily or compulsively—turned into techno-enthusiasts who grasp the utopian potential of the new technology. Additionally, the internet and especially social media have fundamentally redefined the notion of the public sphere and our own place in it as social actors. As Lovrinić (2019, 91; my translation) argues, the effect of social media is such that "due to digital mediation, almost every aspect of life has been cast in a new symbolic dimension as an event, object or process, while people become more visible, more conscious, and 'shareable.'" In *The Circle*, we see the outline of this new regime that gives the effect of transmuting the characters' old selves into a new symbolic dimension that is mediated through technology but shared with other human beings. The character of Mae Holland starts out from the skeptical perspective toward the impositions of the new technology (proposition 2) but in the course of her apprenticeship and work in the company sheds her old second-modernity notion of the self with all its cumbersome additions and launches herself into a new future by the end of the novel (proposition 1).

The key motivation presumably driving her initially reluctant and later enthusiastic embrace of the company's vision are the entangled ideas of sharing, transparency, and communication, captured in the TruYou, a revolutionary new application that allows the Circle to embark on its project of encompassing the entire world. The idea is to redefine, or symbolically redesign, the old notions of privacy, individualism, personal responsibility, and freedom, and to make them fit the new networked principle. Emotions, thoughts, and relationships, removed from their individualistic and private setting, now come to figure in a huge experiment based on "emotional contagion" (Lovrinić 2019, 94; my translation), where what matters is the circuit and transferability rather than the content of emotions or the immediate context in which they arise, all supported by machine intelligence. If in the first novel Mae and some of the people around her still understand or care about the difference between the authentic and the simulated (the individualistic and the networked), the second novel shows how the boundary is more elusive and difficult to maintain.

This is not to say that Eggers's vision capitulates in the face of ambiguities surrounding post-9/11 debates about surveillance. Indeed, as some sociological literature points out, surveillance might not be all that bad (Lovrinić 2019, 94), and we could argue that this was one of the lessons learned at high price in the nearly two years of our submission to the pandemic surveillance measures. As sociological models suggest, surveillance might be construed as intrusive, authoritarian, and insidious (Fuchs et al. 2019; Mathiesen 2012; York 2020); but we could also utilize a more horizontal approach and think of it as participatory surveillance, conducted laterally rather than vertically, and therefore more difficult to detect, observe and obviate, if that is still something that we would want to do (York 2020; Karatzogianni et al. 2016). David Lyon's (1994, 17) nuanced approach to the problem of surveillance suggests that surveillance does not necessarily equate with evil designs on our privacy and freedom but that, nevertheless, the rise of electronic surveillance poses a huge challenge to the otherwise acceptable or necessary forms of population management or data collection in modern societies.

For Eggers, however, this normalization is precisely the problem that he develops as the theme of the second novel, *The Every*, its title suggesting an allegorical scope of action pertaining potentially to every one of us, which takes the plot a step further into a shared, networked culture, where social and private friction is reduced to a mere temporary malfunction of the system. Delaney, also a humanities student like her predecessor Mae, is now an experienced, seasoned opponent of the hive mentality sustained by data collection, surveillance, transparency, and shareability. The transformation of the public spaces and the private sphere is nearly complete, so that the only socially and economically viable spaces are those that connect, while the unseen, the unsurveilled, disconnected, or off-the-grid sites are ghettoes peopled by nontechnological savages, called "trogs" in the novel. More problematically, Delaney seems to have mastered newspeak and equipped herself with firm intellectual and philosophical rebuttals to the arguments of humanists and techno-skeptics (*E* 222). Still, much like her more famous predecessor, Orwell's Winston Smith, the everyman of totalitarian society, it is her mind that gets manipulated and, we may assume at the end of the novel, nearly co-opted into the Every's total vision. In a bleak ending, Delaney is physically vanquished by Mae, whose new biopolitical version of the human triumphs.

Another point to make about "the shadow text" (Zuboff 2019) of the new Big-Tech monopolies is the question of power through knowledge—or, rather, asymmetrical knowledge. According to Zuboff, a new stage of capitalism wields "an unprecedented new species of power" (352) by joining technology with the exclusive access to knowledge, given that knowledge is now the main source of capital. Zuboff contends that its aim is to "remake human nature" by exposing it routinely and endlessly to "behavioral modification" (352), and she calls this early twenty-first-century stage the era of instrumentarianism, unlike Orwell's and Arendt's notions of twentieth-century totalitarianism. As suggested before, the way the protagonists in Eggers's novels—even against their entrenched humanist notions, their philosophical arguments against the intrusive technology, and against their experience—eventually succumb to the collectivist mentality urges us to rethink the usefulness of twentieth-century categories for the present. We should, additionally, remember Arendt's (2015, 339) claim that one of the goals of twentieth-century totalitarianism was to change human nature. No longer carried out by totalitarian politics, the anticipated modification is now effected by an instrumentarian agenda.

Part of the dissonance that the characters experience and try to navigate comes from a dual effect that we can ascribe to social media, embedded in digital culture. On one hand, social media advertise easy access, transparency, freedom of expression, democratization, and expansion of the public sphere, and there are findings that support these effects (Cohen 2016, 208; Bohman 2004). Increasingly, however, we come to understand that these benefits are offset by the dark side of the third modernity, as it relies on concentration of power and knowledge through electronic surveillance (Cohen 2016, 218). The Every knows that one of the key strategies is to colonize language, history, individual memory, and different forms of culture from literature to fashion, thus acquiring total control over human nature for the purpose of enabling an instrumentarian, hive society. As Jure Vujić (2021, 15; my translation) contends, "To exit the semiotic world, as a counterpart to exiting the symbolic and history itself, rounds off the process of technological and virtual dehumanization covered by hidden layers of neural and algorithm networks."

In conclusion, neither of Eggers's dystopian novels offers much hope in the way of an individual standing up against the conglomerate of digital technology and machine learning set up by humans in order to use other humans as objects of control, submission, or profit-making. Furthermore, they inquire into the vulnerability of our social instincts to conform and adapt to collectivist behavior, manipulation, and modification entailed in the idea of "hive mentality." In Dinnen's (2018) words, they challenge us to lift the veil of banality and inevitability from the application of technology. Furthermore, the literature of the digital frontier is finding ways to explore the full potential of the ideas hijacked by the instrumentarian disposition in charge of the new technologies, ideas such as individualism, the self, authenticity, freedom, privacy, transparency, secrecy, and sharing. In doing so, this literature also extends and reaffirms the unfinished project of the human that we should not so easily relinquish to a techno-humanist paradigm blithely announced by the techno-corporate complex, which may amount to a new version of biopolitical nightmare.

Works Cited

Arendt, Hannah. 2015. *Izvori totalitarizma*. Zagreb: Disput. First published 1951.
Ball, Kirstie, et al., eds. 2012. *Routledge Handbook of Surveillance Studies*. London: Routledge.
Bauman, Zygmunt. 2000. *Liquid Modernity*. Cambridge: Polity.
Bauman, Zygmunt, and David Lyon. 2013. *Liquid Surveillance: A Conversation*. Cambridge: Polity.
Bohman, James. 2004. "Expanding Dialogue: The Internet, the public sphere and prospects for a transnational democracy." In *After Habermas: New Perspectives on the Public Sphere*, edited by Nick Crossley and John Michael Roberts, 131–55. Malden, MA: Wiley-Blackwell.
Cohen, Julie E. 2016. "The Surveillance-Innovation Complex: The Irony of the Participatory Turn." In *The Participatory Condition in the Digital Age*, edited by Darin Barney et al., 207–26. Minneapolis: University of Minnesota Press.
Dinnen, Zara. 2018. *The Digital Banal: New Media and American Literature and Culture*. New York: Columbia University Press.
Eggers, Dave. 2013. *The Circle: A Novel*. New York: Penguin.
———. 2021. *The Every*. New York: Vintage.
Ferguson, Niall. 2017. *The Square and the Tower: Networks, Hierarchies and the Struggle for Global Power*. New York: Penguin.
Fox, Nick. 2020. "Organizing the world's information: where does it all come from?" The Keyword. December 3. blog.google/products/search/information-sources-google-search/.
Franklin, Benjamin. 2012. *Benjamin Franklin's* Autobiography. Norton Critical Edition. Edited by Joyce E. Chaplin. New York: W. W. Norton.
Fuchs, Christian, et al. 2012. "Introduction: Internet and Surveillance." In *Internet and Surveillance: The Challenges of Web 2.0 and Social Media*, edited by Christian Fuchs et al., 18–56. London: Routledge.
Galow, Timothy W. 2014. *Understanding Dave Eggers*. Columbia: University of South Carolina Press.
Giddens, Anthony. 1990. *The Consequences of Modernity*. Cambridge: Polity.
Herman, Peter C. 2018. "More, Huxley, Eggers, and the Utopian/Dystopian Tradition." *Renaissance and Reformation/ Renaissance et Réforme* 41, no. 3 (Summer): 165–93.
Karatzogianni, Athina, et al., eds. 2016. *The Digital Transformation of the Public Sphere: Conflict, Migration, Crisis and Culture in Digital Networks*. London: Palgrave Macmillan.
Kelly, Adam Maxwell. 2016. "The New Sincerity." In *Postmodern/Postwar— and After: Rethinking American Literature*, edited by Jason Gladstone, Andrew Hoberek, and Daniel Worden, 197–208. Iowa City: University of Iowa Press.
Kirby, Alan. 2009. *Digimodernism: How New Technologies Dismantle the Postmodern and Reconfigure Our Culture*. New York: Continuum.

Lovrinić, Barbara. 2019. "Nadzor i žudnja u društvenim mrežama: O diskursu kapitalista." *Medijska istraživanja* 25, no. 2: 89–10.
Lyon, David. 1994. *The Electronic Eye: The Rise of Surveillance Society*. Cambridge: Polity.
———. 2018. *The Culture of Surveillance: Watching as a Way of Life*. Cambridge: Polity.
Marks, Peter. 2015. *Imagining Surveillance: Eutopian and Dystopian Literature and Film*. Edinburgh: Edinburgh University Press.
Marx, Leo. 1964. *The Machine in the Garden: Technology and the Pastoral Ideal in America*. Oxford: Oxford University Press.
———. 1984. "On Heidegger's Conception of 'Technology' and Its Historical Validity." *Massachusetts Review* 25, no. 4 (Winter): 638–52.
Mathiesen, Thomas. 2012. "Preface." In *Internet and Surveillance: The Challenges of Web 2.0 and Social Media*, edited by Christian Fuchs et al., 10–17. London: Routledge.
Orwell, George. 1989. *Nineteen Eighty-Four*. London: Penguin. First published 1949.
Pignagnoli, Virginia. 2023. *Post-postmodernist Fiction and the Rise of Digital Epitexts*. Columbus: Ohio State University Press.
Rabinow, Paul. 2008. *Marking Time: On the Anthropology of the Contemporary*. Princeton, NJ: Princeton University Press.
Selisker, Scott. 2018. "The Novel and WikiLeaks: Transparency and the Social Life of Privacy." *American Literary History* 30, no. 4 (Winter): 756–76.
Shapiro, Stephen. 2008. *The Culture and Commerce of the Early American Novel: Reading the Atlantic World-System*. University Park: Penn State University Press.
Suvin, Darko. 1979. *Metamorphoses of Science Fiction: On the Poetics and History of a Literary Genre*. New Haven, CT: Yale University Press.
Taylor, Charles. 1996. *Sources of the Self: The Making of the Modern Identity*. Cambridge, MA: Harvard University Press. First published 1989.
———. 2007. *A Secular Age*. Cambridge, MA: Belknap Press of Harvard University Press.
Vujić, Jure. 2021. "Od špiljskih slika Lascauxa do numeričkih tragova." *Vijenac*, no. 717–18 (September 9): 15.
York, Jillian C. 2020. *Silicon Values: The Future of Free Speech under Surveillance Capitalism*. Kindle ed. London: Verso.
Zappe, Florian, and Andrew S. Gross, eds. 2020. *Surveillance/Society/Culture*. New York: Peter Lang.
Zuboff, Shoshana. 2019. *The Age of Surveillance Capitalism: The Fight for a Human Future at the New Frontier of Power*. London: Profile Books.

12: "The Joy of Confession": Narratives of Disclosure in Jonathan Franzen's *Crossroads*

Jesús Blanco Hidalga

1. Introduction: Secrecy Revisited

IN HIS NOVEL *Purity* (2015), American novelist Jonathan Franzen found a new concern to add to his long-standing preoccupation with the intersection of large sociocultural processes and individual lives within families. This new interest, which took a central role in the book, was secrecy. *Purity* channeled a concept of secrecy as the foundation of personality, as well as a key factor in the proper functioning of human relationships, that seemed much in consonance with the thought of the German thinker Georg Simmel. In fact, as I have argued in my analysis of *Purity*, Franzen did not hesitate to put words into his characters' mouths that read very much like a transcription of some of Simmel's ideas.[1]

As I show in this chapter, Franzen's novel *Crossroads* (2021), the first installment of an intended transgenerational trilogy, is yet another Simmelian novel. Franzen seizes on these ideas of secrecy and privacy and delves even deeper in his exploration of their role in interpersonal relationships. Each of the protagonists, belonging to a suburban Midwestern family living in the early 1970s, is defined by a gnawing secret that is the driving force behind their frequently compulsive behavior. Meanwhile, as he did in his previous novel, Franzen takes full advantage of secrecy as a way to provide characters with depth and conflict.

In *Crossroads* Franzen also revisits confession, another theme that was already important in *Purity*, and examines it extensively, as in *Crossroads* virtually all significant characters have their moment of confession. These confessional acts—which often involve the presence of shame—form the core of the novel and provide it with a considerable part of its narrative momentum.

Closely related to confession is the melodramatic character of the novel's plot. Melodrama, a genre where secrets, revelations, guilt, and

---

1   See Blanco Hidalga (2021).

moral conflict are central, becomes Franzen's main formal means to articulate his exploration of the ways secrecy and confession shape our lives. Elements from this genre were hardly absent from Franzen's previous novels, but they were secondary to other narrative configurations such as bildungsroman and, especially in the case of *Purity*, romance. In *Crossroads*, Franzen unabashedly embraces melodrama, and the emotional temperature of the novel never goes down as we go through lover's obsession, adultery, abortion, sexual abuse, and drug addiction.

Finally, I will be examining how, even though in *Crossroads* Franzen refrains—for the first time ever—from including his usual diatribes on contemporary politics and culture, his enduring concern with community is present here as well.[2] Franzen travels back in time for his new novel, but his portrait of youth groups and troubled middle-class families in the 1970s resonates with contemporary culture. Significantly, the novel takes its title from the name of a Christian youth group whose main community-building procedure is, precisely, disclosure. In his depiction of the social dynamics at work in that group, Franzen shows a clearly adversarial notion of social transparency, one that identifies the latter as impoverishing as regards human relationships, and ultimately totalitarian in the political realm.

2. Family Secrets and Shadowed Zones: "God-fearing mother, unregretting sinner"

The novel follows the six members of the Hildebrandt family in the middle-class suburb of New Prospect, near Chicago, in the days before Christmas of 1971 and in the following months. Besides that, there are several lengthy, interspersed flashbacks reaching as far as the 1920s that illuminate the characters' life trajectories and current states of mind. The novel opens with the midlife crisis of Russ Hildebrandt, associate pastor at New Prospect's First Reformed Church, as he tries to develop an illicit relationship with the flirtatious Frances Cottrell, a recently widowed, younger parishioner. Russ was raised a Mennonite but became estranged from his faith, mostly as a result of meeting his wife-to-be, the tormented Catholic Marion, in 1946. Russ, however, now resents his motherly and overweight wife, Marion, for the dullness of their marriage and, in an indirect and rather unfair way, also for the stagnation of his career as a pastor. We also learn that three years before the opening of the novel, Russ was forced to leave the church's youth group, named Crossroads, in a rather humiliating way. He was replaced by the new youth minister, Rick Ambrose, hugely popular among the group's members.

2   For an extensive analysis of Franzen's communitarian preoccupations see Blanco Hidalga (2017).

The most striking subplot is surely Marion's story. It is all the more compelling because the intensity of her previous and present experience is unsuspected by the rest of her family (and the reader). The novel goes as far as the Depression Era to show how Marion's bankrupt father committed suicide in San Francisco after the stock exchange crash of 1929. As she could not depend on her selfish mother, Marion's teenage years and early youth were characterized by financial and emotional insecurity. In the 1940s, working as a secretary in an automobile dealership in Los Angeles, she is seduced by one of the salesmen, a loquacious married man named Bradley Grant. Marion is carried away in a torrid affair that turns into an obsession for her. When Bradley ends the relationship, Marion has a severe mental breakdown. To compound her predicament, she is pregnant and jobless. Utterly destitute, she is accommodated by an amoral man who helps her get an abortion but demands her submission to sexual abuse in return. She ends up suffering another crisis, which leads to her admission to a mental asylum. It is after being dismissed from the institution that she meets Russ, a young Mennonite who is completing his alternative service as a conscientious objector in Flagstaff, Arizona. Marion, still psychologically fragile, has taken refuge with her uncle there and cultivates a personal kind of Catholicism obsessed with sin and guilt. The couple fall rapidly in love. Afraid to confess the truth about her past but unwilling to deceive Russ completely, Marion tells him that she had been briefly married while living in California. At first, this provokes revulsion in Russ, but eventually he comes to terms with the revelation.[3] They get married, which forces Russ to forsake his Mennonite community, and Marion adopts her husband's Protestantism. Russ goes on to become a pastor and, after a stint in Indiana, the couple end up in New Prospect, Illinois, where they raise their three sons and daughter.

Back in the present, Marion's old obsession with Bradley Grant reappears when she learns about Russ's flirtation with Frances Cottrell. Angry and deeply displeased with her life, she traces Bradley's current whereabouts and, while Russ is away on the yearly charitable trip to a Navajo reservation organized by the Crossroads youth group, Marion travels to

---

[3] Russ's revolt has its origin in the sudden awareness of Marion having a sexual life before knowing him. He tries to move on and forget about it, but "his anger and his disgust had a life of their own. He'd thrown away his virginity on a woman who'd given hers to someone else, and now her nakedness was repellent" (446). The fact is that Russ never manages to forget—and forgive—Marion's having had sexual experience with someone else. When, many years later, he is at last having sex with Frances Cottrell, the thought that at last he is even with Marion in that sense is the most prominent in his mind, "freed, at long last, from the weight of his inferiority" (478).

California determined to revive her affair with her former lover. On meeting him, she is disappointed and disgusted by Bradley. She realizes her mistake and walks away from his home.

Meanwhile, we have also met Perry, the couple's teenage son, who is prodigiously intelligent but also psychologically frail and prone to drug addiction. In the last months, out of sight of his self-absorbed parents, he has developed a cocaine habit with money stolen from his family and is on track to a mental breakdown. His deterioration achieves its climax during the aforementioned trip to the reservation when he sets a barn on fire under the effect of the drug. He is subsequently admitted to a mental institution and diagnosed with manic depression after a suicide attempt. It is worth mentioning that this incident, which brings dire financial trouble to the family, happens just as Russ is sexually consummating his liaison with Frances and Marion is in California resolved to commit adultery with Bradley. It is Perry's misfortune and the guilt involved that bring Russ and Marion together again. Stricken by guilt, Russ confesses to Marion his affair with Frances. Marion consoles and accepts him but does not reciprocate. She does not tell Russ about Bradley Grant, thus sparing Russ the blow and embracing secret guilt as her due penitence.

As I advanced above, *Crossroads* elaborates on themes of secrecy and confession that were already central in Franzen's previous novel, *Purity*. In both works, Franzen's views on secrecy resonate strongly with Georg Simmel's thought. In a seminal article from 1906, the German thinker claims that in any act of human interaction the mutual knowledge of the participants is rather limited compared to the much more extensive areas of the other that remain unknown. This means that what we know about the people we interact with rests upon a much vaster expanse of their being and experience that remains obscure to us. Because such part of the other is always unknown to us, it is possible to state that secrets structure and shape social relations, which are ultimately based on mutual faith. In Simmel's (1906, 445) words, "Life rests upon a thousand presuppositions which the individual can never trace back to their origins, and verify; but which he must accept upon faith and belief." This kind of implicit pact governing social interaction was also identified and discussed by Jacques Derrida. In his study of Derrida's approach to secrecy, Charles Barbour (2017, 25–26) claims that for the French philosopher "every social relation or interaction relies on a (typically silent or implicit, but nonetheless effective) promise, pact or sworn agreement to say what one believes and to believe that the other is doing the same." As Franzen shows, however, living by that pact is anything but a straightforward matter.

Franzen is especially keen on exploring precisely those dark areas of the other mentioned by Simmel, the zones whose preservation was posited as essential in *Purity*.[4] In *Crossroads*, these shadow zones are sometimes shown to be dizzying chasms of unknown experience that shape the lives of those who are closest to us, with little left for us to do about it. The novel shows how such ignorance of the other inevitably leads us to misunderstand them, sometimes with catastrophic consequences. Throughout the novel, Franzen conducts a comprehensive depiction of those areas of consciousness that each character conceals from the other and how they negotiate these shadowed areas in their daily interaction. It would seem that the faith in the other described by Simmel as a foundation of our daily social interaction also includes the implicit hope that the other is not ultimately wholly other, in contradiction to Derrida's (2008, 82) famous aphorism "tout autre est tout autre." As a result, when the other's confession offers us an indication of the complete alterity of those who are closest to us, the result is a kind of vertiginous dread. *Crossroads* shows how the exposition of the complete otherness of our closest ones can be frightening. When young Marion tells Russ that she has been married—as a way to admit that she has had a sexual past without revealing the whole of her turbulent story—he is truly scared, afraid of the other Marion hidden beneath the one he has construed: "It was as if his Marion were imprisoned in a Marion he didn't know at all" (Franzen 2021, 447). Indeed, the most arresting case in the novel of the opacity of the people we share our life with is that of Marion, who hides her tempestuous life previous to her marriage as well as her current frustration. During an argument with Russ, her mere hinting at that unknown area of her experience sounds menacing:

> "You don't have the faintest idea who you married."
> "Since I'm so stupid maybe you should go ahead and tell me."
> "No, you'll just have to wait and see."
> "What does that mean?"
> She came over to him, stood on her toes, and tilted her face toward his. For a moment, he thought she might kiss him after all. But she merely blew a puff of air at him. It stank of tar and alcohol.
> "Wait and see." (367)

In fact, not only does Marion conceal from Russ the truth about her premarital life, but for a great part of the novel she also hides from him the

---

4   One of the characters in *Purity* is quite explicit about it: "How do you know that you're a person, distinct from other people? By keeping certain things to yourself. You guard them inside you, because, if you don't, there's no distinction between inside and outside. Secrets are the way you know you even have an inside. A radical exhibitionist is someone who has forfeited his identity" (Franzen 2015: 275).

vexing fact that she is aware of his affair with Frances Cottrell—a circumstance known to us, as the novel's omniscient narrator renders the characters' thoughts in free indirect style. Marion keeps this information to herself because she feels guilty for having lied to Russ before and to protect the unity of the family, but this knowledge embitters her more each day. Clearly more perceptive than her rather naive husband, Marion proves that while an enhanced awareness of the other's shadow zone can provide us with an advantage in our interaction with them—especially when some kind of power over the other is at stake—it can also become a heavy burden.

The case of the secrecy between Marion and Russ is the most prominent in the novel, but in fact, Franzen is quite meticulous in showing how this kind of ignorance of the other holds in the relationships between all the members of the Hildebrandt family. Thus, Perry hides himself from his father: "Since Perry seemed unable to argue with him without crying, he habitually concealed as much as he could for as long as he could" (29). When Perry confesses to his mother that he has been smoking and selling marijuana for quite a while, Marion reflects, "It occurred to her that the Perry in her head had been nothing but a sentimental projection, extrapolated from the little boy he'd been. She didn't know the real Perry any more than Russ knew the real her" (294). In turn, Perry is deeply destabilized by her mother's confession of the mental problems she had suffered in her youth, as well as by knowing about her father's suicide. In fact, with Perry's case the novel also explores the way our psyche harbors dark areas hidden from our conscious self. His mother's disclosure illuminates a previously shadowed zone in his own identity, which Perry now feels as a growing "crater" in his mind that threatens to engulf him. He doubles down on his drug use as way to run away from that hole:

> Pursued by the crater's edge, he made his way to First Reformed. [. . .] His mother had lost her mind. She'd been committed to a looney bin, her father had drowned himself, *and she'd named these facts to Perry*—named two outcomes that had lurked behind doors in his head which he'd never permitted himself to open, not even on the most sleepless of nights. [. . .] He would tell her nothing more. Not now, not ever. In a sense, the crater he was fleeing was his mother. (349; emphasis in original)

The novel shows how sometimes the areas of shadow in the other can be tantalizing, as is the case for Russ when he is considering taking the initiative in his anticipated affair with Frances Cottrell: "It was a torment not to know what she was thinking" (395). At other times, the trains of thought and expectations of two people talking to each other are so wildly different that it becomes a source of comedy, as when Becky is expecting Tanner Evans to kiss her, but the latter can only think about his folk band (206). Franzen also makes a point of showing how the impression we leave on other people is frequently concealed from us. Perry is perplexed when he faces his sister Becky's hostility toward him: "He struggled to think of a thing he'd ever done to harm her, a thing more visible than the occasionally unkind thoughts he had about her, to explain her hatred" (37).

These areas of shadow in the other are suddenly illuminated for the characters in the novel's abundant confessional scenes. These are the moments when they encounter evidence of the true alterity of the other, of those vast secret expanses in the other's experience we know nothing about and yet make up a fundamental part of their self. In its confessional scenes, *Crossroads* shows the shock that befalls us when the pact advocated by Simmel is revealed as a lie, when we realize that our assumptions about the other—about the convergence of their experience and ours, about their sheer benevolence—were completely out of place. On these occasions we may also find that our theory of the other is, in fact, an unsurmountable obstacle to our understanding of them, and conversely. As Jean Starobinski (1988, 255) shows in his book on Jean-Jacques Rousseau, in his quest for interpersonal transparency the latter finds that "the most awesome and insuperable of all obstacles is none other than the false image of Jean-Jacques that exists in the minds of others and robs him of his transparency."

It is important to notice, however, that while the characters may be opaque to each other, they are not so for the novel's omniscient narrator, and hence for the reader. Marion's revelation to her therapist about her tempestuous past does come as a true surprise for the reader, but in general we are consistently given a position of privileged knowledge over the secrets that the characters hold from each other, as Franzen shows us the characters' thoughts by means of free indirect speech. Franzen's emphasis on secrecy does contrast with the explicit and comprehensive way his omniscient narratorial voice reveals his characters' thoughts, feelings, and motives. It could be argued that a less explicit rendering of the characters' minds would lead to a kind of ambiguity that would open room for more layers of interpretation and thus would be more in consonance with what the novel seeks to show about the centrality of secrecy in human relations. There is an obvious contradiction between Franzen's defense of the role of privacy and otherness in human interaction and his meticulous exploration of his characters' minds. This is a consequence of Franzen's use of free indirect speech by an omniscient narrator as his staple storytelling form. As the introduction to this volume shows, this is, in fact, a kind of narrative conflict that may be traced in other works of fiction that posit a core of deep otherness in human beings, which they proceed to explore by means of an omniscient narrator, as in the case of Nathaniel Hawthorne's *The Scarlet Letter* (1850). In any case, after Marion's shocking revelation, we are mostly free to enjoy our access to the characters' minds as we watch over the trouble and suffering that their mutual misreading brings upon them. Actually, this misunderstanding among characters becomes a key point of interest and a major source of suspense in the novel, as we anticipate the next moment of revelation for them, while at the same time we sympathize with their tribulations. Franzen thus follows a pattern very much in the way of classic nineteenth-century novels such as Jane Austen's *Pride and Prejudice* (1813) and *Emma* (1815), George Eliot's *Middlemarch* (1871), or Thomas Hardy's *Tess of the D'Urbervilles* (1891), with plots based on the characters' mutual misinterpretation. *Crossroads* illustrates well J. Hillis Miller's (2001, 69) simile that compares our neighbor to a text that we always misread because that reading is mediated by our own desires and needs.[5] In this regard, Franzen's omniscient narrator does show the self-deception and false rationalization often involved in our dealing with those desires and needs. Thus, for example, Russ makes the massively embarrassing mistake of telling Sally Perkins, one of the teenage members of Crossroads, that "he and his wife rarely made love anymore" (Franzen 2021, 230). This precipitates his shameful exit from the group. Yet, he manages to convince himself that Marion is to blame for that: "By a curious alchemy, as the months went by, he came to feel that Marion herself had been the cause of his humiliation, by having become unattractive to him" (231).[6] Similarly, when Clem, the Hildebrandts' oldest son, renounces his college deferment to be drafted during the last part of the Vietnam war, he avows to himself that he does it for moral reasons, but the narrator leaves clear that his true intention is to hurt his pacifist father (114).

---

5   As Starobinski shows in his study of Rousseau, in the course of his endeavour for transparency the Genevan writer becomes aware of the impossibility of being properly interpreted by the other, even if they are our closest ones: "I see from the way in which those who think they know me interpret my actions that they know nothing. I see that those who live on the most intimate terms with me do not know me and attribute most of my actions, whether good or ill, to motives other than those that caused them" (quoted in Starobinski 1988: 181).

6   The explanation of the reasons that lead Russ to so unwisely make this confession to Sally Perkins is one example of Franzen's arguably excessive explicitness in the description of his characters' motives: "Made giddy by attention from a popular girl, Russ had imagined that he'd mastered the skill of honesty himself and could somehow erase his own timidity as a teenager, retroactively become a boy at ease with the likes of Sally Perkins" (228).

3. The Power of Disclosure: "Please forgive me. I want to be yours forever"[7]

In Franzen's previous novel, *Purity*, the characters perform several acts of disclosure. For the most part, however, they cannot be accurately described as confessions. Rather, they are acts of secret sharing, mostly done with manipulative intentions: to gain someone's trust, to create a new community of knowledge—often with the purpose of severing the recipient of the secret from a preexisting community—and, in short, to inflict an unwanted bond on someone.[8] In contrast, in *Crossroads* we mostly find more straightforward acts of confession destined to find atonement and absolution, liberation from the inner burden of a previous transgression.[9] Indeed, confession holds a central place in Franzen's novel as all significant characters have their confessional moment. Young Marion tells Russ a false version of her previous life. Years later, she tells the truth to her therapist. In a reconciliation scene, Russ tells Marion about her affair with Frances Cottrell and about the real reason behind his fall from grace in the Crossroads group: as we have seen, he had told one of the girls in the group he was not sexually attracted by Marion anymore.[10] Perry tells his mother about his drug consumption and trafficking, and in return, she tells him about her mental problems in her youth. Clem tells Marion he has left both college and his girlfriend.

In addition, Crossroads, the youth group led by the charismatic vicar student Rick Ambrose, relentlessly uses public confession as its main community-building procedure. Even the names of the novel's two main characters are meant to show the centrality of confession in the work, paying tribute to the founder of modern confessional speech. "Russ" evokes Jean-Jacques Rousseau, the author of *Confessions* (1782). Russ's

---

7   This is an abridged version of Marion's plea to Russ after she (falsely) tells him she has been married before getting to know him (446).

8   See Blanco Hidalga (2021, 199–201).

9   This basic pattern of confession—as opposed to the shady acts of secret sharing in *Purity*—does not exclude certain unacknowledged surplus enjoyment on the part of the confessants in *Crossroads*, derived from the disruptive power of displaying alterity before the other. In his essay, Simmel (1906, 466) refers to "the joy of confession, which may contain that sense of power in negative and perverted form, as self-abasement and contrition."

10 The actual reason for Russ leaving Crossroads is another secret that overhangs the novel for quite some time. Since the beginning of the novel, we know, from Russ's inner monologue, that he had to leave the group in a humiliating way. It is not until a dialogue between Russ and Ambrose in a flashback episode (225–29), however, that we learn the truth about the incident. Marion gets to know about it when a devastated Russ confesses to it after Perry's breakdown (526).

wife is Marion, namesake of the maid who suffers the consequences of Rousseau's acts in the famous "stolen ribbon" episode at the end of the second book of that work. The distinctive shameful character of Rousseau's confession may also be observed in the acts of disclosure in *Crossroads*, as we will see.

The preeminence of confession is wholly consistent with the melodramatic configuration of *Crossroads*, as melodrama is characterized, in Peter Brooks's (1995, 4) words, by "the desire to express all," leaving nothing unsaid and giving voice to the deepest feelings. Brooks relates melodrama to the modern individual's necessity of expressing his or her uniqueness, embodied by Rousseau's decision to "say all" (16) in his *Confessions*. This need to bring to light what was hidden relates melodrama to psychoanalysis. In Brooks's words,

> Psychoanalysis can be read as a systematic realization of the melodramatic aesthetic, applied to the structure and dynamics of the mind. Psychoanalysis is a version of melodrama first of all in its conception of the nature of the conflict, which is stark and unremitting, possibly disabling, menacing to the ego, which must find ways to reduce or discharge it. The dynamics of repression and the return of the repressed figure the plot of melodrama. (201)

It is then logical that the most melodramatic subplot of *Crossroads* should emerge in Marion's confessional flashback at her therapist's office. In an attempt to overcome her dissatisfaction with her life, Marion is using secret savings to furtively see an affordable psychiatrist in New Prospect. She has repressed her past and in a way her own *melodramatic* self for more than twenty years, and she only very reluctantly shares it with her therapist. A measure of Marion's isolation is that she has no trivial secrets to share and thus create bonds with other people, while the important ones are far too shocking to reveal:

> However short on money she was, perennially, she was even poorer in the currency of friendship, the little secrets that friends share to build trust. She had plenty of secrets, but they were all too large for a pastor's wife to safely betray.
>
> What she had instead of friends, on the sly, was a psychiatrist, and she was late for her appointment with her. (Franzen 2021, 127)

Marion, a very clever and well-read person, is actually skeptical about psychoanalysis, which she compares unfavorably to the more elevated Catholic confession: "the immensity of the Church's edifice, the majesty of its history, which made her sins, grievous though they were, feel like tiny drops in a very large bucket—richly precedented, more manageably antique" (129). It is possible to sense some skepticism in Franzen's opinion about psychoanalysis as well, as he exposes—through Marion's biased but sharp perception—her therapist's own commonplace assumptions and inconsistencies. Franzen seems to vindicate literature over psychoanalysis as a privileged access to the self. After all, we get to know the fundamental issues of Marion's past in an omniscient narrator's account of her thoughts while she is at the therapist's office, not in the actual interaction with her analyst, as that specific communication is elided in the narrative.

Catholicism, in turn, has a striking presence in the novel, related to its more melodramatic aspects. Young Marion is a fervent though tormented and unorthodox Catholic, and her religious views emphasize guilt and confession, damnation and redemption. In hindsight, Marion even identifies her Catholicism with her mental illness:

> It was as if, in her Catholic phase, she'd lived under a vault that made the sunniest day dark. She'd been obsessed with sin and redemption, prone to being overwhelmed by the significance of insignificant things . . . and paranoid with the sense that God was watching everything she did. When she'd fallen in love with Russ, and had received the wonderfully concrete blessings of her marriage to him, one healthy child after another, . . . she'd closed a mental door on the years when the sun had been dark and her only friend, if one could call an infinite Being a friend, had been God. (128)

In contrast, Russ's Protestant Christianity is represented as prioritizing ethics and community, free of the anxieties and luridness of Marion's religion: "Christianity as Russ preached and practiced it laid very little stress on sin. Marion had long been inspired, intellectually, by Russ's conviction that a gospel of love and community was truer to Christ's teachings than a gospel of guilt and damnation" (129). Leaving aside the obvious stereotyping at work here, it is clear that Marion's Catholicism is a source of depth, conflict, and intensity in her character, one that affords an additional dose of narrativity and interest. In addition, the religious beliefs of the characters—both Marion's and Russ's—create an ideological framework that intensifies the significance of certain events, such as adultery or drug addiction, which would be banal within a different moral code and are therefore instrumental for the narrativity of the novel. In a way, it could be argued that the novel's plot makes sense precisely because of the religious and moral codes of the characters. This preeminence given to moral conflict in the novel is, of course, typically melodramatic. Brooks (1995, 200) explains the centrality of ethical conflict in melodrama by reference to the original moral function of the genre, which was to reconstruct an intelligible moral universe in the modern, postsacred world of the novel.

Against Marion's sacralizing view of confession, the novel sets in contrast the group dynamics based on disclosure that Rick Ambrose establishes in the youth group Crossroads. This fictional group is based on the Christian group frequented by Franzen in his teenage years, which he describes in his memoir, *The Discomfort Zone* (2007)—a group named Fellowship, sponsored by the First Congregational Church. In that work, Franzen affectionately remembers the serious communitarian impulse underlying the group, which seemed to reconcile the counterculture of the 1970s and what he describes as a typically Midwestern egalitarian and Christian ethos. The depiction of Crossroads is rather different, however, and often steps into satire. There is little religion going on in the group. In fact, his leader is well liked by the teenagers because he does not attempt to teach any Christian doctrine.[11] Crossroads actually resembles more a support group, and it is a place where New Prospect's teenagers socialize in relative freedom from the hierarchies of high-school life. Therefore, rather than a chance to explore religious implications, Crossroads affords Franzen a possibility to show group dynamics of disclosure and, more specifically, to channel his criticism of imposed social transparency. In general, "exercises" in Crossroads promote disclosure and transparency as community building. One of Ambrose's exercises involves participants telling each other what they admire in them, as well as telling their partners "something they're doing that's a barrier to getting to know them better" (26). Another one requires participants to "share something you're struggling with that the group might help you with" (74). In this way, after being caught drunk—something strictly forbidden—Perry confesses publicly in an emotional breakdown that elicits waves of compassion and support in the group:

> He was also thrilled by the quantity and intensity of attention he was getting. [. . .] When he broke down in tears, weeping with shame, authentically, the group responded in a kind of ecstasy of supportiveness [. . .] it was a crash course in the fundamental economy of Crossroads: public display of emotion purchased overwhelming approval. [. . .] Perry wanted more of that drug. (31)

Even if Franzen is describing a situation and characters located in the early 1970s, his depiction of group dynamics at Crossroads inevitably

---

11 In his own act of disclosure, Ambrose confesses to Russ's daughter his fears about the irreligious direction taken by the group under his leadership: "I'm a little worried about what we've unleashed. What *I've* unleashed. I'm worried that, if it doesn't end up leading us back to God, it's just an intense kind of psychological experiment. Which could just as easy end up hurting people as liberating them" (74; emphasis in the original).

brings to mind the way he has criticized in his essays and interviews the disappearance of privacy in the mediasphere.[12] What is more, in *Purity* he went so far as to draw an explicit parallelism between the totalitarian, panopticon state of East Germany and internet culture, which is seen by one of the characters as governed by fear: "the fear of unpopularity and uncoolness, the fear of missing out, the fear of being flamed or forgotten" (Franzen 2015, 449). It is easy, then, to feel that in his rendering of Crossroads, Franzen is aiming at a contemporary culture dominated by public displays of emotion and pleas for forgiveness in TV reality shows and social media.[13] Perry, a newcomer to Crossroads, soon gets to master the group's game: "Where his tears on the night of drinking gin had been cathartic, his tears later on came more easily and were a more fungible currency, redeemable for progress toward the inner circle" (Franzen 2021, 31–32). Jeremy Gilbert (2007, 37) has referred to the current ubiquity of public disclosure in relevant terms:

> We now find ourselves inhabiting a culture constituted by moments of (often sensational) disclosure in the space where the public sphere used to be. This links the cult of psychotherapy with the rise and rise of reality TV, both of which might be said to thrive on the practice of positing, delineating, and exposing to view the "secret" interior workings of the self, or the group, or the household, or the celebrity life.

Unsurprisingly, the continuous practice of public disclosure has turned Crossroads into a rather unanimous community, where critics and dissidents like Laura Dobrinsky tend to leave soon, and Ambrose's leadership and practices are uncontested. As Byung-Chul Han (2015, 7) has argued in his description of contemporary neoliberal society, total transparency disables questioning of the status quo and the articulation of political opposition. In this sense, Crossroads is in accordance with his claim that "compulsive transparency stabilizes the existing system most effectively." The narrator confirms this with an ironic reference to Stalinism: "In good

---

12 See, for example, nonfiction works such as *The Kraus Project* (2013); or the collection of essays *The End of the End of the World* (2018), especially in pieces such as "The Essay in Dark Times" or "Capitalism in Hyperdrive."

13 Franzen's indirect criticism of contemporary confessional culture inevitably harks back to his famous dispute with Oprah Winfrey that led to the latter's revocation of Franzen's invitation to discuss *The Corrections* in her hugely popular Book Club in 2001. In his book on contemporary American fiction, Jeremy Green (2005, 90) describes the controversy with Winfrey as the product of two conflicting views of the self: as constructed through theatricalized therapeutic confession for Winfrey and her followers; and for Franzen as intellectual and emotional property—the "private reserve of the writer."

Stalinist show-trial fashion, with a display of strong emotion, Isner confessed that he was guilty of this himself. The group immediately drenched him with approval for his courageous honesty" (Franzen 2021, 25–26). Once more, as he had done in *Purity*, Franzen presents an idea of social transparency that is basically conceived as a flattening, totalitarian threat to his concept of individuality.

4. Shameful Confession as a Generator of Narrative: "A sickening disclosure. Jealousy and uncleanness, both bodily and moral"[14]

In one of Crossroads's "exercises," Ambrose makes the following demand of the group: "I want each of us in the group to talk about something we've done that was wrong. Something we're ashamed of" (68). This request calls attention to shame as a fundamental element in confessional narratives, as in Rousseau. For J. M. Coetzee, there is a libidinal component to Rousseau's shame-and-confession sequence that works as a feedback loop. As Coetzee (1985, 193) points out, Rousseau's knowledge of the shameful nature of his own desire

> both satisfies the desire for the experience of shame and fuels a sense of shame. And this sense of shame is both experienced with satisfaction and recognized, if it is recognized, by self-conscious searching, as a further source of shame; and so on endlessly.

Since, for Rousseau, confession is libidinally invested, for him the value of desire lies in its being shameful and as such confessable. As Coetzee puts it, "*Shamefulness* and *value* are thus interchangeable terms. For—in the economy of confession—the only unique appetites, the only appetites that constitute confessable currency, are shameful appetites. A shameful desire is a valuable desire" (212; emphasis in original). In this way, we can speak of a confessional capital formed by shameful desires, which would amount to a correlative narrative capital. If this is the case, administering such confessional capital in the way Rousseau does can be compared to the process of managing a narrative. In fact, confession becomes a very effective generator of narrativity. Moreover, just as a narrative is usually conceived of as a sequence aimed at closure, effective confession—be it religious or secular—forms part of a sequence created, according to Coetzee, by transgression, confession, penitence, and absolution (194). The latter constitutes the closing of the sequence, although, as we will see, this can become rather problematic. No doubt, in *Crossroads*, Franzen takes full

14 *Crossroads*, 445.

advantage of this narrative quality of confession, and especially of the narrative potentiality of shame. From the very beginning of the novel, we see Russ lusting after Frances Cottrell in a rather embarrassing way. It is not that he is unaware of the shameful character of his desire, "but on his bad days he was unable not to do things he would later regret. It was almost as if he did them because he would later regret them. Writhing with retrospective shame, abasing himself in solitude, was how he found his way to God's mercy" (Franzen 2021, 11).

As the novel goes on, we get to know of the shameful way Russ had to leave Crossroads, his embarrassing escape from Frances Cottrell's house under the effect of a marijuana-induced panic attack, and, in a paroxysm of shame, his confession to Marion that "I was committing adultery while our son tried to kill himself!" (525). In fact, we may say that Russ has incorporated shame as a mainstay of his identity: "Shame and self-abatement were still his portals to God's mercy. The old paradox—that weakness, honestly owned, made a man stronger in his faith—still obtained" (385–86). At this point, we may also remember how Franzen's previous male protagonists—Chip Lambert, Walter and Joey Berglund—tend to go through highly shameful experiences, a circumstance that reveals that the sequence formed by shame, self-abasement, and confession has been widely exploited by Franzen in his novels to build his characters' arcs.[15]

In *Crossroads*, Franzen is also concerned with certain problems that the confessant may face during the process of confession. As stated above, for Coetzee, the natural closing of the confessional process is absolution—which sometimes takes the form of self-forgiveness. As in psychotherapy, this requires the confessant to come to terms with some kind of truth—though not necessarily objective, factual truth. In Coetzee's (1985, 230) words, "The end of confession is to tell the truth to and for oneself." Especially, however, when confession takes the form of introspection, and the subject is characterized by heightened consciousness or self-awareness, it can deviate into what Coetzee defines, after a phrase by Myshkin in Dostoevsky's *The Idiot* (1869), as "double thoughts." For Coetzee, self-consciousness can be a disease when "it feeds upon itself, finding behind every motive another motive, behind every mask another mask" (220). The result of such disease is double thought, which the

---

15 For example, we may think of Chip Lambert stealing from an upmarket grocery or participating in a scam in Lithuania in *The Corrections* (2001), Walter Berglund being beaten by West Virginian hillbillies he had insulted in *Freedom* (2008), or Joey Berglund searching in his excrement for an engagement ring he had accidentally swallowed in the same novel. All these characters start by doing wrong by their close others, deceiving other people and themselves, until different sobering blows—a kind of reality principle—force them to avow and assume the truth about themselves.

South African defines as "the doubling back of thought that undermines the integrity of the will to confess by detecting behind it a will to deceive, and behind the detection of this second motive a third motive (a wish to be admired for one's candor), and so on" (222–23). Ultimately, the confession is unable to arrive at any truth and thus comes to an end. This kind of double thought is perceptible in the two most intelligent characters in the novel, Marion and her son Perry, as their trains of thought are rendered by the omniscient narrator in free indirect speech. In this way, while young Marion is looking after her depressed, bankrupt father, she feels that "there was no telling if the glow she felt was purely love or also the satisfaction of being a better daughter than her sister" (Franzen 2021, 143). But the character who is most clearly beset by double thought is certainly Perry. He is characterized by an unstable sense of identity, plagued by excessive awareness. Early in the novel, in what seems to be a high-school essay, he writes, "Why am I me and not someone else? Let's peer into the dizzying depths of this question" (19).[16] Later on, he reflects,

> Never mind the nine-year-old Perry: fifteen minutes ago Perry was a stranger to him! Did his soul change every time it achieved a new insight? The very definition of a soul was immutability. Perhaps the root of his confusion was the conflation of soul and knowledge. Perhaps the soul was one of those tools built to do exactly one specific task. *To know that I am I*, and was mutable with respect to all other forms of knowledge? (40–41; emphasis in the original)

Like his mother before him, Perry questions the true motives behind his goodness. In another apparent school essay, he wonders about the selfishness inherent in goodness: is it not compromised if one is aware of the advantages accruing from charitable acts? In a comical but revealing scene at Reverend Haefles's party, he engages while drunk in theological conversation with a reverend and a rabbi on the true, secret value of outward, visible goodness. The atheist Perry is in fact desperately trying to get through the maze of second thoughts in his mind, but the answer he receives from Reverend Walsh is unlikely to solve his questioning: "Only your heart can tell you what your true motive is. [. . .] Only faith in Christ redeems us. Without him, we're lost in a sea of

---

16 Franzen has taken to including texts purportedly written by characters in his novels. Thus, *Freedom* and *Purity* feature lengthy confessional narratives written by Patty Berglund and Tom Aberant, respectively. Here, Perry's reflections on the problem of identity appear in two texts apparently written by him as high-school assignments. In all three cases, these manuscripts serve as a complement and a monotony-breaking change from the narrator's ever-present free indirect speech.

second-guessing our motives" (254–55). The scene is completed with Perry's own moment of shame, when his drunkenness becomes apparent. The fact is that the confessional sequence from transgression to absolution described by Coetzee—where the confessor may be another person or just oneself—does not work for Perry, as it is thwarted by constant double thought.

In a piece of nonfiction, Franzen makes an interesting remark on the correlation between identity and narrative: "Our identities consist of the stories we tell about ourselves" (Franzen 2018, 8). This statement is relevant here, since a confessional narrative is essentially a story about us, whether told to a confessor or to oneself in a kind of introspection that takes on a dialogic form. Similarly, for Coetzee (1985, 214) confession becomes part of the confessant's identity: "The more deeply he has avowed the truth of this confession, the more deeply its truth has become part of his personal identity. Yielding subsequently to the new truth entails damage to that identity." It must be noted that this claim implies a performative notion of identity, according to which it can no longer be considered a stable entity that we keep inside us but something that is somehow created, or at least transformed, in the process of confession. Inevitably, this entails some degree of destabilization and vulnerability for the confessant. Perry's insecure sense of identity is then consistent with the instability and ineffectiveness of his confessional process—and, in one of Franzen's characteristic dabs of factual realism, also with his rampant use of drugs. He is unable to reach any closure for his confession just as he is incapable of attaining any kind of stable truth about himself. When we meet him at the end of his process of deterioration, he is in the grip of delirium.

There is another instance of foiled confession in the novel; namely, that of Marion. After Russ has confessed to Marion his adulterous relation to Frances Cottrell in the wake of Perry's disaster, she overcomes the impulse to respond by telling Russ her whole story, both previous and subsequent to her marriage. Once again, she opts for a very incomplete confession instead. She does not avoid full confession out of excessive shame or to elude any kind of punishment. Nor is she pursuing, in her rejection of the liberation brought about by confession, the masochistic pleasures of self-abasement. Quite the opposite, she refuses to confess and takes on the burden of guilt for the sake of Russ and what remains of her family. As she acknowledges, guilt can be a structuring principle of the self, a kind of buttress and support, which can help both Russ and her:

> His confessions had been piteously sincere, like a little boy's, and it was time to make her own confession. [. . .] And yet: what if she didn't? What exactly would be gained by dragging him through Bradley Grant, through Santa, through the abortion, through

Rancho Los Amigos? She could clear her conscience by groveling in the dirt, but was it really a kindness to her husband? ... He was like a boy, and a boy needed structure in his life, and wasn't remorse a kind of structure? ... Might this not be kinder than dumping her complexities on him? ... the temptation didn't feel evil. It felt more like punishment. To not confess her sins to Russ—to renounce her chance to be chastised, maybe pitied, maybe even forgiven—would be to carry the burden for the remainder of her life. The unending burden of being alone with what she knew. (Franzen 2021, 530)

There is another important side to Marion's refrain from confession, related to that vision of identity as formed by the stories we tell (us) about ourselves, as well as the performative character of confession as regards identity. Marion has built a story about her, "the story Marion told Sophie [her therapist] about herself, a story she'd worked out in the hospital and in her years of Catholic introspection" (144). When she meets Bradley Grant again after twenty-six years, she considers telling him her whole story—including the abortion of the child he had fathered—but she rejects the idea:

It was confounding to recognize how *much* she had, compared to him. Not only many more years to live but full knowledge of their history. The story resided in her head, not his, and she felt a curious reluctance to share it, because she was its sole author. He'd merely had been the reader. (509; emphasis in original)

As in the case of her avoidance of full confession to Russ, there is something more at stake here than merely sparing someone else the burden of knowledge, and it is different from the typical acts of renunciation we can often find in Franzen's novels as well. In a way, refusing to tell the story one has created about oneself amounts to remaining in control of one's sense of identity, avoiding the destabilizing effects of confession, and retaining a certain sense of agency.

5. Conclusion

In this article we have seen how Franzen continues his exploration of the role of secrecy in human relationships. To be precise, Franzen's focus in *Crossroads* lingers on the way people negotiate their inevitable ignorance of vast parts of their close other's experience—a negotiation that includes guessing, hope, abysmal misconstructions, and sometimes plain self-deception. At the same time, the novel shows the shock that the encounter with the other's alterity can provoke. The fundamental means for such an encounter is confession, and, accordingly, disclosure becomes the main motif of the novel. Indeed, from the Catholic Church to bedroom intimacy to the therapist's office, *Crossroads* is organized upon a series of acts of confession, including those taking place at the Christian youth group that lends the novel its name—a transparency-driven assembly whose constant reliance on public disclosure and display of emotion resonate with Franzen's criticism of contemporary cultural trends perceptible in the mediasphere, which he has expressed outspokenly in his novels and nonfiction pieces. Here Franzen evinces the same adversarial, negative view of enforced transparency that he had explicitly articulated in *Purity*. Franzen's censure of excessive transparency and his emphasis on the necessary centrality of secrecy in human relations, however, contrast with the explicit way he renders his characters' thoughts and motives, an incongruity that is in part determined by his extensive use of free indirect discourse by an omniscient narrator.

Franzen's interest also lies in the relation between confessional discourse and identity: a confessional process where one's identity is at stake and that sometimes can be finally mastered by the confessant, as the case of Marion shows, while some other times it is inevitably derailed by the effect of what Coetzee describes as double thoughts, as illustrated by Perry. In the process of these explorations, as the allusion to Rousseau's *Confessions* in the names of the protagonists in *Crossroads* suggests, Franzen has probably become more conscious of the wealth of narrative capital afforded by shameful confession than he was in his previous novels, especially when it is incorporated in downright melodramatic form. This does not mean that protagonists involved in shameful situations were absent in Franzen's previous fiction, by any means, but the prominence and the narrative productivity achieved by shameful confession in *Crossroads* indicates a higher degree of awareness. It is quite apparent that melodrama suits Franzen's purposes well, not only because of its inherent narrativity and emphasis on moral conflict, always welcome in a suburban novelistic environment naturally prone to uneventfulness, but also because the genre is absolutely congenial to the investigation of secrecy and disclosure undertaken by the author.

Works Cited

Barbour, Charles. 2017. *Derrida's Secret: Perjury, Testimony, Oath*. Edinburgh: Edinburgh University Press.

Blanco Hidalga, Jesús. 2017. *Jonathan Franzen and the Romance of Community: Narratives of Salvation*. New York: Bloomsbury.

———. 2021. "'Whilst our souls negotiate': Secrets and secrecy in Jonathan Franzen's *Purity*." In *Secrecy and Community in 21st-Century Fiction*, edited by María J. López and Pilar Villar-Argáiz, 189–205. New York: Bloomsbury.

Brooks, Peter. 1995. *The Melodramatic Imagination: Balzac, Henry James, Melodrama and the Mode of Excess*. New Haven, CT: Yale University Press. First published 1976.

———. 2000. *Troubling Confessions: Speaking Guilt in Law and Literature*. Chicago: University of Chicago Press.

Coetzee, J. M. 1985. "Confession and Double Thoughts: Tolstoy, Rousseau, Dostoevsky." *Comparative Literature* 37, no. 3 (Summer): 193–232.

Derrida, Jacques. 2008. *The Gift of Death, Second Edition & Literature in Secret*. Translated by David Wills. Chicago: University of Chicago Press.

Franzen, Jonathan. 1992. *Strong Motion*. London: Picador-Farrar.

———. 1996. "Perchance to Dream: In the Age of Images, a Reason to Write Novels." *Harper's Magazine* (April): 35–54.

———. 2001. *The Corrections*. London: Picador-Farrar.

———. 2007. *The Discomfort Zone: A Personal History*. New York: Harper Perennial.

———. 2010. *Freedom*. London: 4th Estate.

———. 2013. *The Kraus Project*. London: 4th Estate.

———. 2015. *Purity*. London: 4th Estate.

———. 2018. *The End of the End of the World*. New York: Farrar, Straus and Giroux.

———. 2021. *Crossroads*. London: 4th Estate.

Gilbert, Jeremy. 2007. "Public Secrets: Being-with in an Era of Perpetual Disclosure." *Cultural Studies* 21, no. 1 (January): 22–41. https://doi:10.1080/09502380601046923.

Green, Jeremy. 2005. *Late Postmodernism: American Fiction at the Millennium*. New York: Palgrave Macmillan.

Han, Byung-Chul. 2015. *The Transparency Society*. Translated by Erik Butler. Stanford, CA: Stanford Biefs.

Miller, J. Hillis. 2001. *Others*. Princeton, NJ: Princeton University Press.

Simmel, Georg. 1906. "The Sociology of Secrecy and of Secret Societies." *American Journal of Sociology* 11, no. 4 (January): 441–90.

Starobinski, Jean. 1988. *Jean-Jacques Rousseau: Transparency and Obstacle*. Translated by Arthur Goldhammer. Chicago: University of Chicago Press. First published 1971.

13: Celebrity 2.0: Female Influencer Figures in Contemporary American Fiction

Julia Straub

1. Introduction

SINCE AROUND 2000, American fiction has, in multiple ways, engaged with the growing presence of digital, and especially social, media in daily life. Web 2.0 and the advent of the smartphone at the beginning of the century have fundamentally changed the possibilities for social interaction and communication. Together with this rise of social media—by now ingrained in our lives and communities to such an extent that digital technologies have been rendered "banal," to use Zara Dinnen's (2018) terminology—a whole array of related literary types or characters has emerged, often evoking real-life personalities. Whistleblowers like Julian Assange and tycoon figures such as Mark Zuckerberg and Elon Musk find their echoes in a number of literary works dealing with new media industries, such as the by-now classic *The Circle* (2013) by Dave Eggers, and Jonathan Franzen's *Purity* (2015). But the twenty-first century has seen this set of types widen into a third group, not least owing to the rapid development of social media platforms such as Instagram and Twitter (renamed X in July 2023).

The years since the publication of these novels especially saw the massive proliferation of the third group of social media "types" mentioned above: bloggers, influencers, and social media entrepreneurs in the broadest sense. They reach huge audiences and work their way toward popularity and financial success by merging self-display with product placement and lifestyle enhancement. While the inevitable ephemerality of many internet fashions and the rapid fall into obsolescence of certain digital technologies poses a challenge to any writing on the matter, it seems fair to say that internet culture, and social media in particular, have produced an array of available personae or professions that thrive on the increasingly blurred threshold between private and public life. Rebecca Watson, the British novelist and author of *little scratch* (2021)—an experimental novel seeking to capture one day in the life of a young millennial woman by interweaving analog communication with the character's online chats—remarked in a 2019 review in the *Financial Times*,

> Ever-expanding, [digital technology's] multiplicities teach us new ways of communication and intimacy, tugging at our attention spans and becoming part of us, while social media profiles stay rigidly curated. This slippery sense of self is a challenge for writers to capture. Fiction is led by characterization, and yet we are still working out the effects of the internet on ourselves—as a clutch of recently published novels show.

In this regard, the three novels discussed in this chapter are literary responses to the increasingly blended spheres of the analog and the digital. They represent the relationship between online and offline realities and the role that social media play in creating private and professional identities that can be both an opportunity and a threat to their moral integrity and emotional well-being. The novel as such, characterized by its "ability, that is, through the coherence of its physical form and the coherence of its narrative act, to represent and to assert the 'real' of the world as one of coherence and connection" (Wilson 2019, 48), has to accommodate characters whose online behaviors cannot be neatly disentangled from their analog identities. The influencer figure, as someone who conflates the public and the private, the real and the artificial, with particular intensity, marks this challenge poignantly.

In fact, a considerable number of anglophone novels of the late 2010s and early 2020s revolve around the rise and fall of such new internet professionals who, more often than not, reach a certain celebrity status. They give various genre inflections to the topic, ranging from thrillers to romcoms. The British author duo writing under pseudonym of Ellery Lloyd published *People Like Her* in 2021, a novel about a mom blogger's advice going wrong. Romance meets murder mystery in Jennifer Weiner's *Big Summer* (2020), and Natasha Stagg's *Surveys* (2016) incorporates influencer celebrity into a coming-of-age narrative. These are just a few examples of the uses to which the perceived hazards, rather than the happy prospects, for lives spent online are often put. This chapter, however, focuses on female influencer figures in three novels by US writers: Kiley Reid's *Such a Fun Age* (2019), Megan Angelo's *Followers* (2020), and Patricia Lockwood's *No One Is Talking About This* (2021). The female characters in these novels provide evidence of the dense connection between the promises of online celebrity, female online entrepreneurship, the regimes of controlling female body images, and motherhood. A very permeable relation between privacy and public visibility is the condition for each, but rather than merely dwelling on this by now hazy divide, these novels embrace a more multifaceted view of what online celebrity can mean for women specifically and adopt critical viewpoints.

The chapter will begin with a discussion of twenty-first century online celebrity in light of approaches coming from sociology and media studies (concepts such as Theresa M. Senft's [2013] "micro-celebrity" and Chris Rojek's [2012] notion of "presumed intimacy"). The new kind of public performance by influencer figures partially derives from older, more traditional forms of celebrity, but also adds new dimensions to what traditionally was called "fame." In societies where transparency has become a "*systemic* compulsion" according to Byung-Chul Han (2015, 2), the human being is being "flatten[ed] out" because it lacks impermeable spaces (3); that is, spaces where it is not on display. In all of the three novels, women successfully use social media to create their own brands, to make themselves heard and seen, to accrue a fan base or followership, or to simply make a living. The online popularity that they can claim for themselves requires them to control, contain, and cultivate a public image, subject as it is to distinct forms of digital surveillance. The novels do not necessarily belong to one distinct genre; while dystopian features play into Angelo's *Followers*, both Lockwood's and Reid's novels, different as they are, evoke the traditional novel of manners. Thus, across different subgenres, the three texts under discussion represent female characters who instrumentalize the unstable public-private divide on which online fame rests. They complicate the aforementioned theoretical notions of celebrity by opening up cautionary perspectives on the moral pitfalls of such success. While online celebrity can appear to be an easy and effortless goal, the novels shed light on the strenuous processes of editing and curating the self that it requires. Furthermore, the highly blurred division between the public and the private that these novels present attests to the dangers inherent in the forms of surveillance that social media thrive on.

2. Fame and Celebrity, Now and Then

Twentieth-century media cultures—ranging from Hollywood cinema to the 1980s pop music industry—have been amply researched in terms of their creation of stardom and celebrity.[1] Broadcast media such as television have had a major impact on the self-promotion of stars but, as Chris Rojek (2012, 124) argues, eventually fostered the "illusion of face-to-face relationships." This led to an asymmetrical relationship between the many and a few that, according to Rojek, introduced a new form of social relationship, the "parasocial" (a term first introduced by sociologists Donald Horton and R. Richard Wohl in the 1950s). Parasocial relationships, Rojek writes, have been normalized in contemporary media culture, but, then as now, they thrive on the experience of a perceived connection between "intimate strangers" (124–26). Rojek calls this

---

1 See Braudy (1986); Redmond (2014); and Schickel (2000).

"presumed intimacy" (124). Lauren Berlant's (2008, viii) notion of "intimate publics"—where participants share "a commonly lived history" and "emotional contact" occurs—is a related concept, as is Richard Schickel's notion of "intimate strangers," presented in his eponymous book from 1985. What unites these concepts is that distinct affective transactions or responses need to take place for a public to experience the kind of illusional togetherness that stardom requires. In the specific case of celebrity culture, these relationships with the public are meant to cover up the unavoidable chasm between the stars and their fans by virtue of suggesting some shared realm of experience:

> Celebrity in the twentieth century fed on second-hand knowledge of celebrities' lives, but it still managed to instill a sense of friendship between fans and their adored stars. Stars appeared on talk shows and in radio interviews, magazines published "home stories"—most of these stars sought to cover common ground with their fans, regardless of how much of a "fantasy relationship" this ultimately was. (Rojek 2012, 140)

In pre-digital times, occasions to see celebrities offstage, so to speak, occurred much less frequently. TV interviews and other forms of eye-to-eye coverage offered rarer possibilities for actors, performers, and the like to show their allegedly human, private side to a mass audience.

Of course, famous individuals had inhabited the collective imagination prior to the twentieth century with its strongly media-reliant popular culture. Going back to antiquity, Alexander the Great is sometimes listed as an eminent example (Braudy 1986, 32–51). In literary history, the case has been argued for eighteenth-century celebrity with the likes of Lady Mary Montagu (Brant 2018). According to Emrys D. Jones and Victoria Joule (2018, 2) celebrity, defined as "the meeting point of public appearance and private desire that we recognize as a mark of modernity," has its origins just then: in the eighteenth century. This is a moment in time known for its distinction between public and private realms in a Habermasian sense, but also for the proliferation of print products and possibilities for consumption. As Stella Tillyard (quoted in Jones and Joule, 5) has argued, "celebrity was born at the moment private life became a tradeable public commodity." A little later, in the nineteenth century, Lord George Gordon Byron reached something like celebrity status also owing to growing media coverage and possibilities for self-performance (Marshall 2016, 16; Mole 2009). With popular entertainment on the rise, actors like Sarah Bernard underlined the performative status of public identity, while the stirrings of what could be labeled "human-interest journalism" catered to the growing hunger for stories that unearthed the "real," hidden lives of famous people (see Ponce de Leon 2002). While these are just few selected examples whose full implications cannot be explored in this chapter, they reflect the importance of visibility as a vector for celebrity figures in the modern period. As P. David Marshall (2016, 17) argued, celebrities are "personas that are both produced and promulgated through forms of exhibition that are highly dependent on media"—and this has a long history.

In the twenty-first century, however, this relationship follows different rules. As Ellis Cashmore (2011, 406) has argued, we are looking at an updated version of older celebrity cultures, which means that a historical continuity can only be established partially. For one thing, radical self-exhibition is part of the formula for online success. As the novels to be discussed in the rest of this chapter will show, the prudent management of social media today can enhance one's visibility factor significantly. No longer do celebrities depend on an invitation to a Saturday night TV show to give a well-timed look into their private lives. Reciprocity and recognition now more than ever before are being enabled by the possibility of instantaneous communication and interaction. In the case of social media celebrities and influencers, fans can hope to actually receive replies from their stars when they add a comment to an Instagram post, and they can engage more easily and productively with other fans. As a result, the power asymmetry inscribed into traditional notions of celebrity seems to be leveled out. If an illusionary intimacy between strangers has been the traditional formula for celebrity success, today's celebrity culture tacitly presumes the reciprocal commodification of the fan-star relationship. Consider pop stars of the 1980s such as Madonna, who were more than just singers but something akin to brands producing not only music but also fan gear, books, films, posters, and other merchandise. This kind of celebrity generated massive commercial interests beyond album sales. Today's influencers place and advertise commercial products of any kind; they launch their own cosmetics or fashion brands and sell their products directly via their internet channels. But fans today, unlike Madonna fans in the 1980s, pay with more than just their money. They share their search histories, providing valuable information by trading in their consumer profiles.

Yet, this new kind of celebrity also means that the "worthiness" of celebrity requires reconsideration. Traditionally, fame has been associated with the public acknowledgment of personal merit or achievement, and it has often been linked to a notion such as charisma, implying, according to Rojek (2011, 60), "the heroic or extraordinary qualities, real or imagined, that an admired person is believed to possess." By contrast, the kind of media-produced celebrity we are likely to encounter today is "the consequence of a public visibility that may or may not have arisen as a result of significant personal achievement" (Turner 2016, 85). Crystal Abidin (2018, 4–5) speaks about "the industry of creating celebrities" that consists of "a networked business comprising entertainment, communications, publicity, representation, appearance, coaching, and endorsement specialists, and it is facilitated with specialized jobs such as managers, agents, publicists, promoters, and magazine editors." This does not mean that celebrities renowned for their professional skills—for example, athletes, actors, musician, artists—lack talent or accomplishments. But they find themselves in the immediate vicinity of lay individuals whose celebrity is owed to clever branding strategies and a talent for self-promotion.

Celebrity today exceeds older practices of self-fashioning and requires the deliberate self-management of one's privacy in order to maintain the kind of "entertainment value" or "captivating power" that attracts attention (Abidin 2018, 6–8). According to Cashmore (2011, 405), today's celebrity is distinct from previous forms, as it "describes a culture, a characteristic set of attitudes and behaviour that absorbs as well as surrounds us." Furthermore, digital media are "more encompassing, more invasive, more rapid, more compelling and less avoidable than ever" (Cashmore 2017). It has become much more difficult to disentangle oneself from media usage today than it still was in the later twentieth century. This affects the immediacy with which online celebrity can be both produced by individuals and witnessed or consumed by an audience. The term "DIY celebrity" (coined by Graeme Turner; see Abidin 2018, 9) is used occasionally to describe how ordinary people can now become famous. Like microcelebrity, a term introduced by Theresa M. Senft at the beginning of the twenty-first century in her study on bedroom webcamming, DIY celebrity thrives thanks to the easy availability of tools and technologies, "a set of practices and self-presentation techniques that spread across social networks as they are learned from other individuals," and which "can be performed by anyone with a mobile device, tablet, or laptop" (Marwick 2016, 333). Filters smooth out skin imperfections and add atmospheric effects; Photoshop allows for the small- and large-scale manipulation of pictures; unwanted, unflattering pictures and tags are prudently removed whenever possible. These are by now common processes in the social media flow practiced by users across all age groups, and they do not require much technical expertise. In essence, they are selective strategies of self-fashioning upon which online celebrity is built. *Curation* is a term that has gained currency in these debates (see Bhaskar 2016); that is, a term that refers to the crafting of strongly controlled self-images. This happens at the expense of unwanted information, which can be edited away. Ultimately, with online celebrity, it is not even always clear whether a real person exists behind the images and posts that are shared online (Cashmore 2011, 406). The popular twentieth-century narrative of a star being born is now replaced by a star being self-made. Carefully curated self-images beckon with the possibility of self-empowerment, but there is no guarantee as to which ends the personal information made available online will be used or abused. Thus, in the figure of the social-media influencer returns a familiar, Orwellian discourse: surveillance, or more precisely today, "participatory surveillance" (Albrechtslund 2013, 311). While broadcast media evoked the scenario of many watching the few, social media now sees both the numbers of performers and audiences widen.[2] Personal information is shared on Facebook profiles and in Instagram posts, meaning that social media users are actively participating in their very own surveillance (see Albrechtslund 2013, 315) or in what has been named "shareveillance" by Clare Birchall, emphasizing the active contribution of data to technologies that collect and evaluate it. As a consequence, dystopian tales of individual freedom being crushed by state surveillance, in a "classical"—read "Foucauldian"—sense, become more complicated, since their underlying power asymmetries have been confused now that surveillance rests on voluntary cooperation.

The three novels that will be discussed below feature plots that are driven by the agency of women who turn themselves into online celebrity figures. In the case of Megan Angelo's *Followers*, social media branding is depicted as the relatively effortless result of a cunning ping-pong game between two friends before growing into a voracious form of reality-TV entertainment that goes sour in the novel's dystopian part; in Patricia Lockwood's *No One Is Talking About This*, a novel outspoken about the absurdities of the Twittersphere, the protagonist reaches international popularity as a Twitter star owing to utterly pointless memes; in Kiley Reid's *Such a Fun Age*, one of the two main female characters turns a skill learned in analog times—how to write letters—into a marketable accomplishment she can teach online for good money. But these novels are not "how to" guides. While the characters are all self-made businesswomen, they have to straddle the muddy private-public divide while curating their self-images. More precisely, they have to find their places in both offline and online communities that are oftentimes ill-defined, unstable, and disconcertingly overlapping, threatening personal integrity.

3. Megan Angelo's *Followers*: A Star Not Born, but Made

Followers is the first novel by Megan Angelo, formerly a contributing editor to the glossy women's magazine *Glamour* (and thus close to the trade that she describes in her novel). Its plot consists of two strands: one is set in 2015, the other in 2051, and in each time frame the notion of celebrity provides the script. The year 2015 sees a twenty-something New York–based character called Orla Cadden work as a staff blogger for a website

---

2   See also boyd and Ellinson (2007).

that goes by the name of "Lady-ish," dedicated primarily to fashion and celebrity news. Orla shares an apartment with Floss, who wants to try her luck as an influencer. A telling moment in the novel shows how Floss "didn't want to be an actress. She wanted to be what she already was, even if nobody knew it: a celebrity" (47). Both friends see no way for themselves to do the thing they actually want to do, even though countless options for individual development seem to be available. In Orla's case this is writing a novel; for Floss it is being a professional singer (141). In this regard, they lower their initial aspirations and rely on technology to reach their new aims, but, as Floss's case shows, to no lesser avail in terms of popularity. For Floss, being famous equals being "a person, exaggerated" (47), and this "making" of her personhood occurs in a highly gender-sensitive context; that is, the kind of influencer that Floss aspires to be owes her success to the selling of beauty products and the artful cultivation of her femininity. No mention is made of a distinct achievement that would be required to claim such popularity. As a contributor to the "Lady-ish" website, Orla begins to blog about Floss's social media posts on Twitter and Snapchat. Easily and quickly she thus provides a platform for a beauty product—brow gel—which in return becomes a huge success, turning Floss into a celebrity who is not only recognized in the streets but also generates immediate revenue:

> Right from the start, it was suspiciously easy. At least, Orla should have been suspicious of how easy it was, two girls hijacking the public eye from the floor of their Chelsea rental. [...] They started the way everyone did: they shared. Floss posted pictures online—of herself, her things, her food—constantly, as if she was someone whose meals became fascinating just by virtue of her being in front of them. (64)

This passage depicts the seemingly easy construction of Floss as an online celebrity by virtue of content sharing. The phrase "public eye" implies the kind of "shareveillance" mentioned above: the making visible of one's own private life that has become a communal activity for those watching and those being watched. Floss's incessant display of her daily activities and routines—"food porn" being the obvious example here—follows the logic of social media influence: a normal person providing normal objects, or commodities, with a hitherto unknown appeal. Among the three novels discussed, *Followers* provides the most explicit comment on online celebrity as infused with the risks of participatory surveillance culture.

Shortly after, Floss becomes even more of a public figure by agreeing to star in a reality show along with Orla (who had so far remained in the background) as her roommate. Floss goes "publicly private," the new formula for success in the twenty-first century (Senft 2013, 351). Tensions soon arise among the various roommates. The friendship between Floss and Orla becomes increasingly artificial, and Orla finds herself the object of a ludicrous meme going viral. More existentially, the reality show culminates in a follower's suicide caused by an accidental but unforgivable post by Floss.

The second plot, set in 2051, evokes a pronounced dystopian atmosphere by introducing a United States after "the Spill," an internet blackout that is never explained in the novel but that triggers deep social changes. The novel does not say much about the new political regime, but an obvious sign of a totalitarian shift is the implementation of severe surveillance practices. The readers are introduced to Marlow, a wife and celebrity figure who has been selected by the government to take part in a radical reality show. Like all the other citizens in Constellation, California, she broadcasts her life on a day-to-day basis, and what appears to be a matter of choice—be it clothing or dating options—is, in fact, scripted. A wrist device connects Marlow's brain directly to the producers' room, from where she receives instructions and immediate feedback from her followers. This second, dystopian plotline offers itself to various readings in terms of surveillance: fairly soon it becomes obvious that its participatory dimension is enforced rather than voluntary, and that Marlow seeks to liberate herself from this state of coerced surveillance. Here lies a decisive dystopian twist to the first plotline, which sees Orla and Floss generously sharing their private lives for the purpose of achieving celebrity status, whereas for the next generation it has become a form of governmental control. But there are more connections between the two plots, most prominently when Floss is revealed to be Marlow's mother. This intergenerational relation adds to the novel's temporal layering, as it is Marlow's need to know her family history that encourages her to break free. While Floss, at the outset at least, basks in her DIY celebrity, Marlow, as the ultimate influencer figure with millions of followers, seeks to escape from all the attention that has been imposed on her.

To a certain extent, the novel aggrandizes the threats of social media as they are perceived today—the selling out of individual privacy and the sacrificing of analog bonds and friendship in favor of instant online success—in a vein that is typical of dystopian writing. Its smart structural feature is the inclusion of two temporally distant plotlines to suggest that there is a "before" and an "after," but that the "before" saw social developments that provided the ground for the more radical transformations of the "after." The unsettling transformation of social media culture in 2015 into a government-run form of total surveillance and product sponsorship in 2051 comes across less as an abrupt incision than as a progression. Following the "Spill" and a resulting coup, the inhabitants of Constellation in 2051 are initially reluctant to embrace what they call "the new web" (191), now completely controlled by the government. They are aware of a time before, of "an internet that had nothing to do with the government," whereas in their own time, "on the new internet, data was constantly gathered. It was kept forever, used and shared at the government's discretion" (192). The novel thus issues a warning that the kind of influencer cult that is telling of social media in the here and now, built on a culture of voluntary sharing (to return to Birchall's notion of "shareveillance"), can all too easily turn into forms of coercion and enforced surveillance if the political tides change.

4. Kiley Reid's *Such a Fun Age*— Celebrity and Privilege

Kiley Reid's debut novel, *Such a Fun Age*, juxtaposes two main characters who could not be any more different. One is (yet another) twenty-something millennial woman, Emira Tucker, who is Black and who, having completed a university degree in English, now finds herself single, unemployed, and without health insurance but with a sick father to take care of. The other woman is Alix Chamberlain, white and in her thirties, a wife and mother of two who has made a name for herself as a luxury-product blogger and letter-writing coach. Her online rise to fame happens swiftly, since,

> seemingly overnight, Alix Chamberlain became a brand. Her propensity for receiving free merchandise quickly turned into a philosophy about women speaking up and taking communication back to basics. In the middle of the night, Alix changed her Instagram bio to #LetHerSpeak. (22)

Once more, as seen in *Followers*, the onset of this kind of fame is instantaneous, but the readers are privy to the motivations and the background stories of these female influencers. Alix herself had perfected a demanding attitude as a young person when writing exuberant letters to companies in the hope of receiving free product samples. While, initially, writing letters allowed Alix to get hold of otherwise unaffordable luxury items, this practice leads to the cultivation of a more abstract attitude of taking a stance. "Let Her Speak" is a brand, but it aspires to be a philosophy at the same time. On this website, Alix gives advice to women on how to write efficient letters to make successful claims, but she sells this rather pragmatic skill as the acquisition of greater self-empowerment. In other words, Alix has successfully coupled money-making with a public agenda of promoting gender as well as social equality.

The novel is set in Philadelphia, where Alix had to move from New York because of her husband's job (he works in television). Alix hires Emira as a part-time nanny, and Emira does a great job keeping Alix's two small daughters happy. Triggered by a racist incident in a nearby supermarket involving Emira, who is accused of having kidnapped Alix's older child, Briar, while looking after her on an emergency night shift, the so far merely professional relationship between Alix and Emira develops a new dynamic. Alix feels a strong desire to bond with Emira. The kind of friendship she seeks with her babysitter reflects an attempt to overcome, from Alix's perspective, the divide between the two caused by race, class, and age. Emira, however, remains largely oblivious to these advances, as she is mainly interested in making a living, and her affection is directed at Briar. Besides, she starts a relationship with a slightly older white man, who, it turns out, is Alix's former boyfriend.

The novel brims with sharp observations on class difference and racism in American society. It also highlights the precarious living conditions of many millennials whose education does not enable them to find full-time employment they can reasonably live on. By contrast, Alix, the female blogger/entrepreneur, embodies privilege on many levels. As mentioned, she began to cultivate the skill of artful letter writing early on in her life with the purpose of obtaining upmarket freebies. While this is part and parcel of customer-business relationships in a capitalist market economy, it reflects essentially a position of entitlement: Alix has learned that her complaints and requests will not go unheard. Yet, Alix's harnessing of digital media allows her to take this kind of analog pattern to the next level and to turn it into something much bigger. What had been her own private pastime now grows into a profit-making profession, one that she shares with a huge audience and one that means that her private and professional roles become to a certain extent indistinguishable. Her breastfeeding her two-year-old while on a discussion panel boosts her popularity (and market value) and teaches her how to turn her own private experience of motherhood into a part of her business model:

> The photographers for the event swarmed the foot of the stage. They backed up into the aisle to get a clear shot of Alix, crossing her ankles, breast-feeding her child above a pregnant stomach, and speaking between two suited men. At one point, a photographer whispered, "Can you adjust the shirt so that the logo is showing?" Alix laughed and said yes. She smoothed out the shirt against the side of Briar's head and let the bottom hang flat. Blocking her daughter's face were black letters spelling out *Small Business Femme*.
>
> That day, Alix earned another thousand followers. (Reid 2020, 28–29)

This is clearly a staged scene meant to signal female empowerment. After all, pregnant, breast-feeding Alix marks a distinct contrast with the men in suits around her. Her two children, one of them unborn, become part of her brand. This sense of power is ambiguous, though, as, unlike the men around her, she uses her own children for her performance as mommy entrepreneur, crossing a boundary that is essential for her to ensure the aura of authenticity as a working mother, while making her children part of her commercial enterprise. And while dubitable because of its blending of the personal with the commercial, her gestures and self-performance as a female entrepreneur remain partly an indicator of privilege (Alix profits from a self-confidence and sense of entitlement she has acquired from childhood on), partly of personality (Emira finds herself unsure what to do with her life and lacks Alix's determination). Besides, for some childless women, like Emira, with no stable income, let alone a suitable partner, the ideal of the successful working mom who juggles commitments as both mother and entrepreneur may well, however exhausting it can be, remain a desirable yet unreachable goal. By interconnecting two very different lifeworlds—that of the successful, well-educated white working mother and that of the financially struggling single Black woman—the novel comments on a number of social inequalities that affect particularly women in the United States. For the purpose of this chapter, however, it is important to note that Alix's plotline complicates the phenomenon of the "instamum"—the mommy entrepreneur or the mommy blogger. Like in *Followers*, the foundations of this kind of fame, often built on edited versions of the self, are shown as fragile, since the self-performance that these characters enact invades not only their privacy but also, inevitably, the social bonds they seek to establish. The novel shows two conflicting sides of Alix: she cultivates a professional persona online that is utterly under the control of her social skills and that stands for (and sells) an ideal of female self-assertion. But Alix is also revealed to be haunted by her own misdoings in the past and deeply insecure as a mother and female friend in the analog world. Emira's character, while floating somewhat aimlessly through life, lacks this artifice and becomes the foil against which Alix's inconsistencies become the more conspicuous. *Such a Fun Age* is a multilayered novel offering itself to several readings in terms of race, class, or its use of satire, but with the figure of the successful businesswoman and blogger Alix it also comments critically on the twisted relationship between the private and the public self in social media.

5. Patricia Lockwood's *No One Is Talking About This*

Patricia Lockwood is best known as an essayist for the *London Review of Books*; an active user of X; the author of both a memoir, *Priestdaddy* (2017), and a poem, "The Rape Joke," that went viral in 2013. Her novel *No One Is Talking About This* came out in 2021 and received considerable media attention, possibly owing to her own status as a critic. More so than the two other novels, *No One Is Talking About This* addresses the elusiveness, if not mindlessness, of social media, especially the Twittersphere, and the difficulty of aligning analog experiences with social media identities. Right from the start we are told that social media, which in the novel are called "the portal," owns the unnamed protagonist. She is an addict, feeding the portal herself with nonsensical tweets, while relentlessly scrolling and consuming those of others. The novel contains many passages that convey a sense of the voracity of social media: there is no end to the pictures, GIFs, memes, hashtags, comments, posts, and videos that the protagonist plows through every day, eclectic concatenations of product recommendations, news, advice-giving, and mere nonsense that suggest that there are no boundaries between the moral and the immoral, the beautiful and the ugly, the disturbing and the edifying. "Why did the portal feel so private, when you only entered it when you needed to be everywhere?" the narrator wonders at the opening of the novel (Lockwood 2021, 4), the portal opening a door into what seems like a vortex of information that is both solicited and unsolicited at the same time:

> She lay every morning under an avalanche of details, blissed, pictures of breakfasts in Patagonia, a girl applying her foundation with a hard-boiled egg, a shiba inu in Japan leaping from paw to paw to greet its owner, ghostly pale women posting pictures of their bruises—the world pressing closer and closer, the spiderweb of human connection grown so thick it was almost a shimmering and solid silk, and the day still not opening to her. What did it mean that she was allowed to see this? (8)

Going online, as depicted in Lockwood's novel, imposes a "presumed intimacy" (Rojek 2012) mentioned at the beginning of this chapter, and the protagonist does not feel at ease with this. The quoted passage ends with a question mark, as the protagonist is irritated by the kind of entitlement the internet offers to see things that she probably should not see. The "presumed intimacy" offered by the internet is too intimate for her. The metaphor of the spiderweb growing thicker and thicker brings to mind the inevitable power relationship between the prey and the predator. Whichever suffering, but also whichever meal, trip, purchase, or puppy is shown, it is brought closer than ever before to one's doorstep, or screen.

The protagonist herself assumes an active role. Following a meaningless viral tweet she posted, she turns into something like a Twitter celebrity and is being invited to give talks at conferences and events abroad:

> She had become famous for a post that said simply, *Can a dog be twins?* That was it. Can a dog be twins? It had recently reached the stage of penetration where teens posted the cry-face emoji at her.

They were in high school. They were going to remember "Can a dog be twins?" instead of the date of the Treaty of Versailles, which, let's face it, she didn't know either. (Lockwood 2021, 13)

"The portal" is described as a place devoid of meaning or genuine human bonds, and the protagonist seems to know how to feed the portal exactly the kind of material it craves. She has found herself a comfortable place in the analog world where her illuminations of the online world are sought after and of value:

All around the world, she was invited to speak from what felt like a cloud-bank, about the new communication, the new slipstream of information. She sat onstage next to men who were better known by their usernames and women who drew their eye-brows on so hard that they looked insane, and tried to explain why it was objectively funnier to spell it *sneazing*. This did not feel like real life, exactly, but nowadays what did? (13–14)

The protagonist does not exactly become an influencer, but she makes a living from explaining to the world how the internet, or more precisely the Twitterverse, works. Her popularity is based on the public perception of her as having a deeper understanding of what, effectively, she fails to grasp herself. In this sense she is as much of a self-made internet celebrity as the other characters discussed in this chapter: she masters the written and unwritten laws of online communication, but she experiences, and also expresses, a profound perplexity given her own involvement and its self-perpetuating success. Questions, moments of hesitation, incoherence, and bland incomprehension shape the protagonist's account of her rise on social media—ironically, seeing that she has been singled out as a social-media expert. This echoes an observation made by Pia Tolentino, staff writer at *The New Yorker* and author of an essay collection titled *Trick Mirror: Reflections on Self-Delusion* (2019). In her essay "The I in the Internet" she admits to her own confusion, that she does not know "what to do with the fact that I myself continue to benefit from all this: that my career is possible in large part because of the way the internet collapses identity, opinion, and action" (19). Lockwood's protagonist is similarly unsure about what her job does to her personality.

The novel's tone and register change significantly the moment her sister gives birth to a child with a birth defect. Henceforth, the protagonist finds herself torn out of her virtual world, spending hours in hospital wards, fully occupied by the baby's struggle to survive. Against all odds, the baby makes progress, and "against all wisdom, and in the face of her bleak gray pictures, she was learning, she could learn" (176). The second part of the novel seeks to recover the emotional depth—ultimately to be found only in the analog world—that had receded from the protagonist's previous on- and offline haze. It also introduces readers to a more private protagonist, and in this sense, *No One Is Talking About This*—as the title suggests—implies that despite the transgressive nature of "the portal," where there are seemingly no more taboos, there remains the possibility to opt out from complete disclosure, that, indeed, protective boundaries can be maintained or reinscribed into one's social life. The protagonist is able to reclaim, in the hospital room, a certain "impermeability" (Han 2015, 3) that protects her from the digital world and its demands for sharing. Lockwood's novel is thus, among the three, the one that comments most outspokenly and critically on the moral stakes for social-media figures.

6. Conclusion

The three novels discussed in this chapter depict the rise of female celebrity figures in technology-based societies and their realist or near-future dystopian settings. By scrutinizing notions such as "microcelebrity," "presumed intimacy," and the "parasocial," this chapter examined the implications of online celebrity and fan-celebrity relationships today in order to explore their treatment in contemporary fiction. The chapter showed that the promise of seemingly quick fame and wealth, especially for women, surfaces in all three works and that it is seen as deeply problematic. In each of the novels, the dangers of the private going public are addressed. The novels differ with regard to the cautionary stance they take, but each offers its own critical view of easy assumptions concerning online celebrity. The harmful implications of participatory surveillance or shareveillance become a most overt concern in Megan Angelo's *Followers*, which puts into question the control individuals have over their allegedly self-designed public identities. *Followers* illustrates how quickly surveillance can turn from a self-chosen means of empowerment to a tool of state control. Lockwood's *No One Is Talking About This*, by contrast, reinstates the importance of offline realities as sites for genuine care and human relationships. Reid's *Such a Fun Age* pursues yet a different theme by juxtaposing the personal problems of one of its female protagonists, Alix, with her flawlessly curated public image as a working mom and online entrepreneur, a contrast sharpened by the race and class differences that define her relationship with her daughter's nanny.

Social media has acted as an equalizing force allowing individuals, possibly without vocational training (and often these are women), to claim a stage for their shared experience. The novels valorize this self-empowerment that gives women access to panel boards, customers, and sponsors. Yet they show that this allegedly instantaneous success is volatile by unraveling the emotional and psychological price these characters have to pay for it. In this regard, these novels invite us to rethink established narratives of fame. Comparisons with previous cases from literary history revolving around characters aspiring to fame lie at hand and can be partly insightful (e.g., Theodore Dreiser's *Sister Carrie* [1900]). But these contemporary novels do not retell the narratives that have traditionally produced "stars" —a term that in itself may have reached the end of its shelf life. They do not represent fame or celebrity as a twisted story of hard work and endurance, or a stellar rise, or a version of the American Dream come true, but as one of lucky circumstance, clever marketing, and the instant gratification of ambitions. For online celebrities in these novels, either the line between the public and the private is collapsing, or the two spaces are seen as dangerously colliding, creating space for new stories to be told.

Works Cited

Abidin, Crystal. 2018. *Internet Celebrity: Understanding Fame Online*. Leeds, UK: Emerald Publishing.

Albrechtslund, Anders. 2013. "New Media and Changing Perceptions of Surveillance." In *A Companion to New Media Dynamics*, edited by John Hartley, Jean Burgess, and Axel Bruns, 311–21. Hoboken, NJ: Wiley-Blackwell.

Angelo, Megan. 2020. *Followers*. London: HQ.

Berlant, Lauren. 2008. *The Female Complaint: The Unfinished Business of Sentimentality in American Culture*. Durham, NC: Duke University Press.

Bhaskar, Michael. 2016. *Curation: The Power of Selection in a World of Excess*. London: Piatkus.

Birchall, Claire. 2018. *Shareveillance: The Dangers of Openly Sharing and Covertly Collecting Data*. Minneapolis: University of Minnesota Press.

Bloom, Harold. 1973. *The Anxiety of Influence*. Oxford: Oxford University Press.

boyd, danah, and Nicole B. Ellison. 2007. "Social Networks Sites: Definition, History, and Scholarship." *Journal of Computer-Mediated Communication* 13, no. 1: 210–30.

Brant, C. 2018. "'I Make a Very Shining Figure': Lady Mary Wortley Montagu and the Intimate Publicity of Authorship." In Jones and Joule, *Intimacy and Celebrity in Eighteenth-Century Literary Culture*, 211–31.

Braudy, Leo. 1986. *The Frenzy of Renown: Fame and Its History*. New York: Vintage, 1997.

Cashmore, Ellis. 2011. "Celebrity in the Twenty-First Century Imagination." *Cultural and Social History* 8, no. 3: 405–13.

———. 2017. "Why Am I Famous?" *Fair Observer*, May 19. https://www.fairobserver.com/region/north_america/fame-celebrity-culture-news-analysis-74082/.

Dinnen, Zara. 2018. *The Digital Banal: New Media and American Literature and Culture*. New York: Columbia University Press.

Docx, Edward. 2013. "The Circle by Dave Eggers—Review." *Guardian*, October 9. https://www.theguardian.com/books/2013/oct/09/circle-dave-eggers-review.

Dreiser, Theodore. 2009. *Sister Carrie*. Oxford: Oxford University Press. First published 1900.

Han, Byung-Chul. 2015. *The Transparency Society*. Translated by Erik Butler. Stanford, CA: Stanford Briefs.

Hayes, Chris. 2021. "On the Internet, We're Always Famous: What Happens When the Experience of Celebrity Becomes Universal." *New Yorker* (September 24). https://www.newyorker.com/news/essay/on-the-internet-were-always-famous.

Horton, Donald, and R. Richard Wohl. 1956. "Mass Communication and Para-social Interaction: Observations on Intimacy at a Distance." *Psychiatry* 19, no. 3: 215–29.

James, Henry. 2009. *The Portrait of a Lady*. Oxford: Oxford University Press. First published 1881.

Jones, Emrys D., and Victoria Joule. 2018. *Intimacy and Celebrity in Eighteenth-Century Literary Culture*. Cham, Switzerland: Palgrave Macmillan.

Lockwood, Patricia. 2021. *No One Is Talking About This*. New York: Riverhead Press.

Marshall, P. David. 2016. "The Genealogy of Celebrity: Introduction." In Marshall and Redmond 2016, 15–19.

Marshall, P. David, and Sean Redmond, eds. 2016. *A Companion to Celebrity*. Malden, MA: Wiley-Blackwell.

Marwick, Alice E. 2016. "You May Know Me from YouTube: (Micro)Celebrity in Social Media." In Marshall and Redmond 2016, 333–50.

Mole, Tom. 2009. *Romanticism and Celebrity Culture, 1750–1850*. Cambridge: Cambridge University Press.

Ponce de Leon, Charles L. 2002. *Self-Exposure: Human-Interest Journalism and the Emergence of Celebrity in America, 1890–1940*. Chapel Hill: University of North Carolina Press.

Redmond, Sean. 2014. *Celebrity and the Media*. Cham, Switzerland: Palgrave Macmillan.

Reid, Kiley. 2020. *Such a Fun Age*. London: Bloomsbury Circus.

Rojek, Chris. 2012. *Fame Attack: The Inflation of Celebrity and Its Consequences*. London: Bloomsbury.

Schickel, Richard. 2000. *Intimate Strangers: The Culture of Celebrity*. Chicago: Ivan R. Dee. First published 1985.

Senft, Theresa M. 2013. "Microcelebrity and the Branded Self." In *A Companion to New Media Dynamics*, edited by John Hartley, Jean Burgess, and Axel Bruns, 346–54. Malden, MA: Wiley-Blackwell.

Tolentino, Jia. 2019. *Trick Mirror: Reflection on Self-Delusion*. London: 4th Estate.

Turner, Graeme. 2016. "Celebrity, Participation and the Public." In Marshall and Redmond 2016, 83–97.

Watson, Rebecca. 2019. "The Art of Fiction in the Age of Social Media." *Financial Times*, November 8. https://www.ft.com/content/f551cc98-fefa-11e9-b7bc-f3fa4e77dd47.

Wilson, Leigh. 2019. "Post-Millennial Literature." In *The Cambridge Companion to British Fiction, 1918–2018*, edited by Peter Boxall, 47–66. Cambridge: Cambridge University Press.

Contributors

TOMASZ BASIUK is a professor at the University of Warsaw. He has served as director of the American Studies Center (ASC) and as president of the Polish Association for American Studies and has been serving as director of the Institute of the Americas and Europe, of which the ASC is a part, since 2016. His research interests include contemporary American fiction and life writing, critical theory, and queer studies. He has authored two monographs and edited or coedited six volumes and special journal issues in American studies and in gender and sexuality studies. He is a founding coeditor of *InterAlia*, a queer studies e-journal established in 2006. He was a principal investigator in the HERA-funded queer history project "Cruising the Seventies" (CRUSEV) and is a Fulbright alumnus.

JESÚS BLANCO HIDALGA is a lecturer in the English Department at the University of Córdoba in Spain. His research interests include modern and contemporary fiction in English, critical theory, and political thought. He is the author of the monograph *Jonathan Franzen: Narratives of Salvation* (Bloomsbury, 2017). He has recently published essays on Jonathan Franzen and the 2002–8 HBO series *The Wire* in collected volumes released by Bloomsbury and Brill.

CRISTINA CHEVEREȘAN is a professor PhD habil. at the West University of Timișoara, Romania, where she teaches American Literature, Culture, and Civilization. She is director of the American Studies M.A. Program, a member of several European and American scientific societies; Ca' Foscari Venice Visiting Professor (2019); past recipient of fellowships from the Salzburg Global Seminar, University College Dublin Clinton Institute for American Studies, and the Cornell School of Criticism and Theory; a Fulbright Senior scholar (Harvard University) and Fulbright Ambassador. She has published nine books in Romanian and English, as well as numerous articles in national and international journals, collected volumes, and the Romanian cultural press. She has translated and edited a dozen other volumes.

MICHEL FEITH is professor in American literature at the University of Nantes, France, head of the English Department, and a member of the Center for Research on Identities, Nations and Intercultural Studies

(CRINI). He has published articles on the multicultural literature of the United States, focusing especially on Maxine Hong Kingston, Gerald Vizenor, N. Scott Momaday, Louise Erdrich, John Edgar Wideman, Percival Everett, and the Harlem Renaissance. His recent work includes a collection of essays edited with Prof. Claudine Raynaud, *Troubled Legacies: Heritage/Inheritance in American Minority Literatures* (Cambridge Scholars, 2015) and the monograph *John Edgar Wideman and Modernity: A Critical Dialogue* (University of Tennessee Press, 2019).

JULIÁN JIMÉNEZ HEFFERNAN is professor of English and Comparative Literature at the University of Córdoba, Spain. He has published extensively on Samuel Richardson, Sir Walter Scott, William Makepeace Thackeray, George Eliot, Henry James, Evelyn Waugh, Iris Murdoch, Nadine Gordimer, V. S. Naipaul, and Thomas Pynchon. He is the coeditor of *Community in Twentieth-Century Fiction* (Palgrave, 2013), the author of three books on Shakespeare—*Shakespeare's Extremes* (Palgrave, 2015), *Limited Shakespeare* (Routledge, 2019), and *Unphenomenal Shakespeare* (Brill, 2023)—and is currently working on a book titled *Prepossessing Henry James: The Strange Freedom* (Routledge, forthcoming).

TIINA KÄKELÄ is a senior adviser in research services at the University of Helsinki. After her dissertation on the social role of death in Thomas Pynchon's fiction in 2007, she has written several essays on Pynchon's work, among which the most recent are "Postmodern Ghosts and the Politics of Invisible Life" (2014), "'This Land Is My Land, This Land Also Is My Land': Real Estate Narratives in Pynchon's Fiction" (2019), and "Death and Afterlife" (2019).

PAULA MARTÍN-SALVÁN is professor of English and American Literature at the University of Córdoba, Spain. Her research interests include American literature, critical theory, and modern political thought. She has coedited the collections *Figures of Belatedness: Postmodernist Fiction in English* (UCOPress, 2006), *Community in Twentieth Century Fiction* (Palgrave, 2013) and *New Perspectives on Community and the Modernist Subject* (Routledge, 2017) and is the author of monographs on Graham Greene (Palgrave 2015) and Don DeLillo (UCOPress, 2009). She has recently finished a monograph on Colson Whitehead.

JUAN L. PEREZ-DE-LUQUE is assistant professor in the Department of English and German Studies at the University of Córdoba, Spain. He has been visiting scholar at Trinity College (Ireland), the University of Nottingham (UK), Brown Univesity (USA) and Wheaton College (USA), and has published several articles and book chapters on H. P. Lovecraft, Edgar Allan Poe, and Jeanette Winterson, as well as a monograph on

Lovecraft. His main fields of interest are ideological and communitarian readings of horror fiction, witchcraft, and fantasy literature in general, as well as science fiction and popular culture.

SASCHA PÖHLMANN is professor of American Literature and Culture at TU Dortmund University in Germany. He wrote his PhD dissertation on "Pynchon's Postnational Imagination" in 2008 (published with Winter Verlag, Heidelberg, in 2010), and received his Dr. habil. degree in 2014, both from the Ludwig Maximilian University of Munich. He has published the books *Future-Founding Poetry: Topographies of Beginnings from Whitman to the Twenty-First Century* (Camden House, 2016), *Stadt und Straße: Anfangsorte in der amerikanischen Literatur* (transcript, 2018), and *Vote with a Bullet: Assassination in American Fiction* (Camden House, 2021). He has edited or coedited essay collections on Thomas Pynchon, Mark Z. Danielewski, Percival Everett, foundational sites in modernity, electoral cultures, unpopular culture, American music, video games, and flyover fictions.

UMBERTO ROSSI holds a PhD from Sapienza University, Rome, and is a schoolteacher, literary critic, and scholar who has published a monograph on Philip K. Dick (*The Twisted World of Philip K. Dick*, McFarland, 2011) and articles on science fiction and postmodernist fiction (dealing— among others—with J. G. Ballard, Jonathan Lethem, Thomas Pynchon, and Joseph Heller). He has also written a monograph on war literature in the twentieth century and articles/book chapters on war narratives (both purely verbal and graphic) and comics. He is a member of the International Comparative Literature Association Standing Committee on Comics Studies and Graphic Narrative.

JELENA ŠESNIĆ, a full professor, teaches in the Department of English, Faculty of Humanities and Social Sciences in Zagreb, Croatia. Her research interests encompass nineteenth-century US literature and culture, US ethnic literatures, methodologies of American studies, transnational cultural processes (with special emphasis on the Anglophone Croatian diaspora), and memory studies. She is the author of two books and editor of two collections of essays. As a cofounder of the Croatian Association for American Studies, she co-organizes the society's annual American studies workshops. She edits, with Sven Cvek, Working Papers in American Studies (https://openbooks.ffzg.unizg.hr/index.php/FFpress/catalog/series/WPAS).

TOON STAES teaches English and American literature at the University of Antwerp and at Katholieke Universiteit Leuven, Belgium. He has published several essays on contemporary fiction and narrative theory and is currently writing a book on the systems novel. His research has been sponsored by the Research Foundation-Flanders (FWO), the Belgian American Educational Foundation (BAEF), and the Estonian Research Council (ETAG).

JULIA STRAUB is full professor of modern English literature at the University of Fribourg, Switzerland. She is the author of *A Victorian Muse: The Afterlife of Dante's Beatrice in Nineteenth-Century Literature* (Continuum, 2009) and *The Rise of New Media, 1750–1850: Transatlantic Discourse and American Memory* (Palgrave, 2017), and has published widely on text-image relationships, contemporary literature and its relation to digital media, transatlantic literary studies, and melodrama. Recent publications include "Canon Theory and the Velocity of Book Histories in Times of Digitization," *Anglia* 39, no. 1 (2021): 224–41, and "Surveillance in Jennifer Egan's Novels of the Information Age," in *Surveillance, Society, and Narrative*, edited by Betiel Wasihun (Ergon, 2019), 111–28.

ALICE SUNDMAN holds a PhD in English literature from Stockholm University. Her research interests include Toni Morrison, place and space studies, ecocriticism, and the intersections between literature and philosophy. She is the author of *Toni Morrison and the Writing of Place* (Routledge, 2022).

Index

Abidin, Crystal, 300, 301
accountability, 3, 6–7, 9, 18, 33, 61, 105, 166, 171, 222, 267
Agamben, Giorgio, 197n2
Albrechtslund, Anders, 302
Alexander, Edward, 163, 165
allegory, 23, 85, 96, 106, 118–19, 136n11, 272
Alloa, Emmanuel, 2, 4n3, 5, 7, 7n8, 8, 10, 12, 16, 34, 36, 37, 162, 166, 186, 194n1, 195, 199, 200
Althusser, Louis, 13, 55
Althusser, Louis, works by: "Ideology and Ideological State Apparatuses," 13; *Sur la reproduction*, 55
ambiguity, 1, 11, 39, 46n24, 47, 49, 59, 60n11, 66–68, 73–74, 76, 85, 88, 98, 105–6, 108, 123, 125–26, 140, 151–54, 159, 190, 203, 204, 208, 270, 271, 282, 306–7
Angelo, Megan, 25, 297, 298, 302–5, 310
Arendt, Hannah, 261, 264, 266, 267, 272
Arnold, Matthew, 64
Ashbery, John, 55, 78
Asselineau, Roger, 36
authenticity, 33, 35, 36, 39–40, 130, 166, 183, 248, 273, 307

Ball, Kirstie, 269
Barbour, Charles, 279
Barkun, Michael, 220, 220n4
Barrett, Leonard E., 182n6
Barth, Fredrik, 118
Barthes, Roland, 41, 120
Barthes, Roland, works by: "The Discourse of History," 120; *Mythologies*, 120

Basiuk, Tomasz, 23, 92n3, 98n6
Bateson, Gregory, 245, 246
Baudrillard, Jean, 10, 135
Bauman, Zygmunt, 155, 255–57, 266, 267, 267n5, 268
Bauman, Zygmunt, works by: *Liquid Modernity*, 267; *Liquid Surveillance*, 255; *Retrotopia*, 155
Baume, Sandrine, 32
Bellis, Peter J., 38
Bennett, Chad, 45n23
Bentham, Jeremy, 5, 6, 9, 13, 104, 140, 199
Bercovitch, Sacvan, 19n19
Bergman, David, 72n36
Berlant, Lauren, 299
Berliner, Daniel, 6, 6n7, 7
Bernstein, Ethan S., 11n12
Berressem, Hanjo, 229n11
betrayal, 123, 148, 149–51, 152, 154, 156, 162–63, 165, 167–68, 171, 175, 186, 195, 224, 252
Bhaskar, Michael, 301
Birchall, Clare, 2–12, 5n6, 7n8, 7n9, 8n10, 9n11, 10n11, 17, 18, 31, 31n3, 33–35, 130, 133, 133n7, 140, 141, 141n15, 167, 177n4, 186, 190, 194, 201, 209, 210, 222, 302, 305
Birchall, Clare, works by: "Aesthetics of the Secret," 31, 194, 201; *Conspiracy Theories in the Time of COVID-21*, 133, 133n7; *Radical Secrecy*, 3, 4, 5n6, 8, 12, 31, 31n3, 130, 140, 141, 186, 222; *Shareveillance*, 302, 303, 305, 310; "Transparency, Interrupted," 2, 8n10, 33, 34, 35, 167, 209
Blake, David Haven, 37, 37n8, 39, 46n24

Blanco Hidalga, Jesús, 25, 276n1, 277n2, 284n8
Blaustein, George, 72n35
Boas, Taylor C., 14, 15
Bobker, Danielle, 44n22
body, 48, 86, 183, 188–89, 223, 265, 297; embodiment, 48, 112, 121
Bohman, James, 273
Bok, Sissela, 174, 179, 184, 186
Boling, Patricia, 32n4, 43n14
Boothroyd, Dave, 8n10, 14, 16, 37, 43n16, 194
Boulter, Jonathan, 173n2
Bourdieu, Pierre, 71n34
boyd, danah, 302n2
Brandeis, Louis, 6, 7
Brant, C., 299
Braudy, Leo, 298n1, 299
Breen, Margaret Soenser, 90n2
Brin, David, 8
Broeders, Dennis, 8n10, 16n14
Brooks, Peter, 285, 286
Brooks, Peter, works by: *The Melodramatic Imagination*, 285
Bruun, Mette Birkedal, 30n1
Burt, Andrew, 11n12
Butler, Andrew M., 131n5

Cadora, Karen, 173n2
Cain, William E., 58, 58n10, 59n10, 69n30, 70n32
Calef, Robert, 17, 18, 18n17
capitalism, 13n13, 31, 42n14, 46n24, 56–57, 58n9, 104, 137, 174, 176, 182n6, 216, 228, 253, 255, 257n1, 269, 272, 306
Cashmore, Ellis, 300, 301
Cavallaro, Dani, 173n2, 182, 183n7, 184
celebrity, 37, 46n24, 135, 154, 183, 249, 263, 271, 288, 296–311
Cervantes, Miguel de, 4n4
Chetwynd, Ali, 221, 229n11
Cheung, Floyd, 244, 244n5, 249
Chin, Frank, 248, 249n7
citizen, citizenship, 6–9, 11, 13, 14, 16, 18, 24, 25, 26, 31, 129, 134, 157, 158, 178, 186, 195, 214, 222, 246–47, 252, 266, 304
Civil War, 36, 70–71, 77, 106, 136
clandestinity, 151–54, 157, 219
class, 36, 83, 110, 111, 117, 152, 154, 161, 176, 215, 239, 241–42, 248, 277, 306–7, 310
Clausson, Nils, 93, 94, 95
Coale, Samuel Chase, 220, 221
Cochoy, Nathalie, 108
Coetzee, J. M., 289, 290, 292, 294
Cohen, Jean L., 42
Cohen, Julie E., 259, 273
Cohn, Dorrit, 4
Cold War, 129, 133–34, 152, 156, 214n1, 222
Collado-Rodríguez, Francisco, 173n2
coming out, 23, 71, 83–101
communication, 4, 13, 21, 33–34, 36, 42–45, 50, 55, 119, 129, 180, 183, 221, 229, 260, 271, 286, 296–97, 300–301, 305, 309; interpersonal communication, 44; transparent communication, 18, 65–66
Communism, 58, 71–72, 79, 117, 121, 147–72, 214, 237, 240, 241, 242
community, 4, 21, 23, 24, 38–43, 45, 47, 50, 57n7, 60–63, 72, 84, 87–88, 91, 121, 123, 125, 141, 148–49, 152, 154–55, 158, 161, 164, 168, 170, 196–211, 216, 233–54, 263, 265, 267, 277, 278, 284, 286, 287, 288, 303
concealment, 3, 64, 121, 124, 129, 151, 171, 177, 195–96, 201–3, 206–7, 209–10, 217, 280–82
confession, 4–5, 21, 25, 31, 33–34, 42, 60–61, 63, 90–91, 96–98, 101, 113, 124, 151, 167, 175, 276–95
confidentiality, 167, 266
conformity, 14, 19, 22, 48, 107, 112, 152, 155, 165, 168, 200, 210, 239, 258–59, 263, 273
Conrad, Joseph, 137
consensus, 7, 12, 13, 85, 104, 105, 181

consent, 44, 84, 224
conspiracy, 19, 33, 55–56, 120, 129, 133, 138, 148, 159, 173, 174, 185, 187–89, 190, 201, 214, 220–22
Copjec, Joan, 74n38
corporations, 2, 11, 14, 57n5, 173–93, 260, 264–65, 270, 273
Coviello, Peter, 49
Crenshaw, Kimberlé, 84
Crimp, Douglas, 93
Crowley, Mart, 23, 83, 95–98
Csicsery-Ronay, Istvan, 174, 176
Currah, Paisley, 84, 87, 90n1
cyberpunk, 24, 26, 173–93
cyberspace, 173, 178–90, 215–19, 228–29, 260

Dean, Jodi, 8n10, 10, 16n14
Debord, Guy, 10, 1n13
Defoe, Daniel, 4–5
Delany, Samuel R., 83, 89, 91, 92, 92n3, 96n5, 101
DeLillo, Don, 25, 63, 223n6, 245
DeLillo, Don, works by: *Cosmopolis*, 223n6; *Libra*, 25
Democracy, 6–8, 11, 15, 31, 37, 46, 56, 105, 106, 112, 117, 125, 147–50, 156, 158, 170–71, 184, 214, 257, 265–69; democratization, 10, 214, 215, 273
Derrida, Jacques, 5n5, 31, 35, 61n14, 75n41, 97, 100, 133, 177, 180, 279, 280
Derrida, Jacques, works by: *Of Grammatology*, 75n41
Dery, Mark, 181
Dick, Philip K., 2, 23, 129–44
Dick, Philip K., works by: *The Cosmic Puppets*, 131, 131n5, 132; *The Divine Invasion*, 144; *The Exegesis of Philip K. Dick*, 137n12; "Exhibit Piece," 134; "Faith of Our Fathers," 134; *The Game-Players of Titan*, 136; *The Man in the High Castle*, 130, 138n13, 142; *The Penultimate Truth*, 134; *Puttering About in a Small Land*, 131n4; *Radio Free Albemuth*, 138n13; *A Scanner Darkly*, 23, 137, 138n13, 140, 142, 143; *The Simulacra*, 129–44; *The Three Stigmata of Palmer Eldritch*, 144n19; *The Transmigration of Timothy Archer*, 138
Dinnen, Zara, 259, 268, 273, 296
disclosure, 1, 24, 25, 45, 64, 70, 72, 104, 113, 118, 140, 147, 153, 157, 167, 171, 195, 205–7, 210, 217–18, 221, 276–95, 310
dispositif, dispositive, 13, 34, 55, 57, 62
dissent, dissensus, 85, 87, 161
dissidence, 149, 167–70, 237, 288
dissimulation, 34, 36, 105, 114, 148, 151–54, 164, 168, 183
Djelic, Marie-Laure, 5n6, 6, 11, 12, 14
Docherty, Thomas, 14, 42, 195
Dos Passos, John, 58, 235
Dostoevsky, Fyodor, 290
Dougherty, James, 31, 38, 43n17
Dreiser, Theodore, 93, 311
DuBois, W. E. B., 115, 126n2
Dunn, John, 61n14
duplicity, 120, 156, 160–61, 171
Dworkin, Ronald, 64n17
dystopia, 8, 10, 11, 23, 25, 26, 138, 159, 17n2, 176–77, 190, 191, 255–75, 298, 302, 304, 310

Edelman, Lee, 86, 87, 90, 91, 97
Eggers, Dave, 2, 25, 255–73, 296
Eggers, Dave, works by: *The Circle*, 25, 255, 259, 260, 262, 263, 265, 268, 271, 296; *The Every*, 25, 255, 259, 260n4, 262, 263, 268, 269, 272
Elliott, David, 43n19
Ellison, Ralph, 3, 23, 104–26, 235
Ellison, Ralph, works by: *Invisible Man*, 23, 104–26, 235; *Shadow and Act*, 112, 124
Ellmann, Richard, 70n31
Emerson, Ralph Waldo, 18, 19, 57n8, 68–70, 74n39, 77, 130, 131

Emerson, Ralph Waldo, works by: "Nature," 18, 130; "Self-Reliance," 18
Enlightenment, 2, 4, 5, 8–13, 17, 18, 3n1, 37, 64, 124, 157, 194n1, 258
Erkkila, Betsy, 36, 45
Erkkilä, Tero, 8, 10
ethics, 20, 24, 50, 60n12, 93, 124, 167, 174, 184, 185, 187, 190, 260, 286; ethical choice/judgment, 154, 170, 175
ethnicity, 104, 151, 154, 234–37, 241, 242n4, 250; ethnic transparency, 117–19
exposure, 1, 7, 10, 18, 20–22, 24, 37, 60, 104–28, 147–69, 185, 194–211, 220, 234, 266; self-exposure, 4, 9, 10–11, 18

fear, 1, 24, 62, 108, 132, 148, 167, 169, 186, 199, 208, 234, 288
Felman, Shoshana, 98, 99
Fenster, Mark, 4, 7, 11–13, 16
Ferguson, Niall, 261, 264, 268
Fluck, Matthew, 222
Foster, Thomas, 173n2
Foucault, Michel, 9, 13, 56n3, 88, 90, 98, 104, 140, 199, 200
Foucault, Michel, works by: *Discipline and Punish*, 140; "Friendship as a Way of Life," 88; *Les anormaux*, 56
Fox, Nick, 263
Franklin, Benjamin, 258, 259
Franzen, Jonathan, 25, 245, 276–94
Franzen, Jonathan, works by: *The Corrections*, 288n13, 290n15; *Crossroads*, 25, 276–95; *The End of the End of the World*, 288n12; *Freedom*, 290n15, 291n16; *The Kraus Project*, 288; *Purity*, 276–80, 284, 284n9, 288, 289, 291n16, 294, 296
Fraser, Nancy, 83
Freedman, Jonathan, 70n31
freedom, 19, 57n7, 58n9, 60n11, 62, 64, 77–78, 100, 112–13, 118, 126, 152, 161, 163, 226, 253, 265, 267, 271–73, 302
Freedom of Information Act, 6
Freud, Sigmund, 68n28, 113, 167
Friedman, Milton, 15, 63n16
Fuchs, Christian, 265, 271
Fukuyama, Francis, 214n1
Fuller, Henry Blake, 23, 72, 83, 93–95
Fuller, Randall, 73
Fuss, Diana, 89

Galow, Timothy, 259, 270
Gates, Henry Louis, Jr., 114, 122, 124
gender, 83, 84, 89, 100, 303, 305
Genoways, Ted, 36n6
Gerstein, Robert S., 43n15
Gibson, William, 2, 24, 173–91
Gibson, William, works by: *Count Zero*, 174, 178, 180–82, 185, 188, 190; *Mona Lisa Neuromancer*, 173, 176, 179, 181, 182, 185, 189, 190; *Overdrive*, 173, 180n5, 183, 188, 189
Giddens, Anthony, 257n1
Gilbert, Jeremy, 1, 16n14, 17, 30n1, 41, 43n16, 113, 130, 140, 153, 196, 288
Glissant, Edouard, 106, 124, 141
Gonaver, Wendy, 71n35
gossip, 45n23, 153, 156, 160, 165, 170, 184, 194, 198–208
governance, 3, 6–7, 9, 12–13, 16, 24, 149, 267
government, 3, 5, 6, 7, 12–13, 129, 132–34, 150, 176, 179, 185, 195, 220, 221–25, 228, 260, 264–65, 267, 269, 304–5
Goyal, Yogita, 126n2
Grant, Glenn, 173
Grantham, Michael, 175n3
Green, Jeremy, 288n13
Green, Michaël Lars Cyril Norgaard, 30n1
Gross, Andrew S., 266, 270
Grossman, Jay, 72n36
Gstrein, Oskar Josef, 224, 224n7

Habermas, Jürgen, 5, 60, 60n13
Hallward, Peter, 75
Halperin, David M., 93
Han, Byung-Chul, 1, 8, 10, 13, 16, 42, 43, 55, 60n11, 60n13, 62, 104, 140, 154, 199, 200, 204, 288, 298, 310
Han, Byung-Chul, works by: *Psychopolitics*, 55n1; *The Transparency Society*, 1, 8, 10, 43, 104, 310
Haralson, Eric, 67n27, 69, 76n42, 76n43, 78
Hardt, Michael, 176
Harvey, David, 57n5, 58n9, 62n16
Haver, William, 99
Hawthorne, Nathaniel, 19–22, 61, 64n21, 283
Hayakawa, S. I., 246–48, 250, 251
Heald, David, 7n8
Heffernan, Julián Jiménez, 23
Hegel, Georg Wilhelm Friedrich, 76n44, 91, 108
Henthorne, Tom, 173n2, 176
Herman, Peter, 269, 270
heteronormativity, 83, 86, 89
heterosexuality, 45, 76n43, 88–89, 91
Heuser, Sabine, 173, 174
Hobsbawm, Eric, 74n38
Hofstadter, Richard, 219
Hollinger, Veronica, 173
Holzner, Burkart and Leslie, 5n6, 7, 11
homoeroticism, 45–46, 50, 72n35, 75
homosexuality, 23, 44–46, 66–68, 72n36, 75–76, 83–101
Honneth, Axel, 43, 43n18, 83, 108
Honneth, Axel, works by: "Invisibility," 43; *Recognition*, 43n18; *The Struggle for Recognition*, 43n18
Hood, Christopher, 7
Horn, Eva, 2, 8n10, 9, 12, 16, 30n1, 32, 130, 132–35, 150, 157–59, 165, 174, 177, 178, 183, 184, 186, 190
Horton, Donald, 298

Houellebecq, Michel, 63
Hughes, Langston, 109
Hurley, Natasha, 67n27
Hutchinson, George, 111
hypocrisy, 23, 90, 98, 105–6, 114–16, 120, 122, 123, 125, 154, 155, 157, 202

ideology, 9, 13, 15, 19, 24, 25, 56, 60, 61, 63, 64, 71, 84, 111, 120, 122–23, 125, 148–52, 159, 162–64, 186, 222–23, 237, 253, 259, 264, 265, 267, 286
illusion, 4n4, 9n11, 77, 105, 110, 115, 118, 119, 120, 157, 163, 199, 200, 209, 210, 223, 245, 298
individual, 7–10, 12, 14–19, 22–23, 31–32, 37–38, 40–44, 56–60, 62, 66, 74n39, 79, 84, 86, 88, 90, 98, 99, 105–6, 108, 113, 130, 132, 147–49, 157–58, 161, 164, 168, 170–71, 174, 175n3, 182n6, 196, 207, 210, 217, 220, 224, 234n2, 236, 239, 242, 243, 258, 259, 261–64, 266, 268, 269–71, 273, 276, 279, 285, 289, 299, 301–4, 310
individualism, 14, 19n19, 31, 37–38, 41, 58n9, 255, 261, 270–71, 273
influencer, 25, 296–311
Innes, Julie C. 41n10, 44
intelligibility, 23, 83–101
intertextuality, 106, 124, 125, 174
intimacy, 1, 3, 23, 30–51, 57, 60n13, 68, 93, 122, 165, 263, 294, 297–99, 300, 308, 310
intrusion, 63, 64, 65, 155, 157, 158–61, 178, 260, 266, 271, 272
invisibility, 23, 104–28, 138, 234

James, Henry, 1, 3, 23, 55–79
James, Henry, works by: *The American Scene*, 59n10, 64; *The Aspern Papers*, 60n12, 65, 65n22, 67; *The Notebooks of Henry James*, 69; *The Portrait of a Lady*, 66n25; *The Reverberator*, 65n22;

Stories of Writers and Artists, 59, 65, 66, 67, 69, 71; *The Tragic Muse*, 65
James, William, 64n20, 74
Jameson, Fredric, 76n44, 137
Johnson, James Weldon, 109, 110
Johnson, Samuel, 149
Johnson, Thomas H., 91
Jones, Emrys D., 299
Joo, Hee-Jung, 109
Joule, Victoria, 299

Khawaja, Noreen, 5n5, 33, 34
Käkelä, Tiina, 24, 214, 228
Karatzogianni, Athina, 272
Kebede, Alemseghed, 182n6
Keenan, Bernard, 178
Kelly, Adam Maxwell, 260
Kermode, Frank, 137, 144
Kharpertian, Theodore, 217n2
Kim, Richard, 89
Kirby, Alan, 260
Knight, Peter, 18, 133, 133n7
Knottnerus, J. David, 182n6
Koivisto, Ida, 4, 5, 7n8, 8n10, 10, 11n12, 216
Kotz, David M., 58n9
Kymlicka, Will, 60n12

Larsen, Nella, 109
Larson, Kerry C., 47n26
Laub, Doris, 98, 99
Lavender, Isiah, III, 181
Lawson, Andre, 36
LeClair, Thomas, 235, 245, 246
Lehrer, Tom, 46
Lejeune, Philippe, 34
Levinas, Emmanuel, 31, 43, 43n16, 74n39
Levine, Lawrence, 122
Liberalism, 2, 10, 11, 14–17, 19, 23, 31, 42n14, 56–82, 74n39, 89, 163, 214, 260, 265, 269, 270
Ling, Yinqi, 233
Locke, John, 56n4, 57, 60–62, 66, 75n40
Lockwood, Patricia, 25, 297, 298, 302, 307–10

Lockwood, Patricia, works by:
No One Is Talking About This, 25, 297, 302, 307–10; *Priestdaddy*, 307; "The Rape Joke," 307
Loeffler, Philipp, 152
Lovrinic, Barbara, 255, 271
Luker, Ed, 34n5, 35, 41
Lyon, David, 255–57, 260, 265, 267, 267n5, 268, 270, 272
Lyon, David, works by:
Liquid Surveillance, 255
Lyotard, Jean-François, 13

Macpherson, C. B., 57n7, 61n14
Mao, Maoism, 239, 242
Margolis, Stacey, 19, 37n8, 235
Marks, Peter, 262, 263
marriage, 7n34, 73, 84, 92, 93, 100, 135, 151, 165, 202, 223, 251, 277, 280, 286, 292; same-sex marriage, 84, 86, 88–89, 100
Marshall, P. David, 299, 300
Martel, Frédéric, 86, 87
Martín-Salván, Paula, 197n2, 234n1
Marwick, Alice E., 301
Marx, Karl, 242
Marx, Leo, 256, 259, 265, 269
materiality, 46, 48, 50, 190
Mathiesen, Thomas, 271
Mattessich, Stefan, 226
Matthiessen, F. O., 23, 55–79
Matthiessen, F. O., works by:
American Renaissance, 57, 70; *From the Heart of Europe*, 58, 59, 71n35, 78; *Henry James: The Major Phase*, 66n24, 68, 70, 71, 71n33, 75; *The James Family*, 67, 69, 70, 73
McCarthyism, 23–24, 147–72
McFarlane, Anna, 174
McHoul, Alec, 217n2, 220n3
McKay, Nellie, 114
McKenna, George, 2n1
McKeon, Michael, 4
mediasphere, 10, 17, 25, 288, 294
mediation, 2, 4, 21, 22, 23, 25, 31–32, 37, 39, 40, 51, 120, 23n1, 255, 271

Mehrpouya, Afshin, 5n6, 6, 11, 12, 14
Meijer, Albert, 7
melodrama, 25, 276–77, 285–86, 294
Melville, Herman, 19–22, 57n8, 76, 132, 136
Melville, Herman, works by: *Billy Budd*, 20, 21
memory, 112, 137, 139, 219, 252–53, 273
Mersch, Dieter, 35
Metelman, Jörg, 37n7, 194
Mill, John Stuart, 62, 66
Miller, D. A., 20, 22, 93
Miller, J. Hillis, 60n12, 283, 137
Miller, J. Hillis, works by: *Other*, 283
Miller, Perry, 17, 91
modernism, 34, 37, 59, 64, 106, 163, 24n3, 264
modernity, 11, 13, 17, 30, 32, 158, 257–58, 267, 269–71, 273, 299
Mole, Tom, 299
morality, 6, 7, 33, 61, 6n25, 68, 74, 76–78, 98, 104, 106, 108, 148, 152, 154–58, 160–62, 165–66, 168, 174, 183, 184–90, 202, 298, 308, 310; moral order/code/rule/norm, 45, 105, 113, 121, 154–55, 209, 258, 264, 286; moral conflict, 277, 294
Morrison, Toni, 2, 3, 24, 118, 194–211
Morrison, Toni, works by: *The Bluest Eye*, 201; *Paradise*, 24, 194–211; *Playing in the Dark*, 118
Moyland, Tom, 186
Murison, Justine S., 45

Nadel, Alan, 124
Nadel, Ira, 148, 155, 158, 163
Naurin, Daniel, 43, 195
Negri, Antonio, 176
Neocleous, Mark, 16, 17, 43n14, 149
neoliberalism, 9, 11, 13–16, 55–59, 62, 104, 288
Neville-Shepard, Ryan, 220, 220n4, 220n5, 222

9/11 attacks, 214–15, 220–23, 228, 229, 259, 269–70, 271
Nixon, Nicola, 173
Novick, Sheldon M., 70n31
Nowviskie, Bethany, 216

Omatsu, Glenn, 237
Opacity, 2, 3, 19, 35, 83, 104, 105, 106, 108, 110, 113–14, 119, 120–26, 129–46, 183, 204, 206, 234, 262, 280, 282
Orwell, George, 20, 140, 144, 261, 262, 265, 272

Paine, Thomas, 6
panopticon, 8, 17, 104, 140, 199, 210, 288
paranoia, 132, 138, 160, 165, 169, 217, 219–23, 229, 286
parody, 4, 23, 106, 109, 122, 124, 142, 223n6, 236
parrhesia, 83, 95–101
Penn Warren, Robert, 25
Peplow, Michael W., 105
Phelan, James, 174, 185
Pierpont, Claudia Roth, 150
Pignagnoli, Virginia, 260
Plato, 85, 87, 97
poetry, 25, 26, 30–51
Pöhlmann, Sascha, 2, 5n5, 23, 25, 219, 228
police, 85, 87, 136, 138–41, 176–77, 185, 252, 261, 266
Ponce de Leon, Charles L., 299
Poole, Adrian, 57n8
postmodernism, postmodernity, 34, 5n4, 105, 130, 14n15, 148, 163, 169, 233, 243, 245
power, 12, 14, 20, 22, 24, 25, 4n21, 57, 6nn14–15, 69, 7n40, 98, 100, 105, 109, 113, 116, 123, 135–36, 139, 149, 152–53, 156, 164, 166, 169, 174–79, 181, 183–91, 195–96, 200, 202, 209–10, 217, 222, 224–26, 235, 248, 265, 267–68, 270, 272–73, 281, 284, 300; empowerment, 252, 301–2, 305–6, 308, 310

presentism, 2, 17, 30, 32, 93, 194
privacy, 1, 2, 3, 6–8, 11, 14, 16–17, 21–23, 30–45, 50, 56, 60, 64, 66, 70, 72, 9n3, 104, 140, 148–49, 158–59, 202, 204, 207–8, 216–17, 255, 260–63, 266, 270–73, 276, 282, 288, 297, 301, 304, 307; private life, 25, 67, 70, 164, 299, 303
publicity, 3, 5–6, 14, 30, 32–33, 37, 39, 41, 59, 60, 64–65, 69, 74, 133, 148, 222, 301
Puritanism, 2–3, 17–19, 22, 5n4, 5n7, 59–62, 74, 76, 90–92
Pynchon, Thomas, 24, 133n7, 134n8, 214–29, 245
Pynchon, Thomas, works by: *Against the Day*, 218, 227; *Bleeding Edge*, 24, 214–29; *Gravity's Rainbow*, 134n8, 217–19, 225, 227; *Inherent Vice*, 215, 218, 221; "Is It O.K. to Be a Luddite?," 215; "Low-lands," 227; V; 217, 218; *Mason & Dixon*, 218; *Vineland*, 218, 224, 227

Rabinow, Peter, 256
race, 23, 83, 84, 104–6, 108, 110–19, 122–23, 126, 154, 159, 181, 197–98, 200–202, 210, 235, 237, 241–42, 248–49, 306–7, 310
racism, 84, 105, 110, 115, 119, 125, 181, 243, 306
Radin, Paul, 121
Ramage, Magnus, 245
Rancière, Jacque, 84, 85, 87, 91
Rancière, Jacques, works by: *Disagreement*, 87
Rawlings, Peter, 57n8, 68n29
realism, 5, 24, 25, 35–36, 93, 105, 120, 13n6, 161, 163, 166, 235, 238, 292, 310
recognition, 43, 74, 83, 85, 90–91, 98, 108–9, 119, 125, 205, 300
Redding, Arthur, 71n35
Redmond, Sean, 298n1
Reid, Kiley, 25, 297, 298, 302, 305, 306, 310

Renza, Louis A., 35n5
resistance, 2, 7, 12, 22, 4n14, 61, 125, 14n15, 148, 167, 204, 210, 227, 238
revelation, 3, 20, 39–41, 44, 60, 66, 70, 75, 78, 113, 121, 135, 137–38, 169, 219, 235, 243, 278, 282–83; self-revelation, 60, 6n28
Richards, Neil, 31, 31n2, 44n21
Rieder, John, 173n2
Rigaud, Milo, 180n5
Robbe-Grillet, Alain, 130
Robertson, Ken G., 186
Robinson, Paul, 90
Rojek, Chris, 298–300, 308
Rossi, Umberto, 23, 129n1, 132, 132n6, 136, 136n11, 138n13, 140, 140n14
Roth, Philip, 2, 3, 23, 24, 108n1, 147–71, 233
Roth, Philip, works by: *The Human Stain*, 108n1, 147n1, 160; *I Married a Communist*, 147–71; *The Plot Against America*, 159
Rouse, Margaret, 227, 228
Rousseau, Jean-Jacques, 4, 5n5, 10 194n1, 31, 33, 34, 36, 61n14, 75n41, 194n1 282, 283n5, 284, 285, 289, 294
Roy, Ravi K., 57n6
Royal, Derek Parker, 159, 161

safety, 5n27, 107, 189, 200, 205, 227
Salmon, Richard, 60n12, 63, 64, 64n21, 65n21
satire, 58n9, 105–6, 109, 110, 113–17, 122, 125–26, 13n10, 148, 160, 163, 260, 287, 307
Savoy, Eric, 67n27, 76, 76n42
Scambray, Kenneth, 93, 95
Schickel, Richard, 298n1, 299
Schlatter, Richard, 72n35
Schmidgall, Gary, 44n22, 50n27
Schmitt, Karl, 60n11
Schneider, Manfred, 5n5, 34, 194n1
Schuyler, George, 3, 23, 104–26
Schuyler, George, works by: *Black Empire*, 126n2; *Black No*

More, 23, 104–26; "The Negro-Art Hokum," 110
Second World War, 70–71, 158, 168, 197, 225, 233, 237, 247
secrecy, 1–3, 5–10, 12, 16, 17–25, 30, 32–33, 40, 4n12, 4n23, 46–47, 5n27, 55–57, 59–60, 62, 65, 70, 74n39, 77, 104, 120, 124, 129, 132–33, 137, 141, 144, 147–51, 154, 158, 165–66, 170, 174–75, 177–79, 181, 183–84, 186, 188–91, 194–98, 200–5, 207, 209–10, 216–17, 222, 234, 273, 276–77, 279, 281–82, 293–94; secrecy effect, 2, 32, 133–34, 177–80, 184, 188, 190
secret, 3, 12, 14, 24, 35, 40–42, 45–46, 49–50, 56, 59–60, 63–67, 69, 73, 75, 78, 111, 113, 118, 121, 124, 133, 134–35, 147, 150–51, 153, 158, 160, 166, 167, 169–71, 173–77, 179, 181, 183–91, 195–96, 198, 201–11, 217, 260, 263, 276, 277–85; state secret, 9, 134–35, 175, 177
security, 1, 24, 176–77, 185–86, 215, 221; national security, 194, 270
Sedgwick, Eve Kosofsky, 67n27, 89, 94, 97, 99–100
Sedgwick, Eve Kosofsky, works by: *Epistemology of the Closet*, 89
Seed, David, 217n2
Seidman, Steven, 88
Senft, Theresa M., 298, 301, 303
Selisker, Scott, 259, 266, 270
sex, 45, 72, 92, 93, 9n5, 142, 27n3
sexuality, 89, 91–92, 94, 97
Shakespeare, William, 55, 57n8, 65n23, 66
Shamir, Milett, 37n8
Shapiro, Stephen, 258
shareveillance, 302, 303, 305, 310
Sheffer, Jolie A., 236, 243, 252
Shipp, Karen, 245
Siegel, J., 216
silence, 39, 76, 97, 99, 121, 177, 178
Simmel, Georg, 181, 196, 276, 279, 280, 282, 284n9

Simmel, Georg, works by: "Secrecy," 196; "The Sociology of Secrecy and Secret Societies," 181, 279, 28n9
Slusser, George, 130
Smith, Adam, 6, 9, 258
Smith, Rachel Greenwald, 234n2
Snowden, Edward, 1, 194, 261
social media, 1, 9–10, 17, 30, 104, 113, 153, 169, 21n1, 226, 255, 258–59, 267, 271, 273, 288, 296–311
socialism, 58, 61, 70, 72, 79
Soifer, Eldon, 4n19
sovereignty, 37, 5n3, 149, 157, 176, 178
Sponsler, Claure, 173
Springer, Simon, 15
Starobinski, Jean, 5n5, 34, 282, 283n5
state, 2, 5–11, 12–15, 1n18, 19, 24–25, 5n5, 6n14, 62, 85, 87, 89, 12n2, 133, 134–35, 141, 144, 154, 157, 163, 174, 175–78, 183–86, 194–96, 199, 216, 260, 264, 288, 302, 310
Steger, Manfred B., 57n6
surface, 4n12, 45, 109, 133, 135, 155, 161, 170, 200, 209, 226
surveillance, 1–3, 7–9, 11–13, 19–20, 22, 24–25, 56–57, 62–63, 89, 104, 113, 139–41, 147, 153, 188, 194, 198, 200, 209–10, 214–17, 223, 226, 233, 255–75, 298, 302–5, 310
Suvin, Darko, 141, 255
Suvin, Darko, works by: "Goodbye and Hello," 141; *Metamorphoses of Science Fiction*, 255
systems novel, 24, 26, 235, 245, 251

Tanner, Tony, 217n2, 225
Taylor, Charles, 257, 258, 263, 264
technology, 9–10, 12n2, 176, 187, 194, 216, 228, 255–57, 259–62, 265–73, 296, 301–3, 310; digital technology, 9, 10, 16, 216, 255, 257, 268–70, 273, 296

Telios, Thomas, 37n7, 194
testimony, 83, 90–91, 95–101
Thomä, Dieter, 7, 7n8, 8, 186, 195, 199
Thorp, Clare, 214n1
Tocqueville, Alexis de, 2n1, 64
Tolentino, Jia, 309
Transcendentalism, 18, 173
transparency studies, critical transparency studies, 2, 3, 7, 8–13, 15–16, 104, 195
trauma, 167, 195–98, 201, 204–5, 208
Travis, Mitchell, 84
Trilling, Lionel, 71
Trump, Donald, 105, 133n7
trust, 43, 113, 148, 151, 154–55, 199, 207–8, 209–10, 284–85
Turner, Graeme, 300, 301

Umemoto, Karen, 237, 238, 246, 247, 252
Utopía, 8, 17, 18–19, 61n14, 140, 144, 159, 173n2, 261, 263, 265–71

Vattimo, Gianni, 9
Vendler, Helen, 46, 48, 50
Vietnam war, 267, 283
visibility, 4, 6, 23, 83–87, 98, 108, 138, 222, 234–36, 243, 265, 297, 300
Vujić, Jure, 273

Waelen, Rosalie A., 43

Walters, Suzanna Danuta, 91
Walton, Jo, 34n5, 35, 41
Warner, Benjamin R., 220, 220n4n5, 222
Warner, Michael, 37, 50, 84, 89, 92
Watson, Rebecca, 296
Weeks, Jeffrey, 87
Weisenburger, Steven, 105
Wells, H. G., 108, 125
Westin, Alan F., 42n13
Whitman, Walt, 1–3, 23, 25, 30–51, 56n21, 70n31, 72n35
Wikileaks, 1, 30n1, 194
Williams, Raymond, 199n3
Williamson, Kevin D., 214n1
Wills, David, 42n12, 169, 217n2, 220n3
Wilson, Leigh, 297
Winthrop, John, 17
Wittgenstein, Ludwig, 42n11
Wohl, R. Richard, 298

Yamashita, Tei, 3, 24, 233–53
Yamashita, Tei, works by: *I Hotel*, 24, 233–53; "Literature as Community," 244n5
York, Jillian C., 259, 264, 271, 272
Yu, Lai Ying, 236, 252

Zappe, Florian, 266, 270
Zhou, Min, 242, 242n4, 248, 250
Žižek, Slavoj, 7n38
Zuboff, Shoshana, 255–57, 262, 265, 268, 269, 272
Zunshine, Lisa, 4

Printed in the USA
CPSIA information can be obtained
at www.ICGtesting.com
JSHW011759031224
74704JS00004B/102